COMPLETE A-Z

Law

HANDBOOK

Jacqueline Martin
Mary Gibbins

3rd edition

Hodder & Stoughton

A MEMBER OF THE HODDER HEADLINE GROUP

D E F G H I J K L M N O P Q R S T U V W X Y Z

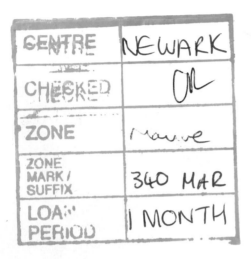
British Library Cataloguing in Publication Data
A catalogue record for this title is available from The British Library

ISBN 0 340 87268 3

First published 1999
Second edition 2002
Third edition 2003

Impression number 10 9 8 7 6 5 4 3 2 1
Year 2007 2006 2005 2004 2003

Cover photograph: Michael Tcherevkoff Ltd/Getty Images

Typeset by GreenGate Publishing Services, Tonbridge, Kent.
Printed and bound in Great Britain for Hodder and Stoughton Educational, a division of Hodder Headline plc, 338 Euston Road, London NW1 3BH, by The Bath Press Ltd.

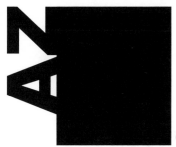

CONTENTS

HOW TO USE THIS BOOK

The *Complete A–Z Law Handbook* is an alphabetical textbook of law in England and Wales. The book contains over 1100 entries and is designed for ease of use. Each entry begins with a basic definition to help students with unfamiliar terms and legal language.

Entries are developed in line with the relative importance of the concept covered. For example, *Diplock courts* are covered in a few lines, whilst *frustration* is a substantial entry. Many topics are expanded with case examples demonstrating how the particular point of law operates. This expansion not only helps students to understand the topic more clearly, but also provides additional material for essays. Diagrams and flow charts are used as a further aid to explain some of the concepts.

The study of a topic can be further developed by making use of the cross-referenced entries. For example, the entry for *auction* refers the reader to *invitation to treat* and *offer*. Cross-referenced entries are identified by the use of italics.

The *A–Z Law Handbook* is a legal glossary covering topics examined by the major boards at A Level. These are:

- English Legal System
- Consumer Law
- Law of Tort
- Contract Law
- Criminal Law
- Family Law

Additional business law terms in employment law, company law and land law are also included making it suitable for use for GNVQ units on business law. ILEX students should also find it a valuable reference book covering inheritance law in addition to all the above topics.

To aid the revision process, carefully selected lists are provided at the back of the book. Those facing examinations can use the lists to make the best use of the *Handbook* during their revision time. The lists are split into modules, for ease of use. Separate lists are provided for the main A level examination boards, OCR and AQA. The relevant modules or units of the specifications are indicated, but candidates should always check the current specification. There are also revision lists for ILEX and GNVQ courses.

We have updated the second edition to include key changes to the law and have included entries showing the changes proposed to the criminal justice system by the Criminal Justice Bill 2002. It had been hoped that this would receive the Royal Assent in the summer of 2003, but the House of Lords' defeat of the proposals to allow trial by jury alone in complex cases or where there was fear of intimidation delayed the Bill. However, students should be aware of these changes as they are likely to start coming into effect in 2004. We have also included comment on proposed changes to the Lord Chancellor's position and the House of Lords as a final appeal court. The Government began consultations on these in the summer of 2003 and major changes are likely to take place by 2005. The law is as we believe it to be in August 2003.

Jacqueline Martin, Mary Gibbins

abatement of a nuisance: the removal or the stopping of a *nuisance*. A person suffering from a nuisance should ask the person responsible to abate the nuisance. If he fails to do this, or in an emergency, the person suffering from it can go onto the other's land and deal with it himself.

abetting: see *aiding and abetting*

absolute discharge: an order that can be made by a criminal court when an offender either pleads guilty or is found guilty of an offence. The effect of an absolute discharge is that, although the conviction is recorded, nothing happens to the offender. It is a complete discharge with no 'strings' attached and is only used when the court thinks that punishment is not necessary. An absolute discharge is rarely given; it is more usual for a court to impose a *conditional discharge*.

absolute liability in the criminal law refers to crimes where a defendant is guilty without the need for any *mens rea* (intention) to be proved. In extreme cases the defendant can be guilty even though the act was also involuntary. This type of situation is known as a state of affairs crime.

Case example: R v Larsonneur (1933)

The defendant, who was French and had left the United Kingdom because permission to stay was refused, was deported from Ireland and brought into the UK by the police. She had no intention to return to the UK, nor did she voluntarily re-enter the country. Despite this she was guilty of 'being found in the UK'.

See also *strict liability offences*.

absolute privilege: a defence in *defamation* giving protection in certain circumstances whether or not the maker is acting through malice (spite). It is a recognition that, sometimes, total freedom of speech is more important than protecting the individual.

Absolute privilege applies to:

- statements made in Parliament by MPs and members of the House of Lords;

- reports of these statements in Hansard, the official record of parliamentary proceedings, and newspaper reports and broadcasts which cover every word that has been said;

- statements made in court during a trial by any of the parties involved including the judge, barristers, the claimant, the defendant and witnesses;

- fair and accurate reports by the media of court proceedings as long as they are published at the time of the trial;

- communications between Ministers of State and other senior officers of state on matters of state.

ACAS stands for *Advisory, Conciliation and Arbitration Service*.

acceptance: an unqualified agreement to all the terms proposed by the *offeror* which creates a contract. The acceptance must be from the person to whom the offer was made. Acceptance can be:

- in writing;
- orally;
- by conduct (see *unilateral contract*).

Once there has been acceptance of the offer a contract is formed.

An agreement which is different in some ways from the terms proposed by the offeror is a *counter-offer*, not an acceptance. The acceptance must be communicated to the offeror even if he has said that this is not necessary, so silence cannot be assumed to be an acceptance (Felthouse v Bindley (1862)). Acceptance should normally be communicated in the same way as the offer was made or in a more efficient way (e.g. if the offer is sent by post, then acceptance should be by post or by a quicker method, such as fax). Where the offeror asks that the acceptance should be made in a particular way (e.g. 'telephone me'), then the acceptance must be communicated in that way. But it may also be communicated in a more efficient way, unless the offeror has made it very clear that only the set way will do.

Acceptance normally takes effect when it is received by the offeror. The *postal rule* is an exception to this rule and means that where an acceptance is sent by post, it takes effect the moment it is posted. See also *communication rules in contract law*.

acceptance in sales of goods occurs when one of the following happens:

- the buyer has told the seller that he has accepted them, provided that he has had a reasonable opportunity to inspect the goods to see whether they conform with the contract;
- the buyer does something with the goods inconsistent with the seller's ownership e.g. alters them;
- a reasonable period of time has passed.

Allowing the seller to repair a defect does not necessarily mean that the buyer has accepted them.

access to justice refers to being able to take legal action when needed. Full access to justice requires an open system of justice that can be easily used by anyone and is also affordable. The cost and complexity of bringing *civil cases* in England and Wales are said to prevent full access to justice.

accessorial liability refers to the liability of a defendant who is an *accessory to a crime*.

accessory to a crime: a person who does not commit the crime itself, but helps with it by *aiding*, *abetting*, *counselling* or *procuring*. Accessories are charged with the same crime as the *principal offender* even though they have only *secondary participation* in a crime.

accomplice: another name for an *accessory* or a *secondary participant* in a crime.

accord and satisfaction: a term used in contract law for new *consideration* provided when both parties agree to amend a contract. Without the new consideration, the new agreement would not be contractually binding and the original contract would still stand.

acknowledgement of service: the procedure the defendant in a *civil case* must carry out when served with a *claim form*. The defendant must fill in a form indicating if he intends defending the case and take or send that form to the court office within 14 days. If the defendant does not do this, then the *claimant* can apply to the court for judgment to be made in his favour without the need for a trial.

acquittal: the term used when a person charged with a criminal offence is found not guilty. It means that the person has been formally discharged from the accusation against them and must be allowed to go free. Under the principle of *autrefois acquit*, that person cannot usually be tried again for that same offence.

Act of God: a defence in *tort* used especially in claims under *Rylands v Fletcher*. The defendant will not be liable if he can show that the escape of the thing which caused the damage was caused by natural forces and it was so exceptional that he could not have been expected to foresee that it might happen or to guard against it.

Act of Settlement 1701: the Act of Parliament which established that superior judges could not be dismissed from office without reason by the monarch. Instead, they held office 'as long as they were of good behaviour' and could only be removed if both Houses of Parliament petitioned the monarch for the judge's dismissal. This is an important feature in guaranteeing *judicial independence*, and the same rule is now set out in the Supreme Court Act 1981 (s11) for judges of the *High Court* and *Court of Appeal*, and in the Appellate Jurisdiction Act 1876 (s6) for the judges in the *House of Lords*.

act of stranger: a defence in *tort* which is used in claims under *Rylands v Fletcher*. A defendant will not be liable if he can show that the damage was caused by a third party over whom he had no control. However, there may still be a claim in *negligence* if it was reasonably foreseeable that someone might act in this way and precautions should have been taken.

action plan order: a *community order* which the courts can impose on offenders under the age of 18 (Powers of Criminal Courts (Sentencing) Act 2000). It is intended as a short intensive programme of community intervention combining punishment, rehabilitation and *reparation* to change offending behaviour and prevent further crime. Such an order will last three months during which time the offender is supervised by a probation officer and has to comply with a series of requirements with respect to his actions and whereabouts. These requirements can be any of the following:

- to participate in set activities;
- to present himself to a specified person at set times and places;
- to attend at an attendance centre;
- to stay away from certain places;
- to comply with arrangements for his education;
- to make reparation.

actionable per se means that a claim can be brought whether or not the claimant suffered any harm. For example, a person who crosses someone else's land without permission can be sued for trespass whether he has damaged anything on the land or not. In this case the claimant will often be seeking an *injunction* against the defendant rather than *damages*.

Acts of Parliament: laws that have been passed by both Houses of Parliament and received the *Royal Assent*. Acts of Parliament are also called statutes. For important new laws, the government will usually issue a consultation document known as a *Green Paper* and firm proposals for new law in a *White Paper*. Then a proposed Act (known as a *Bill*) is drawn up. A Bill must go through several stages in both the House of Commons and the House of Lords and must be passed at each stage if it is to become law as an Act of Parliament. These stages are shown below.

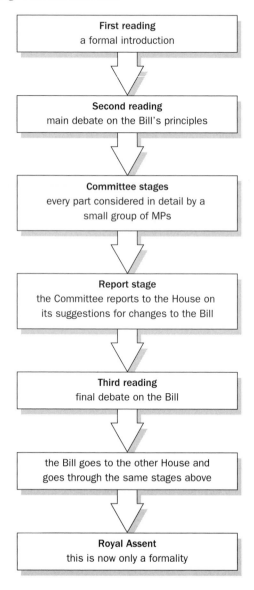

First reading
a formal introduction

Second reading
main debate on the Bill's principles

Committee stages
every part considered in detail by a
small group of MPs

Report stage
the Committee reports to the House on
its suggestions for changes to the Bill

Third reading
final debate on the Bill

the Bill goes to the other House and
goes through the same stages above

Royal Assent
this is now only a formality

About 70 Acts of Parliament are passed each year. There are criticisms that many Acts are too complex and use obscure language which is difficult to understand. The problems over language can lead to court cases on *statutory interpretation* when the court has to decide what particular words or phrases within an Act mean.

actual bodily harm: a term used to describe a level of injury in criminal cases. The courts have held that it means any hurt or injury which interferes with the health or comfort of the victim (Miller (1954)). The hurt or injury need not be serious or permanent and the definition includes bruising and swellings as well as such injuries as loss of a tooth, a broken nose or other minor fractures. It also includes psychiatric injury (Chan Fook (1994)). (See also *assault occasioning actual bodily harm*.)

actus reus: the Latin phrase for the 'guilty act' which must be proved in a criminal case. Each crime must be looked at individually to see what must be proved to establish its actus reus. The actus reus may be an act or it may be a failure to act (see also *omissions as actus reus*). For some crimes, it may also be necessary to show that a particular consequence has happened or that a certain state of affairs exists.

Examples:

- *Burglary:* the actus reus (s9(1)a of the Theft Act 1978) is an act of entering a building (or part of a building) as a trespasser;

- *Criminal damage:* the actus reus is any act which has the consequence of destroying or damaging property belonging to another;

- *Going equipped to steal:* the actus reus involves a state of affairs, as the defendant must have with him any article for use in the course of a theft but this must be while 'not at his place of abode'.

These examples show that actus reus is a wider concept than an 'act', as it covers all the elements of the definition of a crime except those which relate to the mental element (*mens rea*). The Law Commission has recommended using the term 'external elements' instead of actus reus.

administration of justice: is the term used to refer to the operation of the whole legal system. This includes the way the police work, the courts and their procedures for civil and criminal cases, and appeals.

administration order: in company law, an administration order can be made by a court if it is satisfied that:

- the company either is, or is becoming, unable to pay its debts; and

- an order is likely to promote the survival of all or part of the business as a going concern or enhance the assets on a *winding up*.

An administrator appointed under such an order is given full management powers by the Insolvency Act 1986 and the directors' powers are suspended.

An administration order can be sought by:

- a majority of the directors;

- the members by ordinary resolution;

- any creditor of the company.

administrative law controls how government ministers and other public bodies such as local councils should operate (see also *judicial review*).

administrative tribunals: all types of tribunal which have been set up by *statute* to deal with specific types of cases, usually to enforce rights given by social and welfare legislation. One of the most important types of administrative tribunals are the *Employment Tribunals* (previously known as *Industrial Tribunals*) which hear cases involving disputes about employment. There are many other types of administrative tribunal, for example:

- Social Security tribunals, which decide whether claims for various benefits should be allowed;

- rent tribunals, which are involved with the fixing of fair rents;

- immigration tribunals to hear appeals on the right of immigrants to enter and live in the United Kingdom.

administrator of an estate: the person(s) appointed by the court to deal with the estate of a person who has died without making a will. They must be the nearest relatives to the deceased person, but if the nearest relative does not want to do it, then the next nearest will be appointed. Up to four administrators can be appointed. (NB The technical term for a female administrator is an administratrix.) The administrator's duties are to prepare a list of all the assets of the deceased, pay any debts, pay any inheritance tax which is due, and then distribute the remaining assets to those who are entitled to inherit. An administrator is given permission to do this by the court granting *letters of administration*.

Admiralty Court: a court in the Queen's Bench Division of the *High Court* which deals with claims for compensation for deaths or personal injury or damage to property arising from a happening at sea, such as the collision of two ships or a ship sinking. It also decides who has the right to the salvage value of a ship which has been wrecked.

adoption: the transfer of all legal parental responsibility from the natural parents of a child to someone else. It brings to an end all legal relationships between the parents and the child although the natural parents may still have a right to contact. Arrangements for adoption are carried out by *adoption agencies* unless the adoption is by a relative. Adoption orders must be made with the consent of the parents (including an unmarried father if he has a *parental responsibility order*), but the adoption agency can apply for a *freeing order* if there is doubt consent will be given.

adoption agency: a body run by a local authority or an approved voluntary body which is responsible for arranging *adoptions*. All adoptions must be carried out through an adoption agency except those by relatives or a person acting under a High Court order.

ADR stands for *Alternative Dispute Resolution.*

adultery in family law is consenting sexual intercourse between a married person and a person of the opposite sex. A married woman who has been raped has not committed adultery, nor has a married person who has sex with someone of the same sex. A *petitioner* who is seeking a *divorce* may use the *respondent's* adultery as evidence that the marriage has irretrievably broken down provided that he also shows that he finds it intolerable to live with the respondent. However, if he goes on living with the respondent for more than six months after he discovers the adultery, he cannot use this in a divorce petition.

adversarial process: the system used in most courts in England and Wales where each side has to prove their own case. The parties are seen as adversaries, or opponents, and it is up to them to decide what evidence they want to put before the court and which witnesses they wish to call. In many continental countries the court has the power to decide which witnesses should be questioned, as the court is viewed as investigating the matter. This system is called an *inquisitorial process*.

adverse possession of land: the taking over of land by a person who is not entitled to be there (a squatter). After 12 years, if the owner has done nothing to reclaim the land, the squatter can claim the right to remain on the land and sell it if he wishes. Under the Land Registration Act 2002, once a squatter has made a formal claim to the land, the owner is given the opportunity to oppose it and start eviction proceedings.

Advisory, Conciliation and Arbitration Service (ACAS): an independent body set up to promote the improvement of industrial relations. It does this in a number of ways.

- It offers advice to employers, employers' associations, trade unions and individual employees on a wide range of matters connected with employment, and it has issued Codes of Practice giving practical guidance and suggested procedures for dealing with such matters as discipline and the investigation of grievances.

- Where an employee has made a claim to an *Employment Tribunal*, a copy of the claim is sent to ACAS, and a conciliation officer will offer assistance in trying to resolve the dispute without the need for a full tribunal hearing.

- Where there is a dispute between a trade union and an employer, ACAS, if requested to do so by one of the parties, may appoint a conciliation officer.

- Where there is a dispute between a trade union and an employer, ACAS can, with the consent of all parties involved, refer the dispute to arbitration to try to resolve it.

advocacy: the art of speaking on behalf of another. In legal terms, it means to conduct a case in court as the legal representative of one of the parties to the case.

advocacy rights: the rights given to lawyers to appear in court and conduct a case on behalf of another person. All barristers have full advocacy rights; this means they can appear in any court. Solicitors have restricted advocacy rights so that they can normally only conduct cases in the *Magistrates' Court* and the *County Court* unless they obtain a *certificate of advocacy* granting them the right to appear in higher courts. The Access to Justice Act 1999 provides for any solicitor who completes the necessary training to have full advocacy rights.

Advocates-General: lawyers drawn from the member states of the *European Union* who assist the *European Court of Justice* with its work. There are nine Advocates-General, and they are highly qualified as they must either be eligible for appointment to the highest judicial posts in their own countries or be highly qualified academic lawyers. Each case at the European Court of Justice is assigned to an Advocate-General who will research the law and present an independent opinion on it to the court.

affidavit: a written document in which a person's evidence is set out and which that person swears as being true.

affirm: a method of promising to tell the truth when giving evidence in court. It is used where a witness does not have a religious belief or has an objection to using a religious book to swear that they will tell the truth.

affirming a contract: an action taken by the innocent party to a *voidable contract* to show that he intends to carry on with the contract, even though he knows he is entitled to revoke (cancel) it. He will still be entitled to *damages*.

affray: an offence under s3 of the Public Order Act 1986. It is committed where a person uses or threatens unlawful violence towards another and this conduct is such as would cause a person of reasonable firmness to fear for his personal safety. Words on their own are not enough to make a defendant guilty of an affray; there must be some action, for example, raising a fist.

agency: the relationship which arises when one person (the agent) is authorised to act as a representative of another person (the principal). In contract law, if the agent makes a contract on behalf of the principal, the principal is bound by the contract. If things go wrong it is the principal who can sue or be sued, not the agent. This may, in limited circumstances, be so even if the other party to the contract does not realise the agent is acting on behalf of the principal.

A person becomes an agent and can commit the principal when:

● he is given express authority by the principal;

● it is reasonable for an outsider to assume that the principal has given him authority; for example:

  – a managing director is assumed to have authority to commit his company;
  – a wife is assumed to have her husband's authority to obtain credit;
  – the manager of a pub is assumed to have the authority of the owner to buy goods.

The principal can make it clear to the outsider that he has not given authority, in which case he will not be bound by any contract the 'agent' enters into, e.g. a husband can write to a trader saying that he will no longer pay his wife's bills.

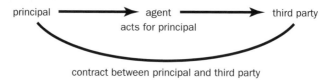

contract between principal and third party

aggravated criminal damage is committed where a person, without lawful excuse, intentionally or recklessly *destroys* or *damages* any property and intends by the destruction or damage to endanger the life of another, or is reckless as to whether the life of another would be thereby endangered. The danger to life must come from the destruction or damage, not from another source in which damage was caused. Recklessness uses the objective test in *Caldwell recklessness*.

aggravated vehicle taking: an offence under s12A of the Theft Act 1968. It is committed when the offence of *taking a vehicle without consent* is committed and any of the following occur:

● the vehicle is driven dangerously;

● injury to a person is caused by the driving;

● damage to something is caused by the driving;

● the vehicle is damaged.

agreement in contract law occurs when both parties to a contract agree not to carry out the contract as originally formed. The new agreement is binding because both parties provide new consideration by giving up the right to insist on the original contract being carried out. If one party has completed his side of the contract already but the other has not, then the party who has not carried out his side of the contract must provide fresh consideration to make the new agreement binding (but see also *estoppel* for an exception to this). The new binding agreement replaces the original contract, which is said to be discharged (see *discharge of contract*).

aiding and abetting: ways in which a person can be guilty of involvement in a crime even though he is not the principal offender. This is known as *secondary participation*, and there are two other ways in which it can occur; these are *counselling* and *procuring*. Although the two words 'aiding' and 'abetting' are often used together, the Court of Appeal in Attorney-General's Reference (No 1 of 1975) said that they had separate meanings.

● 'Aiding' means giving support or assistance. This can be before the crime takes place, for example by lending safe breaking equipment to another person, or at the scene of the crime, for example by acting as the getaway driver.

● 'Abetting' is considered to be encouragement given at the scene of the crime, for example, by shouting words such as 'go on – hit him'.

To be guilty, the aider or abettor must know of the type of crime the principle is intending to commit and must intend to help him with it. Secondary parties to a crime are charged with the same crime as the principal offender and may be tried and punished in the same way.

ALAS scheme: an advice service for those who have been injured in an accident and wish to know whether they can claim compensation. Volunteer solicitors offer free initial interviews.

alibi: a defence where an accused claims that, when the crime with which he is charged occurred, he was somewhere else. When a case is to be tried at the Crown Court, the defendant must disclose if the defence involves an alibi and give the prosecution details of it.

allocation questionnaire: a document sent to the parties in a *civil case* to obtain information so that the court can decide which track the case should be allocated to. This procedure will only happen if a case is defended and a court hearing is necessary. See also *fast-track cases*, *multi-track cases* and *small claims*.

Alternative Dispute Resolution: any method of resolving a dispute without having to go to court. The advantages of using ADR instead of taking court proceedings are that it is cheaper, quicker, less formal and private. The main methods of ADR are:

● *negotiation*;

● *conciliation*;

● *mediation*;

● *arbitration*.

analogy, reasoning by: a method of coming to a decision in a case where there is no previous *precedent* on any similar point. It means that the judge draws parallels between the situation in the present case and different situations which have occurred in earlier cases. For example, in Hunter and others v Canary Wharf Ltd (1995), it was argued that interference with television reception by a tall building was analogous to (i.e. on a parallel with) to loss of a view due a building being erected.

ancillary relief: a term used in divorce for *financial relief*.

Animals Act 1971 sets out when a *keeper* of an animal is liable for damage or injury caused by it. *Strict liability* is imposed on the keeper of a dangerous species of animal but the keeper of a *non-dangerous species* of animal will only be liable where:

- the animal was likely to cause damage of the type that it did actually cause; alternatively the animal, if it did cause damage, would be likely to cause severe damage, and

- this was because of the characteristics of that particular animal or because it is usual in that species but only at particular times and

- the keeper (or animal's possessor aged under 16 in his household) knew about these characteristics.

A defendant will not be liable if an injury was wholly the fault of the claimant or the claimant willingly took the risk of injury. If the claimant was a trespasser the defendant will be liable only if the injury happened through the unreasonable use of a guard animal.

The Act also covers liability for damage caused by straying livestock and liability for damage to livestock by dogs.

annulment: a term used in family law for a declaration that a marriage is not valid. A decree of *nullity* is issued if it is shown that the marriage was either *void* or *voidable*.

antecedents: the past history and previous convictions of a defendant in a criminal case. When a defendant is being sentenced for an offence, the court will be told his antecedents, and this information is likely to be important in deciding the sentence the defendant should receive. If a defendant pleads not guilty, his or her previous convictions are not usually made known to the *jury* (or *magistrates*) during the trial. This is to prevent prejudice against the defendant, although it is argued that if the defendant has previous convictions for similar types of offence, this should be part of the evidence given at the trial.

anticipatory breach of contract occurs when one party shows by words or actions that he intends not to perform his contractual obligations. The other party is entitled to sue for breach of contract, even though the time limit for completing the contract has not passed (Hochster v de la Tour (1853)).

anti-dumping laws: *European Union* laws aimed at preventing goods being sold in an export market at a price below their normal value in the home market, and so causing unfair competition. Anyone (person or business) which considers itself to be affected by this type of unfair competition can lodge a complaint to the *European Commission*, which will investigate and, if necessary, bring proceedings against the 'dumper'.

anti-social behaviour order: an order which can be made by the Magistrates' Court when any person aged ten or over has acted in a manner that caused or was likely to cause alarm and distress to another person who is not in the same household as the defendant (Crime and Disorder Act 1998 s1). Only a local authority or a chief constable can apply for such an order. Proceedings for an anti-social behaviour order are civil, but the standard of proof is the criminal one of beyond reasonable doubt. If proved the court can make any necessary order to prevent recurrence of the behaviour which led to the order being made; for example, a *curfew order*, an order excluding the defendant from a named place or an order that the defendant must not make contact with named individuals. Breach of such an anti-social order is a criminal offence.

Anton Piller order: a court order in a civil case that the defendant must allow the claimant to search the defendant's premises and remove any documents or other material which could help the claimant to prove his case. If it is thought that the defendant might destroy relevant documents, then the claimant may apply to the court *ex parte*, that is without telling the defendant about the application. As it is an *equitable remedy*, it will only be ordered if court thinks it is just and convenient to do so. Under the 1999 *Civil Procedure Rules* this order is re-named a 'search order'.

apology: a defence in *defamation* where the defamatory statement was made inadvertently. It is not often used, the defence of *offer of amends* is usually used in these cases.

appeals: the usual way of challenging a decision made by a court or tribunal. The main appeal routes are shown below. See also *civil appeals* and *criminal appeals*.

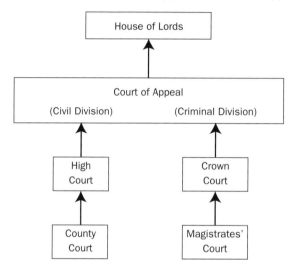

approbation means approval and is a bar to the granting of a decree of *nullity* in family law. A decree of nullity will not be granted if the *respondent* can show that:

- the *petitioner* led the respondent by his behaviour to believe that he would not seek to have the marriage annulled; and
- at the time he knew he had grounds for an annulment; and
- an annulment would result in injustice to the respondent.

appropriation: a key part of the definition of *theft*. The *actus reus* of theft is that a person must have appropriated property belonging to another. Section 3 of the Theft Act 1968 states that 'any assumption of the rights of an owner amounts to an appropriation'. This definition is very wide. It covers obvious situations such as taking money from a handbag or goods from a shop. It also includes situations that are not so obviously theft, such as destroying property (since only an owner has the right to destroy it and so there is an assumption of the rights of an owner).

Case example: R v Gomez (1992)

Gomez, an assistant shop manager, told his manager that cheques which Gomez knew were stolen were 'as good as cash' so that the manager handed over to Gomez's accomplices several thousand pounds' worth of electrical goods. It was held that there was appropriation even though the manager had consented to the taking of the goods.

In Gomez the consent to take the goods had been obtained by deception. However, in R v Hinks (2001) the House of Lords held there could be appropriation where the owner fully consented to the taking and there was no deception involved. Appropriation was a neutral word meaning 'any assumption of the rights of an owner'. Whether it amounted to theft or not depended on whether the defendant had acted dishonestly.

arbitration: a method of resolving a dispute without a court case. The parties agree to go to arbitration, and their dispute will be heard by an arbitrator in private. The arbitrator is usually chosen by the parties and may be a lawyer or a businessman or someone with technical knowledge. The date, the place, the time and the method are all matters for the parties to decide in consultation with the arbitrator. They may choose to have a 'paper' arbitration where the arbitrator makes a decision after reading the documents of the case or they may have a hearing more like a court case in which people give evidence. Many commercial contracts include what is called a *Scott v Avery clause*, which is a clause in the original contract where the parties agree that, in the event of a dispute arising between them, they will have that dispute settled by arbitration instead of going to court.

arraignment: the process in which the accused is called into court and asked whether he pleads guilty or not guilty. In the *Crown Court*, each of the charges in the *indictment* is put to the defendant and he is asked how he pleads to them.

arrest: when a person is taken into custody, usually because they are suspected of committing a crime. That person must be told of the reason for the arrest. The main *police powers of arrest* are set out in ss24 and 25 of the Police and Criminal Evidence Act 1984. Private citizens also have the right to make an arrest, but only in limited circumstances. See *citizen's arrest*.

arrestable offence: an offence for which the police can arrest immediately without having to get a *warrant of arrest* from the court. Arrestable offences are:

- any offence for which the sentence is fixed by law (e.g. murder, which has a fixed sentence of life imprisonment);
- any offence for which the maximum sentence is at least five years' imprisonment; examples are theft (maximum sentence seven years) and robbery (maximum sentence life imprisonment) (NB this is not necessarily the sentence the offender will actually receive);
- any offence which Parliament has specifically made an arrestable offence, even though the maximum possible sentence is less than five years.

(See also *police powers of arrest*.)

arson: a crime under the Criminal Damage Act 1970. It involves causing criminal damage by destroying or damaging property belonging to another by setting fire to it. To be guilty, the defendant must either intend to do the criminal damage or be objectively reckless as to whether criminal damage is caused.

Article 234 (Treaty of Rome) sets out when national courts in the Member States of the *European Union* can refer a case to the *European Court of Justice* for a preliminary ruling on a point of European law. If the national court is the final court of appeal, then the matter must be referred. The European Court of Justice rules on the point of law and the national court then applies this ruling to the case.

Article 249 (Treaty of Rome) states that the *European Union* has the power to issue various types of orders. These are:

- *Regulations*, which are automatically 'binding in every respect and directly applicable in each Member State';

- *Directives*, which are binding on all Member States 'as to the result to be achieved' but allow each Member State to pass its own laws to bring the directive into effect (see also *horizontal direct effect* and *vertical direct effect*);

- Decisions, which are addressed to specific people, organisations or states and are binding on them;

- Recommendations and opinions, which are not binding.

Articles of Association: one of the compulsory documents needed when a company is set up, and which must be sent to the Registrar of Companies. The articles of association set out the internal administration of the company and normally include:

- rules for the appointment of *directors*;

- the powers of directors;

- rules in relation to members' meetings and voting;

- the types of shares and the rights attached to the share categories.

If a company fails to supply a set of articles, then the model articles which are contained in the Companies Act 1985 will apply. These are known as Table A Articles.

asbestos cases: cases where a claimant has developed cancer (mesothelioma) through working with asbestos. The illness usually appears years later and it is difficult to prove which contact triggered the claimant's illness. In these cases the claimant can successfully sue his employer in *negligence* if he can show the employer's negligence materially increased his risk of developing cancer; he does not have to prove that it actually caused the cancer (Fairchild v Glenhaven Funeral Services Ltd (2002)).

See also *limitation of actions*.

assault as a tort: an action which causes the claimant to fear that he is about to suffer physical violence, e.g. trying to punch him. It is part of the tort of *trespass to person*.

Case example: Thomas v NUM (1985)

In this case, it was held that no assault had occurred when striking miners made threatening gestures to working miners who were being taken to work in a bus. Although it was a frightening situation, the working miners had no reasonable grounds for fearing immediate violence, because the striking miners were being held back by a police cordon.

There must be some movement by the defendant, standing still is not enough (Innes v Wylie (1844)), and the defendant must intend to frighten the claimant.

13

assault (criminal law): an act by which a person intentionally or recklessly causes another to fear immediate and unlawful personal violence. This means that there is no need for any contact. Examples include:

- raising one's fist as though to hit the other person;
- threatening someone with a knife or other weapon;
- throwing a stone at someone (even though the stone misses them).

It is possible that words alone are enough to be assault if they cause the victim to fear the possibility of immediate violence (R v Ireland (1997)). An assault is a *summary offence* and will be dealt with in the *Magistrates' Court*.

assault occasioning actual bodily harm: a crime under s47 of the Offences against the Person Act 1861. There must be an *assault* or *battery* which causes *actual bodily harm*. There is no need to prove that the defendant intended to cause any injury. It is only necessary for the prosecution to prove that the defendant intended to cause (or was subjectively reckless as to whether he caused) another to fear immediate and unlawful personal violence or that the defendant intended to inflict (or was subjectively reckless as to whether he inflicted) personal violence on another.

assembly: the meeting of a group of people. Article 11 of the *European Convention on Human Rights* protects the right to freedom of assembly. However, under English law, there are certain situations in which an assembly can be unlawful, for example:

- under the Public Order Act 1986, where 12 or more people present together use or threaten violence for a common purpose, this may be a *riot.*;
- under the Criminal Justice and Public Order Act 1994, the police may order people to leave where there is a gathering of 100 or more in the open air for a 'rave' party.

attachment of earnings order: an order to an employer to deduct a certain amount of money each week from an employee's wages. The employer sends that money to the *claimant* to pay off a judgment debt (i.e. money owing under a court order that a sum of money be paid to another person) owed by the employee.

attempt to commit a crime may be an offence, even though the defendant did not succeed in committing the full offence. A criminal attempt is defined by s1(1) of the Criminal Attempts Act 1981: 'If, with intent to commit an offence…, a person does an act which is more than merely preparatory to the commission of the offence'. The accused must have intended to commit the full crime, but not completed it. It can be difficult to decide what is 'more than merely preparatory'.

Case example: R v Campbell (1990)

The defendant had on him an imitation gun, sunglasses and a threatening note, when the police stopped him outside a post office. It was held that these were only preparatory actions and that he had not done enough to be guilty of attempting to rob the post office.

See also *impossible attempts*.

attendance centre order: an order which can be imposed on offenders under the age of 21. Such an order means that the offender will have to attend at a special centre for two or three hours a week (usually on a Saturday). This for a maximum of 24 hours for those aged

10 to 15 and a maximum of 36 hours for those aged 16 to 20. The centres are run under the supervision of the probation services.

attendance centre requirement: under the Criminal Justice Bill 2002 it is proposed that such a requirement can be made as part of a *community order* for those under the age of 25.

attestation clause: a form of words which should be included at the end of a *will* just before the witnesses' signatures to show that the will has been properly signed and witnessed. The usual words used are 'Signed by the *testator/testatrix* in our joint presence and by us in his/hers'. This means that the end of a will should look like this:

Testator's signature A.B. Jones

Date 22 March 1998

Signed by the testator in our joint presence and then by us in his

Witness signature T.L. Smith

of 2, The Street, Anytown (address)

Witness signature E.R. Windsor

of 5, Vine Avenue, Anytown (address)

Attorney-General: the government's chief legal advisor. He or she must be a *barrister* and a Member of Parliament and will be chosen by the Prime Minister. The Attorney-General may personally act as the prosecuting advocate in high-profile criminal cases and can also represent the government or a government department in *civil cases*. Other important duties are:

- to give permission for certain types of prosecutions, such as corruption cases;
- to grant immunity from prosecution;
- to refer criminal cases to the Court of Appeal for consideration of a point of law following an acquittal of a defendant (see also *Attorney-General's reference*);
- to appeal against sentences which are too lenient.

Attorney-General's reference: a right of the *Attorney-General*, under s36 of the Criminal Justice Act 1972, to refer a point of law to the Court of Appeal. This will occur where the defendant in the case has been acquitted at the Crown Court, but the law needs to be made clear. The decision of the Court of Appeal on the point of law will not affect the defendant in that case, but will set a *precedent* for future cases.

auction: a method of selling. In contract law, when the auctioneer invites people to make bids, he is making an *invitation to treat*. Each bid is an *offer* which the auctioneer can accept or reject. The auctioneer accepts an offer by banging on the desk a hammer and saying 'sold'. This is the moment the contract to sell is formed; before this point, the bidder can withdraw his offer or the auctioneer can withdraw the item from the sale. However, if an auction is advertised as 'without reserve', the auctioneer must sell to the highest bidder.

audi alteram partem: a Latin phrase which means that both sides have a right to be heard. This is a rule of *natural justice*. It is also important that the person is told of the nature of the charges against them and given adequate time to prepare a defence. If this rule of natural justice is not followed, then the aggrieved person can apply for an order of *certiorari* to quash the decision.

Case example: R v Norfolk County Council, ex parte M (1989)

M's name was placed on a register of child abusers by the County Council after a brief one-sided investigation. They did not tell M about the allegations nor give him a chance to refute them. The court held that this was a breach of natural justice and ordered the Council to remove M's name from the list.

automatism: a defence to a criminal charge. It means that the defendant's action was involuntary and has been defined as 'an act done by the muscles without any control by the mind of the person such as a spasm, a reflex action or a convulsion; or an act done by a person who is not conscious of what he is doing such as an act done while suffering from concussion or whilst sleep-walking' (Bratty v Attorney-General for Northern Ireland (1963)).

There is difficulty in distinguishing between *insane automatism* and *non-insane automatism*. If the cause of the automatic behaviour is external, such as a blow which causes concussion, then this is non-insane automatism and provides the defendant with a complete defence so the defendant is not guilty. If the automatic behaviour is caused by an internal factor, such as epilepsy, then this is insane automatism and comes under the defence of *insanity*; the defendant will be found not guilty by reason of insanity (see also *self-induced automatism*).

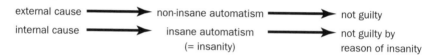

autrefois acquit: a special plea in a criminal case which means that the defendant claims he has already been acquitted of the offence and so cannot be tried for it again. A small exception to this rule has been created under the Criminal Procedure and Investigations Act 1996 where a defendant who has been acquitted because the jury or witnesses were interfered with can be retried.

The Criminal Justice Bill 2002 will allow a re-trial after an acquittal for very serious offences such as murder, rape, manslaughter and armed robbery where there is new and compelling evidence.

autrefois convict: a special plea in a criminal case which means that the defendant claims he has already been convicted of the offence and therefore cannot be tried for it again.

bail: release on a promise to return (either to a police station or court). A person on bail is allowed to be at liberty, rather than held in custody, while awaiting the next stage of the case in criminal proceedings. The Bail Act 1976 states that there is a presumption that a defendant should be granted bail, but it can be refused if there are substantial reasons for believing that the defendant:

● would not surrender (i.e. would not come back for the next stage); or

● would commit further offences while on bail; or

● would interfere with witnesses.

When bail is granted, conditions may be imposed, such as requiring the defendant to live in a bail hostel or to report to a police station daily.

balance of probabilities: the standard of proof required in a civil case. This is a much lower standard than that required in criminal cases, where the case must be proved *beyond reasonable doubt*. In civil cases, the level of proof can be thought of as just tipping the scales of justice in favour of one party or a 51 per cent target. If this is reached, the case is won on the balance of probabilities.

banking cases in contract law: cases where a husband has persuaded his wife to sign a second *mortgage* or charge using the family home as security and has then failed to maintain payments. When the bank (or lender) applies for repossession of the house, the wife argues that her husband had exercised *undue influence* over her and that the contract between her and the bank should be rescinded. The husband would still owe the money to the bank, but the bank would not be able to take possession of the house.

The wife must prove there has been actual or presumed undue influence and that the bank knew or ought to have known about it. Banks are deemed to know that there might be undue influence in all non-commercial loans. They can demonstrate there has been no undue influence by showing that they have explained to the wife in a private interview the risk she is taking and have ensured that she has taken independent legal advice (Royal Bank of Scotland v Estridge (2001)).

bankruptcy: where a person's debts are more than his assets so that he is unable to pay his debts. There are various restrictions on a person who has been declared bankrupt by a court; in particular, they cannot be a company director.

bankruptcy proceedings: court proceedings in which a bankrupt person or any of the *creditors* applies for an order that the bankrupt's assets should be divided among his creditors. Where there is not enough money to pay all creditors, tax and National Insurance debts are paid first, followed by debts to secured creditors. If there is any money over after these have been paid, then it is paid in proportion to the debt owed. For example: if £100,000 is owed but the bankrupt only has £60,000, then creditors will be paid 60 pence for each pound they are owed. So for a debt of £10,000, only £6,000 will be repaid.

Bar Council refers to the General Council of the Bar. It is the governing body of the *barristers'* profession. It is run by officials elected by the members of the Bar and is responsible for the Bar's Code of Conduct and disciplinary matters. The Council describes its function as 'pursuing the interests of the Bar and expanding the market for the Bar's services and is also a watchdog regulating its practices and activities'.

Bar Vocational Course: the post-graduate qualification that those who wish to practise as barristers must pass. The course emphasises the practical skills needed at the bar, such as drafting documents for use in court, knowledge of the law on evidence and *advocacy* skills.

bare promise: a term used in contract law for a promise made by one party to another where nothing is promised or passed in exchange. Because there has been no exchange of *consideration*, no contract comes into existence and the bare promise will not be enforced by the courts.

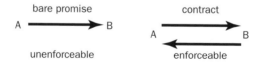

Bare promise versus contract

bargaining power, inequality of: refers to situations in contract law where one party to the contract is in a much less powerful position than the other, either because he is inexperienced in business matters or because he is in great need at the time. This is not normally a reason for the courts to set aside a contract, but the courts do have the power in equity to set aside a grossly unfair bargain, and it may also be possible to bring a claim for *undue influence*, *duress* or *misrepresentation*. It is also a factor taken into account when deciding whether a term of a contract is unfair under the *Unfair Terms in Consumer Contracts Regulations*.

barristers: one branch of the legal profession. They must be members of one of the four *Inns of Court*; there are about 10,000 barristers in independent practice. Barristers are self-employed and are not allowed to form partnerships. They have the right to present a case in any court, and most barristers will concentrate on this, but there are some, especially those specialising in tax or company law, who will rarely appear in court. Clients cannot normally go directly to a barrister but must go to a *solicitor* who will then, when necessary, brief a barrister. After practising for ten years, barristers have the right to apply to the Lord Chancellor to be appointed a *Queen's Counsel*, which means that they are recognised as senior barristers and will be offered more complex cases and paid higher fees. In 2003 a review of the system of Queen's Counsel was announced and all applications were suspended pending the results of the review. This means there may be major changes to the system.

basic award: an award by an *employment tribunal* for unfair dismissal. It is an amount of money calculated according to the employee's age and length of service:

- service below the age of 22: half a week's pay for each year of service
- service between the ages of 22 and 41: one week's pay for each year of service
- service between the ages of 41 and 65: one and a half week's pay for each year of service

At the moment the amount is limited by a maximum of 20 years' service and £260 per week pay. This means that the maximum that can be awarded is £7,800. The employee may also be awarded a *compensatory award*.

basic intent: the term used to describe the level of intention that the prosecution must prove in offences for which the *mens rea* is intention or *recklessness*. The term basic intent is used because the prosecution can succeed if the defendant is proved to have been reckless. This contrasts with *specific intent* crimes in which the prosecution must prove that the defendant had the necessary intention; for these the prosecution cannot rely on any lower level of mens rea such as recklessness. An example of a basic intent crime is criminal damage. The prosecution can prove either that the defendant intended to do the damage or that he was reckless as to whether the damage was done.

battery (criminal law): the application, intentionally or recklessly, of unlawful force to another person. Examples include:

- punching, kicking, slapping or pushing someone;
- hitting another person with a stick or any other object;
- throwing a stone at someone so that it hits them.

If the force does not cause any injury, then the attacker can be charged with common assault under s39 of the Criminal Justice Act 1988. If the attack causes injury which is *actual bodily harm,* then the offence is charged under s47 of the Offences against the Person Act 1861.

battery as a tort: the direct and intentional application of physical force to the claimant which may or may not be forceful enough to cause injury. The defendant must intend to make physical contact but he does not have to have any hostile intention (F v West Berkshire Health Authority (1989)).

battle of the forms: a term used in contract law where both parties to a contract use standard forms setting out their terms of business. One party will send the other details of the contract set out on their standard form giving the terms and conditions. The other party will reply by sending back the terms of the contract set out on their own standard form. It then has to be decided at what point there has been a matching *offer* and *acceptance* rather than a *counter-offer* and, as a result, at what point the contract has been made and on whose terms.

Case example: Butler v Ex-Cell-O Corporation (England) Ltd (1979)

Butler offered a machine tool for sale on their standard terms form. Ex-Cell-O placed an order on their own standard terms form. Butler accepted the order by signing and sending back an acknowledgement attached to Ex-Cell-O's order, but also wrote saying that it was on their terms of business. When a dispute arose, the court had to decide whether the contract was covered by Butler's terms or Ex-Cell-O's. It was held that the contract was complete when Butler signed the acknowledgement slip and sent it back. At this point there was matching offer and acceptance. The contract was therefore on Ex-Cell-O's terms.

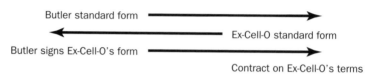

Butler standard form

Ex-Cell-O standard form

Butler signs Ex-Cell-O's form

Contract on Ex-Cell-O's terms

behaviour: in divorce, one of the ways of showing that the marriage has irretrievably broken down. The *petitioner* must show that the *respondent* has behaved in such a way that the petitioner cannot be reasonably expected to live with him. Common examples are violence, verbal abuse or excessive drinking, but account is taken of the petitioner's character, and much less extreme behaviour will support a divorce petition if the petitioner has a timid or nervous nature. It is irrelevant whether the respondent intends to distress the petitioner by his or her behaviour, the fact that it does is sufficient.

belonging to another: for the purposes of theft, property is considered as belonging to any person having possession or control of it, or having any proprietary right in it (s5(1) Theft Act 1968). This means that property can be stolen from a person who is not the owner of it.

Case example R v Turner (No 2) (1971)

The owner of a car was held guilty of its theft from a garage which had carried out repair work on it, when he took it without informing the garage and without paying for the repairs. The garage was held to be in control of the car and had the right to keep it until it was paid for the repairs.

S5(3) also states that when a person receives property from another and is under an obligation to deal with that property in a particular way, the property shall be regarded (as against him) as belonging to the other.

Case example: Davidge v Bennett (1984)

The defendant was guilty of theft when she spent money given to her by the other flat sharers to pay the gas bill.

beneficial contract of service: a contract of employment which gives the employee something more than a salary, such as the opportunity to learn a skill or a trade, and which overall is not to the disadvantage of the employee. If the employee is a minor (under 18), the contract will only be enforceable if it is beneficial.

Case example: De Francesco v Barnum (1890)

A 14-year-old girl entered a seven-year apprenticeship with De Francesco who would teach her stage dancing. The terms were that she was not to marry during the apprenticeship; she could not work for anyone else without permission; she was not guaranteed work; and the rate of pay was very low. He could send her abroad and could end the agreement at any time if he considered she was unfit. It was held that although she was learning a skill, overall the contract was not for her benefit and therefore the contract was invalid.

See also *minors' contracts*.

beneficial interest: a right to some of the benefits of money or property but not outright ownership; for example, the right to interest from capital but not to the capital itself.

beneficial owner: the person who enjoys or is entitled to the benefits of property, even though the legal ownership of that property is not in his name. *Trusts* are an example of this. For instance, if a child aged five is left a house in someone's will, that child is too young to be the legal owner. So, *trustees* are appointed and the property is put into their names. But, the benefit of the house belongs to the child; the child is the beneficial owner.

beneficiary: a person who inherits something under a will. This can be money or a house or a gift such as a painting or jewellery.

beneficiary under a trust: the person who receives money or other advantage, such as a house to live in, under a *trust*. The trust property is held by trustees who must administer the trust for the benefit of the beneficiary.

bequest: the term for a gift which is left by a will.

beyond reasonable doubt: the standard of proof required in a criminal case. In order for a defendant to be found guilty, the prosecution must prove the defendant's guilt beyond reasonable doubt. This phrase is usually explained by the judge telling the jury that they should only convict if they are satisfied so that they are sure of the defendant's guilt.

bigamy: a criminal offence under s57 of the Offences against the Person Act 1861. It is committed when a person goes through a marriage ceremony whilst still being married to someone else. The second 'marriage' is *void*, and the person who knowingly commits bigamy can be prosecuted. If that person believes on reasonable grounds that the first spouse is dead (R v Tolson (1889)) or that the first marriage has been dissolved by divorce (R v Gould (1968)), they have a defence to the charge of bigamy. However, even if the parties reasonably believe that the former spouse is dead, the second marriage is still void.

If a continuous period of seven years has passed with no evidence that the former spouse is still alive, it is then possible for the spouse to be presumed to be dead. A second marriage would not then be bigamy.

Bill of Rights: a law setting out the rights that individuals can normally expect, such as freedom of the person, freedom of religion, freedom of speech and freedom from discrimination. In England and Wales this is now done in the *Human Rights Act 1998* which incorporates the *European Convention on Human Rights*.

Bills: draft Acts of Parliament. When a new law is proposed, it is set out in a Bill. This Bill must then go through all the necessary stages in Parliament, and it is only if it is passed by both the House of Commons and the House of Lords and receives the Royal Assent that it will become an *Act of Parliament*.

binding over order: an order that can be made in a criminal case. It means that the person is bound over not to break the peace. The person bound over must agree to such an order. It will be for a set time, usually one year, and for a certain sum of money. If the terms of the binding over order are broken, then the person will have to forfeit (pay) that sum of money to the court. Binding over orders are often made in cases of minor assault or criminal damage where the people involved in the incident which led to the criminal charge are neighbours. Both the defendant and the victim can be bound over.

binding precedent: a rule of law decided in an earlier case which the judge must apply in the present case. A precedent will be only binding if the court that made it is more senior in the court structure (or, for some appeal courts, a previous decision of their own) and if the facts of the second case are sufficiently similar to the earlier case (see also *judicial precedent*).

blackmail: a criminal offence defined in s21 of the Theft Act 1968. It involves making demands with menaces, and the defendant must intend to make a gain for himself or cause a loss to another through those demands. Menaces means threats; these can be threats of violence or threats of doing something such as telling a wife that her husband is having an affair.

blasphemy: the publication of indecent or offensive language likely to shock or outrage the general community of Christian believers. It is a criminal offence, and the fact that the defendant did not intended to shock is not a defence (Lemon v Gay News (1979)). The law on this is criticised as it only applies to the Christian religion, and reformers want other religions to be protected as well.

Bolam test (in negligence): judges a defendant's actions against those of an ordinary, experienced person doing that particular job. It is used to decide whether a defendant has breached the duty of care. A doctor is expected to reach the standard of an average doctor who is qualified to do that particular task. The Bolam case also established that where there are different opinions within a profession about how to carry out a procedure, a defendant has not breached his duty of care if he follows one of them as long as it is accepted by a responsible body of medical men.

bona fide: a Latin phrase meaning 'in good faith'.

bona vacantia: goods or a whole estate for which no owner can be found. The term is used for an estate under *intestacy* when there is no relative to inherit it. In this case, the goods go to the Crown.

breach of confidence: a tort where a defendant has without permission published confidential information about the claimant to the claimant's detriment, such as a doctor writing a book about a famous patient. Confidential information is information that has been imparted in circumstances importing an obligation of confidence. The defendant has a defence if publication was in the public interest and a fair-minded person would not consider it offensive to disclose the information.

breach of contract occurs where one party:

- does not carry out what he agreed to do; or
- only does part of what he agreed; or
- does it badly.

The other party then has no further obligation to perform his side of the contract. The consequences of a breach of contract depend on the type of term breached. Damages can always be claimed. If there has been a breach of a *condition* or there has been a breach of an *innominate term* and the effect of this has been serious, the injured party is also entitled to rescind (end) the contract. Exceptionally, the innocent party may be entitled to an order that the other party complete the contract (*specific performance*).

If the contract specifies what will happen if the contract is breached, this will take effect even though the contract has come to an end (Photoproduction v Securicor (1980)).

The wronged party is entitled to sue for breach of contract before the time limit for carrying it out has passed if the other party has made it clear that he has no intention of complying with it. See also *anticipatory breach of contract*.

breach of duty of care in negligence occurs when a person fails to act in a reasonable way.

Where someone is using a skill, he will be in breach of the duty of care if he does it less skilfully than the ordinarily competent person. For example:

- Where a person such as a doctor is using a skill, a breach of the duty of care occurs if the doctor fails to reach the standard of a reasonably competent doctor of the level who would normally be expected to do that task (Wilsher v Essex AHA (1988)).

- A learner driver will be judged against the standard of an ordinary driver, not a learner driver (Nettleship v Weston (1971)).

With other activities, the court will balance:

- how likely an accident is to happen (Bolton v Stone (1951)); and

- the likely seriousness of any injury that might be caused; and

- the effect of any injury on the people who might be injured (Paris v Stepney BC (1951))

against:

- the cost and practicality of taking precautions (Latimer v AEC (1953)); and

- the social utility of the activity (Watts v Hertfordshire CC (1954)).

If the person sued has not taken the precautions that a reasonable person would have taken, then he has breached the duty of care. See also *duty of care* and *causation in negligence*.

breach of the peace: behaviour which causes harm to a person or, in his presence, to his property or makes a person fear that such harm is likely to happen. When this occurs, both police and private citizens have the right to arrest the person who is breaking the peace.

breach of statutory duty: a *tort* enabling a *claimant* to sue when the *defendant* has breached (broken) a duty laid down by an Act of Parliament, e.g. a claimant can sue if he is injured at work because his employers have broken industrial safety regulations passed under the Health and Safety at Work Act 1974. Some Acts specifically state that an individual can sue in the event of a breach, but many do not refer to this point and it is then up to the court to decide whether the right exists or not. The court is more likely to find that it does if:

- the Act was intended to give protection to a limited class (group) of people; and

- it appears Parliament intended to give the members of that class the right to sue in the event of a breach. This is more likely to be the case if no other remedy for a breach is provided.

Some breaches of a statutory duty can only result in a criminal prosecution, whilst some will both result in a prosecution and give the individual affected the right to sue in the civil courts.

bumping: a term used in employment law to describe a *redundancy* where an employee is dismissed in order to give his job to another employee whose position is redundant.

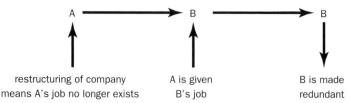

restructuring of company means A's job no longer exists	A is given B's job	B is made redundant

burden of proof refers to who has to prove a matter in court. In criminal cases, the normal rule is that the burden of proof is on the *prosecution*. It is for the prosecution to prove that the defendant is guilty; the defence does not have to prove that the defendant did not commit the crime. However, where the defendant wants to rely on certain defences, such as insanity, the burden of proving these is on the defence. In *civil cases*, the normal rule is that the burden of proof is on the *claimant*.

burglary: a criminal offence defined in s9 of the Theft Act 1968. This has two parts. Section 9(1)a states that a person is guilty of burglary if he enters a building or part of a building as a trespasser with intention to do one of the following:

- steal anything in the building;

- inflict grievous bodily harm on anyone in the building;

- rape anyone in the building;

- damage the building or anything in it.

This means that a defendant with the intention to do one of these things is guilty the moment he enters the building.

Under s9(1)b, a person is guilty of burglary where, having entered as a trespasser, he steals something in the building, or attempts to do so, or inflicts grievous bodily harm on someone in the building, or attempts to do so. This allows for a person to be convicted of burglary, even though when they entered the building they did not intend to steal or cause grievous bodily harm.

For both s9(1)a and s9(1)b, entering the building does not mean that the defendant has to get right into the building; leaning in through a window is enough. The test is whether the entry is effective (R v Brown (1985)).

'but for' test in negligence: used to decide whether the defendant's negligent actions caused the claimant's injuries. Unless the claimant can prove this, he will not be able to claim *damages*. The court will ask itself: 'Would the damage not have occurred but for the *breach of the duty of care* by the defendant?' If the injury would have happened anyway, the defendant will not be liable, even if he was negligent. See also *causation in negligence*.

by-laws: a form of *delegated legislation*. They are laws made by local councils for the area covered by that council or by certain public authorities to cover their field of operation. For example, Kent County Council can make by-laws for the whole of Kent, while a district council such as Sevenoaks District Council can make by-laws for just their part of Kent, such as parking restrictions and one-way streets. Other bodies which operate public services, such as London Transport, can make by-laws about behaviour on their property; for example, banning smoking on underground stations.

What other subjects are you studying?

A–Zs cover 18 different subjects. See the inside back cover for a list of all the titles in the series and how to order.

Caldwell lacuna: a loophole in the definition of *Caldwell recklessness*. It means that, if the defendant can show that he did consider whether there were any risks, but came to the conclusion that there were none, he is not guilty under the Caldwell definition. However, in practice, this argument has not succeeded in any case.

Case example: Chief Constable of Avon and Somerset v Shimmen (1987)

Shimmen was trying to show how expert he was at a form of Korean martial art. To do this, he kicked towards a shop window, meaning to miss it by two inches. He smashed the window. He was found guilty of criminal damage as he knew there was a risk the window might be broken, though he thought that he had minimized it.

Caldwell recklessness refers to the level of intention required for certain crimes. Before R v Caldwell (1981), recklessness meant that the defendant must have seen the risk and decided to take it. This is the idea of *subjective recklessness* (see also *Cunningham recklessness*). In Caldwell, the House of Lords extended the meaning of reckless with Lord Diplock saying:

'A person is reckless as to whether or not any property would be damaged if he does an act which creates an obvious risk that property would be destroyed or damaged and, when he does that act, he either (1) has not given any thought to the possibility of there being any such risk or (2) has recognised that there was some risk involved and has none the less gone on to do it.'

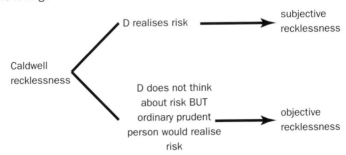

The first part extends the meaning of recklessness, since it includes situations where the defendant has not realised there is a risk although an 'ordinary, prudent individual' would have realised the risk. This is referred to as objective recklessness; the courts are no longer considering what the defendant realised; they are imposing an external test of what others would have realised. This can make a defendant criminally liable even though he or she was incapable of realising the risk (Elliott v C (1983)). In the 1980s, the House of Lords even applied this version of negligence to manslaughter (R v Seymour (1983)), but in R v Adomako (1994), they reverted to the subjective recklessness test for manslaughter. Objective recklessness appears now to apply only to crimes of criminal damage.

capacity in contract law: the ability to understand what is being agreed. If the parties are unable to understand what has been agreed, this may be grounds for declaring the contract *void*. It is assumed that an adult over 18 has full legal capacity and has therefore entered into a *valid* contract unless it can be shown:

- he was mentally incapable or drunk at the time the contract was made; and

- the other party knew he was incapable at the time; and

- he bought goods or services which were not *necessaries* (if they are necessaries, he will only be expected to pay a reasonable price for them).

Minors (under 18 years) can make contracts but are held not to have the same capacity as adults. See also *minors' contracts*.

capacity in criminal law means the ability to understand one's actions and form the necessary *mens rea* (intention) for the crime. This rule is important for those who are considered insane under the criminal law and for children. Those suffering from insanity are held not to have the capacity to commit a crime (see also *insanity as a defence to crime* and the *M'Naghten rules*). Children under the age of ten are said to be *doli incapax*, that is incapable of crime. This means that they cannot be found guilty of any crime.

Until the Crime and Disorder Act 1998, children aged from ten years up to their 14th birthday were presumed incapable of committing an offence. However, if the prosecution could produce clear evidence that the child knew the act was seriously wrong, that he had what is called 'mischievous discretion', then the presumption could be rebutted and the child could be convicted. The Crime and Disorder Act abolished this rule, so now children aged ten and over are considered fully responsible for their criminal acts.

Caparo test (in negligence) establishes that a *duty of care* exists if the damage caused was reasonably foreseeable, there was sufficient proximity between the claimant and the defendant and it is just and reasonable to impose a duty of care.

capital punishment means the death penalty for criminal offences. In England and Wales the death penalty was abolished for murder in 1965. After this date, capital punishment was still technically available for treason and piracy but was never used. It was abolished for these crimes by the Crime and Disorder Act 1998.

care order: a court order giving *parental responsibility* for a child to a local authority. The responsibility is shared with the child's parents, but the local authority decides to what extent the parents are capable of carrying out their responsibilities. Care orders will only be made if it is shown that the child is likely to suffer significant harm because:

- he is not being given the care that a reasonable parent would give; or

- the child is out of the parents' control.

Carlill v Carbolic Smoke Ball Co (1893): the company advertised its smoke ball claiming that it prevented flu. They promised that if customers caught flu despite using the smoke ball the company would pay them £100 and to show their good faith they had deposited £1,000 in a bank. Mrs Carlill bought the smoke ball from a shop. She used it properly but caught flu. She sued the company when they refused to pay her £100.

The court held that this was a *unilateral contract* between the company and Mrs Carlill. The company had made a definite *offer*. It was not a *mere puff* because the company had shown its intention to enter into a contract by depositing the £1,000 in the bank. In a unilateral contract, *acceptance* takes place when a member of the public complies with the *offeror's* request; there is no need for her to communicate with the offeror until she had carried out the required actions. A contract had been made, and Mrs Carlill was entitled to £100.

case law: the term used for law made by the decisions of judges in cases. Case law is important in *common law* jurisdictions. This is because the law of the country is not fully written down in a code but has been largely developed by decisions in past cases. Case law is practical in that it is based on actual cases. See also *judicial precedent*.

case stated, appeal by way of: a method of appealing after a criminal case has been tried by the *Magistrates' Court*. The prosecution or the defendant can appeal on a point of law to the *Queen's Bench Divisional Court*. The magistrates are asked to set out the facts of the case as they found them to be; this is the 'case stated'. There is no dispute about the facts, and the appeal at the Queen's Bench Divisional Court is argued on the law assuming those facts to be correct. If a defendant has appealed from the Magistrates' Court to the Crown Court, an appeal by way of case stated can be made to the Queen's Bench Divisional Court from the Crown Court. Case stated appeals are not common. There are usually less than 200 each year out of over two million cases tried in the Magistrates' Court.

After the Queen's Bench Divisional Court makes its decision, there is the possibility of a further appeal to the House of Lords. However, this can only happen if there is a point of law of general public importance involved in the case and either the Queen's Bench Divisional Court or the House of Lords gives leave (permission) to appeal. These appeals routes are shown in the diagram below.

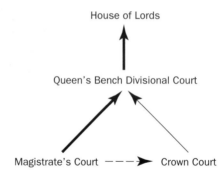

causation in criminal law is important where, for the full crime to be committed, there must be a consequence of the defendant's act. For example, to prove murder, the prosecution must show that the defendant did an act such as shooting or stabbing and that this act caused the victim's death. The act need not be the only cause or even the main cause, but it must be a 'substantial and operating cause'. If there is another act independent of that done by the defendant which caused the death, then the defendant will not be guilty of murder; the *chain of causation* will be broken as shown on the next page.

D has not caused V's death because the shooting injury has not killed V or directly contributed to V's death. The injuries received in the ambulance crash broke the chain of causation.

D shoots V.
V is seriously injured
by the gunshots.

V dies from the
head injuries.

Ambulance taking V to
hospital crashes. V suffers severe
head injuries in the crash.

If the second act is not so independent from the defendant's act, then the defendant may be held to have caused the death.

Case example: R v Lewis (1970)

A husband threatened to kill his wife; in fear she jumped from the window of her third floor flat and broke both her legs. The husband was convicted of causing her grievous bodily harm. The wife's act of jumping did not break the chain of causation as it was caused by the husband's threats and was not independent of his acts.

See also *medical treatment and the chain of causation*.

causation in negligence: the *breach of the duty of care* must directly cause the injury that the *claimant* suffered and must not just be one of the possible causes (Wilsher v Essex AHA (1983)). In deciding whether the defendant's actions caused the claimant's injuries, the court will decide whether the injury would have happened if the defendant had not breached the duty of care.

Case example: Barnett v Chelsea and Kensington HMC (1968)

A night watchman became ill and went to the hospital. The doctor on duty did not see him and he was told to go home and call his own doctor if he did not get better. When he died, his widow sued the hospital as employer of the doctor. She was able to prove that the hospital owed her a *duty of care* and that this had been breached by the doctor failing to examine her husband. However, she was not successful in her claim because it was proved that, even if her husband had been examined, it would have been too late to save him; he had accidentally taken arsenic which had caused irreversible damage by the time he reached the hospital.

A different approach is taken in *asbestos cases*.

See also *chain of causation*.

caution (by police before interview): before the police question a suspect, they must caution him or her. The wording of this caution is normally: 'You do not have to say anything. But it may harm your defence if you do not mention when questioned something which you later rely on in court. Anything you do say may be given in evidence.' This is set out in *Code of Practice* C made under the Police and Criminal Evidence Act 1984. This caution should also be given when a person is arrested. The words of the caution which state that 'it may harm your defence if you do not mention when questioned something which you later rely on in court' reflect the changes made to the law by the Criminal Justice and Public Order Act 1994. This Act restricted the so-called *'right to silence'* of suspects.

caution (instead of charge): a way of dealing with those who have committed a crime but it is not thought necessary that they should be taken to court. The Crime and Disorder Act 1998 limits the number of cautions that can be given to a young offender. On the final *warning*, the offender must be referred to the *youth offending team*. Any further offence after this must be dealt with in court.

caveat: a notice entered at a probate registry to prevent the *grant of probate* of a will being made without notice being given to the person who entered the caveat. A caveat will be entered where there is some doubt about the validity of a will or where there is a dispute about who is entitled to act as executor.

caveat emptor: a Latin phrase meaning 'let the buyer beware'. In contracts, buyers are expected to check that the goods they are buying are of the right quality and what they want before entering into the contract. If they fail to do so, they cannot later bring a claim against the seller. This rule does not apply to *consumer contracts*.

Centre for Dispute Resolution: a centre in London which offers to try to resolve civil disputes between businesses, so that the parties will not need to go to court. Many major companies belong to this centre, including many of the big London law firms.

certainty in contract law means that the key terms of an agreement must be quite clear to both parties. If the terms are too vague, a court will hold that no contract has come into existence.

Case example: Scammell v Ouston (1941)

It was agreed that some of the purchase price would be paid 'on-hire purchase terms'. It was held that this phrase was too vague because no details were given as to when instalments would be paid, how much they would be and how much interest would be charged. There was therefore no contract.

certificate of advocacy: a qualification which allows *solicitors* to act as advocates in the higher courts. All solicitors have the right to act as advocates and represent clients in the *Magistrates' Court* and *County Court*. But until the Court and Legal Services Act 1990, their *rights of audience* in other courts were limited. This Act allowed solicitors to apply for a certificate of advocacy for higher courts. In order to qualify, a solicitor must have experience of advocacy in the lower courts, take a short course and pass examinations on the rules of evidence. The first certificates of advocacy were granted in 1994 and, by mid 2003, only about 1,840 out of a total of over 80,000 solicitors had obtained one. Many of these had been exempt from the short course and examination as they had previously qualified as barristers before becoming solicitors. Solicitors with an advocacy certificate are eligible to be appointed as *Queen's Counsel* and also to be appointed to the higher judicial posts.

certificate of incorporation: the document issued by the Registrar of Companies to show that a *company* has been legally created. In order to obtain a certificate of incorporation, the promoters of the company must pay the relevant fees and send the following documents to the Registrar of Companies at Companies House in Cardiff:

- the *Articles of Association*;
- the *Memorandum of Association*.

certiorari: the first word in a Latin phrase certiorari volumus which means 'we wish to be informed'. Certiorari is one of the prerogative orders by which the higher courts can control the activities of inferior courts and other decision-making making bodies such as tribunals, local authorities, immigration officials and even government ministers. The other prerogative orders are *prohibition* and *mandamus*. Certiorari is used to bring the matter before the *Queen's Bench Division* of the High Court so that the legality of any decision can be examined in *judicial review* proceedings. If the decision is found to be invalid for any reason, then the Queen's Bench Division can quash the decision.

Case example: R v Marylebone Magistrates Court ex parte Joseph (1993)

The stipendiary magistrate hearing the case against Joseph did not appear to be paying sufficient attention to the case. He was looking at his diary and at other papers during the trial. Despite this the magistrate convicted Joseph. The conviction was quashed on an application for certiorari as the trial had to be seen to be fair.

chain of causation in criminal law means that there must be a direct and unbroken link between the defendant's act and the necessary criminal consequence. If the chain of causation is broken by an outside act, the defendant will not be guilty of the crime. See also *causation in criminal law* and *medical treatment and the chain of causation*.

chain of causation in the law of tort means that there must be a direct link between the defendant's actions and the injury caused to the claimant. This link can be broken by a second negligent action by a third party or the claimant. In this case the defendant is not responsible for the claimant's injuries, even though he started off the chain of events which led to them. However, if the second action is a natural and probable consequence of the defendant's actions, then the chain of causation is not broken and the defendant remains liable. See also *novus actus interveniens* and *'but for' test in negligence.*

challenge to a juror can be made if a potential juror is disqualified from being a juror or ineligible (see also *jury qualifications*). A challenge can also be made if there is reason to believe that a juror is likely to be biased, for example because they are related to the defendant or to a witness. The challenge must be made before the juror is sworn in to try the case (s12 Juries Act 1974).

Chancery Division of the High Court: one of the three divisions of the High Court. The main business of this division involves cases of insolvency, both for individuals and for companies, the enforcement of *mortgages*, disputes relating to the administration of trust property, disputes over copyright, trade marks and patents, matters involving company law, and contested *probate* actions. All cases are heard by a judge. Juries are never used in the Chancery Division.

The president of the Chancery Division is the *Lord Chancellor*, but in practice he does not sit to hear cases, and the vice-president is the effective head of the court.

Chancery Divisional Court: the name given to the *Chancery Division of the High Court* when the court is acting as an appeal court. Two judges from the Chancery Division will sit in the Chancery Divisional Court to hear appeals on taxation issues from decisions of the Commissioners of Taxes.

charge certificate: document relating to a property which is issued by the Land Registry to the mortgagee of a property. It is a record of the property details kept at the Land Registry which include the name of the owner, the type of title (freehold or leasehold), a description of the property with plan and details of the charges and any other rights that other people have over the property and a copy of the mortgage deed.

charter party: a contract for the hire of a ship between the owners of the ship and the charterers who want to use it.

checklist in family law refers to the factors a court should take into account when making decisions about children. These are set out in s1(3) of the *Children Act 1989* and are:

a) their wishes and feelings, taking into account their age and understanding;

b) their physical, emotional and educational needs;

c) the likely effect on them of their change in circumstances;

d) their age, sex and background and any other relevant characteristic;

e) any risk of harm;

f) the capabilities of their parents and any other relevant adults;

g) the range of orders available to the court.

child: anyone under the age of 18 (Family Law Reform Act 1969). There are restrictions which have been set by Parliament on what children can do. The age varies for different matters. Some of the limits are shown below.

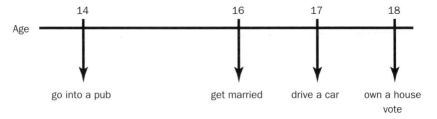

A child of 16 and over can give consent to medical treatment under the Family Law Reform Act 1969. A child under 16 is able to do this when he is mature enough to understand the implications of what he is doing (he is *Gillick competent*).

child curfew order: s14 of the Crime and Disorder Act 1998 gives local authorities power to impose local short-term curfews for children under the age of ten in specified areas. Any such curfew can only be made if the authority has consulted with the chief constable(s) of the area(s) concerned and the scheme must be confirmed by the Home Secretary. Where a local curfew scheme is set up it can only be within the following parameters:

•   for children under ten

•   in a specified area (and applies to only public places in that area)

•   between the hours of 9 p.m. and 6 a.m.

•   for up to 90 days.

The curfew would not apply to a child who was in the effective control of a parent or responsible adult aged 18 or over.

S15 Crime and Disorder Act 1998 allows a constable who has reasonable cause to believe that a child is in breach to remove that child to the child's home. Breach of curfew is also one of the factors that can trigger a *child safety order* under s11 of the Crime and Disorder Act 1998. Curfew orders (along with child safety orders, *parenting orders* and *youth offending teams*) will be piloted in four areas of England and Wales for a period of 18 months from October 1998.

child destruction: the crime of intentionally killing an unborn child which is capable of being born alive (s1 Infant Life (Preservation) Act 1929). However, it is not a criminal offence if a pregnancy is terminated to preserve the life of the mother or by a doctor acting lawfully under the Abortion Act 1967.

child, financial provision for: a parent or person with *parental responsibility* has a duty to maintain any child under the age of 16 (or 19 if in full-time education). This duty can be enforced by:

● the divorce court when the parents divorce or obtain a judicial separation;

● the Magistrates' Court on application of the parent with whom the child is living;

● the High Court in wardship proceedings and other family proceedings;

● the *Child Support Agency*.

Any of the courts can make an order for *periodical payments*, *lump sums*, *settlement of property* and *transfer of property*.

child of the family in family proceedings is:

● a child of both the parties;

● any other child who has been treated by both parties as a child of the family, apart from foster children placed by the local authority or another agency (Matrimonial Causes Act 1973).

This is wide enough to cover the child of just one of the parties who has been treated as part of the family and even a child who is no blood relation but has lived with the parties under a private fostering arrangement.

child safety order: an order that can be made by the Family Proceedings Court in the local Magistrates' Court in respect of any child under the age of ten (s11 Crime and Disorder Act 1998). An order can only be applied for by a local authority with social service responsibilities. A court can only make an order if:

● the child has committed an act which, if he had been aged ten or over, would have constituted an offence; or

● it is necessary for the purposes of preventing the child from committing such an act; or

● the child has broken a local curfew order; or

● the child has acted in a manner that caused or was likely to cause harassment, alarm or distress to one or more persons not of the same household as himself.

The order places the child under the supervision of a social worker or member of a *youth offending team* normally for a period of three months, though in exceptional circumstances, this can be extended to 12 months. An order also requires the child to comply with requirements specified by the court. Draft Home Office guidance suggests the following as possible requirements:

● attending school or extra-curricular activities;

● avoiding contact with disruptive and possibly older children;

- not visiting certain areas, such as shopping centres, unsupervised;

- being at home during certain hours, probably the evenings;

- attending particular courses or sessions to address specific problems (e.g. educational support or behavioural management).

There has been much criticism of this measure; for example, the National Association of Probation Officers has argued that it 'reduces the age of criminal responsibility to zero'. A *parenting order* could be made in the same case.

Child Support Agency assesses, collects and enforces maintenance payments by an absent parent to the parent with care of children under the age of 16 (19 if in full-time secondary education). The CSA deals with both married and unmarried parents. Parents with care are expected to apply to the CSA for financial provision if they are on benefit and may do so voluntarily if they are not. Maintenance is assessed according to a formula, and there has been criticism that this has led to unjust results. The formula has been amended several times. Another criticism has been the high level of mistakes in the assessments. An assessment by the CSA does not stop the parent with care applying to the court for additional maintenance in divorce or separation proceedings.

Children Act 1989 was passed to provide a consistent set of principles and orders which will apply in all courts where the welfare of a child is being considered. Its philosophy is that the State will not intervene in the affairs of a family unless it is necessary to stop a child suffering significant harm, and even then every effort will be made to keep the child with his family.

The principles of the Act are:

- the welfare of the child is paramount (takes priority) (see also *welfare principle*);

- there should be no delay in court proceedings;

- when making an order concerning a child, the court should take into account the wishes of the child, his needs, the effect on him of his changing circumstances, whether he is at risk of harm and how capable his parents and any other relevant adults are (see also *checklist in family law*);

- no court order should be made about a child unless it is better than not making an order.

The Act also introduced a new range of orders a court can use concerning a child:

- *residence order* which states who the child will live with;

- *contact order* which sets out when a child will see any parent or other relevant adult whom he does not live with;

- *prohibited steps order* which stops a parent carrying out an specific action which he would normally carry out as a parent, e.g. taking the child abroad;

- *specific issues order* which gives the court's decision about a question of a child's upbringing where the parents are in dispute, e.g. whether a child is to go to a private or a state school.

chose in action: an intangible piece of property, which has to be represented by a piece of paper stating the right on it. Examples of choses in action are cheques and share certificates.

chose in possession: something that can be touched and physically possessed, such as a car or furniture.

CICB stands for the Criminal Injuries Compensation Board. It is state funded and was set up to provide compensation for victims who suffer physical injury as the result of crime because many victims are unable to sue their assailant because he is unknown or has no money to pay adequate compensation. The board has been criticised for using a standard-ised scale of payments and for the low level of payments.

cif contract means 'cost includes insurance and freight'. Often used in shipping, the price the seller has quoted includes not just the cost of the goods but also the cost of transport-ing them and insuring them in transit.

circuit judges: judges who sit to hear cases at the *Crown Court* and at the *County Court*. Candidates for such posts must either have had *rights of audience* in the Crown Court or the County Court for at least ten years or have been a *recorder*. Since 1995, posts for circuit judges are advertised, and applicants are interviewed by a panel which includes a serving judge, an official from the Lord Chancellor's Department and a lay person. The panel's views are then put to the *Lord Chancellor* who makes the appointment. The Lord Chancellor can also dismiss a circuit judge for incapacity or misbehaviour. This has occurred only once, in the case of a judge who was convicted of evading customs duty on cigarettes and whisky.

There is criticism that the majority of circuit judges are white and male. For example, in 2003 out of the 550 or so circuit judges, only one per cent were ethnic minority judges and ten per cent female judges.

Citizens Advice Bureaux: advice agencies which were first set up in 1938; today there is a bureau in most towns. They give free advice on a variety of matters, mostly connected to social welfare problems and debt. They also advise on some legal matters and some may have arrangements with local solicitors who attend at the bureau on a regular basis to give free legal advice. Individual bureaux may bid for the right to be a fundholder under the legal help schemes and operate the government funded Form 10 for legal advice.

citizen's arrest: under s24 of the *Police and Criminal Evidence Act* powers of arrest are given to ordinary citizens to arrest anyone:

- who is in the act of committing an *arrestable offence* or whom he has reasonable grounds for suspecting to be committing such an offence;

- who has committed an arrestable offence or whom he has reasonable grounds for sus-pecting to be guilty of it.

The key point is that an arrestable offence must be in process of being committed or have been committed. If it turns out that no arrestable offence is being or has been committed, the citizen making the arrest can be sued in the law of tort for *false imprisonment*. See also *police powers of arrest*.

civil appeals: the normal appeal route for *civil cases* is to the *Court of Appeal* (Civil Division). Leave (permission) to appeal to the Court of Appeal was introduced from 1 January 1999 for all appeals. This requirement is intended to reduce the number of inap-propriate appeals.

The Access to Justice Act 1999 changed the appeal system for *fast track cases* and small claims. The system is:

- small claims cases heard by a district judge – appeal to circuit judge
- fast track cases heard by a district judge – appeal to circuit judge
- fast track cases heard by a circuit judge – appeal to High Court judge

For *multi-track cases* the normal route of appeal is to the Court of Appeal.

civil and criminal cases contrasted: civil cases and criminal cases are heard in different courts and have different procedures. The main differences are shown below.

Civil cases	Criminal cases
• individual starts case	• state usually prosecutes
• heard in County Court or High Court	• heard in Magistrates' Court or Crown Court
• case decide by a judge (very rarely jury) (see *civil juries*)	• case decided by magistrates (Magistrates' Court) or jury (Crown Court)
• case needs to be proved on the balance of probabilities	• case must be proved beyond reasonable doubt

civil cases: those which involve civil law. A civil case is started by the individual or business who wishes to make a claim against another person.

civil courts: courts which hear cases involving *civil law*. This means that they deal with disputes between individuals, or an individual and a business or between two businesses. The main civil courts are the *County Court* and the *High Court*. The *Magistrates' Court* also has jurisdiction to hear some civil cases, mainly involving family proceedings.

civil juries: only used in cases which involve allegations about the character or reputation of one of the parties. These cases are:

- *defamation*;
- *false imprisonment*;
- *malicious prosecution*;
- cases where there is an allegation of fraud.

In such cases, the jury decide both whether the case is proved and also the amount of damages which will be awarded to the claimant. A major criticism is that the amounts juries award are inconsistent. For this reason, juries are not thought suitable for use in personal injury cases (Ward v James (1966)).

Civil Justice Council: created in 1998 to monitor the progress of reform of the civil justice system and advise the Lord Chancellor. The members of the Council include judges, lawyers and non-lawyers who are involved in various consumer organisations, such as the National Consumer Council.

Civil Justice Review reported in 1988 on the problems of civil cases. The report led to a number of changes being made in the civil court structure by the Courts and Legal Services Act 1990. The main changes were:

- an increase in the jurisdiction of the small claims court;
- removing the limit on the amount of claim that could be made in the County Court;
- increased flexibility in transferring cases between the County Court and the High Court.

Despite these changes, the civil justice system was still thought to be unsatisfactory and a further review was carried out by Lord Woolf in 1996. See also *Woolf Report*.

civil law: also referred to as private law. Its function is to regulate legal relations between individuals and/or businesses. There are many branches of civil law; the main ones are:

- Contract Law;
- Law of Tort;
- Family Law;
- Company Law.

civil legal aid: government-funded help and representation for taking or defending *civil proceedings*. In order to qualify for civil legal aid, a person must pass a *merits test* showing that they have reasonable grounds to take or defend proceedings and a *means test* proving that they are poor enough to qualify for financial help. Those below minimum levels of *disposable income* and *disposable capital* are given legal aid free; those above the minimum level and below the maximum level have to pay a contribution; those above the maximum figures do not qualify for legal aid.

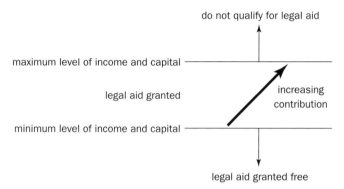

The income levels in the means test have not kept up with inflation, so few people qualify to use the scheme. Those who are granted legal aid have to pay the Legal Services Commission out of any money they win in the court case (see also *statutory charge*). Civil legal aid is not available for:

- *small claims cases*;
- undefended *divorce* proceedings;
- personal injury cases;
- *defamation* actions;
- most tribunals.

civil liberties: the fundamental rights of people. The most important rights are the right to liberty, which means that a person is protected from unjustified arrest and detention, *freedom of association*, *freedom of speech*, *freedom of religion* and freedom from *discrimination* on the grounds of race or sex. See also *Human Rights Act 1998*.

Civil Partnership Registration: a formal declaration giving a same sex couple legal recognition of their relationship. Once registered, the couple acquire rights such as parental responsibility for each other's children, joint state pension benefits, inheritance under the intestacy rules and a fair property division if the partnership dissolves. The scheme was proposed by the government in 2003 and anticipated to be brought into effect in 2004/5.

Civil Procedure Rules set out all the rules for *civil* cases both in the *High Court* and the *County Court*. Cases are started by issuing a claim form.

civil proceedings: the actions taken to bring a civil case to court and the actual conduct of the case through the court. To start a case, the *claimant* must send a claim form to the defendant setting out what is claimed.

civil remedies: the orders that a court can make in a case when the case has been decided. The main remedy is *damages*. This is an amount of money which the losing party must pay the winning party by way of compensation. Another remedy is an *injunction*: this orders the losing party to do something or, more usually, to stop doing something. Other remedies which can be given for breach of contract are *specific performance*, *rescission* and *rectification*.

claim form: the document which is used to start any *civil case*. Prior to April 1999, cases were started by different methods and this was thought to be confusing to people who wished to take a case without using a lawyer. See also *Civil Procedure Rules*.

claimant: the legal name for the person starting a *civil case*. Prior to April 1999 the term used in most cases was 'plaintiff'. See also *Civil Procedure Rules*.

class actions: civil cases taken jointly by several people who have suffered from the same problem. An example is where several *claimants* claim that they have been injured by a drug because the drug manufacturers failed to take proper care in developing the drug (this is under the tort of *negligence*). As the same legal principle is involved in each case, a class action is taken to establish whether there is a breach of duty under the tort of negligence. This saves the court from having to hear the same legal arguments in each case. If the class action is successful, then the court will then hear the individual cases to decide how much compensation each claimant should receive.

clean break: in divorce, the aim of a court when making a financial settlement between the parties so that the parties can put the past behind them and begin a new life. It is not possible to achieve a clean break if there are children who need maintaining, or if the children are young and the parent looking after them does not work. Under the Matrimonial Causes Act 1973, the court has a duty to consider whether a clean break is possible or can be achieved in the future by ordering that maintenance is paid for a limited period only.

Codes of Practice are considered 'soft' law. This is because they are not actual law but are merely guidelines issued on specific areas. However, when deciding a case, tribunals and courts will often consider what a Code of Practice recommends. The most important Codes of Practice are those on *police powers* and those on *discrimination* in employment.

codicil: a document which makes changes or additions to a *will*. A codicil can be made any time after the original will is made, but must be signed by the *testator* and witnessed by two witnesses.

codification of the law: bringing all the law together in one complete code. A code of law has the advantage that the law is easy to find. Many European countries use this method of stating their law. The law in England and Wales is not codified, but in some areas of law there have been attempts to produce an Act of Parliament stating all the law on one topic. Examples are the Sale of Goods Act 1979, the Theft Act 1968 and the Land Registration Act 2002.

cohabitee: a person who lives with someone else. It is commonly used where a man and a woman are living together as a couple but are not married; however, the term has no legal significance. Recently, many of the legal differences between people who are married and those who are living together have disappeared, but there are still some significant differences especially with regards the house in which they are living.

A comparison between:

People who are married	People who are living together
Children are legitimate.	Children are illegitimate.
Both parents have a responsibility to maintain children.	Both parents have a responsibility to maintain children.
Both parents have parental responsibilities, e.g. decide where children go to school.	Mother has parental responsibility, father must apply for a *parental responsibility order.*
Children will inherit from both parents if they die *intestate.*	Children will inherit from both parents if they die intestate.
A spouse who is not an owner of the matrimonial home has a right to occupy it.	A cohabitee who is not the owner of the joint home has no right to occupy it.
On divorce, the matrimonial assets are divided according to both parties' needs and earning capacity.	On separation, the assets are divided according to who paid for them.
Where a spouse dies, not leaving anything to the other, a claim can be made for an appropriate sum from the estate.	Where a cohabitee dies without leaving anything to the other, a claim can be made for an appropriate sum from the estate if they have lived together for two years.

See also *same sex couples.*

coincidence of actus reus and mens rea: the *actus reus* and the *mens rea* must be present together for an offence to have been committed. However, if there is a sequence of events or acts then the defendant will be guilty if he had the necessary mens rea at any point during that sequence (Thabo Meli (1954), Le Brun (1991)). Also if there is an on-going act, then the existence of the necessary mens rea at any point during that act is sufficient.

Case example: Fagan v Metropolitan Police Commissioner (1969)

Fagan was asked to stop his car by a police officer. When he did so, he accidentally drove one wheel onto the foot of the police officer. At this point he did not have the mens rea for an assault. However, as he refused to move the car when the policeman pointed out what had happened, he then had the necessary mens rea and at this point he committed the offence of assaulting a police officer in the execution of his duty.

collateral contract: a second contract which runs at the same time as the main contract and is related to it but is between one of the parties to the main contract and a third party.

Case example: Charnock v Liverpool Corporation Garage (1968)

A car owner took his car to a garage for repairs after an accident. The repairs were to be paid for by his insurance company. When the garage took an unreasonable length of time to carry out the repairs, the car owner successfully sued the garage. It was held that the main contract was between the insurance company and the garage but there was also a collateral contract between the owner and the garage; the consideration the owner provided was giving the garage the opportunity to enter into a contract with the insurance company.

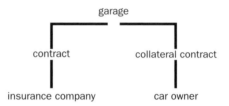

Collateral contracts sometimes seem to be artificial contracts which the courts recognise to avoid the problems of *privity of contract*. If no collateral contract had existed in the case example, the car owner would not have been able to sue the garage.

collective agreements: agreements made between trade unions and employers about the terms and conditions of employment. Such an agreement is not normally a legally enforceable contract unless it is in writing and contains a provision which states that it is intended to be legally enforceable. Individual workers are likely to be affected by a collective agreement, for example it may agree hours of work or amounts of pay, but it is not part of their *contract of employment* unless the terms have been specifically made part of that contract.

commercial arbitration: a method of resolving civil disputes in business cases without going to court. Usually the agreement to go to *arbitration* will be in writing. The Arbitration Act 1996 applies to such written arbitration agreements and states that the object of arbitration is to 'obtain the fair resolution of disputes by an impartial tribunal without any unnecessary delay or expense'. The parties agree that an independent third party will act as arbitrator and decide the matter. The date, time, place and method of arbitration are all matters for the parties to decide in consultation with the arbitrator. The decision made by the arbitrator is called an award and cannot be challenged unless there has been a serious irregularity in the proceedings. See also *Scott v Avery clauses*.

Commercial Court: a special court in the *Queen's Bench Division* of the High Court. It hears cases about banking, insurance disputes, problems over the meaning of documents used in mercantile cases, such as *negotiable instruments* and *charterparties*. The judges are judges of the Queen's Bench Division who have special knowledge and experience of such cases.

Commission for Racial Equality (CRE): established by the Race Relations Act 1976 with the aims of working towards the elimination of *discrimination* on racial or ethnic grounds, promoting equality of opportunity and keeping the legislation under review. The Commission may give advice to individuals and help them to pursue remedies in tribunal hearings. It can also take action itself; for example, in cases of discrimination in the work place, it has the power to issue a non-discrimination notice against the employer. The Commission has issued a Code of Practice for the elimination of discrimination and the promotion of equality of opportunity in employment.

commissioner for local administration: *Ombudsman* appointed to investigate complaints of maladministration against local authorities.

committal proceedings: where a defendant is sent by magistrates to be tried at the *Crown Court*. This only happens if the charge against the defendant is a *triable either way offence* and either the defendant has chosen to be tried at the Crown Court or the magistrates are of the opinion that the offence is too serious to be tried by them. Committal proceedings can be held either:

- under s6(1) Magistrates' Court Act 1980 where the magistrates will read all the prosecution evidence against the defendant and decide if there is enough evidence to send him for trial; or

- under s6(2) Magistrates' Court Act 1980 where, with the agreement of the defendant's legal representative, the magistrates do not look at the prosecution evidence, but formally commit the defendant for trial. This type of committal is often called a 'paper' committal.

Committal proceedings are to be abolished under the Criminal Justice Bill 2002. Instead all cases will be transferred to the Crown Court under s51 of the Crime and Disorder Act 1998.

committals for sentence can be made where *magistrates* do not feel that they have sufficient sentencing powers to deal with a defendant who is guilty of a *triable either way offence*. The magistrates send the defendant to the *Crown Court* to be sentenced there.

common law: law which has been developed by the judges. The term can be used in different ways as shown in the table below.

Different meanings	Distinguishes it from
• The law developed by the judges in the 12th and 13th centuries to form a law which was uniform or common throughout England and Wales.	• The local laws used prior to the Norman Conquest.
• The law which has continued to be developed by the judges through the doctrine of *judicial precedent*.	• Laws made by a legislative body, such as *Acts of Parliament*, *delegated legislation* or *European law*.
• The law operated in the common law courts before the reorganisation of the courts in 1873–1875.	• *Equity*, the law developed by the early Lord Chancellors and operated in the Chancery courts.

common mistake occurs when both parties entering into a contract make the same mistake about an essential part of it. If this happens, the contract is void. Common mistake arises where both parties mistakenly think:

- the goods exist at the time the contract is made;
- the goods are owned by the seller

A mistake about the quality of the goods, however, does not make the contract void.

Case example: Leaf v International Galleries (1950)

The gallery sold Leaf a picture that they both believed to be by Constable. Later Leaf found out that it was by someone else and therefore less valuable. It was held that the contract was a valid one because there had been no mistake about which picture Leaf had bought, the only mistake was about one of its qualities.

See also *frustration* for where goods cease to exist after the contract is made.

Commonwealth courts: courts in Commonwealth countries which operate on the same principles of *judicial precedent* as in England and Wales. Decisions in these courts can have an influence on decisions made in England and Wales and are considered as *persuasive precedent*.

communication rules in contract state when an *offer*, an *acceptance* and a *revocation* take effect. The main rules are:

1 Offer

An offer takes effect when the *offeree* knows about it, e.g. when a letter containing the offer is received or a telephone call is made.

2 Acceptance of an offer

An acceptance takes effect when the *offeror* knows about it, e.g. when the telephone call is made, provided that it is made in the way the offeror requested or in a more efficient way. Acceptance always has to be communicated to the offeror, even if the offeror has said that this is not necessary.

Exceptions:

- using the post: acceptance is effective when the letter is posted, even if the letter is lost in the post;
- reward offers: acceptance takes place by the person to whom the offer is made carrying out the terms of the contract and then informing the offeror;
- using a fax (and probably the Internet): acceptance takes place when it can be reasonably assumed that it has been read.

See also *acceptance, communication of*.

3 Revocation of an offer

A revocation takes effect when the person to whom the offer is made knows about it. It is irrelevant whether he is told by the offeror or someone else (Dickinson v Dodds (1876)). Unlike an acceptance, a letter of revocation takes effect when it is received. This means that it is possible for a contract to be made by the *offeree* posting a letter of acceptance, even though the offeror has changed his mind and there is a letter of revocation already in the post. This is shown by the time sequence in Byrne v van Tienhoven (1880).

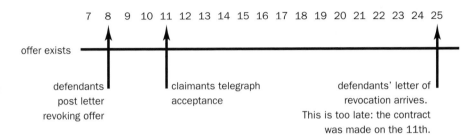

offer exists

7 8 9 10 11 12 13 14 15 16 17 18 19 20 21 22 23 24 25

defendants
post letter
revoking offer

claimants telegraph
acceptance

defendants' letter of
revocation arrives.
This is too late: the contract
was made on the 11th.

community legal service (CLS) fund: in 2000 this replaced legal aid for civil and family cases in cases which cannot be funded by some other method (e.g. *conditional fees*). There is a set budget for the CLS fund, with two sub-budgets (civil and family) and the *Legal Services Commission* has limited flexibility to switch money between the two. The Commission allocates budgets to its regional offices, though a central budget is retained for very expensive cases.

Under the Community Legal Services fund there is priority for funding legal services to:

- social welfare cases; e.g. cases about people's basic entitlements such as a roof over their heads and the correct social security benefits;

- other cases of fundamental importance to the people affected, for example involving major issues in children's' lives such as care or adoption issues;

- cases involving a wider public interest; e.g. important new legal issues or Human Rights cases.

community order is a proposed sentence under the Criminal Justice Bill 2002 for offenders aged 16 or over. This order is intended to replace all the separate community sentences and allow the court to impose any requirement which it decides is suitable from the following:

- an unpaid work requirement (formerly a *community service order*)

- an activity requirement

- a programme requirement

- a prohibited activity requirement

- a curfew requirement (formerly a *curfew order*)

- an exclusion requirement

- a residence requirement

- a *supervision requirement* (formerly a *probation order*)

- treatment requirements, e.g. mental health, drug rehabilitation, alcohol treatment

- an *attendance centre requirement* (for those under 25).

community sentences: sentences which affect a defendant's liberty but are served in the community rather than in prison. Under the Powers of Criminal Courts (Sentencing) Act 2000, a community sentence can only be imposed by a court if:

- the offence or offences committed by the defendant are serious enough to warrant a community sentence;

- the combination of orders is suitable for the particular defendant; and

- the restriction on liberty is commensurate with the seriousness of the offence(s).

There are four types of community sentence:

- community rehabilitation order, previously *probation order*;

- community punishment order, previously *community service order*;

- community punishment and rehabilitation order;

- *curfew order*.

Under the Criminal Justice Bill 2002 these orders will be replaced by a *community order* which can have different requirements attached to it.

community service order: a *community sentence* which can be imposed on offenders aged 16 and over. It requires the offender to work for between 40 and 240 hours on a suitable project organised by the probation service. The exact number of hours is fixed by the court, and those hours are then usually worked in eight-hour sessions, often at weekends. The type of work will vary, but is likely to involve such things as painting school buildings or working on a local conservation project. A criticism is that the number of hours is not enough; other countries, which run similar schemes, can impose much longer hours. (Now called a community punishment order.)

community support officer are civilians who work with the police and have some police powers. These include being able to issue fixed penalty notices, to ask the name and address of someone who has committed a fixed penalty offence or an offence causing injury, alarm, distress or damage **and** if the person refuses to do so, to detain that person for up to 30 minutes (using reasonable force if necessary) pending the arrival of a police officer.

See also *corporate personality*.

companies and partnerships compared: there are many legal differences between a *company* and a *partnership*. The most important are:

Companies	Partnerships
• Formed by registering under the Company Acts.	• Formed by agreement between the partners; this agreement may even be implied from conduct.
• Can have any number of members.	• Between 2 and 20 members (except for some professions, e.g. solicitors).
• Separate legal personality.	• No separate legal personality.
• Limited liability – members only liable for company debts to value of their shares.	• Unlimited liability – partners liable for partnership debts.

company: an artificial legal personality that can make contracts, commit torts and crimes and sue and be sued. A company comes into being when a *certificate of incorporation* is issued.

compensation order: an order made by a criminal court that a convicted defendant must pay a sum of money to the victim of the crime. In the *Magistrates' Court*, the maximum amount that can be ordered is £5,000.

compensatory award: an award which can be made by an *employment tribunal* in a case of *unfair dismissal* in addition to the *basic award*. The compensatory award is to compensate the employee for the loss he has suffered as a result of being unfairly dismissed. The tribunal consider such matters as immediate and future loss of earnings, loss of fringe benefits and pension rights and expenses of having to look for another job. However, there is a fixed maximum amount (in 2003 £53,000) that can be awarded, so the award may not fully compensate the employee.

complete defence: a defence in criminal law which, if successful, will mean that the defendant is acquitted. For example, a defendant who as assaulted someone will be acquitted if he can show that he acted in self-defence.

conciliation: a method of *alternative dispute resolution* where a third party tries to help parties to resolve their differences. The conciliator will take an active part in suggesting the possible basis for a settlement of the dispute or giving opinions on points at issue.

condition as a term of a contract: an important term of a contract dealing with the most essential parts of it. If one party to the contract breaches (breaks) a condition, the other party is entitled to rescind (cancel) the contract and claim *damages*.

Other terms of a contract are *warranties* and *innominate terms*, and a court, when deciding what category each term falls into, will first look at the contract. The parties may have decided during negotiations which terms are important enough to be conditions and have included this in the contract. Otherwise the court will look at the whole agreement and decide which terms are fundamental to the contract and therefore conditions.

conditional caution can be used where there is evidence to charge a suspect, he admits the offence and agrees to being cautioned. A condition aimed at rehabilitation or reparation can be made. Failure to comply with the conditions could mean the taking of the case to court for the original offence.

conditional discharge: a method by which a criminal court can deal with a convicted offender. The effect of the order is that, provided the defendant is not convicted of another offence within a time limit set by the court (up to three years), the defendant will not receive any further punishment. If the defendant does commit another offence within the time limit, he can be brought back to court and re-sentenced for the original crime.

conditional fees: a way of funding a legal case. The person who wishes to take or defend a civil case agrees with his *solicitor* a fixed sum for the cost of the case. This agreement will also contain an agreed extra amount known as the success fee which will be paid to the solicitor if the case is won. If the case is lost, this extra amount will not be paid. Conditional fees are often referred to as 'no win, no fee', but this is not strictly true as usually the original amount agreed must be paid even if the case is lost. However some claim firms do not make any charge if the case is lost.

conditional sale agreement: an agreement where the debtor borrows money from a credit company to buy goods. Like a hire-purchase agreement, he takes possession of the goods straight away but does not become owner of them until the last repayment is made. During the repayment period the goods remain the property of the credit company.

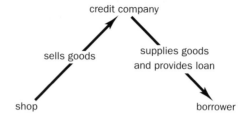

Conditional sale agreements are covered by the *Consumer Credit Act 1974,* subject to the exemptions.

consensus ad idem: a Latin phrase meaning 'agreed about the same thing'. In contract law, a contract is held not to come into existence until both parties are agreed about all the details.

consent and offences against the person: in some circumstances, the fact that the other person consented to an assault will mean that no crime has been committed. For example, if a person consents to sexual intercourse then it is not rape. Also for minor assaults, the victim's consent will usually mean that the assault is not a criminal offence. However, there are certain situations where, even though the victim consented, the law states that a criminal offence has been committed. These are:;

- offences in which a serious injury has been caused
- injuries caused through acts which are not in the public interest, such as fighting (A-G's reference (No 6 of 1980) (1981));
- injuries caused through sado-masochistic acts (R v Brown (1993)).

consent in tort: a defence which is used in *trespass to person*. A claim cannot be brought for *battery* if the claimant agreed to it and it served a socially useful purpose, e.g. surgical operations and physical contact sports. The claimant's consent must have been freely given, not under duress. The claimant must also have fully understood what will happen and the risks involved.

Consent can be in different forms:

- in writing;
- by words;
- by implication, e.g. joining a game of rugby.

The defence does not apply if the defendant went beyond what was agreed to, e.g. a footballer who injures another player by foul play. This defence is similar to *volenti non fit injuria* which is used in negligence.

consideration: what both parties undertake to do in a contract and the reason for the contract being made. It is one of the five essential ingredients of a contract. (See also *offer, acceptance, intention to create legal relations* and *capacity.*) Consideration is usually:

- the exchange of goods; and/or
- the exchange of services; and/or
- the exchange of money.

The courts have also, especially in the 19th century, treated as consideration any benefit that one party to the contract receives which is a detriment to the other party.

The main rules on consideration are:

1) Both parties must give consideration for a contract to come into existence. Where only one party agrees to do something, this is a *bare promise* and there is no contract. The person to whom the promise was made cannot enforce that promise.

2) Whatever is given as consideration does not have to be of the same value as what is given in exchange.

Case example: Chappel & Co v Nestlé (1960)

Records were sold for 1/6d (8p) plus three chocolate wrappers. These wrappers were thrown away as soon as they were received, but it was held that they were consideration even though their value was very small. Legally they were sufficient consideration.

The following have been held not to be consideration:

- *past consideration,* that is something which has already happened;

- illegal acts, such as smuggling goods (Foster v Driscoll (1929));

- paying only part of a debt in settlement even where the other party agrees to accept part payment. This known as the rule in *Pinnel's case*;

- carrying out an act where there is already a legal duty to do it. In Collins v Godefoy (1831), a lawyer did not provide consideration by promising to give evidence in court as he had already received a court order to do so;

- carrying out an act where there is already a duty under a contract to do it (see *existing contractual duty*).

consolidation of statutes: the bringing together of all existing *statutes* on a topic in one *Act of Parliament*. This makes the law easier to find and apply. An example of a consolidating statute is the Employment Rights Act 1996, which brought together all the existing law on employment rights.

conspiracy: an inchoate criminal offence. Inchoate means 'just begun or undeveloped', in other words the main crime has not been completed but the law still recognises that the offender has committed an offence.

Most conspiracies are now charged under the Criminal Law Act 1977. This provides that the offence is committed if two or more persons agree to carry out a course of conduct which will 'necessarily amount to or involve the commission of any offence or offences by one or more of the parties to the agreement, or, would do so but for the existence of facts which render the commission of the offence impossible'. So the essence of conspiracy is that there is an agreement to carry out conduct which amounts to a criminal offence. It does not matter that the parties do not actually do anything more, the agreement and the intention to carry it out is enough for them to be guilty. The defendant will be charged with conspiracy to commit the relevant crime, for example conspiracy to murder or conspiracy to steal.

There are still three types of conspiracy which are referred to as *common law* conspiracies, as they are not defined under the Act. These are:

- conspiracy to defraud;
- conspiracy to corrupt public morals;
- conspiracy to outrage public decency.

Note that an agreement to commit a tort is no longer a criminal offence.

constitution: the basic law of a state which regulates how it is governed and sets out the rights and duties of the state and its citizens. Most countries have a written constitution. The United Kingdom does not have a complete written constitution; instead, our constitution is to be found in a variety of sources of law, including *case law*, *Acts of Parliament* and *custom*.

constitutional law defines the government's powers and the relationship between the three types of governmental powers (*legislative*, executive and judicial) (see also *Montesquieu's theory of the separation of powers*). It also defines the relationship between the government and the citizen.

constructive dismissal: the term used where an *employee* is forced to resign from work because of the employer's behaviour. This concept is set out in the Employment Rights Act 1996 s95(1)(c) which states that where an employee terminates the employment contract 'in circumstances in which he is entitled to terminate it without notice by reason of the employer's conduct', the employee is dismissed. The employer's conduct must amount to a 'significant breach going to the root of the *contract of employment*' (Western Excavating (ECC) Ltd v Sharp (1978)). Constructive dismissal may also be *wrongful dismissal* and/or *unfair dismissal*.

constructive manslaughter: a killing where an accused, who does not have the necessary intention for *murder*, kills the victim in the course of an unlawful act. It is called constructive manslaughter as the crime is constructed or made out of a less serious crime which has resulted in a death. This crime is also referred to as unlawful act manslaughter. In order for a defendant to be guilty, it must be shown that:

- he intentionally did an unlawful act; and
- the act was dangerous in that 'sober and reasonable people would inevitably recognise' that there was the risk of some injury, although not necessarily a serious injury; this is an objective test, the defendant does not have to realise that any injury might be caused; and
- the act caused the death.

Case example: R v Newbury and Jones (1977)

Two youths pushed a paving stone off a bridge onto a train passing underneath. The stone hit the train and killed the guard. The youths were guilty of constructive manslaughter as they had intentionally done an unlawful act (criminal damage); this act was clearly dangerous, as a reasonable person would realise that someone on the train could be injured; the act caused the guard's death.

constructive trust: a trust which arises in cases involving land to prevent a person who has acted fraudulently, inequitably (unfairly) or in breach of trust from benefiting even though he legally is entitled to do this.

Case example: Bannister v Bannister (1948)

A sister sold two cottages to her brother, relying on his spoken agreement that she could go on living in them until her death. Once he became the owner, he tried to evict her, arguing that he was not bound by the agreement because it was not in writing as required by the Law of Property Act 1925. It was held that a constructive trust had been created, the brother was the legal owner of the property but he held it for the benefit of his sister so that she could go on living in it.

There is an overlap between constructive and resulting trusts; however, constructive trusts can be created not just where money has been contributed towards the purchase of land but also where the claimant has done any act which gives the defendant an interest in land. For example, giving up a claim to a tenancy so that the defendant acquires it.

consumer: an individual, rather than a business, who makes a contract with a business. Where a company buys goods, it can still be a consumer if it is acting like an individual and buying goods which are normally for private use.

Case example: R & B Customs Brokers Ltd v UDT (1988)

A freight-loading company bought a car for the Managing Director's use. It was held that, as the car was not going to be used for an integral part of the company's business, the company was acting as a consumer; it would have been different if they had bought a fork-lift truck.

Consumers are given protection by the *Unfair Contract Terms Act 1977* and the *Unfair Terms in Consumer Contracts Regulations 1994* which regulate exclusion clauses imposed by businesses when dealing with consumers. In recognition of the fact that individuals are unable to deal with businesses on equal terms, consumers have been given added protection when buying goods and services under the *Sale of Goods Act 1979* (as amended) and the *Supply of Goods and Services Act 1982*.

consumer contract: a contract between a *consumer* and a business or individual who is in the business of selling. A consumer contract always includes terms implied by the *Sale of Goods Act 1979* and the *Supply of Goods and Services Act 1982*.

consumer credit: in consumer law, an agreement between an individual borrower and a company whose business it is to make loans. Typical consumer credit agreements are:

- a *hire-purchase agreement*;
- a *conditional sale agreement*;
- a *credit sale agreement*;
- buying goods using a *credit card*;
- borrowing money by using a credit card to withdraw cash to buy goods;
- obtaining a personal loan from a bank or building society;
- using an overdraft facility.

Consumer credit agreements are regulated by the *Consumer Credit Act 1974*, subject to exceptions.

Consumer Credit Act 1974 regulates credit and hire agreements which *consumers* enter into where the sum borrowed, without interest, is less than £25,000, although some agreements are exempt (see also *Consumer Credit Act 1974, exempt agreements*).

The Act gives borrowers certain protection by:

- regulating the formation, terms and enforcement of credit and hire agreements;
- setting up a licensing system for people who provide credit or advise on credit;
- ensuring that lenders explain their interest rates in the same way to give a true picture and so that borrowers can make fair comparisons;
- requiring warnings about the consequences of not keeping up mortgage repayments to be included in all pre-contractual information
- requiring complete information on all charges be given on low-start mortgages;
- controlling door to door canvassing by lenders and creating criminal offences to stop unsatisfactory practices;
- giving borrowers, in some circumstances, a *cooling-off period* during which they can change their minds about the contract;
- giving enforcement powers to the *Director-General of Fair Trading* and local Trading Standard Officers;
- making it impossible to contract out of the Act.

Consumer Credit Act 1974, exempt agreements: not all credit agreements are regulated by the Consumer Credit Act. The main agreements which are exempt from the regulations of the Act are:

- most first mortgages;
- *debtor-creditor-supplier agreements* where there is a maximum of four payments and repayments have to take place within 12 months.
- debtor-creditor-supplier agreements where repayment of a running account must be made in full by a single payment, e.g. an American Express account, where the amount owed must be paid off in full each month;
- *debtor-creditor agreements* where the rate of interest is low (not more than 13 per cent or 1 per cent above UK banks' base rate).

consumer credit agreements, formalities: every consumer credit agreement must show:

- how much each repayment is and when it is due;
- the total charge for credit (the Annual Percentage Rate), this must be done in a standard way so that the borrower can make a true comparison between credit companies;
- what protection and remedies are available to the borrower under the *Consumer Credit Act 1974*.

The borrower must receive a copy of the agreement at the time the contract is made. If the borrower fills in forms applying for credit, he must receive one copy at the time he makes an application and must be sent a second copy within seven days of the credit company accepting his application. If the formalities are not complied with, the credit company will only be able to enforce the contract with the permission of the court, which has power to reduce or extinguish the debt owed by the borrower.

consumer protection: protection given to an ordinary person buying goods or services (*consumer*) by Parliament against businesses who would otherwise be able to dictate terms because of their greater power. The main Acts which control which terms will be included in a *consumer contract* are:

- *Consumer Protection Act 1987*;

- *Sale of Goods Act 1979*;

- *Supply of Goods and Services Act 1982*;

- *Unfair Contract Terms Act 1977*;

- *Unfair Terms in Consumer Contracts Regulations 1994*.

If these Acts are breached, the consumer can make a claim in the civil courts.

Other Acts have been passed which make some actions by businesses criminal offences. For example, under the *Trades Descriptions Act 1968*, it is an offence to give goods a misleading description.

See also *Office of Fair Trading*.

Consumer Protection Act 1987 gives a *consumer* or anyone injured by a defective product the right to sue the producer without having to show that the producer was negligent, provided that the defective product caused death, personal injury or damage to property to the value of at least £275.

Defect can be caused by:	Product can be:	Producer can be the:
the design, the process or manufacturing or lack of proper warnings or clear assembly or installation instructions	anything that has gone through a manufacturing process, including gas and electricity; fresh food which has not been processed is not included.	manufacturer or company which labels the goods under its own brand name or company which imports the goods into the European Union

The Act does not cover damage to goods which are either not normally intended for private use or not being used for private use, so that a business cannot use this Act to sue a producer of defective factory machinery.

The Act also creates some criminal offences for breaches of safety regulations, now mainly replaced by the *General Product Safety Regulations 1994*.

Consumer Protection (Distance Selling) Regulations 2000 protects consumers buying goods or services by telephone, mail order, fax, Internet or other distance selling where the supplier's business is selling goods in this way. Clear details must be given to the buyer before the contract is made about the supplier and the goods and a right to cancel within seven working days. Goods must be supplied within 30 days. Where unauthorised payments are made on a buyer's credit card, debit card, etc., the credit card company must refund the buyer and reclaim the money from the supplier.

See also *Electronic Commerce (EC Directive) Regulations 2002*.

consumer sale: a sale of goods where the buyer is purchasing as a *consumer* and not in the course of business and the seller is selling in the course of business.

contact order: a court order requiring the person with whom a child is living to allow the child to visit or stay or otherwise have contact with the person named in the order. The court sets out the details of what contact there is to be, e.g. how many hours visits will last or when overnight stays will take place. When considering what order to make, the court's first consideration will be the welfare of the child (see also *welfare principle*).

contempt of court: disobeying a court's *judgment* or order or breaking an undertaking (promise) given to a court or any act which is calculated to obstruct or interfere with the proper administration of justice. Examples of such acts are jurors who attend court in a drunken state, protesters who interrupt court proceedings, or newspapers which publish information which might prejudice a fair trial. Contempt of court can be punished by the court with a fine or by imprisonment.

contingency fees: the payment of a percentage of the client's *damages* to his lawyer when the lawyer wins the case. If the case is lost, the lawyer is not paid anything. This percentage system is operated in the United States of America but is not allowed in England and Wales. Instead, a system of *conditional fees* is used.

continuity of employment: working for the same *employer* for a continuous period of time. In order to qualify for certain employment rights, especially the right not to be unfairly dismissed and the right to claim redundancy payment, an employee must have at least one year's continuous employment. Where there is a takeover in a business, an employee's rights are protected, and continuity of employment is preserved even though the employer has changed (see also *transfer of undertakings*).

contra proferentum rule: a Latin phrase meaning 'against the person putting it forward'. This concept is used where a contract has terms which limit one party's liability in the event of the contract not being completely carried out. If there is any doubt at all about the exact meaning of the term, the courts will choose the meaning that is the least favourable to the party who tried to limit their liability.

Case example: Wallis, Sons and Wells v Pratt and Haynes (1911)

A contract for the sale of seeds included a clause that the sellers gave 'no warranty express or implied' about the description of the seeds. The seeds were not as they had been described, but it was held that the sellers' liability was not excluded by the clause. The court decided that the description of the seeds was such an important part of the contract that it was a condition of the contract rather than a warranty. Therefore the exclusion clause did not apply. Although the sellers had intended to limit their responsibility in the event of the contract going wrong, the wording they used did not exactly cover the situation that arose, and the court would not allow them to avoid liability.

contract: a legally binding agreement made between two parties, usually to exchange goods, services or money. It can be made orally or in writing or even by actions alone. For a valid contract to come into existence, there must be:

- a clear *offer* made by one party to the other; and
- a clear *acceptance* of the offer by the person to whom the offer was made; and

- an exchange of *consideration* (this can be an actual exchange of goods, services or money or a promise to do so in the future); and

- an intention by both parties to enter into a legal contract (see also *intention to create legal relations*); and

- an understanding by both parties of what they are agreeing to (see also *capacity*).

Unless all five are present, a legally enforceable contract will not be created.

contract for services: an agreement by an *independent contractor* to provide services for another person. An example is where a house owner agrees with a painter that the painter will decorate the outside of the house. The house owner is making a contract for services with the painter. It is not a contract of employment. It is not always easy to decide if someone is an independent contractor or an *employee*. The courts have put forward a number of tests to decide this. (See also *employment contrasted with self-employment*.)

contract of employment: a contract between an employer and an employee. Normal rules of contract apply, so it does not have to be in writing (except for employment as a merchant seaman or an apprentice). However, under s1 of the Employment Rights Act 1996, employers must provide employees with a written statement of the main terms of the employment within two months of the employment starting. This *written statement of employment* is not the contract of employment but can be evidence of the terms of the contract.

The employer and the employee will agree the main terms of the employment, but there are also terms implied by law which impose duties on both employer and employee. The main ones of these are:

Employer	Employee
• Pay the wages of the employee.	• Obey reasonable lawful orders.
• Treat the employee with respect.	• Exercise reasonable care and skill.
• Take reasonable care to ensure the health and safety of the employee.	• Give faithful service (e.g. must not disclose confidential information).

contract of service: a *contract of employment*. It must be distinguished from a *contract for services,* which does not create an employment situation. See also *employment contrasted with self-employment*.

Contracts (Rights of Third Parties) Act 1999: see *third parties, rights under contract*.

contributory negligence: an action by the claimant which justifies reducing the amount of damages (compensation) payable by the defendant. If the defendant can show that the claimant contributed towards the accident which caused the injury or the injury he suffered was made worse by his actions, e.g. not wearing a seat belt, his damages will be reduced in proportion to how much he was to blame (Law Reform (Contributory Negligence) Act 1945). Contributory negligence only occurs if the injured person could reasonably have foreseen that he ran a risk of injury through his actions.

Case example: Sayers v Harlow UDC 1957

Mrs Sayers was injured trying to climb out of a lavatory owned by Harlow UDC. It was proved that Harlow had been negligent because the lavatory had a faulty lock, but Mrs Sayers' damages were reduced because she had partly contributed towards the accident by standing on the lavatory-roll holder. It was held that it was reasonably foreseeable that this would turn over, causing Mrs Sayers to fall.

conveyance: a document used to transfer ownership of land from one person to another where the land has not been registered at the Land Registry.

conveyancing: the legal transfer of ownership of land. This includes buying and selling houses. *Solicitors* used have a monopoly (sole right) over conveyancing. This was changed by the Administration of Justice Act 1985 which allowed people other than solicitors to become licensed conveyancers. In 1990, the right to carry out conveyancing was also given to banks and building societies.

cooling off period: is time given customers to reconsider a *consumer credit agreement* they have entered into. The customer has five days to change his mind from the time of receiving from the credit company either a notice of cancellation rights (if the agreement has already been signed) or a copy of the agreement to sign, provided that:

- the agreement is a consumer credit agreement; and
- oral (spoken) negotiations have taken place before the agreement was reached; and
- those negotiations took place in the presence of the customer (i.e. not on the telephone); and
- the negotiations took place away from the credit company's premises (this is usually at the customer's home).

Notice of this change of mind must be sent in writing to the credit company.

Coroners' courts inquire into violent or unnatural deaths, sudden deaths where the cause in unknown and deaths in prison. They also have jurisdiction to decide whether items found are *treasure* under the Treasure Act 1996 and must go to a museum. Cases are heard by a Coroner, who is either legally or medically qualified. A *jury* of between seven and 11 members must be used if the death being investigated occurred:

- in prison;
- in police custody or resulting from an injury caused by a police officer in the execution of his duty;
- in an industrial accident or through an industrial disease;
- in circumstances where there is a possible risk to the health and safety of the public.

A jury may be used in other matters at the discretion of the Coroner.

corporate liability for crimes: a corporation has a separate legal personality and can therefore be guilty of a crime. As a company has no physical existence and cannot act or think, the law assumes that the acts and thoughts of certain people within the corporation are the acts and thoughts of the corporation itself. The problem is in identifying which people are considered sufficiently high ranking to be considered as the corporation's mind and will. In Bolton Engineering v Graham (1957) it was said that:

'Some people are ... nothing more than hands to do the work...Others are directors and managers who represent the directing mind and will of the company, and control what it does. The state of mind of these people is the state of mind of the company and is treated by the law as such.'

This clearly includes directors and the company secretary, but in Tesco v Natrass (1971), it was held that a branch manager was not sufficiently senior to be considered the 'mind and will' of the company.

A corporation can also be liable for the wrongful acts of its employees under the principle of *vicarious liability*.

corporate manslaughter: under the principle of *corporate liability*, it is possible for a corporation to be convicted of *manslaughter*. This occurred in 1994 when OLL Ltd was found guilty of the manslaughter of four teenagers in a canoeing tragedy. The managing director was aware that safety precautions were inadequate, and his 'guilty' state of mind made the company liable. (The managing director was also personally found guilty of manslaughter.) To make it easier to convict corporations, the Law Commission has proposed a special crime of corporate manslaughter, under which the prosecution has to prove that:

- a management failure is the cause of a person's death; and
- that failure constitutes conduct falling far below which can reasonably be expected of the corporation in the circumstances.

corporate personality means that a business which has been legally incorporated has a separate identity from the people who are involved in the business. As it has its own legal personality, the *corporation* can make contracts, commit torts and crimes and sue and be sued. Most corporations have limited liability, so that in the event of the corporation being unable to pay its debts, the members are not liable for these debts.

Case example: Salomon v Salomon (1897)

Mr Salomon formed a company in which he, his wife and children were the only shareholders. When the company became unable to pay all its debts, Mr Salomon claimed that he had first priority on the company's assets, as it owed a secured debt to him. Other creditors argued that Mr Salomon and the company were not separate legal personalities and he should not be allowed to claim this debt. The House of Lords held that the company was a separate legal personality and Mr Salomon was entitled to claim.

corporation: an artificial legal personality which has a separate identity. A corporation can be created by:

- registration under the Companies Act 1985 and the issue of a *certificate of incorporation* (this is the most usual way);
- by an Act of Parliament (for example, local authorities have been incorporated in this way);
- by Royal Charter; this is very unusual, but the BBC and some of the modern universities have been created as corporate bodies by Royal Charter.

(See also *corporate personality*.)

corporation aggregate: a group of people who have become in law a single legal personality which exists independently of those people, through being incorporated. Incorporation can be by:

- Royal Charter (e.g. universities);
- statute (e.g. local authorities);
- registration under the Companies Act 1985.

(See also *corporate personality*.)

corporation sole: a legal personality which exists because of a special position held by an individual. This allows the legal personality to continue beyond the lifetime of that individual. The Crown is a corporation sole; its legal position continues, even though individual kings and queens come and go. The advantage of having this artificial legal personality is that the property belongs to it, not to the individual who holds the post at any one time.

costs: in civil law, the financial costs of bringing a claim to court. These are mainly solicitors' and barristers' bills, but also include the cost of experts' reports and court fees. At the end of a case, the judge usually orders the losing party to pay the winning party a sum of money which will cover his costs. But the judge may decide not do this if he considers that the winner should not have brought the case or has acted inappropriately. The costs of the claimant and defendant added together are usually more than the amount in dispute, so deciding who will pay each party's costs is an important part of settling a case.

Council of Europe: an international organisation formed after the Second World War and which was instrumental in drawing up the *European Convention on Human Rights*. Most European countries are members of the Council. This Council is not part of the European Union, but a separate organisation.

Council of Ministers: one of the four main institutions of the *European Union*. It comprises one minister from each member state. Usually the Foreign Minister is a state's main representative, but another minister may attend; for example, if the principal subject matter under discussion is agriculture, then the Minister for Agriculture may attend. Twice a year, the heads of each state meet in the European Council to discuss broad issues of policy. The Council is the principal decision making body of the European Union. Voting in the Council is on a weighted basis, with each country having a number of votes roughly in proportion to the size of its population.

Council on Tribunals: the body that supervises and keeps under review the working of over 2,000 *administrative tribunals*. It was set up by the Tribunals and Inquiries Act 1958 and has 15 members who observe tribunal hearings and receive complaints about tribunals. It publishes an annual report. The Council has been criticised for being too small to deal with the vast number of tribunals and for having very little power, as it can only make unenforceable recommendations.

counselling as secondary participation in a crime: one of the ways in which a person is liable as a secondary party to a crime. The other methods of secondary participation are *aiding*, *abetting* and *procuring*. Counselling means advising, encouraging or giving information on a crime. The counsellor does not have to be present when the crime is committed, but it is necessary to show that the crime committed by the principal offender is 'within the scope of the counselling'.

Examples of counselling are:

- giving information about the security system of a bank to a burglar;
- hiring someone to commit a crime, as in R v Calhaem (1985) where the defendant hired another person to kill the victim; the defendant was guilty of murder.

counter-claim: where a defendant in a civil case makes a claim against the *claimant*. This frequently occurs in cases where the claim arises from a car crash. The claimant will make a claim against the defendant for loss and injury suffered in the crash: the defendant will deny it is his fault and will counter-claim against the claimant for loss and injury which he, the defendant, suffered.

counter-offer: in contract law, a reply to an *offer* which does not accept the offer but puts forward different terms. It is not an *acceptance* because it does not agree to the terms of the offer. The person who made the original offer (the *offeror*) can either accept or reject the counter-offer. If the offeror accepts the counter-offer, there is a contract made on the basis of the terms of the counter-offer.

When a counter-offer is made, it revokes (cancels) the original offer, so that this original offer cannot be accepted later by the person making the counter-offer.

Case example: Hyde v Wrench (1840)

Wrench offered to sell his farm to Hyde for £1,000. Hyde replied saying he would buy for £950 (counter-offer). Wrench refused to sell at this lower price. Hyde then wrote saying he would buy the farm for £1,000, but Wrench refused this. Hyde argued that there was a contract as he had now 'accepted' Wrench's original offer. It was held that there was no contract between the parties, as when Hyde had made his counter-offer of £950, this had revoked Wrench's original offer. The final letter which Hyde wrote could not, therefore, be an acceptance of the original offer, as that offer no longer existed.

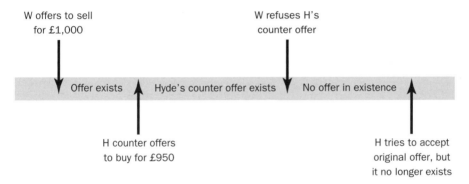

A request for further information, such asking if the offeror would let the other party buy on credit, is not a counter-offer (Stevenson v McLean (1880)).

County Courts: local courts which hear *civil claims*. Since the Courts and Legal Services Act 1990 and the High Court and County Courts Jurisdiction Order 1991, there is no longer any strict financial limit on the amount of money that can be claimed in contract and *tort* cases in the County Court. However, if a case involves a claim of more than £50,000, or if it involves complex law or facts, then it is probable that such a case, even if commenced in the County Court, would be transferred to the *High Court* for trial.

Cases are normally started by the person making the claim (the *claimant*) requesting the court to issue a *claim form*, which is then sent to the other party (the defendant). Nearly 2 million claims are issued each year but, in many cases, judgment is given by default. This means the defendant has failed to respond to the claim within 14 days of its being served on him. In other cases, the claimant accepts the defendant's offer to pay all or part of the claim. Only about 125,000 cases are actually tried at court. For these, there is the problem of delay, as there is a waiting time of about 18 months before cases are heard, but a fast-track procedure has been brought in, under which the judge sets a strict timetable for each case.

Claims in the main part of the County Court are tried by a circuit judge. It is possible for a jury of eight jurors to sit to hear cases of malicious prosecution or false imprisonment, but this is very rare. Claims for less than £5,000 are heard by a *district judge* under the special procedure for *small claims*.

course of dealings: in contract law, a regular series of contracts between the same people over period of time. If they have happened frequently enough, the court will assume that terms that were included in previous contracts will have been included (implied) into the current contract, even though the parties have not discussed them. This often arises when one party wants to say that he is not liable for a breach of contract because, in previous contracts, liability was excluded. Whether a series of contracts amounts to a course of dealings depends on the circumstances: 100 similar contracts over a three-year period has been held to be a course of dealings while three or four contracts over five years was not.

course of employment (discrimination law): an important concept under s41 of the Sex Discrimination Act 1975 and s32 of the Race Relations Act 1976 for deciding whether an employer is liable for sexual or racial harassment of one *employee* by another employee. The phrase 'course of employment' has a wider meaning than under *vicarious liability*. An employer can be liable for acts done by an employee even though the acts may not be part of the work of that employee.

Case example: Jones v Tower Boot Ltd (1997)

Jones, a mechanic working for the defendants was of racially mixed parentage. His fellow workers subjected him to a number of incidents of racial harassment. These included burning his arm with a hot screwdriver, throwing metal bolts at his head and repeatedly calling him names such as 'chimp', 'monkey' and 'baboon'. Although these acts were not part of the work that the fellow workers were employed to do, the incidents took place in the work context and so the employers were liable.

course of employment (negligence): an employee is said to be acting in the course of his employment if he is doing something which he has been authorised to do by his employer. This applies even if he does it in a way that is against his employer's rules provided that it benefits his employer.

Case example: Limpus v London Omnibus Co (1862)

A bus driver injured a pedestrian through his negligent driving whilst racing another driver which was against his employer's rules. It was held that the employer was acting in the course of his employment; he was carrying out what he had been authorised to do.

Court of Appeal: the main court hearing appeals. It has two divisions, criminal and civil. The Civil Division hears appeals against decisions of the *High Court* and the *County Courts*. It also hears appeals against decisions by the *Employment Appeal Tribunal*, the Immigration Appeal Tribunal and the Lands Tribunal. The Criminal Division deals with appeals from the *Crown Court* against conviction and/or sentence. A further appeal from the Court of Appeal may be made to the *House of Lords*, but only with permission of either the Court of Appeal or the House of Lords.

Court of Chancery: developed in the Middle Ages to hear cases referred to the Chancellor where the *claimant* was unable to obtain a remedy in the ordinary courts. The Chancellor decided cases on the basis of fairness and conscience and developed law known as *equity*.

In 1873–1875, the court structure was completely reformed, and the Court of Chancery was abolished. In its place, the modern *Chancery Division of the High Court* was created.

covenant: a promise. They are usually found in contracts of employment or contracts for the sale of a business. A covenant concerning land must be made by *deed*. See *restrictive covenants*.

covenantee: a person to whom a covenant (promise) is made and who gets the benefit of it.

covenantor: a person who makes a covenant (promise).

credit agreement: in consumer law, an agreement where a borrower is lent money which is to be repaid over a period of time. Consumer credit agreements where the borrower is an individual or partnership are regulated by the *Consumer Credit Act 1974*, subject to any exceptions.

credit card: used by a borrower by agreement with the credit card company to pay for goods or withdraw cash. The borrower can only use the card to buy goods at shops which already have an agreement with the credit card company. The shop passes goods to the borrower and claims the cost from the credit card company; the borrower is sent a statement every month. He has a running account whereby he is given a pre-set credit limit. Some credit card companies, such as American Express, must be paid off by a single payment each month, while companies such as Visa must be paid a minimum each month and interest will be charged on the remainder. Where the card is used to withdraw cash, interest is charged from the day of withdrawal. A credit card agreement is a *debtor-creditor-supplier agreement*.

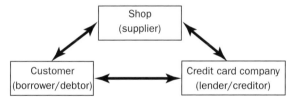

credit sale agreement: in consumer law, an agreement between a borrower and a shop which provides goods and credit. The borrower becomes the owner of the goods straight away and makes repayments to the shop over a period of time. This is different to a *hire-purchase agreement* where the buyer does not become the owner of the goods until all payments have been made. If the goods are faulty, the borrower can claim under the *Sale of Goods Act 1979*, and the financial arrangement is regulated by the *Consumer Credit Act 1974*, subject to exceptions.

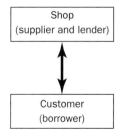

creditors: those to whom money is owed.

criminal appeals: there are different appeal routes for cases depending on whether the case was tried in the *Magistrates' Court* or the *Crown Court*. For cases tried in the Magistrates' Court the normal appeal for the defendant is to the Crown Court, where the case is heard by a judge sitting with two *lay magistrates*. There is normally no further appeal from this hearing However, if a point of law is at issue, both the defendant and the prosecution have the right to appeal to the Queen's Bench Divisional Court (see *case stated appeal*). This appeal can be direct from the Magistrates' Court or from the appeal at the Crown Court.

Where a case has been tried at the Crown Court the defendant may appeal to the *Court of Appeal* (Criminal Division). Leave (permission) to appeal is needed. If there is a point of law of general public importance, it is possible for either the defendant or the prosecution to appeal from the Court of Appeal's decision to the House of Lords.

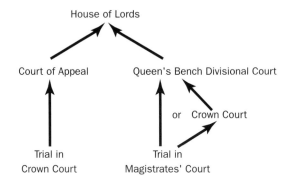

Criminal Cases Review Commission: set up by the Criminal Appeal Act 1995 as an independent body to investigate possible miscarriages of justice in criminal cases. There are 14 members of the Commission who can order a re-investigation of a case. If the Commission considers that there is a real possibility that a conviction would be overturned, it can refer the case to the Court of Appeal (Criminal Division). The first case to be referred was that of Mahmood Mattan who had been convicted of murder and hanged in 1952. The conviction was quashed as unsafe after the evidence of the main prosecution witness was shown to be unreliable. The case of Derek Bentley, who was hanged for murder in 1958, was also referred to the Court of Appeal and the conviction quashed. Both these cases show that the Commission is prepared to investigate even long-standing cases.

criminal damage: a crime under s1 of the Criminal Damage Act 1971. It is defined as destroying or damaging property belonging to another and either intending to do that damage or being *reckless* as to whether such damage is caused. Being reckless means that the defendant either realised there was a risk that the damage would occur or he failed to think about possible risks, but an ordinary, careful person would have realised that there was a risk the damage might happen (see also *Caldwell recklessness*).

If the criminal damage endangers someone's life, then the crime is more serious and can be punished by life imprisonment. Criminal damage caused by fire is charged as *arson*.

Criminal Defence Service: a new method of funding advice and representation for defendants in criminal cases. Under the Access to Justice Act 1999 the previous *criminal legal* *aid* scheme was replaced by the Criminal Defence Service in 2001. Most work is done by private lawyers under contracts. However, the Criminal Defence Service is also able to employ lawyers directly as salaried defenders in the *Public Defence Service (PDS)*. By 2003 there were eight PDS offices operating. The Government accepts that these plans will involve some restriction on the choice of defendants as to their representative.

Criminal Injuries Compensation Board: set up in 1964 to award compensation to victims of crime. There is no automatic right to compensation, but where it is awarded, it is on a set tariff according to the crime and the injury received. This use of a fixed tariff has led to criticisms, as the amounts for victims of certain crimes, such as rape, are regarded as being too low.

Criminal Law Revision Committee: a part-time body of lawyers and judges which considered areas of law referred to it by the Lord Chancellor and recommended changes and reforms. It operated from 1959 to 1986. One of its main achievements was the report that led to Parliament passing the Theft Act 1968, which completely reformed the law on theft and related offences.

criminal legal aid: government-funded provision of legal representation for a defendant in criminal proceedings. The defendant must show that it is in the interests of justice for legal aid to be given. To decide this, five factors set out in the Access to Justice Act 1999 are considered:

1. If convicted, is the defendant likely to lose his liberty or his job or suffer serious damage to his reputation?

2. Does the case involve a substantial point of law?

3. Is the defendant able to understand the proceedings? For example if the defendant is deaf or does not speak English, legal aid should be granted.

4. Is it necessary to trace and interview witnesses or does the case involve the need for expert examination of witnesses?

5. Is representation desirable in the interests of another person, for example a child witness in a sex-abuse case?

cross purposes mistake: see *unilateral mistake*.

Crown Court: the main criminal court. There are 91 courts sitting in different towns and cities throughout England and Wales. The court hears the following types of criminal case:

- all *indictable offences*: these are the most serious crimes, such as murder and rape, and can only be tried at the Crown Court;

- *triable either way offences*, such as theft, where the case has been sent to the Crown Court for trial from the *Magistrates' Court*.

If a defendant pleads not guilty, the case is tried by a judge and a *jury*. If the defendant pleads guilty, a judge sitting alone decides the sentence. The Crown Court also deals with defendants who have been sent by the magistrates to the Crown Court to be sentenced and appeals from decisions of the Magistrates' Court.

Crown Prosecution Service (CPS): established by the Prosecution of Offences Act 1985 as a national prosecution service to conduct prosecutions on behalf of the State. The *Director of Public Prosecutions* is the head of the CPS. The main functions of the CPS are:

- to give advice to police on admissibility of evidence;

- to review all cases passed to them by the police to see if there is sufficient evidence for the case to proceed;

- to conduct cases in the *Magistrates' Court*;

- to act as prosecutors in the Crown Court or to instruct lawyers with the necessary *certificate of advocacy* to act as prosecutors in the *Crown Court*.

The main criticism of the CPS is that it discontinues too many cases. Two main factors are taken into account in deciding whether a case should go to court or not. These are:

- the evidential test, which is concerned with whether there is a realistic prospect of conviction;

- the public interest test which takes into account a wide range of matters, such as the seriousness of the offence and the age and health of the defendant.

Under the Criminal Justice Bill 2002 it is proposed that the CPS take over from the police the charging of suspects. Pilot schemes showed that the charges were more accurate and less likely to lead to cases being discontinued.

Cunningham recklessness: named after the case of R v Cunningham (1957). In this case the defendant was charged with 'maliciously administering a noxious thing so as to endanger life' when he tore a gas meter from the wall in an empty house in order to steal money from it; as a result, gas leaked in to the next-door house, making the woman who lived there ill. The court decided that the word 'maliciously' meant either:

1. an actual intention to do the particular type of harm that was in fact done; or

2. *recklessness* in the sense that the defendant, when acting, realised there was some risk of such harm occurring.

This second meaning is known as *subjective recklessness* because the defendant realises there is a risk. This meant that Cunningham could not be guilty unless he at least realised that there was a risk that escaping gas could injure someone. (See also *Caldwell recklessness*.)

curfew order: allows a court to order that an offender should remain at a fixed address for between two and 12 hours in every 24 hours. This order can last for up to six months. The aims of such an order are to prevent re-offending and protect the public. In order to make sure that an offender complies with the curfew order, the court can order that he is electronically tagged. (See also *electronic tagging*.)

curia regis: the King's Council or King's Court under the Norman Kings. This Council had the power to act as a court and decide disputes.

custodial sentences: punishments that involve taking away the offender's freedom.

There are different types of custodial sentence:

- *mandatory sentences* where the court has to impose a particular sentence such as a life sentence for murder;

- discretionary sentences where the court has a choice of whether or not to impose a custodial sentence and can also decide the length of the sentence;

- *minimum sentences* where the court has to give a certain minimum period although longer can be given.

If an offender is aged 21 or over, the custodial sentence is served in a prison. If the offender is aged ten to 20, the sentence is served in a detention and training unit (Crime and Disorder Act 1998). An offender aged ten to 14 can be sent to such a unit only if they are persistent offenders or if they have committed a very serious offence. The Power of Criminal Courts (Sentencing) Act 2000 states that a discretionary sentence should not be passed unless:

- the court considers that the crime was so serious that only a prison sentence is justified; or
- the case involves a violent or sexual offence, and only a prison sentence would be adequate to protect the public.

custody officer: a police officer who is responsible for making sure that all people detained at a police station are treated in accordance with the rules in the *Police and Criminal Evidence Act 1984 (PACE)* and the *Police Codes of Practice* issued under this Act. The officer must keep a custody record for each person, recording all events such as interviews, periods of rest and refreshment, police visits to cells and consultation with a legal advisor. The custody officer must also review the reason for detention at the start of the detention period and at regular intervals throughout.

custody plus is a short prison sentence followed by a community programme. A prison sentence of up to 3 months is followed by a period of compulsory supervision in the community within an overall sentence of 12 months.

custom: a source of law. It was important in forming the law of business and commercial practice. Nowadays, it is rare that any custom will be recognised as creating new law, but it is possible for a local custom to be recognised and given legal effect, provided it can be shown that:

- the custom existed from time immemorial (set as 1189);
- the custom has been exercised peaceably, openly and as of right during this time;
- the custom is definite as to locality, nature and scope;
- the custom is reasonable.

custom in contract law: an established practice of a particular trade or market. Where a custom is well known, it will be incorporated (implied) into any contract unless the parties to the contract specifically agree to exclude it. For example, if in a market the normal practice is payment in cash when goods are delivered, then a court will assume that when two market traders make a contract they intend that this will apply whether they have discussed it or not. See also *implied terms*.

damages in civil law: an award of a sum of money to be paid by the losing party to the winning party. The object of an award of damages is to compensate the claimant for loss caused by the other party.

damages in contract law: the money paid by a person who has *breached a contract* to the other party to compensate them for any financial loss they have suffered. Compensation will only be paid for the actual financial loss that the innocent party has suffered. If they have suffered no loss, they will not receive any damages. The innocent party is expected to do his best to make the best of the situation e.g. finding an alternative buyer (see also *mitigation of loss*).

Compensation will only be paid for:

* losses that are a usual result of the breach of contract;
* unusual losses that both parties knew at the time the contract was made would occur if the contract was breached.

Case example: Victoria Laundry (Windsor) Ltd v Newman Industries Ltd (1949)

The claimants were launderers and dyers who wanted another boiler to expand their business and also to do high-profit dyeing work. They ordered a boiler from the defendants, who knew it was wanted for immediate use. The boiler was not delivered until five months later. The claimants claimed the 'normal' profits they had lost on the business they could have done with the boiler. They also claimed the extra profits they could have made on the dyeing. The Court of Appeal held that, as the defendants knew the boiler was wanted for immediate use, they had to pay damages to cover the 'normal' profits. However, the defendants did not know about the dyeing work, so they were not liable for the profit on this.

Other rules are:

* Damages are not usually given for non-financial loss such as injured feelings unless the whole object of the contract is providing pleasure, such as a holiday (Jackson v Horizon Holidays (1975) or freedom from discomfort had been made an important object of the contract (Farley v Skinner (2001)).
* If the contract specifies what the damages will be if the contract is breached, then this sum will be the sum payable (*liquidated damages*) as long as it is a realistic assessment of the loss to the wronged party and not intended to penalise (punish) the party who breached the contract (Dunlop Pneumatic Tyre Co v New Garage and Motor Co (1915)).

See also *speculative damages* and *reliance loss*.

damages in contract and tort: the following table provides a comparison.

Contract	Tort
• Aim of damages is to put claimant in position he would have been in, if the contract had been successfully concluded.	• Aim of damages is to put claimant in position he would have been in, if the tort had not happened.
• Damages can only be claimed for losses that are a usual result of the breach of contract and for any unusual results that the parties knew might happen when the contract was made.	• Damages can only be claimed for type of damage that it could reasonably be foreseen would happen.
• Damages can only be claimed to cover the financial loss that the claimant has actually suffered.	• Damages can be claimed for financial loss or to punish the defendant.
• A specified amount of damages payable in the event of a breach can be included in the contract.	• No pre-estimation possible.
• Parties can exclude or limit amount of damages payable except businesses cannot exclude liability for death or personal injury caused by negligence or where exclusion clause is unreasonable.	• Not possible to exclude liability for death or personal injury caused through negligence.

damages in negligence (remoteness of): damages can only be claimed for injuries if they are directly caused by and closely connected with a *breach of the duty of care*. Injuries that are a result of the defendant's actions but not closely connected with the breach are said to be too remote. In *The Wagon Mound (1961)*, it was held that damages could only be claimed for injury or damage that is reasonably foreseeable.

It is sufficient to show that the damage is a possibility (reasonably foreseeable), not that it is likely to happen. A claim will be successful as long as the TYPE of damage is foreseeable, even if it is much more extensive than could have been foreseen (Bradford v Robinson Rentals (1967)) or if it happens in a way that could not have been foreseen (Hughes v Lord Advocate (1963)). See also *eggshell skull rule*.

dangerous driving, causing death by: an offence under s1 of the Road Traffic Act 1988. 'Dangerous' means that the driving was so far below the standard of the ordinary careful and competent driver that such a person would say it was dangerous. This is an objective test, as the intention of the driver is not considered.

dangerous species: an animal that is not normally domesticated in the UK and which, if not restricted, is likely to cause severe harm or, any damage it might cause is likely to be severe. The *keeper* is strictly liable for any damage caused. See also *Animals Act 1971*.

death sentence: used to be the penalty in England and Wales for murder until 1965 when it was abolished. The death sentence has also been abolished in most European countries, but is still used in some American states and in some African and Asian countries. It is argued that the death penalty is ineffective in preventing crime, as the murder rate in states and countries which have retained it is often higher than in those which have abolished it.

debenture: a security issued by a company for money it has borrowed. Debentures are an alternative to shares for raising capital for a company. The advantage for debenture holders is that the debt owed them by the company takes priority over other debts if the company becomes *insolvent*.

debtor: a person or a business who owes you money. If the money is not paid, there is a *breach of contract* and it is usually possible to sue the debtor for the money in the *civil courts*.

debtor-creditor agreement: in consumer law, an agreement where the creditor lends the debtor money which he can spends as he likes. For example, withdrawing money from a bank using a *credit card*; the borrower has the cash in his hand and can spend it freely. This applies even when he borrows money for a particular purpose and uses it for something else; he is in breach of contract with the lender, but the agreement remains a debtor-creditor agreement.

debtor-creditor-supplier agreement: in consumer law, an agreement where the creditor makes a loan to the debtor for a particular purpose and there is a legal link between the supplier of the goods and creditor. In hire-purchase, conditional-sale and credit-sale agreements, the creditor and the supplier are the same people. But in credit card agreements, the supplier of the goods, e.g. a shop, has an agreement with the credit card company that it will supply goods and be paid by the credit-card company later.

Unlike a *debtor-creditor* agreement, the borrower can only buy specific goods with the loan. In a hire-purchase agreement, he chooses a particular car and then applies to have it on hire purchase, and in a credit-card agreement, he chooses a particular item and then asks the shop if he can use his credit card for payment.

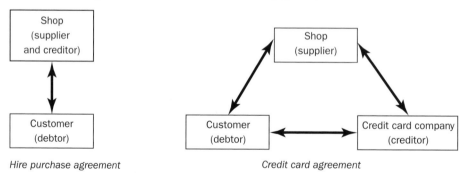

Hire purchase agreement
Conditional sale agreement
Credit sale agreement

Credit card agreement

Types of debtor-creditor-supplier agreements

deceit (as a tort) arises when the defendant has deliberately deceived the claimant. To bring a claim, the claimant must show that: the defendant knowingly or without any belief in its truth made a false representation of fact which he intended to cause the claimant to act in a particular way, and the claimant did act in that way, and the claimant suffered damage as a result.

Case example: Langridge v Levy (1837)

The defendant sold a gun to the claimant's father, falsely stating that it was free from defects. The claimant was injured when it burst. He could not sue the defendant in contract because he was not one of the parties to the contract. But he was able to successfully sue in the tort of deceit; the seller knew that the claimant would rely on his statement because his father had told him that he intended his sons to use the gun.

Where the statement is a statement of opinion or it is made negligently, rather than deliberately, then a claim is made in *negligent misstatement*. If the statement is made as part of negotiations leading to a contract, a claim is made for *fraudulent* or *negligent misrepresentation*.

deception offences: offences under various sections of the Theft Acts 1968 and 1978. They cover *obtaining property by deception*, *obtaining services by deception* or a pecuniary advantage by deception and *evading liability by deception*. The deception must be deliberate or reckless and can be by words or conduct as to fact or intention. It must deceive another person. Putting a fake coin in a machine to obtain goods is not a deception offence (though it may be *theft*), as a machine is not a person, so no person is deceived.

declaratory theory of law: the idea that judges, when deciding cases, do not create law but merely declare what the law has always been. This was a widely held view until the end of the 19th century; for example, Lord Esher, a judge in the *House of Lords*, said in 1892:

> 'There is no such thing as judge-made law, for the judges do not make the law though they frequently have to apply existing law to circumstances as to which it has not previously been [applied].'

Nowadays, it is accepted that, although judges follow *judicial precedent*, they do make law when new situations arise for which there is no precedent.

decree absolute: the final stage of a *divorce*. It is a court order which brings to an end a marriage. After the decree absolute, the parties are legally free to marry again.

decree nisi: a Latin phrase meaning a court order will be made unless a valid objection is made to it. It is the second to last stage of divorce proceedings and is followed by the *decree absolute* (final divorce) after a minimum period of six weeks. Normally, the *petitioner* applies for the decree nisi to be made absolute, but if he or she fails to do so, the *respondent* can apply after three months.

deed: a formal legal document which irrevocably commits the person signing it. A deed must:

- be in writing;
- show from its contents that it is intended to be a deed, e.g. include the sentence, 'This Deed of conveyance is made the 1st day of September 1999';
- be signed by the person making it in the presence of a witness;
- be signed by the witness;
- be delivered; this occurs when the person signing does something which shows that he accepts the document as his own. In practice this usually happens when it is dated; before this the deed is not complete.

Deeds are necessary to convey or transfer most interests in land or create an enforceable *bare promise*.

deed of partnership: a formal written agreement creating a *partnership*. It will normally state:

- the name of the partnership and the type of business;
- the date on which it is to commence;
- the names of all the *partners*, the amount of capital each is providing, their liability and their share of the profits;
- the effect of the retirement or death of any of the partners.

However, it is not necessary to have a deed of partnership for a partnership to be created. Under the Partnership Act 1890, the law recognises that there is a partnership where people carry on business 'in common with a view of profit', even if there is no written agreement.

defamation: the publication of a statement which is likely to lower the person referred to in the estimation of right-thinking members of society. Defamation is either:

1 *libel*: a statement which is made in a permanent form, e.g. writing, print, picture, broadcast, stage play, waxwork. The claimant does not have to show that he has suffered any financial or material loss to bring a claim; or

2 *slander*: a statement made in a temporary form, usually spoken. The claimant usually has to prove that financial or other material loss has been suffered as a result of the slander.

To bring a claim in defamation, the claimant has to prove:

- the statement was defamatory; this means that it would tend to lower the claimant in the estimation of right-thinking members of society (see also *innuendo*);
- the statement referred to the claimant, i.e. that the statement referred to the claimant by name or it was clear from what was said who was being referred to;
- the statement was published: i.e. it was communicated to a third party; if the defendant makes the statement to the claimant, this does not count as publication, nor does making it to the defendant's spouse. Each time the statement is repeated is a new publication.

The main defences to defamation are:

- *justification*: the statement was substantially true;
- *absolute privilege*: includes statements made in Parliament and in court, and full reports of these;
- *qualified privilege*: statements made because of a moral or legal duty, provided they are not prompted by malice;
- *fair comment*: an opinion rather than a statement of fact given on a matter of public interest.

See also *offer of amends*.

defamation cases: civil cases which are usually tried in the *High Court* and can be tried by a *jury* and a judge. The jury decides whether the claimant has been defamed and also the amount of *damages* they should receive.

defective goods: where a buyer has bought defective goods, he can sue various people. The chart on the next page shows the different rights a buyer has.

It is also a criminal offence under the *Consumer Protection Act 1987* and the *General Product Safety Regulations 1994* to sell unsafe products.

The buyer may be able to sue under the *Sale of Goods Act 1979* or under the contract. The buyer and also other people injured by the goods (e.g. the buyer's child) can sue under the Consumer Protection Act 1987 or under the law of *negligence*.

	Who buyer can sue	Grounds for claim
Sale of Goods Act 1979	Seller of goods	Breach of term implied under s14 that goods must be of satisfactory quality.
Consumer Protection Act 1987	Manufacturer; or company which gives the good their own brand name; or company which imported goods into EU	Defective product has caused death or personal injury or damage to property amounting to more than £275.
Contract	Other party to contract	Breach of contract if contract specified that goods were to be in good condition; or mis-representation if seller assured buyer that goods were in good condition.
Negligence	Manufacturer	Breach of duty of care if manufacturer negligent and buyer suffered physical damage to himself or his property.

defective product: defined by the *Consumer Protection Act 1987* as one where the safety of the product is not such as persons are generally entitled to expect. A product can be defective because of a defect through:

- design; or
- manufacturing or processing; or
- misleading or inadequate instructions or a lack of warning which means that the product may be used, installed or assembled in an unsafe way.

Where a defect causes damage of more than £275 or any injury, the consumer can sue the 'producer' (see also *Consumer Protection Act 1987*). The producer may have a defence if he can show that the state of scientific and technical knowledge at the time of production meant that the defect could not have been known about or discovered. This is the *state-of-the-art defence*.

deferred sentence: where a court believes that there is about to be a major change in a defendant's life, such as a new job, which may reform him, the court can decide to defer (put off) sentencing that defendant for a period of up to six months in order to see if his behaviour does improve.

delegated legislation: law made by some organisation or body other than Parliament but with the authority of Parliament. This authority is given in an *enabling Act*.

Delegated legislation can be made by:

- the Queen and the Privy Council who can make Orders in Council in times of emergency when Parliament is not sitting;
- ministers and government departments who can make regulations called statutory instruments on matters connected with the particular department;
- local authorities who can make *bylaws* for their own area.

Advantages of delegated legislation	Disadvantages of delegated legislation
• Saves Parliamentary time.	• Undemocratic – made by unelected ministers.
• More detailed than an Act of Parliament	• Limited Parliamentary controls over it.
• Can be made quickly and is flexible.	• Large volume – difficult to discover the law.
• Uses expertise of specialist departments.	

democracy: the concept that government should be 'by the people, for the people'. In Western nations, democracy is achieved by the general public electing representatives to govern them. In the United Kingdom, there must be a general election every five years, so that the government is accountable to the electorate.

denunciation of crime: one of the aims of *sentencing*. Under this aim, the punishment should show society's disapproval of the crime. It reinforces the moral boundaries of acceptable and unacceptable behaviour and can mould public perception of certain conduct. For example, drink driving has become less acceptable as the law imposes severe penalties for this crime.

Department for Constitutional Affairs is the government department taking over most of the work of the *Lord Chancellor's Department*. This new ministry was announced in June 2003. Initially the head of the ministry will still be called the *Lord Chancellor*. However, the Government intend to reduce the number of roles of the Lord Chancellor and may even completely abolish the post.

deposit: a payment made by one party to a contract to the other party, usually at the time the contract is entered into. It is a form of security and will be forfeited if the payer fails to complete the contract, even if the deposit is more than the other party has lost because the payer failed to complete the contract. This is different from a *part payment*. If there is a part payment, anything in excess of the innocent party's loss can be reclaimed by the payer. When deciding whether a payment is a deposit or part payment, the court will usually accept the description that was given to it in the contract even though in reality the parties may not have realised the legal significance of the different terms.

desertion: in *divorce*, one of the ways of showing that the marriage has irretrievably broken down. To prove that there has been desertion, the *petitioner* must show that:

- the parties are physically *living apart*; and
- the *respondent* intended to live apart from the petitioner permanently; and
- the separation was against the wishes of the petitioner, i.e. there was no agreement to separate; and
- there was no good reason for the separation (a good reason might be medical grounds or the petitioner's behaviour).

All four conditions must exist for two continuous years immediately before the presentation of the divorce petition.

destroys or damages in *criminal damage* includes where property has been made useless even though it is not completely destroyed. Damage includes non-permanent damage which can be cleaned off; for example, water-soluble paint (Hardman v Chief Constable of Avon and Somerset Constabulary (1986)), or mud (Roe v Kingerlee (1986)).

detention and training order: a custodial sentence that can be passed on offenders under the age of 18 under the Powers of Criminal Courts (Sentencing) Act 2000. It is for a period of between 4 and 24 months. It can be given to defendants as young as 12, but for those under 15, an order can only be made if they are persistent offenders. There are provisions to extend the sentence to ten and eleven year olds but only where it is necessary to protect the public from further offending.

detention by police can occur after arrest if it is necessary to question the suspect or obtain other evidence. The decision as to whether there is good reason to detain an arrested person is made by the *custody officer*. The detention must be reviewed at regular intervals and can only last for 24 hours for most crimes. The critical time factors are shown below.

Time factor	Event(s)
Start of detention	Arrested person arrives at police station, and custody officer decides there is reason to detain him/her.
Within 6 hours	First review by custody officer.
Every 9 hours thereafter	Subsequent reviews by custody officer.
24 hours	Police must charge or release detainee unless it is a *serious arrestable offence*.
36 hours	For serious arrestable offences, the maximum time of detention by police. Can only detain further with authorisation of magistrate.
96 hours	Maximum period of detention.

Note that the Criminal Justice Bill 2002 has provision for the period of detention to be increased to 36 hours for all arrestable offences.

detention officer is a civilian working for the police who has the power to take fingerprint samples, make intimate and non-intimate searches and take non-intimate samples.

deterrence of crime: one of the aims of *sentencing*. The deterrence can be individual or general. Individual deterrence is aimed at making the offender less likely to re-offend. Penalties intended to have this effect are prison sentences, suspended prison sentences and heavy fines. General deterrence is aimed at potential offenders and involves punishing one offender severely in order to deter potential offenders through fear of a similar punishment. Critics point out that deterrence does not work, as most crimes are committed on the spur of the moment and offenders are unlikely to consider the consequences. Statistics show that many offenders are reconvicted within two years of serving their original sentence.

diminished responsibility: a partial defence to a charge of *murder* which reduces the offence to *manslaughter*. It is defined in s2 of the Homicide Act 1957 as suffering from an abnormality of mind which substantially impairs the defendant's mental responsibility for the killing. This is a wide definition and has been held to cover such diverse conditions as psychopathic behaviour (R v Byrne (1960)) and battered-wife syndrome (R v Ahluwalia (1992)). The reducing of the charge to manslaughter allows the judge discretion in sentencing instead of having to impose the life sentence which is mandatory for murder.

Diplock courts: courts in Northern Ireland in which a judge will hear certain criminal cases alone without a jury. They were introduced in 1973 because of the fear of sectarian bias and/or threats to a jury.

direct applicability: a concept of *European Union law* which means that certain EU law applies directly in member states without the member state having to make its own law on the matter. This particularly applies to *regulations*, which are directly applicable under *Article 249 (Treaty of Rome)*.

direct discrimination occurs when a person is treated less favourably on the grounds of race or sex. The key point is that the discriminatory act is done because of the person's race or sex. The motive for the discrimination is irrelevant.

Case example: Greig v Community Industries (1979)

There were only two girls on a work-experience scheme for painting and decorating, all the other trainees were male. When one girl left, the management withdrew the other girl from the scheme 'for her own good'. It was held she had suffered direct discrimination.

direct effect: a concept in *European Union law* under which individuals can rely on European law even though their national government has not implemented that law. Direct effect can be vertical or horizontal. Vertical means that the law can be enforced against the state or any state agency (arm of the state); horizontal means that the law can be relied on against non-state businesses and organisations. Treaties and *regulations* have *vertical direct effect* and *horizontal direct effect*, but *directives* only have *vertical direct effect*.

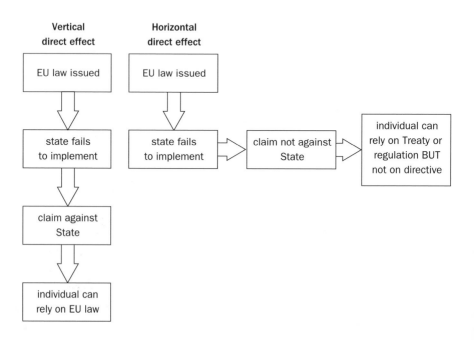

directed acquittal occurs where a judge in a trial at the Crown Court decides that there is insufficient prosecution evidence to allow the case to continue. In such situations, the judge directs the jury that they must return a verdict of Not Guilty.

directives: the main way of harmonising laws throughout the member states of the *European Union*. The European Union has power to issue directives under *Article 249* of the *Treaty of Rome*. Member states must then pass their own laws to implement the directive within a time limit set by the *European Commission*. If a state does not implement a directive, it may be possible for citizens of that state to rely on the effects of the directive if:

- the directive is sufficiently clear (Van Duyn v Home Office (1974));
- the claim is being made against the state or an 'arm of the state' (Foster v British Gas (1990)); this is the concept of *vertical direct effect*.

Where a state has not implemented a directive but the individual cannot rely on the directive because the claim is against a private agency, it may be possible to sue the state for loss caused by its failure to implement the directive (Francovitch v Italian Republic (1991)) (see also *Francovitch principle*).

Director-General of Fair Trading: the head of the *Office of Fair Trading* which was set up by the Fair Trading Act 1973. He:

- receives reports from Trading Standards Offices and reviews consumers' problems;
- issues reports;
- makes proposals for changes in law;
- can makes changes himself by statutory instrument, e.g. Business Advertisements (Disclosure) Order 1977 which stops businesses representing themselves as private sellers in advertisements;
- can obtain assurances from traders who act in a way detrimental to consumers' interests and publish these in the Annual Report of the Office of Fair Trading. If they persist, he can take proceedings against them in the Restrictive Practices Court;
- issues licences to those who provide credit and enforces the *Consumer Credit Act 1974*.

Director of Public Prosecutions (DPP): the head of the *Crown Prosecution Service* and responsible for its organisation and policy. The DPP through the CPS is also expected to advise police on matters relating to criminal offences. In addition, the DPP conducts certain important criminal proceedings personally in court and appears for the prosecution in certain appeals.

directors: those who exercise all the powers of a company. The Companies Act 1985 says that anyone doing this is considered a director, regardless of the actual title given to that person. Directors can be appointed:

- by being named as such in the statement of first directors sent to the Registrar of Companies on the forming of a new company;
- by being named in the *Articles of Association*;
- by being appointed at an annual general meeting of the company's *shareholders*.

disability discrimination: the Disability Discrimination Act 1995 makes it unlawful for an employer to treat a person less favourably because of a disability. 'Disability' is defined as a physical or mental impairment which has a substantial and long-term adverse effect on the person's ability to carry out normal day-to-day activities. Examples of discrimination would be refusing employment or failing to consider for promotion. An employer has a duty to make reasonable adjustments to the workplace such as providing ramps for wheelchair users. However, an employer can claim that the discrimination is justified in certain circumstances, for example, where there would be a real risk to the health and safety of the disabled person or other workers.

The Disability Discrimination Act also has provisions to make it unlawful to discriminate against a disabled person in:

- the supply of goods and services;
- education;
- public transport.

These provisions are being brought into effect gradually to give shops, hotels, schools, etc. the chance to make the necessary modifications to their premises.

Disability Rights Commission is an independent body set up to help eliminate discrimination against disabled people. It provides help and advice for disabled people, employers and service providers. It also helps solve problems and, where necessary, will support legal action.

discharge of contract: the ending of a contract. This will happen where:

- both parties carry out what they have agreed to do (*performance*);
- both parties agree to do something different and a new contract is created (*agreement*);
- one party refuses to carry out his part of the contract (*breach of contract*);
- the contract becomes impossible to carry out through no fault of either party (*frustration*).

Where there has been performance of the contract or agreement, the parties have no further obligations under the contract. Where there has been breach of contract or frustration, the courts will decide how losses will be divided between the parties.

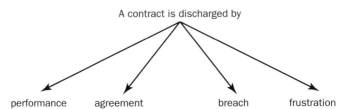

A contract is discharged by

performance   agreement   breach   frustration

disclaimer: in tort, a notice given which excludes or restricts legal responsibility in the event of negligence. Provided that sufficient effort is taken to bring the notice to the claimant's attention before or at the time and the exclusion is reasonable, the defendant will not be liable. It is similar to an *exclusion clause* in contract. Under the *Unfair Contract Terms Act 1977,* it is not possible to restrict liability for death or personal injury. See also *Hedley Byrne v Heller (1964)* for an example of the use of a disclaimer.

disclosure of evidence: in both civil and criminal cases, each side is under a duty to disclose certain evidence to the other side. The aim of disclosure is to identify the issues in the case, prevent unnecessary cases and speed up trials.

In criminal cases, the Criminal Procedure and Investigations Act 1996 places a duty on the prosecution to disclose any material which, in the prosecutor's opinion, might undermine the case against the accused. The defence must give a written statement to the prosecution setting out the defence case in general terms and giving details of any *alibi*.

In civil cases, both parties must disclose all documents on which he relies and all documents which:

- adversely affect his own case
- adversely affect another party's case
- support another party's case.

Privileged documents such as letters between solicitor and client do not have to be disclosed.

discrimination in employment occurs if an employer treats a person less favourably because of their sex, race or disability. In all such cases, the person discriminated against can make a claim in an *employment tribunal*. (See also *disability discrimination*, *racial discrimination* and *sex discrimination*.)

dishonesty: an essential part of the *mens rea* of *theft* and related offences against property. The Theft Act 1968 does not define what is meant by dishonesty, though s2 gives three situations which are not to be regarded as dishonest. These are when the defendant believes:

- he has the right in law to take the property;
- he would have the consent of the owner of the property if the owner knew of the *appropriation* and the circumstances of it;
- the owner of the property cannot be found.

Section 2(2) also states that a person's appropriation of property may be dishonest even though he is willing to pay for it.

As there is no other guidance in the Act on what is meant by dishonesty, the courts have developed guidelines (R v Ghosh (1982)) under which it must first be considered whether what the defendant did was dishonest by the standards of ordinary people and, if so, then whether the defendant realised that what he was doing was dishonest by those standards.

dismissal from employment occurs where:

- the contract of employment is terminated by the employer;
- a fixed-term contract comes to an end and is not renewed;
- the employee is entitled to terminate the contract because of the employer's conduct; this is known as *constructive dismissal*;
- a female employee who has taken maternity leave and given the correct notice that she wishes to return to work is not permitted to return to work after childbirth.

See also *unfair dismissal* and *wrongful dismissal*.

disposable capital: the amount of assets owned by a person, such as money in a bank or building society, land, stocks, shares and other investments. Disposable capital also includes the home that is owned by a person, but only if the value of the home is more than

£100,000 after deducting any mortgage which is still owed. On an application for legal help or representation, a person who has more than a set minimum amount of disposable capital will be asked to contribute all of it if they wish to receive funding. In civil proceedings, there is also a fixed maximum above which the person will be disqualified from receiving funding.

disposable income: the amount of income available to a person after deducting fixed rates of basic living expenses. On an application for legal help or representation, a person who has more than a set minimum amount of disposable income will be asked to pay a contribution for as long as the case lasts if they wish to receive legal funding. In civil proceedings, there is also a fixed maximum above which the person will be disqualified from receiving legal funding.

disqualification from driving: a penalty which can be imposed by the courts on those found guilty of certain driving offences. The length of the period of disqualification depends on the seriousness of the offence. For example, a defendant guilty of drink-driving must be disqualified for a minimum of one year, but if the amount of alcohol in his body is very high then the period of disqualification is likely to be longer.

distance selling: selling goods through mail order, Internet, telephone, fax, etc. Where this is done by a business to private individuals (consumers), protection is provided by the *Consumer Protection (Distance Selling) Regulations 2000*. Protection is also provided by the *Electronic Commerce (EC Directive) Regulations 2002* for everyone, including businesses, buying or receiving advertisements through the Internet and telephone texting.

distinguishing (in judicial precedent): a method by which a judge avoids having to follow what would otherwise be a *binding precedent*. It means that the judge finds that the material facts of the case he is deciding are sufficiently different from the previous precedent that he can draw a distinction between them.

Case example: Merritt v Merritt (1971)

There was a question of whether an agreement made between a husband and wife was a legally binding contract. This would depend on whether they had an intention to create legal relations when they made their agreement. The judge held that there were sufficient differences from an earlier case of Balfour v Balfour (1919) that he did not have to follow that decision.

Balfour v Balfour	Merritt v Merritt
• Husband and wife not separated.	• Parties had separated, but not divorced.
• Verbal agreement.	• Written agreement.
• Agreement for H to pay wife housekeeping money while he worked abroad.	• Agreement that wife would take over payment of mortgage and house would be hers.
• Held: domestic arrangement NOT a contract.	• Held: legally binding contract.

district judge: a judge who works in the *County Court* hearing *civil cases*, especially *small claims cases*. To become a district judge, it necessary to have practised as either a barrister or a solicitor for at least seven years, though in reality nearly all district judges are former solicitors. As with all levels of the judiciary, there is a lack of women, with only about 19 per cent being female.

district judge (Magistrates' Court): the new title for *stipendiary magistrates* (Access to Justice Act 1999).

divisional courts: each division of the *High Court* has a special court which has the power to hear special appeals from lower courts. These appeal cases will be decided by a panel of two or three judges from that division. The most important of the divisional courts is the *Queen's Bench Divisional Court*, which also hears cases of *judicial review* and applications for *habeas corpus*.

divorce: the legal ending of a marriage leaving both parties free to marry again. A court will issue a divorce when it is satisfied that the marriage has irretrievably broken down. This is done by proving to the court the existence of one of the *five facts* set out in the Matrimonial Causes Act 1973. Proceedings cannot be started until the parties have been married for one year. The divorce is issued in two stages: the *decree nisi* and the final *decree absolute*. The court may also, at the same time or later, issue orders concerning maintenance and other *financial provision* and concerning the *children of the family*. (See also *divorce, grounds for* and *Family Law Act 1996*.)

divorce, effect on will: a divorce has the effect of cutting your ex-spouse out of your will. This means that any property left by the will to the ex-spouse will not go to them. Instead, it goes to whoever would have inherited it had the spouse died at the time of the divorce. Also any provision in the will appointing the spouse as executor of the will or as guardian to children of the family will be cancelled.

divorce, grounds for: the only grounds for a divorce is that the marriage has irretrievably broken down. This can be proved in five different ways (the *five facts*) which are set out in the Matrimonial Causes Act 1973. See also *Family Law Act 1996*.

divorce, mediation in: helping divorcing couples to come to an agreement over issues concerning children and finances rather than contesting matters in court. The *Family Law Act 1996* was intended to make mediation more central to divorce proceedings by requiring couples to attend a meeting where mediation was explained. However pilot schemes were unsuccessful and this part of the Act was not brought into force.

doli incapax means that a child under the age of ten is not responsible for his or her criminal actions. Even if a child of nine deliberately stabs someone, intending to do it and understanding that it will cause serious injury, the rule of doli incapax means that child cannot be found guilty of any criminal offence in relation to the stabbing.

domestic violence: the term used for violence which takes place in family situations and particularly between couples, whether married or unmarried. A victim of domestic violence can obtain various court orders against the abuser under the *Family Law Act 1996*. These civil orders are in addition to any criminal prosecution the police may bring for assault:

- *non-molestation order*: an order to stop serious pestering or harassment;
- *occupation order*: an order that the abuser does not enter the victim's home even if it is his home as well. This has replaced the *ouster order*.

The court has the power to send to prison a person who breaches either of these orders.

Donoghue v Stevenson (1932): a case which established modern *negligence*. Mrs Donoghue was bought a drink of ginger beer by a friend in a café. The drink contained a decomposed snail, and Mrs Donoghue suffered gastro-enteritis. She could not sue the café in contract because she had not bought the drink, and her friend could not sue because he had not suffered any injury.

She therefore sued the manufacturer in *tort*. She had no difficulty in proving that he had been negligent in the preparation of the drink but the House of Lords had to decide how far his responsibility extended. It was held that he owed a *duty of care* to his 'neighbour', that is anyone he could reasonably foresee would be affected by his actions. As it could be reasonably foreseen that the consumer of the beer would be affected by what the manufacturer did when preparing the beer, Mrs Donoghue won her case.

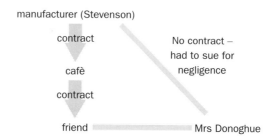

double jeopardy refers to the principle that no-one should be at risk of being tried a second time for the same offence. The Criminal Justice Bill 2002 proposes removing the double jeopardy rule for very serious offences such as murder, rape, manslaughter and armed robbery if 'new and compelling evidence' comes to light.

Evidence is new if it was not available or known to an officer or prosecutor at or before the time of the acquittal. Evidence is compelling if:

a   it is reliable

b   it is substantial; and

c   when it is considered in the context of the outstanding issues, it is highly probable that the person is guilty of the offence.

Draft Criminal Code: produced by the *Law Commission* in 1989. The Code was an immense work which would have brought much of our criminal law together in one piece of legislation. It laid down general principles and definitions of key concepts such as intention. It also set out the extent of defences such as duress. However, Parliament did not enact it as law, possibly because of the vast extent of it and the time needed to consider it. Since then, the Law Commission has published smaller sections of proposed reform of the criminal law, but as yet only the reforms of sexual offences (which made rape of a man a crime) have been enacted. A draft *Offences against the Person Bill* was sent out for consultation in 1998, but it has not yet been included in the Government's legislative programme.

drug treatment and testing order: a new community penalty created by ss61–64 of the Crime and Disorder Act 1998 of drug treatment and testing for offenders age 16+. Such an order can last for between six months and three years. An order can only be made if the offender is willing to comply with it and the court must also be satisfied that arrangements have been made or can be made for the treatment. The treatment can be residential or non-residential. The court sets the minimum number of tests required from the offender each month. The court must hold reviews of the order in which the offender must attend at court and a written report of progress, including results of drug testing, must be provided before each review. If the offender does not co-operate the court has power to revoke the order and re-sentence him.

duress in contract law occurs when one party is forced into the contract so that no real agreement is given. The result is that the contract is *void* or *voidable* depending on the type of duress. There are two types:

- common law duress: where physical force or the threat of force is used, such as a threat to put someone in a mental hospital (Cumming v Ince (1847)), the contract will be void;

- *economic duress*: where 'illegitimate' financial pressure is used, the contract will be voidable. The court will declare the contract invalid if it seems just in the circumstances to do so.

duress as a defence to a criminal charge: where a defendant has a defence to a criminal charge because he only did the criminal act because he or his family (or possibly any other person) was threatened with death or serious injury if he did not agree to do the crime. Duress is defence to all crimes except:

- murder (R v Howe (1987));

- attempted murder (R v Gotts (1992));

- some forms of treason (R v Purdy (1946)).

For the defence to be successful, the defendant must show that he really did believe the threats and felt compelled to do the crime and also that a sober person of reasonable firmness would have responded to the threats in the same way. The flow chart below shows the key elements of duress. See also *duress of circumstances*.

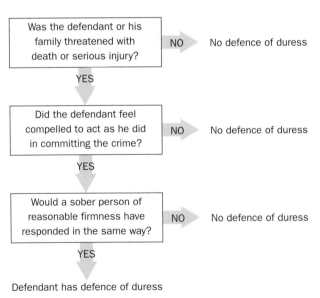

duress (effect on marriage): threats or pressure which overwhelm the will of the individual and destroy the reality of consent to a marriage. If a spouse can show that she or he only entered into a marriage because of such threats, the marriage will be annulled because no true consent was given. The spouse's nature and circumstances will be taken into account and what will be duress for one person will not necessarily amount to duress for a more robust person.

Case example: Hirani v Hirani (1982)

A 19-year-old Hindu girl was told by her parents to give up her Muslim boyfriend and marry a man of their choice or 'pick up her bags and go'. Because she was totally dependent on her parents, this was held to amount to duress and the marriage was annulled.

As a *voidable* marriage, it will have existed until it is annulled, and any children conceived during the marriage will be *legitimate*.

duress of circumstances: a recent extension of the defence of *duress as a defence to a criminal charge*. The same tests apply as for duress by threats (see diagram on previous page); the difference is that the duress and the threat of death or serious injury are not made directly by another person, but occur from the surrounding circumstances.

Case example: R v Conway (1989)

The defendant was driving a car with a passenger who had recently narrowly escaped death in a gun attack by two men. Two men approached the car and the defendant believed that his passenger was in danger of being attacked again. In fact, they were police officers, not attackers, but the defendant did not realise this, he genuinely believed that his passenger's life was at risk. He drove off in a dangerous manner. It was held that this amounted to duress of circumstances.

In Shayler (2002) the defendant tried to argue that he had a defence to his disclosure of secret information, that of duress of circumstances or *necessity*. The court rejected the defences of duress or necessity holding that for the defences to be made out the following requirements had to be fulfilled:

- the act must be done only to prevent an act of greater evil;
- the evil must be directed towards the defendant or a person or persons for whom he was responsible;
- the act must be reasonable and proportionate to the evil avoided.

The Court of Appeal did not distinguish between duress of circumstances and necessity. They treated them as part of the same defence, which seems odd as necessity was accepted as a defence to murder in Re A (conjoined twins) (2000), while duress cannot be a defence to murder.

duties of directors arise from both general common law principles of the *duty of care* and from the fact that directors are *quasi-trustees* of the assets of the company and owe a *fiduciary duty* as a result. A duty of care is owed to the company, and a director should not act negligently in managing the affairs of the company. The normal standard of care is that of a reasonable man in looking after his own affairs, but if a director has particular experience or qualifications, then the standard is higher. An executive director, that is one employed because of his business skills, also owes a higher duty of care in his dealings.

duty of care in negligence: the legal responsibility owed by one person to someone else not to act carelessly. If this duty is broken and the other person is injured as a result, compensation (damages) must be paid by the person causing the injury. In deciding if the duty of care is owed by one person to another, the court will take into account:

- foreseeability: whether it is reasonably foreseeable that the other person will be affected by the actions of the person who acted negligently (*Donoghue v Stevenson (1932)*);

- proximity: whether the two people are close to each other. This usually means that they have a close relationship or close contact with each other, so that it is obvious that the actions of one party will affect the other (Yuen Kun Yeu v A-G of Hong Kong (1987)). It can also mean geographical closeness (Home Office v Dorset Yacht Co (1970));

- whether it is just, fair and reasonable to hold that there is a duty of care (Marc Rich & Co v Bishop Rock Marine Co (1995));

- whether there are any public policy reasons for deciding that a duty of care should not exist. It has been decided that no duty of care is owed by a judge for his actions in court, the police when investigating a crime and, usually, a fireman when putting out a fire. See also *breach of duty of care*.

duty solicitor schemes operate both in police stations and at Magistrates' Courts. A person who has been detained by the police at a police station has the right to consult a solicitor and must be told of the duty solicitor scheme. Anyone appearing at a Magistrates' Court can ask to see the duty solicitor of the day. Both these schemes are free.

Duxbury calculation: used in divorce when calculating financial provision to work out what investments are needed to provide a certain income.

Dworkin, theories of: Dworkin sees law as a set of principles on which all legal rules are based. This is in direct contrast to Professor Hart, who defines law as a set of rules. (see also *Hart, theories of*). Dworkin also argues that the principles of law will supply a right answer to every possible problem. According to this theory, judges have no real discretion when deciding cases, as the legal principles will supply an answer. This aspect of Dworkin's theories is criticised, as most legal writers accept that there are situations in which judges have considerable discretion, and that judges do create law.

easement: a right a land owner has over someone else's land, for example, a right to have pipes under a neighbour's land.

Economic and Social Committee of the European Union advises the *European Commission* and the *Council of Ministers* on economic matters. It is made up of unelected representatives of businesses, employers, trade unions and consumers and must be consulted on proposals for new European laws.

economic duress: in contract law, 'illegitimate' financial pressure on one party to the contract imposed by the other, either to enter into the contract or to accept an amendment to an existing contract. As there is no real consent to the contract, it is voidable and the court will declare it invalid if it seems just in the circumstances to do so. It may refuse to do so if, for example, there is a long delay in disputing the contract (e.g. North Ocean Shipping Co Ltd v Hyundai Construction Ltd (1979)).

Case example: Atlas Express v Kafco (1989)

A national delivery company agreed to transport goods to Woolworths for a small company. Later, the delivery company wanted to increase their prices in breach of the contract. The company could not find another delivery company and would have been in great financial difficulties if they had failed to deliver their goods to Woolworths, so they agreed but later refused to pay. It was held that they had only entered into the second agreement through economic duress and this second contract was not valid. The company did not have to pay the extra charges.

See also *duress in contract law*.

economic loss in negligence: a financial loss, such as loss of earnings or loss of profit. Where a defendant has been negligent, economic loss can only be claimed if it is:

*   loss which is a result of physical injury to a person or their property, such as loss of earnings after a road accident;
*   loss which is a result of what the defendant said or wrote (*negligent misstatement*) rather than his actions (Hedley Byrne v Heller (1963)).

If the defendant's negligent actions cause only financial loss and no physical injury, no claim can be made.

Case example: Spartan Steel & Alloys v Martin & Co (1973)

The electricity supply to a factory was negligently cut off. The factory was able to claim for the loss of the work in progress that was damaged by the electricity being cut off (physical damage) and the profit that would have been made on that work in progress (economic loss). They were not able to claim for the loss of profit on work that they would have carried out during the rest of the day but were unable to do so because of the failure of the electricity.

eggshell skull rule in negligence means that a claimant who is more vulnerable than an ordinary person can claim extra damages when they have been injured by someone's negligence because they have suffered more. This will only apply if the type of harm they suffered would have affected an ordinary person as well, although to a lesser extent.

Case example: Smith v Leech Brain & Co Ltd (1962)

The claimant was splashed with molten metal through another employee's negligence. He suffered a burn as any ordinary person would have done but, because of his state of health, developed cancer and died, which an ordinary person would not normally have done. It was held that his family could recover damages for both the burn and the ensuing cancer.

ejectment: now called recovery of land through the courts. The claimant applies to the court for an order that trespassers leave his property so that he can take possession of it again.

ejusdem generis rule: a rule of *statutory interpretation* which means 'of the same kind'. Where general words follow a list of specific words or phrases, the general words are taken only to include things of the same kind as the specific words.

Case example: Powell v Kempton Park Racecourse (1899)

The defendant was charged under the Betting Act 1853 with keeping a 'house, office, room or other place for betting'. He had been operating betting at Tattersall's ring, which was outdoors. It was held that, as the specific words were all indoor places, the general phrase 'other places' could only include indoor places. So betting at an outdoor place was not illegal.

Electronic Commerce (EC Directive) Regulations 2002 provides protection for everyone, including businesses, who buys through the Internet and telephone texting. The seller (trader) must give full and permanently accessible details of name, geographic address, terms and conditions and when the contract is formed. The order must be acknowledged promptly. The order and acknowledgement are deemed to take effect when the recipient is able to gain access to them by going online. The regulations also apply when a buyer receives advertisements by electronic means but later buys the goods in person or another non-electronic means.

electronic tagging: a method of making sure that a defendant keeps a *curfew order* imposed on him by a court. A device is worn by the offender which cannot be removed. This device has to be connected up to electronic monitoring equipment at the defendant's home to prove that he is keeping the curfew order. Electronic tagging began in England and Wales in 1995 with small scale pilot studies to see how effective it was and has been gradually extended. Surveys show that about 75 per cent of tagging orders are successful.

electronic tagging of released prisoners: under the Powers of Criminal Courts (Sentencing) Act 2000 short term prisoners (serving between 3 months and 4 years) can be released on licence with a curfew condition. The period of curfew is increased with the length of sentence.

emergency protection order: in family law, an order made by a magistrate with regard to a child where there are reasonable grounds for believing that the child is likely to suffer significant harm if he is not removed to accommodation provided by the applicant. The order gives *parental responsibility* for the child to the applicant (usually the local authority or NSPCC) who can then take steps to safeguard him or protect his welfare. The order can also direct that a particular person give details of where the child is and gives the applicant permission to search premises. The order lasts for eight days with only one extension of seven days allowed. The police have similar powers to remove a child where they believe the child is likely to suffer significant harm.

employee: a person who is employed. Being employed gives certain rights under the Employment Rights Act 1996, particularly after one year's continuous employment with the same employer. (This is likely to be reduced to one year.) An employee must be distinguished from an *independent contractor* who is not in an employment situation. The main differences between the two are:

Employee	Independent contractor
• employed to work fixed periods of time	• employed to carry out a particular of of job
• paid for time worked on a regular basis	• paid for work that has been done
• does not usually profit if he manages his work extra well	• can make more profit if he manages his work well
• usually under the control of the employer	• usually makes own decisions as to how to carry out a job
• tools provided by employer	• provides own tools
• has to carry out the work himself	• can usually decide who carries out work, either himself or a substitute
• tax and insurance contributions deducted by employer	• tax and insurance contributions paid direct by contractor

When deciding the status of a worker, the court will weigh up the factors that show that he is an employee and the factors that show he is an independent contractor and decide which are more important (Ready Mixed Concrete (South East) Ltd v MPNI (1968)).

The status of a worker is particularly important in:

- *negligence*: an employer is *vicariously liable* for the actions of an employee but not usually those of an independent contractor;
- *occupiers' liability*: an occupier does not usually have a responsibility towards independent contractors and is not responsible for the actions of independent contractors, but he does have responsibilities with regards employees;
- employment law: an employee has many more rights than an independent contractor.

See also *employment contrasted with self employment*.

employee representative represents employees in discussions with management. There can be *trade union representatives*, *health and safety representatives*, and works council representatives. Such representatives have the right not to be subjected to a detriment as a result of acting as a representative (Employment Rights Act 1996 s47). Dismissing a person because of their role as a representative is considered *unfair dismissal*.

employee's duties: included in the *contract of employment* and also implied by common law. The main duties are to:

- obey reasonable lawful orders;

- exercise reasonable care and skill in work;

- give faithful service.

If there is a serious breach of any of these, it can justify an employer dismissing the employee.

Case example: Denco v Joinson (1991)

An employee who misused a computer password by hacking was not giving faithful service and could be instantly dismissed from his job.

employer's duties to an employee are to:

- pay wages as agreed;

- ensure the *health and safety at work* of the employee;

- treat the employee with respect;

- indemnify the employee against liability or loss incurred within the course of employment.

If the employer is in breach of any of these duties, the employee may claim for any loss suffered and in some circumstances may be able to claim *constructive dismissal* if the breach is serious enough to justify leaving work.

Case example: Courtaulds v Andrew (1979)

An assistant manager criticising a worker in a derogatory way was held to have breached the duty of the employer to treat the employee with respect. This justified the worker leaving and claiming that he had been constructively dismissed.

Employment Appeal Tribunal (EAT) hears appeals from decisions by *employment tribunals*. The appeal is usually heard by a judge and two lay people who are on a special panel drawn from employers' representatives and trade unions. The decisions of the EAT are binding on employment tribunals. There is the possibility of further appeal to the Court of Appeal and from there to the House of Lords.

employment contract: a contract between an employer and an employee. See also *contract of employment*.

employment contrasted with self-employment: there are a number of important legal effects between employment and self-employment. The main ones are:

Employed	Self-employed

• Has employment rights including:
  – not to be unfairly dismissed;
  – right to redundancy pay;
  – right to maternity pay;
  – right not to be discriminated against on the ground of race, sex or disability.
	• No employment rights except the right not to be discriminated against on the ground of race, sex or disability;

• Employer owes a high standard of care in regard to the *health and safety* of employees.	• More limited duty of care owed to an *independent contractor*.

Employed	Self-employed
• Employer *vicariously liable* to other people for the wrongful acts of an employee committed during the course of employment.	• In general, no liability for wrongful acts of independent contractors.
• Employer deducts tax and National Insurance payments.	• Self-employed pay own tax and National Insurance payments.

employment tribunals decide disputes which arise from employment and connected matters, such as *unfair dismissal*, failure to pay agreed wages and *discrimination*. There is usually a panel of three hearing the case: a legally qualified chairman and two lay people who have experience in industry; one from management and one from workers. Employment tribunals used to be known as industrial tribunals and have existed since 1964.

enabling Act: an *Act of Parliament* which gives power to other bodies to make laws or rules. The law then made is known as *delegated legislation*. Examples of enabling Acts are:

- the *Police and Criminal Evidence Act 1984*, which allows the Home Secretary to issue *Codes of Practice* giving guidance on how police powers to stop, search, detain and interview suspects should be used;
- the Civil Procedure Act 1997, which gives power to the Civil Court Rule Committee to make rules on procedure in the *civil courts*.

Delegated legislation made under an enabling Act must not go beyond the power given under the Act. If it does the courts can hold that it is *ultra vires* and void (not effective).

enforcement of a judgment: making sure that the losing party in a civil case complies with the court order that has been made against him. Usually the court order will be for an award of a sum of money to be paid to the other party (*damages*). If the money is not paid, it is up to the winning party to take the necessary steps to enforce the judgment. There are various ways this can be done:

- warrant of execution against goods belonging to the person, under which goods are seized by the court bailiff and sold to raise the money owed;
- attachment of earnings, where the court orders the debtor's employer to deduct a certain amount each week from his wages;
- garnishee orders, under which money from a bank account or other savings account is ordered to be paid to the claimant.

Equal Opportunities Commission: established by the Sex Discrimination Act 1975. Its main functions are:

- to work towards the elimination of *discrimination*;
- to promote equality of opportunity between men and women;
- to keep the law on discrimination under review;
- to help claimants bring cases of discrimination.

The Commission has produced a Code of Practice for employers to follow aimed at eliminating discrimination in the workplace.

equal pay for men and women is a principle set out in Article 141 of the *Treaty of Rome*. When the United Kingdom joined the *European Union*, it was necessary that our law should support this principle, so the Equal Pay Act 1970 was brought into effect. Under this, there are three ways of claiming the right to equal pay. These are:

- showing that the work is 'like work', that is the same or broadly similar;
- having the work rated as equivalent under a *job evaluation scheme* showing that the work is equivalent in such matters as skill, effort and decision-making;
- showing that the job is of equal value; this is where the employer will not carry out a job evaluation, so on an application by the employee to an *employment tribunal* the tribunal will commission an independent expert to evaluate the two jobs; the tribunal will then decide if the work is of equal value.

equitable means fairly. In legal terms an equitable principle or remedy is one that was created by the law of *Equity*.

equitable estoppel: another term for *promissory estoppel*.

equitable interest: a right which does not comply with the legal formalities but which it would be inequitable (unfair) for the court not to recognise and enforce. For example: a mother gives her son money to help him buy a house and shares it with him. Although her son is the owner of the house, the mother has an equitable interest in the house and cannot be evicted from it. On sale of the house, she will be entitled to a share of the proceeds unless she has made it very clear that she does not want the money back.

equitable maxims: sayings on which the principles of fairness and *equity* are based. The most important maxims are:

- he who comes to equity must come with clean hands: if the claimant has not acted fairly, he cannot use equitable principles or claim an *equitable remedy* (D & C Builders Ltd v Rees (1965));
- delay defeats equity: if a claimant waits too long before starting a case, then he cannot claim an equitable remedy (Leaf v International Galleries (1950));
- equity will not suffer a wrong to be without a remedy: this allows equity to create new remedies if needed; this led to the *Anton Piller Order* and the *Mareva injunction*.

equitable remedies: discretionary remedies which a court can order in a *civil case*. This means that the court does not have to make such an order, even though the *claimant* has won the case. The court will only grant the remedy if it is fair in all the circumstances. In deciding whether it is fair, the court will consider any delay in bringing the action, whether the claimant acted fairly and whether on the balance of convenience it would be fair to grant an equitable remedy. The main equitable remedies are:

- *injunctions*;
- *specific performance*;
- *rescission*;
- *rectification*.

Case example: Miller v Jackson (1977)

The claimant successfully brought an action for *nuisance* regarding cricket balls which were frequently hit into his garden. He asked the court for the equitable remedy of an injunction banning cricket matches from being played on the village green. The court exercised its discretion and refused to grant the injunction, as cricket had been played on the ground for over 70 years and public enjoyment of the sport had to be balanced against the nuisance to the individual. The claimant was awarded *damages* instead.

Equity: the law developed from the 13th century to the 19th century by the King's Chancellors and the Court of Chancery to provide justice in cases where the *common law* was too rigid and did not have effective remedies. Historically, this was an important source of law and developed concepts such as *mortgages* and *trusts*. Equity also created new remedies of *injunctions, specific performance, rescission* and *rectification*. Equity is not a complete set of laws; it fills in the gaps of the common law and has been described as the 'gloss on the common law'. Following the reform of the court structure by the Judicature Acts 1873–1875, equitable principles can be applied in any civil court. (See also *equitable maxims* and *equitable remedies*.)

estate refers to the total assets of a person after any debts they owe have been deducted. In inheritance law, the value of a person's estate on their death is important because tax has to be paid on estates over a certain value.

estoppel: an *equitable* concept used by the courts to stop a person taking unfair advantage by going back on his word. Where A by his words or conduct has led B to believe that a certain set of facts exist and B acts on that belief to his prejudice, A is not permitted to then gain advantage by saying that a different set of facts existed at that time.

Case example: Avon County Council v Howlett (1983)

Howlett was overpaid by the Council. When they tried to recover the money, Howlett successfully argued that they had told him that he was entitled to the money and that in reliance of their assurances he had spent the money. It was held that they were therefore estopped from claiming the return of the money.

There are different types of estoppel, such as estoppel by representation, *proprietary estoppel, promissory estoppel* and *waiver*. Because it is an equitable concept, the courts will only use it to benefit a person who has acted equitably (fairly).

European Commission: the executive body of the *European Union*, consists of 20 Commissioners who act in the interests of the EU rather than in the interests of their home countries. Commissioners are appointed for a four-year term, and each one heads a department with special responsibility for an area of Union policy. The Commission's main functions are proposing policies and presenting draft legislation to the *Council of Ministers* for consideration, implementing the Union's budget, and ensuring measures adopted by the Union are properly implemented in the member states.

Where a member state has not implemented Union law or has infringed the law in some way, the Commission can refer the matter to the *European Court of Justice*. This may result in a judgment against the member state. The Commission also has powers to investigate and prevent monopolies and anti-competitive trade behaviour, such as price fixing. Where such behaviour is proved, the Commission has the power to impose large fines. An example of this occurred in 1998, when fines were imposed on British Sugar and Tate and Lyle for fixing the price of sugar.

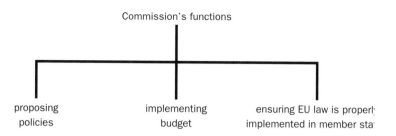

Functions of the European Commission

European Convention on Human Rights: drawn up after the Second World War in order to try to prevent abuse of people's rights by their government. It sets out the rights and freedoms that the people of Europe are entitled to expect. The main ones are that:

- the right to life shall be protected by law, though it is recognised that states have the right to impose the *death penalty* for certain crimes;

- no-one shall be tortured or suffer inhuman or degrading punishment;

- slavery is not allowed;

- everyone has the right to liberty except where the law allows for arrest or detention;

- people have the right to a fair and public hearing of any court case;

- everyone has the right to freedom of thought, conscience and religion;

- all these rights and freedoms should exist without any discrimination on any ground.

Although Britain signed the Convention in 1959, it was not incorporated into our law until the *Human Rights Act 1998* was passed. A complaint about an alleged breach of human rights can be made to the *European Court of Human Rights*.

European Court of Human Rights: established in 1959 to hear cases in which a breach of the *European Convention on Human Rights* is alleged. The court sits in Strasbourg. In 1998, it became a full-time court with judges from each of the 40 countries that have signed the Convention. Individuals can make a complaint to the court that their rights have been infringed. A committee of three judges considers the complaint to see if it should go before the court. If they decide that it should, the case is then heard by a panel of seven judges. A decision does not have any binding effect on the state against whom it is made; however, the British government has, on some occasions, changed our law to prevent further infringements of rights.

Case example: Golder v United Kingdom (1975)

The court held that the Prison Rules which did not allow a prisoner to send confidential letters to his solicitor, nor to bring an action against a prison officer, were in breach of the Convention. After this ruling, the British Government changed the Prison Rules.

European Court of Justice: the court which ensures that the law of the *European Union* is observed and applied uniformly throughout the member states. The court sits in Luxemburg and has 15 judges, one from each member state, who are appointed under Article 223 of the *Treaty of Rome* for a term of six years. The court hears cases referred to it by the *European Commission* on whether member states have failed to implement

European Union law. It has the power to fine any state which is in breach of the law. It also decides points of law referred to it by courts of member states for a preliminary ruling under *Article 234 of the Treaty of Rome*. There is also a court of first instance which hears complex economic cases as well as disputes between the European Institutions and their employees. A major development by the European Court of Justice has been the concept of *direct effect*.

European Economic Community (EEC): formed in 1957 by the *Treaty of Rome*. The original member states were France, Germany, Italy, Belgium, The Netherlands and Luxemburg. The aim was to establish a common market with no trade barriers between the countries. This aim was taken further by the Treaty of European Union in 1993, and the EEC was renamed the *European Union*.

European Ombudsman: a post created by Article 195 of the *Treaty of Rome* and appointed by the *European Parliament* to investigate maladministration by *European Union* institutions.

European Parliament: directly elected by the citizens of the member states of the *European Union* in elections held every five years. The Parliament does not have any law-making powers; it is a consultative body. Its main function is to discuss proposals put forward by the *European Commission*. It has some power over the Union budget and plays an important role in deciding whether new member states should be admitted to the Union.

European Union: originally the *European Economic Community*, established in 1957. In 1993, the name was changed to European Union to reflect the aims of the Union which are set out in Article 2 of the *Treaty of Rome*. These aims are:

- the establishing of a common market;
- economic and monetary union;
- to promote harmonious and balanced development of economic activities;
- to promote a high level of employment and of social protection and the raising of the standard of living within the member states.

The European Union has four main institutions which help to promote these aims. These are:

- the *Council of Ministers*;
- the *European Commission*;
- the *European Parliament*;
- the *European Court of Justice*.

European Union law: law which affects all member states. The main source of EU law is the *Treaty of Rome*. This sets out basic principles such as the right to the free movement of goods (Article 30), the right of free movement of workers (Article 39) and the right not to be discriminated against on the basis of sex (Article 141). The Treaty is directly effective in all member states, (see also *direct effect*). So far as Britain is concerned, this is also stressed by the European Community Act 1972 which says that rights and powers under the Treaties are 'without further enactment to be given legal effect and used in the United Kingdom'. The Treaty of Rome also gives power for further EU law to be made by *regulations* and *directives*. New treaties, such as the Treaty of European Union, can also create law. Before new EU law is created, there is a lengthy consultative process as shown on the following page.

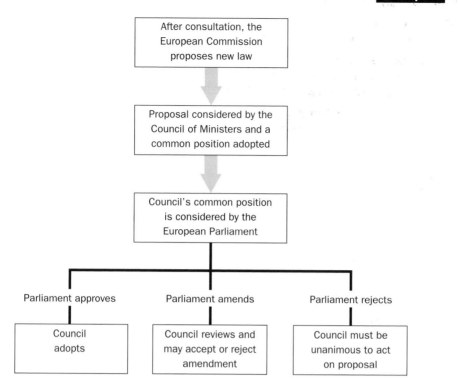

euthanasia: the practice of painlessly putting someone to death, especially where the person is suffering from an incurable and painful illness. In some countries, for example, The Netherlands, euthanasia is lawful provided the sufferer wishes to die. In England and Wales, euthanasia is illegal and any such killing is murder.

evading a liability: an offence under s2 of the Theft Act 1978. This creates three separate ways in which the offence may be committed. These are:

- *dishonestly* securing the remission of the whole or part of any existing liability to make payment, whether his own liability or another's; this covers situations where someone who owes money tells a false story, so that the creditor agrees to the debt, or part of it, not being repaid;

- dishonestly inducing the creditor to wait for payment; this applies to situations where the creditor is persuaded to put back the date for repayment;

- dishonestly obtaining any exemption from or abatement of liability to make payment; this covers showing an out-of-date season ticket or lying about one's age so that a reduced fare is paid.

evidence: the means of proving a case. Evidence can be given verbally in court with a witness stating what they know and being questioned about it, or it can be written. There are strict rules of what evidence is admissible in court.

ex parte means 'without one party or side' in a case. If an application is made to a court ex parte, only one side is present, the other party has not been informed that the court case is taking place. This can only be done in cases of emergency where there is not time to contact the other side or in cases where it is feared that the other side will do something such as leave the country or destroy evidence if they know about the court case.

ex turpi causa non oritur actio means an action in *negligence* cannot be based on an illegal action. This stops people whose injuries are inextricably linked with their criminal activities being awarded *damages* if they have been injured.

See also *illegality doctrine (in tort)*.

Case example: Ashton v Turner (1981)

Two men carried out a burglary and made their escape in a car which crashed injuring the passenger. He sued the driver and, although it was proved that the driver had been negligent, it was held that the passenger should not be awarded damages because at the time of the accident he was carrying out a criminal activity.

exclusion clause: a *term* of a *contract* which limits or excludes one party's liability if he breaches (breaks) the contract. For example: a car-park owner will not have to pay *damages* to car owners if their cars are damaged while parked in his car park, if he displays a notice saying 'Cars parked at owners' risk'. Normally, an exclusion clause must be clear and will only be effective if the other party knew about it at the time the contract was made or sufficient effort was made to draw his attention to it (Chapleton v Barry UDC (1940) and Olley v Marlborough Court (1949)). It may, however, be implied into the contract if the parties have frequently done business with each and the same clause has always been used in the past (there has been a *course of dealing*).

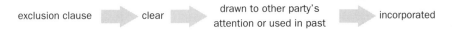

exclusion clause ⟹ clear ⟹ drawn to other party's attention or used in past ⟹ incorporated

Even if incorporated into the contract, an exclusion clause will not always be upheld by the court.

* If there is any ambiguity in the wording of the clause, the court will construe (interpret) it in a way that is least favourable to the person who is trying to limit his liability (see also *contra proferentum rule*).

* Liability for death or personal injury caused by negligence cannot be excluded (*Unfair Contract Terms Act 1977*).

* Liability for other loss caused by negligence cannot be excluded unless it is reasonable to do so (*Unfair Contract Terms Act 1977*).

* Exclusion clauses in *consumer contracts* will not be upheld if they are unfair (*Unfair Terms in Consumer Contracts Regulations 1999*).

exclusion order: a court order that can be made banning an offender from going into the place where he committed the offence, or even from other places where it is likely that he will commit further offences. It is usually used to ban those convicted of offences connected with football hooliganism from going to football matches.

executed consideration: the term given to an action amounting to *consideration* made in response to a reward offer. When a reward offer has been made, the *offeror* does not know who has accepted the offer until after the action which amounts to consideration has been carried out, such as returning a lost dog. Normally, consideration which happens before an offer has been accepted is not *good consideration*. However, an exception is made in reward offers provided that the person accepting the reward offer knows about it before carrying out the consideration. See also *past consideration*.

executor/executrix: a person named in a *will* to get *probate* of the will, deal with the deceased's estate and make sure that the terms of the will are carried out. Executor refers to a man and executrix is the female form of the word (although executor can be used to cover men and women). Executors are also called personal representatives.

executory consideration: promises made by both parties to a contract to exchange money, goods or services in the future rather than immediately. A promise to exchange in the future is just as good *consideration* as an actual exchange, and a contract comes into existence when the promises themselves are exchanged.

exemplary damages (also known as *punitive damages*): damages in *tort* which are more than are needed to compensate the claimant for his loss and are intended to:

- punish the defendant; or

- deprive him of any benefit he has gained by the tort; e.g. where a newspaper deliberately prints a defamatory article calculating that their increased profits from sales will be more than they will lose in a defamation case; or

- protect the individual against oppressive conduct by government officials, such as police officers.

Exemplary damages are very rarely awarded and they are not available for breach of contract (but see *restitutionary damages*).

exemption clause: see *exclusion clause*

existing contractual duty: a duty which exists from a previous contract between the parties. This existing duty, which one party is already legally obliged to do, cannot be *consideration* for a new contract unless the nature of the duty has changed considerably because of a change in circumstances.

In both of the two cases below, sailors agreed a wage for a complete voyage. In both cases, some of the crew deserted and the captain agreed to pay the remaining crew extra. When the ships returned to England, the captains then refused to pay the extra wage and the sailors sued. One case succeeded while the other failed because of the different circumstances.

Stilk v Myrick (1809)	Hartley v Ponsonby (1857)
• two sailors deserted out of a crew of 11	• 17 sailors deserted out of a crew of 36 leaving only five able seamen
• work done on return voyage was similar to that done on the outward voyage	• return voyage dangerous because of the lack of crew
• sailor did nothing more than he had originally agreed to do	• sailor did more than he had originally agreed to do
• no consideration was given for second agreement, only doing existing duty	• consideration was given for second agreement
• no new contract	• new contract had come into existence
• sailor not entitled to extra wage	• sailor entitled to extra wage

Sometimes one party may be held to have provided extra consideration for a second contract, even though he appears to be doing only what he had originally contracted to do, if the other party receives some extra benefit from the new contract.

Case example: Williams v Roffey (1990)

The owner of a block of flats contracted with builders to renovate them. They in turn contracted with a carpenter to do some of the work. When he began to fall behind, a second agreement was reached that he would be paid extra for each flat he completed on time. It was held that, although he was bound to do this anyway under the original contract, he was providing new consideration for the second contract. This was because it gave the builders the benefit of avoiding having to pay compensation to the owners for late completion.

expectation interest: the benefit that a party to a contract expects to get out of it. If he does not get this benefit because the other party has breached (broken) the contract, he is entitled to *damages* that will put him in the position he would have been in if the contract had been completed. These are assessed by looking at how the wronged party is worse off because of the breach of contract or by looking at how much it would cost to put right.

Case example: Radford v De Froberville (1977)

The claimant sold part of his land to the defendant who agreed to build a wall between the two properties. He failed to do so and when sued argued that the amount of damages should be the amount that the claimant's land had fallen in value because the wall had not been built. The court, however, decided that the amount of damages should be the cost of having the wall built by someone else, which was a much higher figure.

express term: a *term* of a contract which has been discussed and agreed by the two parties. Terms of a contract which have not been discussed but implied into the contract by the courts or Parliament are called *implied terms*.

expressio unius est exclusio alterius: a rule of language in *statutory interpretation* which means that where specific matters only are mentioned, then it is assumed that all other matters are not included.

Case example: Tempest v Kilner (1846)

It was held that the words in the Statute of Frauds 1677 (now repealed) which required a contract for the sale of 'goods, wares and merchandise' for £10 or more to be evidenced in writing, did not apply to a contract for the sale of stocks and shares. The words 'stocks and shares' were not mentioned in the Statute and so it was assumed that they were excluded.

extortionate credit bargain: one where an individual borrower is required to make payments which are grossly exorbitant or which contravene ordinary principles of fair trading. Under the *Consumer Credit Act 1974*, the court has the power to re-write the agreement. Each case is taken on its own facts but, in practice, the borrower is not often successful.

extrinsic aids to statutory interpretation: sources outside the Act or other law in question, which may help to make the meaning of disputed words or phrases clear. Extrinsic aids include:

- previous *Acts of Parliament* on the same topic;
- the historical setting;
- case law;
- dictionaries of the time.

These are all accepted as aids which should be used.

Case example: DPP v Cheeseman (1990)

The defendant was charged under s28 of the Town Police Causes Act 1847 by which it was an offence to 'indecently expose his person in a street to the annoyance of passengers'. To find the meaning of the word 'passenger', the judges consulted the Oxford English Dictionary which was in use in 1847. This gave the meaning of 'a passer-by or through; a traveller (usually on foot); a wayfarer'. As a result, the defendant was found not guilty, as the only people to see him were policeman waiting to catch him, and the court held that they were not passers-by.

There are also other extrinsic aids which are now allowed to be consulted in limited circumstances to find the intention or purpose of the law. These are:

- *Hansard* (the report of debates in Parliament) in which only the statements made by the promoter of the law can be considered (see also *Pepper v Hart (1993)*);
- reports of law reform bodies such as the *Law Commission* which can be considered to see what gap the law was designed to deal with;
- international conventions or *directives* which the English law is trying to implement.

Do you need revision help and advice?

Go to pages 259–99 for a range of revision appendices that include plenty of exam advice and tips.

fair comment: a defence in *defamation*. The defendant must show that:

- he was giving his opinion rather than making a statement of fact; and

- it was made without malice, it was an honest expression of his own view; and

- it was about a subject of public interest and not a purely private matter (Slim v Daily Telegraph (1968)).

The difference between fair comment and *justification* is:

Fair comment	Justification
covers a statement of the defendant's opinions;	covers a statement of fact made by the defendant;
defendant must show that his statement was his genuine opinion made without malice; he does not have to show it was true.	defendant must prove that his statement was substantially true

Fair Trading Act 1973: set up the *Office of Fair Trading*, which is headed by the *Director-General of Fair Trading*, to protect consumers' interests by proposing and making changes to consumer legislation, pursuing traders who act in a way detrimental to consumers' interest and licensing credit providers.

false imprisonment (trespass to person): preventing someone from exercising freedom of movement. This is usually locking someone in a room or otherwise preventing them from leaving, but includes preventing a person from going in the direction he wants to go in, unless there is a suitable alternative route. A claim for false imprisonment can be brought even if the claimant did not realise at the time that he was unable to leave the room he was in (Meering v Grahame-White Aviation Co Ltd (1919)). An *arrest* which is unlawful will also amount to false imprisonment.

Family Division of the High Court hears cases involving the family. It is the only court that can hear applications to make a child a *ward of court*. It also has jurisdiction to deal with:

- all cases involving children under the *Children Act 1989*;

- all matrimonial cases;

- *grants of probate* which are not disputed.

Family Divisional Court hears appeals on family matters from decisions by the *Family Panel in the Magistrates' Court*. There are usually only about 40 of these cases each year, and they are heard by two judges of the Family Division sitting together.

Family Law Act 1996 was passed but only the sections concerned with *domestic violence* have come into force. It has been decided to repeal the provisions concerning divorce after unsuccessful pilot schemes. The main aim of the Act was to encourage parties who are thinking of divorcing to make every effort to effect a reconciliation. If this was not possible, the divorce was to be carried out in a way that caused the least distress to the parties and their children. The five stages of a divorce or separation were to be:

- the parties attend an information meeting;
- a statement of marital breakdown is filed at the court by one or both parties;
- there is a period for reflection and consideration;
- a statement of financial arrangements is filed at the court together with a statement of arrangements for the welfare of the children; these arrangements can be the result of negotiations between the parties or the result of a court order;
- one or both parties apply to the court for a divorce order which will be made on the basis that the marriage has irretrievably broken down provided the above steps have been taken. It is possible for one of the parties to apply for an order preventing divorce if it can be shown that he or she will suffer substantial financial hardship or it would be wrong in all the circumstances.

The process was to take a minimum of 12 months (18 months if there are children involved).

Family Panel in Magistrates' Court consists of specially trained *lay magistrates* who hear family cases in the Magistrates' Court. *District judges* can also hear these cases, but they usually sit with one or two lay magistrates. Cases dealt with include anything connected with the family, such as disputes over *residence* and *contact orders* for children, applications for financial provision for a spouse and applications for *non-molestation orders* where there has been domestic violence. They cannot grant divorces.

fast track cases: civil cases usually for claims of more than £5,000 but less than £15,000. The decision as to whether a case is suitable for the fast track is made by the court after considering the replies to an *allocation questionnaire*. The cases will be subject to a fixed timetable which will usually require a hearing within 30 weeks of allocation to the fast track. There are capped costs on advocacy fees and the government has consulted about further possible controls on costs.

fault based liability: liability which only arises if a defendant is at fault in some way by deliberately committing a tort or acting negligently or failing to take reasonable precautions. In torts of *strict liability* the defendant is liable even if he took all reasonable precautions. Fault based liability is seen as fairer because the defendant only pays compensation if he has not been careful enough. However, a person who needs money because he has been injured may find it impossible to prove the defendant's fault. New Zealand introduced a non-fault compensation system but has found it very expensive.

fiduciary duties of directors: as directors are *quasi-trustees* of the assets of a company, they have special duties towards the company. These are:

- to account to the company for any personal profit made in the course of dealings with the company property; that is a director must give the company any profit he makes unless a general meeting of *shareholders* consents to his keeping the profits;
- to use their powers for the benefit of the company.

fiduciary relationship: a term used in contract law for a relationship where one party is much more dominant or more experienced than the other or there is another reason for placing great trust in him. These can include the relationship between:

- *solicitor* and client;
- doctor and patient;
- *trustee* and *beneficiary*;
- parent and child.

Where the two parties enter into a contract, the dominant party must take more care than usual to ensure that the other party understands what he is undertaking, otherwise the contract may be set aside for:

- *misrepresentation* if the dominant party has failed to tell the other party all the relevant facts; or
- *undue influence*, unless the dominant party can show that the other party had independent advice.

financial provision on divorce: the division of matrimonial assets and arrangements for maintenance for the spouses and any *child of the family* on divorce or separation. If the parties cannot come to an agreement over these, the court can make various orders:

- financial provision orders
    - *periodic payments order*
    - *secure periodic payments order*
    - *lump sum order*
- property adjustment orders
    - *transfer of property order*
    - *settlement of property order*
    - *variation of marriage settlement order*
- order for sale of matrimonial assets, e.g. matrimonial home
- *pension attachment order* and *pension sharing order.*

When considering what orders to make, the court will apply the factors set out in the *Matrimonial Causes Act 1973 s25.* When making the order, the court will be more concerned with both parties' needs and a fair division rather than the financial contribution each party has made to the marriage and will try, if possible, to achieve a *clean break.*

See also *White v White* and *Welfare Reform and Pensions Act 1999.*

financial relief: a term used in divorce for *financial provision.*

fines: a method of punishment used for a wide range of offences. Nearly all motoring offences are dealt with by way of a fine, though the court may also disqualify the offender from driving. About one third of other offenders appearing in the Magistrates' Court will also be fined. This will include those guilty of theft, criminal damage and minor assaults. Only about four per cent of offenders are dealt with by way of a fine in the Crown Court; this is because the cases generally involve offences which are too serious to be given a fine.

fingerprinting: *PACE* gives the police powers to take fingerprints from anyone with their consent. The police can also take fingerprints without the person's consent if:

- a senior police officer authorises it; or

- the person is suspected of involvement in a criminal offence and it is believed that fingerprints may prove or disprove their involvement; or

- a suspect has been charged with a recordable offence.

S64 of PACE has been amended by the Criminal Justice and Police Act 2001 so that fingerprints can be kept by the police even if the suspect is not charged.

fit for the purpose: a term used in s14 of the *Sale of Goods Act 1979* to describe the standard expected of goods. The seller in all sales of goods implies that the goods he sells are:

- fit for the purpose they are normally used for;

- fit for an unusual purpose provided that the buyer explains what he intends to use them for, and the seller has told him that the goods are fit for that purpose and it was reasonable for the buyer to rely on the seller's assurances;

- fit for the purpose that the buyer wants them for if the buyer has checked this with the seller and it has been reasonable to rely on the seller's assurances.

For example, if a buyer asks for a computer ink cartridge by name, the seller implies that the cartridge will work in the printer it was designed for. But if the buyer asks for an ink cartridge suitable for a particular type of computer, then the seller implies that it will work for that type of computer provided that the buyer has gone to a specialist shop.

five facts: used in divorce law to prove that a marriage has irretrievably broken down. They are set out in the Matrimonial Causes Act 1973.

The *petitioner* must show one of the following :

- the *respondent* has committed *adultery*, and the petitioner finds it intolerable to live with the respondent. This cannot be used if the petitioner continues living with the respondent in the same *household* for more than six months after finding out about the adultery;

- the respondent has behaved in such a way that the petitioner cannot reasonably be expected to live with him (see also *behaviour*). This cannot be used if the petitioner continues living with the respondent in the same household for more than six months after the last event complained of;

- the respondent has deserted the petitioner for a continuous period of two years immediately prior to the presentation of the petition (see also *desertion*). The two-year period can be interrupted by one or more periods of reconciliation not amounting to six months in all. But these periods of reconciliation do not count towards the two years; e.g. if a couple separate in January 1996 and are reconciled for three months in 1997, divorce proceedings cannot be started until April 1998;

- the parties to the marriage have *lived apart* for a continuous period of two years immediately preceding the presentation of the petition, and the respondent consents to the decree being granted. As with desertion, the parties can be reconciled for up to six months.

- the parties have lived apart for a continuous period of five years immediately preceding the presentation of the petition. As with desertion, the parties can be reconciled for up to six months.

floodgates argument: the idea that if one particular claim were allowed, this would open the gates to thousands of other similar claims. It is an argument against extending negligence claims to include wider recognition of *economic loss* or to allow *nervous shock* cases to succeed where the claimant is not closely connected to the victim.

foreseeability and the duty of care: in *negligence*, a *duty of care* is only owed to people it can reasonably be foreseen will be affected by the defendant's actions. For example, if a person drives his car negligently, it is reasonably foreseeable that other road users may be affected by this. This rule originated in the case of *Donoghue v Stevenson (1932)* and is used to limit the number of people who can bring a claim. The test is an objective one, so that it is irrelevant whether the defendant realised that his actions would affect others or not.

Case example: In Bourhill v Young (1943)

A motor-cyclist negligently overtaking a tram hit a car and was killed. A woman behind the tram heard the accident but did not see it. She later saw blood on the road where the accident happened. She suffered from *nervous shock* and had a miscarriage. It was held that although the motor-cyclist owed a duty of care to the car driver, it was not reasonably foreseeable that the woman would suffer injury, and she failed in her claim.

Establishing reasonable foreseeability is the first step towards showing that the defendant owed the claimant a duty of care. The claimant must then show:

- proximity (that there is a close connection between the parties);
- that it is just, fair and reasonable to impose a duty of care;
- that there are no public policy reasons against imposing a duty of care.

foreseeability and its effect on damages in tort: *damages* can only be claimed for damage which could be reasonably foreseen as a result of the defendant's negligence. This is an objective test, so it is irrelevant whether the defendant foresaw that the damage would arise or not. As long as the type of damage is foreseeable, a claim can be made even if:

- the way the damage was caused was not foreseeable;
- the extent of the damage is much greater than was foreseeable;
- the extent of the damage is much greater than was foreseeable because the claimant was particularly vulnerable (the *eggshell skull rule*);
- the precise nature of the damage was not foreseeable;
- the damage was caused by a third party, provided it was very likely that this would happen as a direct result of the defendant's negligence (see also *chain of causation* and *novus actus interveniens*).

See also *Wagon Mound (1961)*.

foresight of consequences: an aspect of the criminal law on *intention*. The issue is whether a defendant who realises that his actions may cause a particular consequence, even though he does not particularly want that consequence to occur, can be said to have the intention to cause that consequence. This is also known as *oblique intention*.

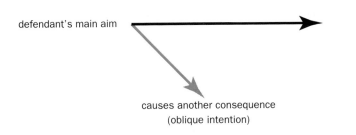

defendant's main aim

causes another consequence
(oblique intention)

Up to 1985, it was held that foresight of consequences was sufficient to prove intention. (Hyam v DPP (1975)). However, the law in this area was changed by decisions in two House of Lords' cases. These are R v Moloney (1985) and R v Hancock and Shankland (1986). The key points from these cases are that:

- foresight of consequences is not the same as intention; it is only evidence from which intention may be inferred (Moloney);

- the greater the probability of a consequence occurring, the more likely that it was foreseen and thus the greater the probability that it was intended (Hancock and Shankland).

In R v Nedrick (1986), the Court of Appeal tried to 'crystallise' these two decisions and suggest how the matter should be considered by a jury who were trying the case. Nedrick states that there are two questions a jury should ask themselves:

1. Was the consequence a virtual certainty of the defendant's actions?

2. Did the defendant foresee that consequence as being a virtual certainty?

If the answer to both these question is 'Yes', then there is evidence from which the jury can infer that the defendant intended those consequences.

In R v Woollin (1998) the House of Lords did not like the use of these two questions but approved of the suggested direction to the jury in Nedrick that they should be told, 'they are not entitled to find the necessary intention unless they feel sure that death or serious bodily harm was a 'virtual certainty' (barring some unforeseen intervention) as a result of the defendant's actions and that the defendant appreciated that such was the case'.

forfeiture orders can be used in criminal cases to deprive convicted offenders of property they have used to commit their crimes. For example, a burglar who used his own car to drive away stolen property could have that car forfeited. The Proceeds of Crime Act 1995 also gives the courts special powers to order forfeiture in drugs cases, so that all profits from drug dealing over the last six years can be taken.

form 10 allows people on low income to receive free initial advice and assistance with legal problems. It is funded by the *Legal Services Commission*. This scheme was previously known as the Green Form scheme.

formal justice: the idea that all legal rules and principles and procedure must be carried out without bias, so that everyone is equal before the law.

formalities of making a will: the requirements are that:

- the will must be in writing; and

- the will must be signed by the *testator* (or some other person on the testator's direction and in the testator's presence); and

- that this signature must be made or acknowledged in the presence of two or more witnesses who are present together; and

- each witness must then sign the will in the presence of the testator.

Foss v Harbottle rule states that where a wrong has been done to a *company* or a where a company wishes to enforce its rights, the company itself is the correct *claimant* to take the case to court. A *shareholder* cannot bring a case on behalf of the company. The reasons for this rule are:

- the company has a separate legal personality from its members;

- there is a right of the majority of members to rule, and an action brought by a single shareholder may be against the wishes of the majority; when a company acts, this is only on the wishes of the majority, either by a directors' resolution or by a resolution of members in a general meeting;

- allowing individual shareholders to take action could lead to a multiplicity of actions.

However, there are exceptions (see also *Foss v Harbottle rule, exceptions to*), particularly where the rule would create an injustice and allow the majority to carry out actions which would amount to a *fraud on the minority*.

Foss v Harbottle rule, exceptions to: although individual members cannot normally take action on behalf of the company, there are exceptions in which it is recognised that the rule in Foss v Harbottle would create an injustice. These exceptions are:

- if the act complained of is illegal or *ultra vires*;

- if the act cannot be confirmed by a simple majority, but needs a greater majority;

- where there is a *fraud on the minority*; this includes:
  - where the company itself has been defrauded
  - where the minority members have been forced out by an alteration of the company's articles;

- unfair use of the majority power.

franchising: a method by which the government gives contracts for legal aid work to solicitors' firms and other legal agencies. The aim of franchising is to ensure quality of work, 'giving value for money to the taxpayer'. To obtain a franchise, firms have to show that they meet set criteria for both legal competence and business management.

Francovitch principle allows citizens of European Union member states to claim compensation from a state for losses caused by the state's failure to implement a *directive*. A claim can only be made if :

- the purpose of the directive was to grant rights to individuals; and

- the directive is sufficiently clear that those rights can be identified; and

- the failure to implement has directly led to the loss.

Case example: Francovitch v Italian Republic (1991)

The Italian government failed to implement a directive aimed at protecting wages of employees whose employer became bankrupt. When the firm for which Francovitch worked went into liquidation owing him wages, he could not use the directive because it had not been implemented. So he sued the government for his loss. The European Court of Justice held that he was entitled to compensation.

Franks Committee: set up to investigate the workings of *tribunals* and other inferior decision-making bodies. It identified three key principles under which these bodies should operate; these were openness, fairness and impartiality. It also recommended that:

- all tribunal chairmen should be legally qualified;
- a *Council on Tribunals* should be set up to oversee the workings of tribunals;
- an *ombudsman* should be appointed to deal with complaints of maladministration by government departments.

All of these recommendations were eventually followed.

fraud cases in criminal law: these are not specifically defined, but generally involve obtaining money or other property by deception or other fraudulent means. In some cases, the offence charged may even be *theft*. Serious allegations of fraud, particularly where company funds are involved, are investigated by the *Serious Fraud Office*. When such a case is tried, it may last for months and be very complicated, with hundreds of documents for the judge and jury to look at. The Roskill Committee (1986) recommended that a jury should not be used in such cases. The Auld Review also recommended juries should not be used. The Criminal Justice Bill 2002 proposes that the prosecution should be able to apply for a judge to hear the case without a jury in complex fraud cases. This part of the Bill was voted against by the House of Lords in July 2003 but the Government has indicated that they will re-instate this part of the Bill and ensure that it is eventually passed.

fraud in contract law: see *mistake* and *misrepresentation*

fraud on the minority: a concept in company law which creates an exception to the normal rule that *shareholders* cannot take an action in court on behalf of a company. Where it would create a serious injustice to allow the majority to commit wrongs against the company and benefit from those wrongs at the expense of the minority, the courts allow individual members to bring an action on behalf of the company.

Case example: Cook v Deeks (1916)

The directors of a company had negotiated a contract on behalf of the company, but then made the contract in their own names and also passed a resolution declaring that the company had no interest in the contract. Cook, who was a shareholder in the company sued the directors, claiming a declaration that the benefit of the contract belonged to the company. The court held that Cook was entitled to bring the case and obtain the declaration, as the actions of the directors were a fraud on the minority.

fraudulent misrepresentation: in contract law, a *misrepresentation* which has been made:

- knowingly; or
- without belief in its truth; or
- recklessly as to whether it is true or not (Derry v Peek (1889)).

The person to whom the misrepresentation has been made is entitled to rescind (cancel) the contract and claim damages under the tort of deceit. The damages will be calculated so as to put the party in the same position he would have been in if the misrepresentation had not been made. Most claims, however, are made in *negligent misrepresentation* because this is easier to prove. See also *damages in contract* and *damages in tort*.

free movement of goods in the European Union: guaranteed by Article 28 of the *Treaty of Rome*. Member states cannot prohibit goods being imported from other member states or set a limit on the amount of goods imported or take any other measures which will limit the importation unless it is necessary to:

- protect public health;
- protect consumers;
- protect the environment;
- protect public morality (R v Henn and Darby (1979));
- protect public security.

Case example: European Commission v Germany (German beer purity case) (1984)

Germany did not allow any beer which contained additives to be sold there. The use of additives was authorised by other member states, and the evidence was that they were not harmful to health. It was held that Germany was in breach of Article 30 as it prevented the free movement of goods without a good reason. Labelling could easily indicate to consumers that a beer contained additives.

free movement of workers in the European Union: guaranteed by Article 39 of the *Treaty of Rome*. There must be no discrimination as regards employment, pay or other conditions of employment against workers from other member states based on nationality, unless it is justified on the grounds of public policy, public security or public health. Workers are allowed to enter another member state to take up employment or to look for work (though they can be deported if they do not find work after six months). Where a worker enters another *European Union* country, his or her family may also enter (*Regulation* 1618/68).

Case example: the Jean Marc Bosman case (1993)

Bosman was a Belgian football player who was prevented from taking up a contract with a French football club because the transfer rules limited the number of foreign players who could play in a country. It was held that the transfer rules were in breach of Article 48 as they did not allow free movement of workers (a football player was held to be worker) into other member states.

Free Representation Unit: run by barristers to provide free representation in a court or tribunal for those who cannot obtain legal funding under the government schemes. Barristers offer to do a small number of cases each year for the Unit free of charge.

freedom of association includes the right to join a trade union or other lawful organisation and to meet with others in public places as well as privately. These rights are upheld by Article 11 of the *European Convention on Human Rights*. In England and Wales there are, however, certain restrictions, especially on the right of assembly in public places. The main restrictions are as follows:

- The Public Order Act 1986 makes it a criminal offence to use violent conduct when 12 or more people are present (*riot*) or when three or more people are present (*violent disorder*).
- The Public Order Act 1986 makes it a criminal offence to wear political uniforms in public.

- The Criminal Justice and Public Order Act 1994 creates the offence of aggravated trespass where people trespass on land in order to demonstrate against a lawful activity.
- Under the Criminal Justice and Public Order Act 1994, the police can also intervene if there is a 'rave' party in the open air at night with loud music and at least 100 people attending it.
- Processions are subject to control and can be banned by the district council for up to three months.

freedom of contract means that individuals and businesses are free to come to any contractual agreement they like. The courts, following this principle, will enforce a contract even if it is a very unfair one, and will enforce all the terms of a written contract whether the parties have read them or not.

Exceptions:

- *minors' contracts* where one of the parties is under 18;
- contracts where one of the parties was suffering from a mental disorder or was drunk at the time the contract was made (see *capacity in contract law*);
- contracts where there has been *undue influence* or *duress* on one of the parties;
- contracts where there has been *misrepresentation*;
- *consumer contracts*: businesses cannot exclude certain *implied terms*.

freedom of the person: a basic human right upheld by Article 5 of the *European Convention on Human Rights*. There are, however, situations in which a person can be deprived of their liberty. The main grounds are:

- that the person has been lawfully arrested (see also *powers of arrest*);
- that a court has ordered that the person should be held in custody while awaiting trial;
- that a sentence of imprisonment has been imposed by a court;
- under the Mental Health Acts.

A writ of *habeas corpus* is available to protect the freedom of the person. Also, if anyone has been unlawfully detained, they may claim damages for *false imprisonment*.

freedom of speech (also called freedom of expression): regarded as one of the key features of a democratic society. In Britain, it is possible to criticise the government and express opinions on current events. There are, however, some restrictions on freedom of speech, for example:

- Defamatory statements are a tort and the victim may sue for damages (see also *defamation*).
- Leaking information which puts national security at risk is a criminal offence.
- Publishing obscene material which is likely to deprave or corrupt is a criminal offence.
- Reporting details of court proceedings which the court has forbidden to be published, such as the identity of a rape victim.

freehold estate is land which is permanently owned, giving the owner the right to occupy it and leave it to his or her heirs or sell it. This is unlike a *leasehold estate* which must be handed back to the owner at the end of the lease period.

freeholder: a person who holds a freehold estate.

freeing order: a court order transferring parental responsibility for a child to an adoption agency prior to *adoption*. Normally the order is made with the parents' consent, but if the child is in care, the agency can apply for their consent to be dispensed with. The consent of an unmarried father is not needed, but the court must be satisfied that he does not intend to make an application for a *parental responsibility order* or a *residence order*. Once the freeing order is made, the natural parents have no say as to who will adopt their child.

frolic of his own in *vicarious liability* means an action or an activity by an employee at work which is wholly unconnnected with the job he is employed to do. While an employer is normally vicariously liable for the actions of his employees at work, he is not liable if an employee is on a frolic of his own. The activity must be nothing to do with the employee's job for the employer not to be liable; if the employee is carrying out his job but in a way that is in breach of the employer's rules, the employer remains liable.

Case example: Beard v London General Omnibus Co (1900)

A bus conductor drove a bus negligently and injured the claimant. It was held that it was not part of his job to drive buses and that he was on a frolic of his own. His employer was not liable for his negligent action.

frustration: an event outside the parties' control which prevents a contract from being carried out. This can happen where:

- carrying out the contract has now become illegal because the law has changed;
- the party who is due to carry out a service under the contract has died;
- the party who is due to carry out a service is unavailable through illness or some other reason, e.g. in Morgan v Manser (1948), an entertainer was unable to fulfil his contract because he had to do military service for over half the period covered by the contract;
- something which is essential to the contract has been destroyed, e.g. in Taylor v Caldwell (1863) the concert hall in which the performance was due to take place burned down;
- circumstances have changed so that it is impossible to carry out the contract;
- circumstances have changed so that the contract is now pointless.

Case example: Krell v Henry (1903)

A room was hired to watch Edward VII's coronation procession. When the coronation was postponed, the contract was held to be frustrated because the hiring of the room had become pointless. If the hirer had got some other benefit from the contract, it would not be frustrated (Herne Bay Steam Boat Co v Hutton (1903)).

If the contract is frustrated, it is terminated from that point. Neither party has to do anything further. *Damages* will be assessed under the *Law Reform (Frustrated Contracts) Act 1943* which tries to spread any loss fairly between the parties.

The contract will not be held to be frustrated if:

- it is still possible to carry out the contract, but in a more difficult or expensive way (Tsakiroglou & Co Ltd v Noblee Thorl GmbH (1962));

- the contract has become impossible to carry out because of one party's actions (Maritime National Fish Ltd v Ocean Trawlers (1935));
- the parties had foreseen the possibility of the contract becoming impossible to perform and had included a term in the contract to cover this;
- the parties should have foreseen the possibility of the contract becoming impossible to perform.

fundamental breach of contract: a *breach of contract* that destroys the whole point of the contract.

Case example: Photo Productions v Securicor (1980)

A security guard supplied by the defendants accidentally burnt down the factory he was supposed to be safeguarding. This was held to be a fundamental breach of contract.

In the past, it was held that it was not possible to exclude liability for a breach of contract that was fundamental to it. However, since the Photo Productions case, it is now possible to exclude liability for a fundamental breach, but only if the wording of the *exclusion clause* is very clear and unambiguous so that the other party understands what he is agreeing to. See also *contra proferentum rule*.

fusion of the legal professions: the concept that there should not be separate professions of *solicitors* and *barristers*, but instead these should be joined into one profession. This is the position in most countries in the world. The arguments for and against fusion are:

Pros	Cons
• Fusion would reduce costs to the client as only one lawyer would be needed.	• Same amount of work would still have to be done so only limited reduction in costs.
• Less duplication of work.	• Two opinions are better than one.
• More continuity.	• Specialist skills of advocacy are needed.
• Students would not have to choose which profession to enter.	• Advice from barristers is available to all solicitors thus allowing small firms to offer a good service.

What other subjects are you studying?

A–Zs cover 18 different subjects. See the inside back cover for a list of all the titles in the series and how to order.

garden leave: the term given to the period of time when an employee is under notice to leave and is still being paid by the employer but is not required to do any work for the employer. The key point is that the employer is enforcing the contract of employment by refusing to let the employee start working for anyone else during the period of notice. This usually only occurs where the employee is high ranking and could take clients away from the employer or when the employee has confidential information about the company (or its inventions) which could be of use to a rival firm.

garnishee order: a method of enforcing a *judgment debt*. Where the debtor has a bank account or other savings account, the *claimant* can ask the court to order the bank or savings company to pay money out of the account to pay the judgment debt.

General Council of the Bar: the governing body of the *barristers'* profession. It is usually referred to as the *Bar Council*.

general damages: a sum of money awarded by a court in a civil case. General damages are compensation for losses which cannot be specifically quantified. For example, if there is claim for injuries received in a car crash, the amount awarded for pain and suffering is general damages. An amount can also be awarded for future loss of earnings, if the injured person is unable to return to work.

general partner in a *partnership* is a partner who is allowed to conduct any of the partnership business. They will have put capital into the partnership and will have a share of the profits. They will also be liable for the partnership debts.

General Product Safety Regulations 1994 make it a criminal offence for a person or business to sell or supply unsafe products as part of a commercial activity. Both producers and distributors have a duty to:

- only supply products which are safe or which carry only a minimal risk which is reasonable taking into account the product's use. When deciding whether a product is safe, a court will take into account the characteristics of the product, whether children will use it, the packaging and instructions for installation and maintenance;
- provide any necessary warnings to ensure safe use of the product;
- act with due care to ensure that products supplied are safe.

genuine occupational qualification: an exception where sexual or racial discrimination is permitted in employment situations under the Sex Discrimination Act 1975 (s7) and the Race Relations Act 1976 (s5). These exceptions are:

- where it is necessary for dramatic performances or other entertainment for reasons of authenticity;

- for personal services promoting welfare when these can most effectively be provided by someone of the same sex or race; for example, a woman could be employed as a counsellor for female rape victims;
- to preserve decency or privacy (sex discrimination only);
- for authenticity in places where food or drink is served, such as Chinese restaurants (racial discrimination only).

Ghosh test: a test for deciding whether the defendant has acted dishonestly in *theft* and other offences under the Thefts Acts. In such cases the jury should be asked to decided whether what was done was dishonest according to the ordinary standards of reasonable honest people. If so, did the defendant realise that what he was doing was dishonest by those standards?

Gillick competent means that a *child* is mature enough to understand the consequences of what he is agreeing to; the more serious the consequences, the older and more mature the child needs to be.

Case details: Gillick v West Norfolk and Wisbech AHA (1985)

Mrs Gillick wanted an assurance from the AHA that her daughters would not be given contraceptive advice when under 16 without her knowledge and consent. The House of Lords held that children could give consent to medical treatment if they fully understood its implications. If children are capable of giving consent, their doctor should not reveal any details of their treatment to their parents.

Once children reach 16 they can give consent to medical treatment under the Family Law Reform Act 1969.

going equipped to steal: an offence under s25 of the Theft Act 1968. The offence is committed when a person who is not at his place of abode has with him any article for use in the course of or in connection with any *burglary*, *theft* or cheat. The term 'any article' makes this a very wide offence; it covers articles such as car keys (if they are to be used to steal a car) and screwdrivers or other tools which are to be used to get into a building to commit burglary. It has even been held to include bottles of wine which a wine waiter intended selling to customers instead of the hotel's own stock (R v Doukas (1978)).

golden rule: one of the so-called three rules of statutory interpretation. It is used where the *literal rule* cannot be used as there are two or more meanings. In this situation, the courts will take the least absurd (R v Allen (1872)). Some judges will also use the golden rule where the literal rule would lead to an absurd result or a repugnant situation. The court will 'modify' the words of the Act to avoid such a result.

Case example: Adler v George (1964)

The defendants were prosecuted under the Official Secrets Act 1920 which made it an offence to obstruct HM Forces 'in the vicinity of' a prohibited place. The defendants obstructed HM Forces actually IN the prohibited place. The strict use of the literal rule would have meant that they were not guilty because they were 'in' rather than 'in the vicinity of'. This was absurd, and the court used the golden rule to find them guilty.

good consideration: in contract, *consideration* that a court considers is valid. Unless good consideration is exchanged by both parties, no *contract* comes into existence. Good consideration is usually goods, services or money, but does not have to be of equal value to the consideration provided by the other party and can be something very trivial, such as used chocolate bar wrappers (Chappel v Nestle (1960)). The following have been held NOT to be good consideration:

- natural love and affection;
- performing a duty where there is already a legal obligation to do it;
- performing a duty where there is already an obligation under a previous contract to do it;
- repaying only part of a debt, even when the creditor has agreed that this will settle the debt (*Pinnel's case*);
- *past consideration*.

good title means legal ownership. In a contract for the sale of goods, legal ownership is passed from the seller to the buyer. A person who buys stolen goods does not acquire good title, however much he has paid for them, because the seller himself does not have good title. The buyer must return the goods to the true owner and can claim his money back from the seller.

In all *consumer contracts*, there is an *implied term* that the seller has good title to the goods under the *Sale of Goods Act 1979*. See also *nemo dat quod non habet*.

grant of probate: a court order under which the will of someone who has died is accepted by the court as being their last will. This grant gives the *executors* of the will the legal authority to deal with the deceased's estate. They are able to collect in all the assets, pay out debts and then distribute the remainder to those who inherit under the will.

grant of representation: the general term which covers the *grant of probate* and the grant of *letters of administration*. In both situations, legal authority is given to representatives of the deceased to deal with the estate.

Green Paper: a consultative document issued by the government on proposed new laws which they wish to enact as an *Act of Parliament*. Anyone with an interest in the topic can send their comments on the proposals to the relevant government department. The proposed law will be then be reconsidered by the government, any changes thought necessary made and a *White Paper* then issued containing a draft of the law. This draft may be put before Parliament for consideration and, if it passes all the necessary stages, it will become law.

grievous bodily harm means really serious injury. It does not have to be life threatening nor cause long-term harm and can be physical injury or psychiatric illness (R v Burstow (1997)). Grievous bodily harm is the necessary level of injury for a person to be convicted of either s18 or s20 Offences against the Person Act 1861 (see also *malicious wounding* and *wounding with intent*). It is also an important concept for *murder*, as an intention to cause grievous bodily harm, if it results in a death, is sufficient for a conviction for murder (R v Vickers (1957) and R v Cunningham (1982)).

gross negligence manslaughter: where a death is caused by a very high degree of negligence. It is difficult to state with any certainty how serious the negligence must be to qualify as gross negligence. In R v Bateman (1925), Lord Hewart put forward the following test:

> '... the facts must be such that, in the opinion of the jury, the negligence of the accused went beyond a mere matter of compensation between subjects and showed such disregard for the life and safety of others as to amount to a crime against the state and conduct deserving punishment.'

So it appears that, to prove the offence, the prosecution must show that:

- the defendant owed the victim a duty of care;
- the defendant was in breach of the duty of care;
- the breach of duty caused the death;
- the breach of duty was so negligent as to justify a criminal conviction.

Case example: R v Adomako (1994)

The defendant was an anaesthetist who failed to notice that a tube from a ventilator had become disconnected. As a result of this, the patient died. The defendant was convicted of manslaughter. The House of Lords held that whether a breach of duty should be characterised as gross negligence depended on the seriousness of the breach and was essentially a matter for the jury to decide.

guarantee: a promise to pay debts or other liabilities of another person if that person does not pay them himself.

A enters into a hire-purchase agreement with B

C guarantees these payments

B

A guarantee must be distinguished from an indemnity, where C takes over the liability of A, so that A is no longer liable. In a guarantee, B can choose to sue A or C, as A is still liable.

A guarantee is one of the types of contract that must be evidenced in writing.

guardian ad litem: a Latin phrase meaning 'a guardian appointed for the purpose of litigation'. He or she is an independent social worker appointed by the court to act in the interests of a child who is the subject of adoption or care proceedings or other proceedings brought by public bodies. The guardian will find out the child's wishes, investigate the background, explore possible options, commission expert reports and appoint a solicitor to represent the child. He will prepare a report for the court making recommendations concerning the future of the child.

From April 1999 the new Civil Procedure Rules use the term litigation friend instead of guardian ad litem.

habeas corpus: a remedy which allows a person who has been detained to challenge the lawfulness of the detention. This is done by applying to the *High Court* for a writ of habeas corpus. The effect of this writ is to order the detainer to bring the detained person before the court immediately so that the court can decide if the detention is lawful or not. If the court decides that the detention is unlawful, it will order the immediate release of the person. Refusal to obey this order is *contempt of court*.

handling stolen goods: a criminal offence under s22 of the Theft Act 1968 of dishonestly receiving or dealing in goods that have been stolen. To be guilty, the defendant must know or believe that the goods are stolen and must either receive the goods or assist another person by:

- retaining (keeping) the goods; or
- removing the goods; or
- disposing of the goods; or
- realising the goods(selling them or getting value for them in some other way).

Hansard: a record of all that is said in debates in Parliament. It is an *extrinsic aid to statutory interpretation*. Up to 1992, the courts were not allowed to read Hansard to assist them in deciding what Parliament meant by unclear words or phrases in Acts of Parliament. However, in *Pepper v Hart (1993)*, the *House of Lords* decided that Hansard could be consulted, but only if all the following conditions are satisfied:

- the legislation in question was ambiguous or obscure, or led to an absurdity;
- the material relied on in Hansard consists of statements by a minister or other promoter of the Bill and any connected matters such as the questions which lead to the statement;
- those statements are clear.

harassment as a crime: section 1 of the Protection from Harassment Act 1997 makes it an offence to pursue a course of conduct (this means on at least two occasions) which amounts to harassment of another and which one knows or ought to know would amount to harassment. Harassment is not specifically defined, but includes following another person or pestering them by letters or telephone calls.

harassment at work: this is not specifically defined in British law, but has been held to come within the concept of discrimination, as it involves treating another less favourably because of their sex (Sex Discrimination Act 1975, Porcelli v Strathclyde Regional Council (1985)) or their race (Race Relations Act 1976). *Sexual harassment* is defined in the European Union Code of Practice on the Dignity of Men and Women at Work as 'unwanted conduct of a sexual nature or other conduct based on sex affecting the dignity of men and women at work'.

Hart-Devlin debate: a debate on whether or not the law should follow morality, which was largely triggered by the report of the Wolfenden Committee, which recommended legalising homosexual behaviour and also prostitution. Professor Hart believed that law and morality are essentially separate and that morality should not dictate what the law should be. Lord Devlin felt that some form of common morality was necessary and that the law should uphold this common morality (see also Wolfenden Report).

Hart–Fuller debate: a debate on the issue of whether there is natural law which must accord with moral principles. Professor Fuller wrote that there was an 'inner morality' of the law and that law and morality are inextricably mixed. This idea of *natural law* comes to the conclusion that where the law of a country fails to accord with morality, either such rules cannot be properly classified as law or the citizen is not bound to obey such law. Professor Hart believed that there should be a clear separation of law and morality. This means that if legal rules are in conflict with morality, the legal rules must be followed. This is the concept of *positivism*. Hart also wrote that, just because an action was considered morally wrong, it should not necessarily lead to legal sanctions.

Hart, theories of: Professor Hart has defined the factors which make up a legal system. These are:

- rules which forbid or compel certain conduct;
- rules requiring people to compensate those whom they injure;
- rules which cover 'mechanical' areas, such a making a will;
- a system of courts to determine the rules and whether or not they have been broken;
- a body who has responsibility for making rules.

Hart also supports the positivist view of law that law and morality are clearly separated and that the law should not be used to impose moral values (see also *positivism*).

Harvey order: an order that can be made when dividing the matrimonial assets on divorce. It states that the spouse who stays in the matrimonial home should pay the other spouse rent, once the mortgage has been paid off. This order is suitable when the house market is static and houses are difficult to sell.

health and safety at work: the law recognises that employees should be protected from unnecessary risks at work and, if injured, should be able to claim compensation from their employer. Employers are also liable to criminal proceedings for serious breaches of health and safety law. The law in this area is very complex and comes from several sources:

1 the common law with decisions in cases by judges: the common law implies general duties on employers to ensure the safety of employees. These duties are to provide:

- a safe place of work
- safe plant and equipment
- a safe system of work
- reasonably competent fellow employees;

2 Acts of Parliament, especially the Health and Safety at Work Act 1974: this Act places general duties on the employer to ensure as far as is reasonably practicable:

- the provision and maintenance of plant and systems of work so that they are safe and without risk to health

- the making of arrangements for the safe use, handling, storage and transport of articles and substances

- the provision of information, instruction, training and supervision

- the maintenance of places of work, including means of access and egress, in a safe condition

- the provision and maintenance of a safe, risk-free working environment with adequate welfare facilities.

The Act also makes breaches of duty criminal offences.

3   European Union law: Article 118A of the Treaty of Rome provides that member states shall encourage improvements in health and safety in the working environment. Several directives have been issued aimed at improving specific aspects of safety at work.

4   regulations made by government departments aimed at specific safety issues, for example the Manual Handling Operations Regulations 1992 which are aimed at preventing injuries through mishandling heavy loads.

An employer, therefore, may be liable for breaches of health and safety in a number of ways.

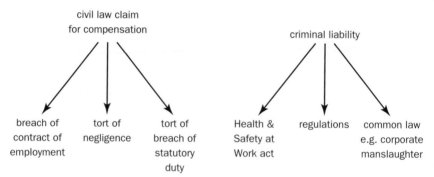

Health and Safety Commission: established by the Health and Safety at Work Act 1974. Its duties include arranging for research on safety matters, promoting training in health and safety at work and acting as an advisory and information service on health and safety issues.

Health and Safety Executive: responsible for appointing inspectors who have the authority to enter work premises to check safety. An inspector who discovers a breach of health and safety regulations can serve a notice on the employer to remedy the matter and, if this is not done, the inspector can issue a prohibition notice directing that work is stopped until the safety requirements are met. The Health and Safety Executive can prosecute employers for breaches of health and safety laws.

health and safety representative: recognised trade unions have the right to appoint safety representatives in the workplace. Such representatives can investigate potential hazards and complaints by another employee. They also consult with the employer and can make representations on health and safety matters. Employment law protects safety representatives by providing that they have the right not to be subjected to any detriment as a result of carrying out their duties (s44, Employment Rights Act 1996). Also dismissal because of carrying out their duties is automatically unfair (s100, Employment Rights Act 1996).

Hedley Byrne v Heller & Partners (1964): the case which established *negligent misstatement*. Before this case, if a person lost money because he relied on what someone told him, he could only sue if he had a *contract* with him or under the tort of *deceit* or for breach of fiduciary duty. The case extended a person's responsibility for the statements he makes. Most of the subsequent cases involve professional advisers.

Case details: Hedley Byrne v Heller & Partners (1964)

Easipower asked Hedley Byrne to place some advertisements for them. This involved Hedley Byrne spending money on behalf of Easipower. They therefore asked their bankers, National Provincial, to check on Easipower's creditworthiness. The bankers asked Heller & Partners, who were Easipower's bankers, for a reference. This was given, but Easipower later went into liquidation, owing Hedley Byrne £17,000. Hedley Byrne sued Heller & Partners, and it was held that Heller & Partners did owe them a legal responsibility for their reference although there was no contract between them; Heller & Partners knew that Hedley Byrne would rely on what they said, they did so and suffered financial loss as a result. However, Hedley Byrne lost their case because Heller & Partners had put a *disclaimer* on their reference.

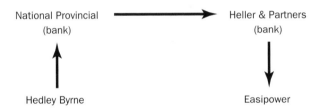

hierarchy of the courts refers to the order of seniority of the courts. This is particularly important in *judicial precedent*, where decisions of higher courts are binding on lower courts. The hierarchy starts with the *European Court of Justice* at the top, as decisions by this court on European law have to be followed by all other courts. The highest domestic court is the *House of Lords*. The figure on page 116 shows the full order of the courts.

High Court of Justice: the main civil court in England and Wales. It has three divisions, which specialise in certain types of cases. These divisions are:

- *Chancery Division*, which deals with matters such as company insolvency, partnership disputes, enforcement of mortgages and copyright disputes;
- *Queen's Bench Division*, which hears cases involving contracts and torts and judicial reviews;
- *Family Division*, which deals with family proceedings and matters affecting children.

Each of these divisions has High Court judges assigned to it. A single judge will sit to try cases, though in the Queen's Bench Division it is possible to have a *civil jury* for a small number of cases. Any appeal from the decision of a High Court judge is made to the *Court of Appeal*.

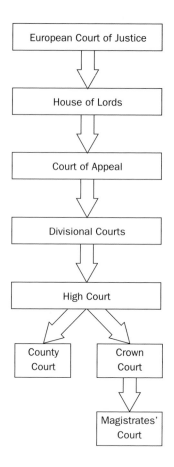

Hierarchy of the courts

High Trees case: see *promissory estoppel*

hire purchase agreement: an agreement that a person makes regular payments in return for the use of goods. At the end of an agreed period of time, he will have the option of buying the goods at a pre-determined price, which is usually a small amount. Although the buyer may feel as though he is buying the goods by making regular payments, in fact he does not become the legal owner until the end of the agreed period. Until the final payment is made, the goods remain the property of the hire purchase company. This means that if regular payments are not kept up, the hire purchase company is entitled to reclaim its goods. Also, if the buyer sells the goods before the end of the agreed period, he cannot pass *good title* (legal ownership). An exception is made under the Hire Purchase Act 1964 in the case of motor vehicles which are sold to *bona fide* private purchasers who are unaware that the vehicle is subject to a hire purchase agreement.

Under the Supply of Goods (Implied Terms) Act 1973, terms concerning title, description, quality and sale by sample similar to those in the *Sale of Goods Act 1979* are implied into every hire-purchase agreement.

If the hirer has paid more than one third of the total price of the goods, the hire-purchase company cannot repossess the goods for non-payment without going through the court, which is entitled to give the hirer more time to pay.

A hire-purchase agreement is usually regulated by the *Consumer Credit Act 1974*.

homicide: the unlawful killing of a person. In English law, homicide is charged as:

- *murder*; or

- *manslaughter*; or

- *infanticide*.

honour clause: a clause in a business contract making it clear that there is no *intention to create legal relations* and the contract is not enforceable through the courts. Normally it is assumed that the parties to a commercial contract intend to be bound by it, but a clear honour clause can rebut (cancel) this presumption. For example, football-pools coupons state that the contract between the pools company and the customer is 'binding in honour only'. This is sufficient to rebut the presumption and make the contract unenforceable.

horizontal direct effect: a concept of *European Union law* by which citizens of member states can rely on provisions of treaties and *regulations* in claims against non-state organisations and businesses where their national government has not implemented the European law.

Case example: Macarthys Ltd v Smith (1980)

A woman who was being paid less than the man who had done the same job immediately before her was able to rely on Article 141 of the Treaty of Rome which guarantees equal pay for men and women in her claim for equal pay. She could not use English law as the Equal Pay Act 1970 only applied where the man and woman were working in the company at the same time.

Directives do NOT have horizontal direct effect. This is shown by Duke v GEC Ltd (1988) where Mrs Duke could not claim for breach of the Equal Treatment Directive when she was required to retire at 60 although men could work until they were 65. This was because she had been working for a private employer.

House of Lords: the final appeal court of the English legal system. Its full title is the Judicial Committee of the House of Lords. The judges are known as the Law Lords. It only hears appeals on points of law. In criminal cases, this must be a point of law of general public importance. It is also necessary to get leave (permission) to appeal from either the House of Lords or the court from which the appeal is coming. Although it is the final court of appeal for points of English law, cases involving European law must be referred by the House of Lords to the *European Court of Justice*. Decisions by the House of Lords on points of law create *judicial precedents* which all other courts in the English legal system must follow.

In July 2003 the Government announced that it intends to remove the judges from the House of Lords (where they also sit as part of Parliament) and create a separate Supreme Court.

household, in the same: a phrase used in family law to describe a husband and wife living together who share some household activities and who both consider themselves as a couple. It is possible for a husband and wife to share a house but not be considered as living in the same household. This occurs when they live separate lives and do not share any joint activities. See also *living apart*.

human rights: it is recognised that all people in this country have basic rights, such as the right not to be imprisoned without a fair trial, and that these rights should be protected by the state. Britain has signed the *European Convention on Human Rights*, and this has now been incorporated into our law by the *Human Rights Act 1998*.

Human Rights Act 1998 incorporates the *European Convention on Human Rights* into our law. Its main provisions are:

- It is unlawful for a public authority to act in a way which is incompatible with a Convention right. Public authority is any person or organisation who has some public function; this includes the courts, but does not include Parliament or a person exercising functions in connection with proceedings in Parliament.

- The courts are under a duty to interpret legislation in a way that is compatible with the Convention. Where a court decides that it is impossible to fit the wording of a law so as to give effect to the Convention, that court can make a declaration that the law is incompatible with the Convention. This law should then be reviewed by the government and, if they decide it needs amending, brought it into line with the Convention; an amendment to this effect will be put before Parliament for its approval.

- Individuals are able to take court action if they feel that their rights have been violated and, if the action is successful, the court can make any order it considers just and appropriate.

This Act came into force in October 2000. Since then individuals have been able to take action in British courts instead of having to go to the *European Court of Human Rights*.

illegality doctrine (in tort): a defence where it is held that, as a matter of public policy, a claimant should not receive compensation for his injuries because they were inextricably linked with his criminal behaviour.

Case example: Ashton v Turner (1981)

Two men carried out a burglary and made their escape in a car which crashed injuring the passenger. He sued the driver and, although it was proved that the driver had been negligent, it was held that the passenger should not be awarded damages because at the time of the accident he was carrying out a criminal activity with the defendant.

However, a burglar can still sue a householder who uses excessive force on him (Revill v Newbury (1995)).

See also *ex turpi causa non oritur actio.*

illegality of contract: when a contract will not be enforced by the court because its purpose is an illegal act or it would be against public policy (not in the general interests of society). Both the courts and Parliament have laid down types of contracts which will not be enforced. This can be because the contract:

- is to carry out an illegal act; for example, an agreement to smuggle goods. This makes the contract void;
- is to carry out a legal act but in a way that is against the law. This normally makes the contract unenforceable by the party who performed his part of the contract in an illegal way;
- has been made illegal by Parliament; for example, the Resale Prices Act 1976 states that a contract between a wholesaler and a retailer that the retailer will sell goods at a fixed price is illegal and void;
- has been made unenforceable by Parliament; for example, it is not illegal to place bets but betting agreements are unenforceable under the Gaming Act 1845.

illegitimate child: one whose parents are not married to each other at the time of his conception or birth, and who do not marry each other after the birth. Many of the distinctions between a legitimate and an illegitimate child have now been abolished. For example, an illegitimate child inherits from both mother and father if they die without making a will. However, an illegitimate child will not inherit from a brother or a sister.

Immigration Appeal Tribunal: set up by the Immigration Act 1977 to hear appeals from the Immigration Adjudicators on whether immigrants have the right to enter or stay in the United Kingdom. There is a further appeal from the Immigration Appeal Tribunal to the Court of Appeal, but only on a point of law.

immunity from suit means that judges cannot be sued for actions taken or decisions made in the course of their judicial duties. This is an important element in ensuring judicial independence in decision-making. Barristers and solicitors used to be immune from being sued for anything they did whilst acting as advocates in the course of a court hearing (Rondel v Worsley (1969). However, in Hall v Simons (2000) the House of Lords ruled that advocates could be sued for negligence in court. They can also be sued for negligent advice given outside the scope of any court hearing.

implied term: a term of a contract which has not been discussed by the parties and expressly included in it, but which the courts will hold is part of the contract. Terms can be implied by:

- statute (e.g. the *Sale of Goods Act 1973* implies terms into all *consumer contracts*);
- custom (the usual practice of a particular trade or market place);
- a court when it decides that a term must have been intended by the parties when making the contract (the *officious bystander test*);
- a court reflecting standard expectations of certain types of contract, notably employment contracts and contracts between landlords and tenants; for example, in all employment contracts, the court will hold that there are implied terms that the employee will serve the employer faithfully and that the employer will treat the employee with respect.

impossible attempts refer to situations where a defendant has attempted to commit a crime but its completion is impossible. This is illustrated by the following examples:

- possible attempt: D fires a gun at V, who is standing ten yards away; the bullet just misses V. V could have been killed by the bullet, so the crime of murder was possible,
- impossible attempt: D fires a bullet at V, who is lying in bed; the bullet hits V in the head, but, unknown to D, V had died from a heart attack an hour earlier. As V was already dead, the crime of murdering him is impossible.

The law used to be very complicated as to when an impossible attempt was considered a criminal act and when it was not. The Criminal Attempts Act 1981 makes it clear that all impossible attempts are now criminal acts.

Case example: R v Shivpuri (1986)

Shivpuri was arrested with a suitcase in his possession that he thought contained a prohibited drug and which he intended selling. In fact, the case contained a vegetable substance which was not a prohibited drug. Shivpuri was found guilty of attempting to deal in prohibited drugs.

in camera means 'in private'. No members of the public are allowed into a court that is sitting in camera. This can occur if the case involves national security. Cases about the welfare of children are also heard in camera.

inchoate offences: offences which are not complete because the substantive crime has not been committed. There are three types of inchoate offence:

- *conspiracy*, in which two or more people plan to commit a crime;
- *incitement*, where one person seeks to persuade another to commit a crime;
- *attempt*, where the defendant tries to commit a crime but, for some reason, does not succeed.

incitement: the crime of seeking to persuade another person to commit a crime. The persuasion may be by threat, encouragement or an inducement such as paying a sum of money for the crime to be committed. The incitor is guilty even if the other person does not commit the crime. For example: D offers to pay A £50,000 if A will murder D's wife. A says he will think about it but actually goes to the police immediately and tells them of D's offer. D is guilty of incitement to murder even though A was not persuaded to commit the crime.

incorporation of terms in contract law means that a term has become part of the contract and is enforceable. In written contracts everything in the contract is incorporated into the contract whether it was read or not (L'Estrange v Graucob (1934)). In oral contracts a term is incorporated if it was clear and drawn to the other party's attention before the contract was entered into (Olley v Marlborough Court (1949). The more unusual the term, the more effort must be put into making sure that the other party is aware of it.

indemnity clause: a clause in a contract stating that one party will recompense the other party for money he has paid out. The *Unfair Contract Terms Act 1977* controls indemnity clauses in *consumer contracts* where the consumer is expected to indemnify the other party if the other party incurs debts through his own negligence or breach of contract. These will only be upheld if they are reasonable.

independence of the judiciary: the theory of the separation of powers states that it is important for judges to be independent from the executive and legislative arms of the government so that they cannot be pressurised into making government-favourable decisions. The main ways in which this is achieved is that:

● judges in the High Court, Court of Appeal and House of Lords cannot be dismissed by the government;

● judges have a certain degree of financial independence as their salaries are paid out of the consolidated fund so that payment can be made without the need to obtain Parliament's authorisation.

However, the Lord Chancellor's powers over the appointment of judges are criticised as being an abuse of this principle of judicial independence. In addition, Professor Griffith points out that many judges are too pro-establishment and conservative (with a small 'c'), and that these attitudes may affect their decision-making. This is seen in the case of Civil Service Union v the Minister for the Civil Service (1984) where the House of Lords upheld the minister's right to ban trade union membership among the workers at GCHQ. See also Montesquieu's theory of the separation of powers.

independent contractor: someone who works on his own account. He is not an *employee* and is not protected by the employment laws. It can be difficult to decide if someone is an independent contractor or an employee. The courts have used several different tests for this. These are:

● the control test: does the person decide how and when a job is done? If so, they are probably self-employed;

● the organisation test (or the integration test): is the work done as an integral part of the business? If so, this is an employment situation;

● the economic reality or multiple test, which stresses that a wide variety of factors must be considered; these will vary according to the type of work involved (Ready Mixed Concrete Ltd v Ministry of Pensions (1968)).

independent contractors, tortious liability: a householder is responsible in occupiers liability for the actions of people working on his premises. However, he will not be responsible for the actions of independent contractors provided that he chose competent contractors, it was reasonable to entrust the work to them and he took steps to ensure that the work was done properly. This means checking the work for any dangers that would be apparent to the ordinary person and, if necessary, employing a professional to supervise the work.

Independent Police Complaints Commission (IPCC) was created by the Police Reform Act 2002 to replace the previous Police Complaints Authority. Complaints can be made to the IPCC by the victim of the police conduct complained of or by anyone who claims to have been adversely affected by it, or who witnessed it, or by someone acting on behalf of any of the above.

indeterminate sentence: a proposed new sentence in the Criminal Justice Bill 2002 for sexual and violent offenders. An offender would serve a minimum period but if assessed as still dangerous could then remain in prison until the Parole Board was completely satisfied that the risk had sufficiently diminished for that person to be released and supervised in the community. The offender would remain on licence for the rest if their life.

indictable offences: those which can only be tried on indictment by a judge and *jury* at the *Crown Court*. Indictable offences are the most serious offences and include murder, manslaughter, rape and robbery.

indictment: the document which formally sets out the charges against the defendant at the *Crown Court*. Each offence is set out as a separate count or point of the indictment, and the jury will be asked to decide if the defendant is guilty or not guilty to each count.

AMBRIDGE CROWN COURT

The Queen v Barbara Betty
charged as follows:

STATEMENT OF OFFENCE
robbery contrary to section 8 of the Theft Act 1968

PARTICULARS OF OFFENCE
Barbara Betty on the 8th day of March 2003 did rob Charles Cane of £200

---

indirect discrimination occurs when an unjustified condition is applied to a situation which will have the effect of discriminating against a particular sex or race. This type of discrimination is forbidden by the Sex Discrimination Act 1975 and the Race Relations Act 1976. To prove indirect discrimination, it must be shown that:

- a condition has been imposed; and
- this condition is not justifiable; and
- the proportion of one sex or race who can comply with the condition is considerably smaller than the other sex or another racial group; and
- inability to comply with the condition is to the complainant's detriment.

Case example: Price v Civil Service Commission (1978)

An age requirement of 17 to 28 was put on promotion to posts of executive officer. This was held to be indirect discrimination against women, as fewer women than men would be able to apply within this age range due to women of those ages having a career break to have children.

individualised sentences: sentences imposed on defendants for which the courts consider the defendant's background and potential for reform as being an important element in deciding what sentence to impose. This is the opposite of *tariff sentences*, where the penalty is imposed because a certain type of offence has been committed.

industrial tribunals have been re-named *employment tribunals*.

inequality of bargaining power see *bargaining power, inequality of*.

inevitable accident: a defence in tort. The defendant will not be liable if he can show that the accident could not have been avoided by taking reasonable care. It does not apply to claims under *Rylands v Fletcher* where *strict liability* applies. This defence is rarely used.

infanticide: the offence of a mother intentionally killing her baby while the balance of her mind is disturbed by the effect of the birth. Under the Infanticide Act 1938, the offence only applies if the child is under one year old. Infanticide is charged rather than murder, as this gives the judge discretion as to the punishment, whereas for murder the penalty has to be life imprisonment.

injunction: an *equitable remedy* in which the court orders one party to do something (a mandatory injunction) or not to do something (a prohibitory injunction). Injunctions are used in a wide range of cases, including:

- domestic violence cases, where the violent partner can be ordered not to assault the other partner and/or not to go within a certain distance of the place where the other is living;
- business cases, where a former employee may be ordered not to disclose trade secrets or a trade union may be ordered not to take unlawful industrial action;
- cases of nuisance to prevent the continuation of noise or pollution.

Case example: Kennaway v Thompson (1980)

An injunction was granted to limit the times and days on which motor boat racing could take place on a lake as the noise was creating a nuisance.

injunction in contract law: a court order to stop one of the parties to a contract breaching it. This is an *equitable* remedy, and the court will only make this order when it seems fair to do so. An injunction will not be granted:

- if it involves performing a personal service; this applies both where the party is trying to avoid carrying out the service or trying to insist on carrying it out;
- where the result would be that the other party would be prevented from earning his living.

Case example: Warner Bros Pictures v Nelson (1937)

An actress agreed to act only in Warner Bros films. When she signed a contract with someone else, Warner Bros were granted an injunction stopping her from carrying this out. It was held that the court could do this, as it was not making her act for Warner Bros, only stopping her acting for anyone else. Also, it was not stopping her earning a living, as she could still do this in a different job.

innocent defamation: see *unintentional defamation*

innocent dissemination: a defence to *defamation* for those involved in the mechanical publication of books, newspapers, etc. They will not be liable if they did not know about the defamation, there was nothing to alert them to the defamation and the reason they did not know about the defamation was not through their negligence.

innocent misrepresentation: in a contract, a *misrepresentation* which has not been made negligently nor fraudulently. If there has been innocent misrepresentation, the claimant is entitled to rescind (cancel) the contract (Misrepresentation Act 1967). However, where this would be unreasonable because the effect of the misrepresentation is minor and rescission would be out of all proportion, the court may, instead, award *damages*.

innocent publication: publishing a defamatory statement which was not intended to refer to the claimant and not realising that other people might take it to refer to the claimant, or a statement about the claimant which was not apparently defamatory, not realising that other people knew of circumstances which made it defamatory.

See *unintentional defamation* and *offer of amends* for when innocent publication can be a defence.

innominate term: a term of a contract which lies between a *condition* and a *warranty* in that the results of breaching an innominate term can vary from the serious to the minor. Breach of an innominate term will entitle the innocent party to revoke the contract if the consequences of the breach are serious and he is deprived of substantially the whole benefit of the contract. However he is only entitled to damages if the consequences are minor.

Case example: Cehave N-V. v Bremer Handelsgesellschaft mbH (The Hansa Nord) (1975)

Citrus pellets were to be shipped 'in good condition' but arrived damaged. This was held to be an innominate term because breaching it could result in the pellets being slightly damaged or being totally unusable. In this case, they were slightly damaged and the buyers were only entitled to damages, they were not entitled to terminate the contract and refuse to accept them.

Unlike conditions and warranties, which can be categorised as soon as the contract is made, it is only possible to decide whether a breach of an innominate term justifies revocation of the contract once the effect of the breach is known (Hong Kong Fir Shipping Co Ltd v Kawasaki Kisen Kaisha Ltd (1962)).

Finding that a term is an innominate term gives the courts the flexibility to do justice in the case in front of them, but they are reluctant to do so as it leads to uncertainty. A term is most likely to be found to be an innominate term if:

- the party in breach of contract was in a stronger bargaining position;
- the breach is a very technical one and is being used as an excuse to get out of the contract (Reardon Smith Line v Hansen Tengen (1976)).

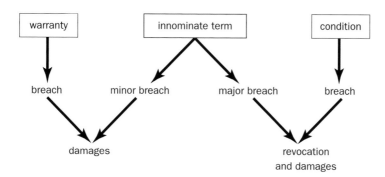

Inns of Court: all barristers must belong to one of the four Inns of Court. The Inns are Lincoln's Inn, Inner Temple, Middle Temple and Gray's Inn. Student barristers have to dine or attend certain functions at their Inn as part of their qualification.

innuendo: in *defamation*, changes what appears to be an innocent statement into a defamatory statement. It happens when the people who read or hear the statement have extra information which gives it a different significance.

Case example: Tolley v Fry (1931)

A drawing of the claimant appeared in an advertisement for chocolate with a verse which made it clear that it was intended to be of him. At first reading, there was nothing defamatory about this, but the claimant succeeded with his claim because he was able to show that golfers reading the advertisement would assume that he had been paid for appearing in it. This would imply that he had been lying when he had competed as an amateur golfer (one who receives no payment for playing).

inquisitorial system of justice: a system in which the court is responsible for inquiring into the case. In some continental countries, a magistrate or judge is given control over the police inquiries into a crime or other situation where investigation is needed. An example of this was seen after the death of Diana, Princess of Wales, in a road accident in France. An examining magistrate was responsible for the investigations into the cause of the accident. See also *adversarial system of justice*.

insane automatism: an automatic state of mind which is caused by an internal factor such as a brain tumour or epilepsy. It gives the defendant in a criminal case the defence of *insanity*.

insanity as a defence to a crime: governed by the M'Naghten Rules which were set out by the judges of the House of Lords in 1843. The first rule is that everyone is presumed sane until the contrary is proved. In order to prove insanity, the defence must show that the defendant was suffering from a defect of reason caused by a disease of the mind and that this caused the defendant either not to know what he was doing or not to know that what he was doing was wrong.

In R v Sullivan (1984), the House of Lords held that 'disease of the mind' included physical as well as mental illnesses. This means that conditions such as epilepsy, brain tumours and diabetes have all been held to make the defendant legally insane. This can be criticised, as the medical definition of insanity does not include such matters.

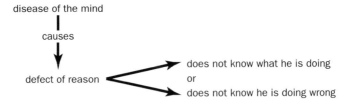

If insanity is proved, then a special verdict of Not Guilty by Reason of Insanity is reached. Under the Criminal Procedure (Unfitness to Plead) Act 1991, the judge then has discretion to make an appropriate order in respect of the defendant. These are:

- to order that the defendant be admitted to hospital (where the charge is murder, there must be an order committing the defendant to a secure hospital);
- to make a guardianship order under the Mental Health Act 1983;
- to make a supervision and treatment order;
- to order an absolute discharge.

insolvency: the state of a company that is unable to pay its debts. In such a case, any creditor can apply to the court for the company to be wound up. (See also *winding up*.)

Institute of Arbitrators trains and supplies arbitrators for *commercial arbitration* cases.

Institute of Legal Executives: responsible for the professional standards of *legal executives*. It supervises the training of legal executives.

intention in criminal law is the highest level of *mens rea*. Usually it is concerned with whether a person intends a particular result or consequence. However, the concept of intention is not defined in any Act of Parliament and the courts have had difficulty in formulating a clear definition. In the case of Moloney, the House of Lords stated that *foresight of consequences* is not intention but only evidence of intention.

The *Law Commission* has suggested that intention should be defined in the following way:

'a person acts … intentionally with respect to a result when

- it is his purpose to cause it, or
- although it is not his purpose to cause it, he knows that it would occur in the ordinary course of events if he were to succeed in his purpose of causing some other result.'

intention to create legal relations: in contract law, an intention by both parties to enter into a contract which can be enforced through the courts. A contract does not come into existence unless this intention exists at the time the agreement was made.

In business situations, it is assumed that an intention to create legal relations exists unless it is proved otherwise. An *honour clause* saying that the contract is 'binding in honour only' is sufficient to show that no intention exists and therefore the agreement is not enforceable (Rose and Frank Co v JR Crompton and Bros Ltd (1925)).

In family and social situations, it is assumed that there is no intention to create legal relations unless it is proved otherwise. See Balfour v Balfour (1919) and Merritt v Merritt (1971) in *distinguishing*.

intention to permanently deprive (in theft) is where someone appropriates property and does not intend to give it back. It includes where a defendant does not mean for the other permanently to lose the thing, but the defendant intends 'to treat the thing as his own to dispose of regardless of the other's rights' (s6(1) Theft Act 1968).

The Theft Act 1968 also states that a borrowing or lending of an item may amount to an intention to permanently deprive if it is 'for a period and in circumstances making it equivalent to an outright taking or disposal' (s6(1)). In Lloyd (1985) it was held that this meant borrowing the property and keeping it until 'the goodness, the virtue, the practical value ... has gone out of the article'.

interim damages: in tort, damages that a court can award before a case is heard. This type of order is used to help a claimant with his immediate problems. However, it can only be used where the defendant has admitted liability (that he committed the tort) but disputes the amount of damages claimed by the claimant.

interim relief: an order for a temporary remedy while waiting for the trial to take place. For example, in a divorce case, the court may order that one spouse pays maintenance to the other in the interim period between the issue of the divorce petition and the granting of the divorce. An *interlocutory injunction* is another order for interim relief.

interlocutory injunction: an *injunction* which is granted to protect one party's rights pending the final trial of the case. In American Cyanamid Co v Ethicon Ltd, the House of Lords laid down guidelines for when such injunctions would be granted. The main factors are that damages would not be an adequate remedy and that the party would suffer irreparable harm if the injunction were not granted. The court is trying to maintain the position between the parties while waiting for the trial.

interlocutory proceedings: preliminary proceedings in a civil case which take place before the actual trial. These can be on administrative points, such as orders for the discovery and inspection of documents, or they may be on preliminary issues, such as whether the claimant is entitled to judgment because the defendant failed to put in defence to the case.

intermittent custody is a new approach proposed by the Criminal Justice Bill 2002 in which a prison sentence and community sentence are served alternately; for example, a prison sentence at weekends (or at night) with a community programme during the week (or during the day).

international law governs relations between countries. Much of this law comes from treaties signed by the heads of state of the countries.

Interpretation Act 1978 sets out some basic rules about the meanings of common words in Acts of Parliament. It says that, unless an Act states anything to the contrary, 'words importing the masculine gender include the feminine'. So, if an Act uses the word 'he', this can also mean 'she'. The Interpretation Act also says that singular words include the plural, so that if an Act says 'he', it also means 'they'. For example: the definition of theft in the Theft Act 1968 is that a person is guilty of theft if 'he dishonestly appropriates property belonging to another...'. The Theft Act only uses 'he', but the Interpretation Act 1978 makes it clear that women as well as men can be guilty of theft and also that theft can be committed by two or more people.

interpretation clause: in an Act of Parliament, a section which explains or defines the meaning of some of the words in the Act. For example in burglary, s9 of the Theft Act 1968, an essential element is that the defendant enters a 'building'. The word building is explained in s9(4) as applying also to 'an inhabited vehicle or vessel'. This means that burglary of a caravan or houseboat is covered under the word 'building'.

interpretation of statutes: see *statutory interpretation*

intestacy: the situation which is created when a person dies without making a will. The law, in particular the Administration of Estates Act 1925, sets out the order in which relatives are entitled to inherit the deceased's property on intestacy (see also *intestate succession*).

intestate: a person who has not made a will.

intestate succession concerns who inherits property when a person dies without making a will. Basically, the nearest relative inherits, but the Administration of Estates Act 1925 sets out detailed rules of how this works. These rules are different depending on whether there is a surviving spouse or not. If there is a surviving spouse, that spouse gets the first £125,000 of the estate and a life interest in half the rest. The remainder is divided between the children. If there are no children, the surviving spouse gets the first £200,000 and half the rest. The other half goes to the parents of the deceased (or, if they are dead, to his brothers and sisters). If there are no brothers or sisters or their children, then the surviving spouse inherits the whole estate. Where there is no surviving spouse, the basic order of inheritance is given in the figure below.

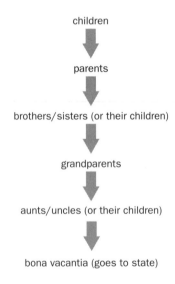

children

↓

parents

↓

brothers/sisters (or their children)

↓

grandparents

↓

aunts/uncles (or their children)

↓

bona vacantia (goes to state)

intimate samples: for the purposes of police investigation, these are defined by s65 of the Police and Criminal Evidence Act 1984 as:

• a sample of blood, semen or other tissue fluid, urine or pubic hair;

• a dental impression;

• a swab taken from a person's body orifice other than the mouth.

Such samples can be taken only by a doctor or a nurse. All samples can be kept even if the suspect is not charged. There are over 2 million DNA samples on the police database.

intimate search: defined as a search which consists of a physical examination of a person's body orifices other than the mouth (s65 Police and Criminal Evidence Act 1984). When a person is detained at a police station such a search can only take place if there are reasonable grounds for believing:

- that the person may have something concealed which could be used to harm himself or another; or

- that the person may have a class A drug concealed on him.

Permission to carry out an intimate search can only be given by a police officer of at least the rank of superintendent and should, where practicable, be carried out by a suitably qualified person, such as a doctor or a nurse.

intoxication may provide a defence in a criminal case if its effect is to make the defendant incapable of forming the necessary intent for the crime he is charged with. The law on intoxication applies to the effects of drugs as well as to drink. To discover if a defendant can use intoxication as a defence, it is necessary to consider:

- the level of intention required for the crime the defendant is charged with; i.e. whether the crime is a crime of *specific intent* or *basic intent*; and

- whether the defendant became drunk voluntarily or involuntarily (e.g. not knowing a drug had been put in his coffee).

For specific intent crimes, the defendant may have a defence, provided he was so drunk that he was incapable of forming the necessary intention. But if he had the intention to commit the crime, he cannot use intoxication as a defence, even if it was *involuntary intoxication* (R v Kingston (1995)). If a defendant decides to commit a crime and gets drunk to do it, then he still has the intention and is guilty of that crime.

Case example: A-G for Northern Ireland v Gallagher (1963)

The defendant decided to murder his wife. He drank a considerable amount of whisky in order to give himself the 'courage' to do the killing. It was held he was guilty of murder. As he had formed the intention to kill, he could not use the defence of intoxication.

For basic intent crimes, the defendant cannot use the defence of intoxication if he has voluntarily taken drink or drugs. This is because basic intent crimes only require proof of recklessness and getting drunk or taking drugs is held to be reckless (DPP v Majewski (1977)). If a defendant has become intoxicated involuntarily or through taking legal medication which he did not know could have an intoxicating effect, he will be able to use the defence even to a crime of basic intent, as he has not been reckless. There is an element of public policy in this area of the law, as the courts are unwilling to allow those who deliberately take an intoxicating substance to use their own actions to absolve themselves from all criminal responsibility.

intrinsic aids to statutory interpretation: matters within the statute itself which help to make certain words or phrases clearer. The main intrinsic aids are:

- the long title of the Act which may briefly explain Parliament's intentions;

- the short title of the Act;

- the preamble which is usually found in older Acts and which explains the purpose of the law;

- sections within the Act which explain the purpose of the Act;

- sections within the Act which contain definitions of words and phrases;

- any other sections in the Act which may make the meaning clearer;

- any heading used before a group of sections;
- schedules attached to the Act.

invitation to treat: negotiations which lead up to the formation of a contract which are not specific enough or which do not show an intention to be committed so as to be an *offer*. For practical reasons, the following have been held to be invitations to treat rather than offers:

- advertisements in newspapers offering goods for sale (Partridge v Crittenden (1968));
- catalogues with goods for sale;
- goods for sale in shop windows (Fisher v Bell (1961));
- goods for sale on shelves in self-service shops (Pharmaceutical Society of GB v Boots (1953));
- an auctioneer asking for bids (British Car Auctions Ltd v Wright (1972)).

If these were offers, it could create some impossible situations. For example, a seller would be committed to sell the goods to everyone who replied to the advertisement, whether he had sufficient stocks or not. Or a customer would be obliged to buy all goods that he picked off the shelf in a supermarket and would not be able to change his mind. In *auctions*, the whole purpose would be lost, as the first bid would form a contract, instead of allowing each bidder to put forward an offer which the auctioneer can accept or reject.

involuntary intoxication refers to a person becoming intoxicated without knowing. This is usually because someone else has 'spiked' their drink by adding alcohol or a drug to a non-intoxicating drink such as coffee. In such cases, if the person commits a crime while in the intoxicated state, it may be possible to use the defence of *intoxication* if they did not have the necessary intention to commit the crime. However, if the defendant, despite his drunken state, was able to form the intention, then he would not be able to use the defence.

Case example: R v Kingston (1995)

The defendant's coffee was spiked with a drug and he was then taken to a room where there was a boy who was also drugged. The defendant indecently assaulted the boy. He claimed that he would not have committed the offence had his inhibitions not been removed by the drug in his coffee. The House of Lords held that he could not use the defence of involuntary intoxication as he did have the intention to assault the boy, even though he was in a drugged state.

involuntary manslaughter: an unlawful killing where the defendant did not have the necessary intention (*malice aforethought*) for *murder*. The term 'involuntary manslaughter' is used to distinguish this type of killing from *voluntary manslaughter* where the defendant did have the intention for murder, but because of the special defences of diminished responsibility, provocation or suicide pact, the crime is reduced to manslaughter. There are two categories of involuntary manslaughter:

- *constructive manslaughter* (also known as unlawful act manslaughter);
- *gross negligence manslaughter*.

There is also possibly reckless manslaughter where the defendant is subjectively reckless as to the risk of death (R v Lidar 2000).

job-evaluation study: comparing two jobs to see if they are equivalent in matters such as effort, skill and decision-making. This comparison will take place when there is a claim for *equal pay* for work done by men and women on the basis that the work should be rated as equivalent (s1(5) Equal Pay Act 1970).

joint and several liability occurs where two different people are responsible for the same *tort*. Both are separately liable to pay the injured party full compensation for his injuries, giving him a choice as to who to sue. If he sues more than one person, he cannot recover more than once.

joint enterprise: where two or more people agree to carry out a crime together. If they commit the crime, they are both guilty of it as joint principals. In addition, if one of them commits another crime in the course of carrying out the agreed one, the others may also be liable as secondary participants for this other crime if they foresaw that something of that nature might happen.

Case example: R v Bamborough (1996)

The defendant and another man went to carry out a robbery at the victim's flat. The defendant knew that the other man had a gun with him, but thought that it was unloaded, though it might be used to beat anyone who interrupted them in the course of the robbery. The other man shot and killed the victim. The Court of Appeal held that the defendant was also guilty of the murder, as he knew that the other man might cause grievous bodily harm with the gun.

See also *secondary participation*.

joint tenants: people who jointly own land, so that when one of them dies, their share automatically goes to the other joint owners.

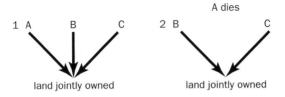

Land can also be owned jointly by *tenants in common*.

joint will: where two or more people express their wishes in one will as to what should happen to their property when they die. The joint will takes effect as the separate will of each person and has to be admitted to *probate* on the death of each person.

judges, appointment of: all judges are appointed from those who have qualified as a barrister or solicitor. The *Lord Chancellor* either nominates or appoints all lower rank judges and also advises the Prime Minister on whom to nominate for appointment to higher judicial posts. In July 2003 the Government began consulting on changing this system. It is probable that in future an independent *Judicial Appointments Commission* will make the appointments. The qualifications needed for each level of the judiciary are set out in the Courts and Legal Services Act 1990 and are based on holding the necessary *certificate of advocacy*. There is criticism that the system for selecting judges, especially to the High Court and above, is secretive and largely based on confidential information and opinions of existing judges. To counter this, there are now advertisements inviting those with the correct qualifications to apply to be a judge. There is also criticism that few women are appointed (less than ten per cent of the full-time judiciary), and very few ethnic minority candidates are appointed (none in the High Court or above).

judgment: a decision by a court. The word is also used for the speech made by a judge at the end of a case in which he explains how he reached his decision. See also *ratio decidendi* and *obiter dicta*.

judgment debt: money owed by one party to another party in a court case as a result of the court's decision in the case. If the money is not paid, the winning party can enforce this judgment debt by a warrant of execution, an *attachment of earnings order* or a *garnishee order*.

Judicial Appointments Commission: a proposed new independent body which would have responsibility for the selection of judges. This proposal was made because of the criticisms made of the Lord Chancellor's powers in this area. In June 2003 the Government began consulting on what form this commission should take. They put forward three models for consideration. These were:

- a Commission which would take over the Lord Chancellor's role in drectly making appointments up to the level of circuit judge and advising the Queen on appointments at that level or above; or

- a Commission which would make recommendations to a Minister as to whom to appoint (or recommend that the Queen should appoint); or

- a Commission which directly appoints junior levels of judges and recommends more senior appointment.

Judicial Committee of the Privy Council: the final appeal court from decisions of courts in some Commonwealth countries. Originally, all appeals from the Commonwealth were heard here but, as countries gained their independence, many have opted out of the system and established their own final court of appeal. The judges include the Lord Chancellor, the Law Lords and some judges from Commonwealth countries. Decisions by the Judicial Committee of the Privy Council create *persuasive precedent* for the courts in England and Wales.

There are also other functions including:

- hearing appeals by doctors, dentists and opticians who have been struck off and prevented from practising by their professional body;

- hearing appeals on some matters connected with the church and the ecclesiastic courts;

- deciding whether any member of the House of Commons is disqualified from being an MP.

judicial independence: see *independence of the judiciary*

judicial precedent: the following of legal principles laid down in previously decided cases. The doctrine of judicial precedent is based on the principle of *stare decisis*, which means 'stand by what has already been decided'. In England and Wales, this doctrine leads to the idea of *binding precedent*, which operates so that:

● lower courts must follow decisions of higher courts;

● appeal courts are normally bound by their own past decisions.

The fact that appeal courts are normally bound by their own past decisions is based on the idea that there should be certainty in the law. However, it is argued that if all courts are bound, then there is no room for the law to change with society. Also, if an error was made by the House of Lords, the judges could not change that mistake in a later case. The problems have led to different rules being developed for the House of Lords and the Court of Appeal.

1 Judicial precedent in the House of Lords

The House of Lords has some discretion and need not always follow its own past decisions. This is as a result of the *Practice Statement* 1966 in which the House of Lords said that they would depart from a previous decision when it appeared right to do so. This flexibility allows the law to develop so that out-dated principles are not applied too rigidly to modern society. However, this flexibility has not often been used.

2 Judicial precedent in the Court of Appeal

The Court of Appeal must follow previous decisions of the House of Lords. The Court of Appeal (Civil Division) is also bound by its own past decisions with a few minor exceptions which were set out by *Young's case* (1944). The Court of Appeal (Criminal Division) can refuse to follow a past decision of its own if the law has been 'misapplied or misunderstood'. This is because in criminal cases, people's liberty may be at stake.

See also *distinguishing* and *persuasive precedent*.

judicial review: the reviewing by judges of decisions and actions of lower courts and other decision-making bodies where there is no further right of appeal from that decision. It is the way in which the *High Court* exercises control over inferior decision-making bodies. Anyone who has been affected by a decision (or a failure to make a decision) can apply for leave to start judicial review proceedings in the High Court. The judicial review is a review of the legality of the decision and will only be successful if:

● there was an error of law; or

● the decision or action was so unreasonable that no reasonable authority would have made it; this is based on *Wednesbury principles* set out in the case of Associated Provincial Picture Houses v Wednesbury Corporation (1948); or

● there was a procedural irregularity in that the authority had failed to act according to standard procedure or had breached the rules of *natural justice*.

judicial separation: a court order that the parties to a marriage no longer have a duty to cohabit. A judicial separation is granted if the *petitioner* can prove one of the *five facts* used in divorce proceedings, but there is no need to prove that the marriage has irretrievably broken down. When granting a judicial separation, a court can also make orders about maintenance and other *financial provision* and about any *child of the family*. Judicial separations are often sought by people who have religious objections to divorce but want to settle financial matters. Under the *Family Law Act 1996*, they were to be replaced by *separation orders*.

Judicial Studies Board supervises the training of judges. It was set up in 1979, and the amount of training given to judges has increased to include human awareness training on racial and gender issues and training in information technology as well as updates on the law.

judiciary: the collective term for judges.

juries in civil cases: now used in only a small number of cases (about 40) each year. When they are used, they decide the liability of the parties in the case and set the amount of damages (compensation). The right to jury trial has been gradually removed, but parties still have the right to jury trial in cases of:

- *defamation*;
- *false imprisonment*;
- *malicious prosecution*;
- *fraud*.

It is also possible to ask for jury trial in a personal injury claim in the *Queen's Bench Division* of the High Court but, in effect, they are not used for such cases. This is because assessing the amount of damages to be paid as compensation for injuries is better done by a judge to maintain consistency between one case and another (Ward v James (1966)).

juries in criminal cases sit in the *Crown Court*. They have the role of deciding the facts of a case and the verdict of guilty or not guilty. The judge rules on any point of law and, if the jury finds the defendant guilty, decides on the appropriate sentence. There are 12 jurors and, if they cannot agree on a verdict, there can be a *majority verdict* of 11–1 or 10–2.

jurisdiction: the power of the court. To say a court has jurisdiction over any matter means that court has power to deal with the matter.

jury equity: the idea that the jury does not always follow the strict letter of the law but can refuse to convict in a case where it thinks that this would be an injustice. Such a decision can also be called a perverse decision as it is one made against the obvious evidence in the case.

Case example: R v Randle and Pottle (1991)

The defendants were charged with helping a convicted spy to escape from prison. This prosecution did not take place until 25 years after the escape, when the two defendants wrote about what they had done. The jury found them not guilty.

jury qualifications: to serve on a jury, a person must be:

- aged between 18 and 70;
- registered as an elector for Parliamentary or local elections;
- ordinarily resident in the United Kingdom, the Channel Islands or the Isle of Man for at least five years since their 13th birthday.

In addition, certain people are disqualified or ineligible and cannot sit on a jury. The main categories are shown on the next page.

Some people, although qualified to sit on a jury, have the right to be excused jury trial. This is an excusal as of right and applies to:

- those who are aged between 65 and 70;
- those who have served on a jury within the previous two years;

- people in essential jobs, such as doctors, nurses and dentists, and the armed forces;
- Members of Parliament;
- practising members of a religious group whose beliefs are not compatible with serving on a jury.

Disqualified	Ineligible
Anyone who:	
• has been sentenced to imprisonment for life or detained during Her Majesty's Pleasure; • has been sentenced to imprisonment of five years or more • has served any custodial sentence, suspended sentence or Community Service Order within the last ten years; • has been on probation within the last five years; • is currently on bail.	• judges and magistrates; • anyone who has, within the last ten years, been a barrister, solicitor or legal executive; • anyone who, within the last ten years, has worked in the courts or connected services, e.g. police, prison or probation service or the Lord Chancellor's Department; • those suffering from mental disorders; • ministers of religion.

The Criminal Justice Bill 2002 proposes abolishing the categories of ineligible and excusable as of right. This would mean that people currently in these categories would have to do jury service unless they were given a discretionary excusal.

jury, role of: a jury is used to decide cases in:

1 The *Crown Court* for criminal trials, where their role is to decide if the defendant is guilty or not guilty.

2 The *Queen's Bench Division* of the *High Court* and the *County Court* for tort cases of *defamation*, *false imprisonment* and *malicious prosecution* and any other civil case where fraud is alleged. In all these cases, the jury decides both whether the case has been proved and the amount of damages to be awarded.

3 The *Coroners' Courts*, where they must be used to inquire into deaths which have occurred in prison or police custody, in an industrial accident, or in circumstances where public health and safety is involved.

jury selection: carried out by an official at the court who selects names at random (this may be done manually or by computer) from the lists of electors for the area covered by the court. The official sends out summons to those selected. The people summonsed must tell the court if they are disqualified or ineligible or excusable as of right (see also *jury qualifications*). The remainder will be expected to attend at court unless the court official agrees to excuse them. The court official has the discretion to excuse people if they have a good reason, for example they are ill or have a holiday booked for the period of jury service.

At court, jurors are usually divided into groups of 15, and when a jury is required for a trial, one group of 15 will be sent to that court. In court, the clerk will select 12 of the 15 at random. It is possible for the prosecution and defence to challenge an individual juror because:

- they are disqualified; or
- they know someone in the case.

The prosecution also has the right to stand by any potential juror. This means that that juror's name goes to the end of the list and he will only be used if there are not enough jurors.

jury trial, advantages and disadvantages of: there is much debate as to whether juries should try cases. In particular, it is often stated that juries should not be used to try complex fraud cases as they are unable to understand the evidence. However, the idea of trial by one's peers (equals) is an important part of democracy. Below is a list of the main pros and cons of jury trial.

Advantages	Disadvantages
• public involvement in the legal system;	• unable to understand complex cases;
• public confidence;	• no reason given for verdict – may
• jury equity;	have decided for unacceptable
• open justice;	reasons, e.g. R v Young where jurors
• trial by one's peers;	held a seance to contact a murder victim;
• cross-section of society.	• influenced by media coverage;
	• high acquittal rates.

jury vetting occurs after the names of potential jurors have been selected and before they start to try any cases. There are two types of vetting:

- a routine police check to eliminate those who have a conviction and are disqualified;
- a wider check on background and political views. This may only be done with the permission of the *Attorney-General* in cases which involve national security or terrorist cases.

justice and law: justice is the aim of the law, but it may not always be achieved in every case. There is the difficulty that what one person thinks is justice may not be the same as another person's views. Applying the same rules equally to all people can be said to produce justice. However, rules that are too rigid may lead to injustice in some cases.

Justices of the Peace: another term for *magistrates*.

Justices' clerk: the qualified legal advisor who sits in the *Magistrates' Court* and guides *lay magistrates* on questions of law, practice and procedure, but must not actually take any part in the decision-making. Clerks are also responsible for the administration of the court and can deal with routine matters such as issuing warrants for arrest and extending *bail* for a defendant who has already been given bail by the police. Their powers to deal with preliminary issues have been extended by the Crime and Disorder Act 1998.

justification (or truth): a defence in *defamation*. If the defendant can show that what he said or wrote was substantially true, he will not be liable, even though the statement was defamatory.

Case example: Alexander v NE Railway (1865)

The railway company publicised the fact that Alexander had been fined for non-payment of his fare with the alternative of three weeks' imprisonment if he failed to pay. He sued for defamation because although the fine was stated correctly, the alternative prison sentence was two weeks rather than three weeks. The railway company successfully argued justification despite the mistake about the prison sentence; the statement had been substantially true.

See also *fair comment* for a comparison between justification and fair comment.

keeper: the owner or possessor of an animal or the head of a household where a member aged under 16 keeps an animal. The keeper of an animal is liable for damage caused by it. See *Animals Act 1971.*

King's Bench Division: the name given to the *Queen's Bench Division* of the High Court when a king is on the throne. In law reports for the years 1901 to 1951, you will see that reports from this division are abbreviated as KB (King's Bench). From 1952, the date Queen Elizabeth II became the monarch, all reports are shown as QB (Queen's Bench).

King's Counsel: the title of senior barristers when the monarch is a king. When a queen is on the throne, they are called *Queen's Counsel.*

law centres: places where local people can get free legal advice. Funding of these centres is a major problem. The Home Office provides some funding, but most rely on their local authority and have suffered cut backs in spending, which has forced some law centres to close.

Law Commission: an advisory body which makes proposals for law reform. It was set up by the Law Commissions Act 1965 to 'keep under review all the law ... with a view to its systematic development and reform'. It is headed by a Chairman and there are four other Law Commissioners plus support staff. Areas of law are researched and a report issued with proposals for reform. Often the proposals are in the form of a draft *Bill* which it is hoped will be put before Parliament for it to be passed as law. Laws which have been made in this way include:

- Occupiers' Liability Act 1984;
- Law Reform (Year and a Day Rule) Act 1996.
- Contract (Right of Third Parties) Act 1999
- Land Registration Act 2002.

The Law Commission has published a *Draft Criminal Code* but this has never been enacted by Parliament.

Law Lords: the judges who sit in the House of Lords. Their full title is the Lords of Appeal in Ordinary. They are appointed from those who hold high judicial office in England and Wales, Scotland and Northern Ireland. The appointments are made by the monarch on advice from the Prime Minister. No woman has ever been appointed as a judge in the House of Lords.

Law Officers of the Crown: the *Attorney-General* and the *Solicitor-General*. Both are appointed from Members of Parliament who are also barristers. The Attorney-General is the Government's chief legal advisor and the Solicitor-General is his deputy.

law reform: making a change to the law. Such changes may be brought about through many different avenues. The main ones of these are:

- government policy: most *Acts of Parliament* are passed to change the law in line with the current government's ideas;
- decisions in cases which create *judicial precedent* for other judges to follow;
- *law reform agencies*, especially the *Law Commission*;
- *European law*.

In addition, changing ideas in society can lead to changes in the law, especially where pressure groups campaign for change.

law reform agencies: bodies which are responsible for researching areas of law and then making proposals for reform of the law. The main agencies are:

- the *Law Commission* (this is the most important law reform agency);
- the *Law Reform Committee*;
- *Royal Commissions*.

Law Reform Committee: a part-time reform body which was set up in 1952 to consider possible reforms of the civil law. Its proposals have led to Parliament passing the Occupiers' Liability Act 1957, the Civil Evidence Act 1968 and the Latent Damages Act 1986.

Law Reform (Frustrated Contracts) Act 1943 regulates what *damages* are payable when a contract has been frustrated (see also *frustration*). The main provisions are:

- money paid in advance must be refunded, although deductions can be made for expenses already incurred at the time the frustrating event took place;
- money that is due to be paid under the contract does not have to be paid;
- where some of the service or goods have already been provided before the contract was frustrated, the provider is entitled to a just sum in payment for the benefit that has been received.

The Act does not cover *charter parties*, contracts of insurance and contracts for the sale of specific goods which perish before the contract is carried out. In these cases, the loss lies where it falls unless there has been total failure of consideration, in which case any money paid must be returned.

law reports: records of decided cases. In the major law reports, such as the All England Reports, the whole of the judgment (judge's speech at the end of the case) is set out. In other series, such as those in The Times newspaper, only key extracts from this judgment are given. Law reports are an important tool in the doctrine of *judicial precedent* as they enable judges to know exactly what legal principles were applied by judges in earlier similar cases. Law reports are now available on the Internet.

Law Society: the governing body of *solicitors* which also acts on behalf of the profession as a whole. The Law Society supervises training and discipline. A solicitor can only practise if he has a practising certificate issued by the Law Society.

lawyer: the general name given to those who are qualified in law. This covers both *barristers* and *solicitors*.

lay assessors: non-lawyers who have expertise in a technical area and who sit with a judge in cases where such technical knowledge is needed. Lay assessors are regularly used in the *Admiralty Court* where they advise the judge on questions of seamanship and navigation.

lay magistrates: ordinary people who sit part time in the *Magistrates' Court* to decide cases. To be appointed as a lay magistrate the only formal qualifications are:

- to be aged between 21 and 65 (though it rare to be appointed under the age of 27);
- to live within 15 miles of the area covered by the court;
- to be prepared to sit as a magistrate at least 26 times a year.

Local advisory committees interview candidates and put forward names of potential new magistrates to the *Lord Chancellor*, who makes the appointment. Although the intention is to draw magistrates from as wide a background as possible, there is criticism that these committees nominate candidates who are from similar backgrounds. This has led to lay magistrates being described as middle aged, middle class and middle minded.

Advantages of using lay magistrates	Disadvantages of using lay magistrates
• local knowledge;	• insufficiently trained for the work;
• sit as panel of three so get a cross-section of views;	• inconsistency in sentencing;
	• rely too heavily on the clerk;
• cheap, as they are only paid expenses.	• likely to believe the police too readily.

lay members of tribunals: people who sit with a legally qualified chairman to decide tribunal cases. They will have special knowledge of the area covered by the tribunal. For example, in an industrial injuries tribunal, the lay members would be medically qualified, whilst in an *employment tribunal* they would be representatives from employer and employee organisations.

lay participation in the legal system: considered desirable as it keeps the law more open and allows decisions to be made by one's peers. The main areas in which ordinary lay people (not legally qualified) are used are:

• *jury* trials in the *Crown Court*;

• *lay magistrates* in the *Magistrates' Court*;

• *lay members of tribunals*;

• *lay assessors* in the *Admiralty Court*.

leapfrog appeal: an appeal route direct from the *High Court* to the *House of Lords*. Under the Administration of Justice Act 1969, such an appeal can be made only if there is a point of law of general public importance:

• which is concerned with the interpretation of a statute; or

• where there is a binding precedent which the trial judge must follow.

The House of Lords must also give leave (permission) to appeal. This type of appeal is very rare, happening only three or four times a year.

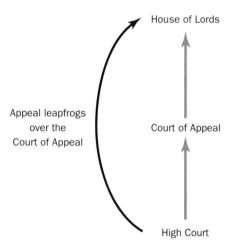

lease: the right to have possession of land for a fixed period of time, usually in exchange for rent. At the end of the period of the lease, the property must be returned to the *free-holder* (owner). It can also mean the document which gives details of the arrangement.

legacy: a gift which is left to someone in a *will*.

legal advice: an important element in ensuring that people's rights are protected. A criticism is that legal advice from lawyers can be very expensive and therefore not available to ordinary people. To counteract this, there are some government funded schemes which provide free legal advice in limited circumstances. The main one is Form 10 which allows those on very low incomes to obtain two hours of advice from a solicitor with no payment. Those who are detained by the police can see a duty solicitor free of charge, and there is also a duty solicitor scheme for those who are appearing in the Magistrates' Court.

As these schemes are limited, free advice is offered by other advice agencies such as:

- *Citizens' Advice Bureaux*;
- *Law centres*;
- trade unions for work-related matters;
- the organisation, Shelter, which gives advice on housing problems;
- the legal profession themselves with schemes such as *ALAS*.

legal aid schemes: government funded schemes which provide legal representation in civil and criminal cases. *Civil legal aid* is available to those who wish to take or defend a case, provided they have a reasonable chance of winning the case. However, if they would only gain a trivial advantage from the case, the *Legal Services Commission* can refuse funding. *Criminal legal aid* is available for any defendant in a criminal case provided it is in the interests of justice. In both civil and criminal cases, there is a *means test* so that only those on low incomes will be offered legal aid. The means test for civil legal aid is much stricter than that for criminal legal aid.

legal executives work in solicitors' firms as assistants dealing with the more straightforward cases and routine matters. To become a legal executive, it is necessary to work for at least five years in a solicitors' office or similar post (e.g. the Crown Prosecution Service) and pass the examinations set by the Institute of Legal Executives.

legal help is one of the services funded by the *Community Legal Service*. It allows people on very low incomes to receive free advice and assistance on legal matters.

legal personality: a being recognised by law as having legal rights. The law recognises two types of legal person:

1 natural persons (human beings);

2 artificial persons (*corporations*).

Human beings have legal personality from the moment they are born to the end of their life, though the rights and duties of those under the age of 18 are restricted (see *child*). However, the law does not recognise a foetus as having any legal rights.

Legal Practice Course: the vocational course which must be passed in order to qualify as a *solicitor*. The course lasts one year and includes practical skills, such as interviewing clients, negotiating, drafting legal documents and doing legal research, and business skills, including keeping accounts. Once this course has been passed, the would-be solicitor must then work for two years in a solicitors' office on a training contract before being admitted as a fully qualified solicitor.

legal profession refers to *barristers* and *solicitors* who are practising as lawyers.

legal relations, intention to create: see *intention to create legal relations*

legal representation means having a lawyer to put your case in court. This can be paid for privately or, for those on low income, it may be possible to have legal representation paid for by the Government. To qualify for government-funded representation in civil cases, the merits of the case in the context of the Government's priorities and available resources must justify public spending. The case must have a high chance of success and the likely *damages* must be more than the case will cost.

legal services: the term given to the range of advice services and representation in court which is available. This covers the services of *barristers* and *solicitors* and also other agencies such as *Citizens' Advice Bureaux* and *law centres*.

Legal Services Commission: set up by the Access to Justice Act 1999 to maintain and develop the *Community Legal Service* and the *Criminal Defence Service*.

This Commission is run by a board of directors appointed by the Lord Chancellor. The intention is that people with a wide range of expertise and experience (advice sector, other legal services, local government and business) are appointed. The Commission's responsibilities are to develop local, regional and national plans to match the delivery of legal services to identified needs and priorities.

The LSC is able to make contracts with providers of all types of legal service.

Legal Services Ombudsman examines complaints against *solicitors*, *barristers* and *licensed conveyancers*, where the complainant is dissatisfied with the way in which the professions' own regulatory bodies have dealt with the matter. The post was created by the Courts and Legal Services Act 1990. If the Ombudsman upholds the complaint, there is power to order that compensation be paid.

legislation: law that is made by the government or with the government's authority. An *Act of Parliament* is legislation passed by Parliament. Legislation passed by other bodies which have been given the authority to do so by Parliament is called *delegated legislation*.

legislature: the law-making body of a country. In this country, Parliament is the legislature.

legitimate child: the child of:

- a woman who is married at the time of conception;
- a woman who is married at the time of the birth;
- parents who, at the time of conception, think they have a valid marriage although, in reality, it is *void*;
- parents who have a *voidable marriage*.

If a husband thinks a child is not his, he can challenge its legitimacy. An application is made to the court, and if tests show that he is not the father, the child will be illegitimate. See also *legitimated child* for children who are born as an *illegitimate child* but later become legitimate.

legitimated child: one whose parents marry after the birth even if they were married to other people at the time of conception. A legitimated child has the same rights and obligations as a legitimate child.

lessee: a person who leases a property. Another term is a 'tenant'.

lessor: a person who grants a lease of his property to a *lessee*. Another term is a 'landlord'.

letters of administration: granted to the *personal representatives* of someone who has died without making a will so that those personal representatives have the authority to deal with the deceased's property.

liability means a legal obligation is owed. If someone commits a *tort* or breaks a contract, they are liable for any damage caused and may be sued for compensation.

libel: a type of *defamation*. It is a statement tending to lower the person referred to in the estimation of right-thinking members of society and made in a permanent form. Usually this is in the form of print, but can include paintings, statues and waxworks. Broadcasts on the television and radio are included as libel under the Broadcasting Act 1990 and stage plays under the Theatres Act 1968.

A claimant bringing a claim does not have to show that he has suffered any financial loss as a result of the libel. See also *slander*, which is the temporary form of defamation.

licence: permission to be on someone's land, e.g. going to the cinema or staying at a friend's house. This permission can be taken away, and the person who has the licence has no rights to stay on the land.

licensed conveyancers: those other than solicitors who have been given the right to deal with conveyancing (the legal transfer of land). Up to 1985, solicitors had the sole right to do this work, but under the Administration of Justice Act 1985, the qualification of licensed conveyancer was introduced. This broke the solicitors' monopoly on conveyancing.

lien: a legal right to hold the property of another as security. For example, a garage that repairs a car has the right to hold on to the car until the bill for the repair is paid.

life interest: where property is left to a person for their lifetime and then it is to go to someone else. The person with the life interest does not own the property, they have only a *beneficial interest* in it. This means they cannot spend the capital, but the interest from the money is theirs.

life sentence: a punishment for a very serious criminal offence which can be given to offenders aged 21 and over. A life sentence must be imposed when someone is found guilty of murder. A judge has the discretion to impose a life sentence on a defendant who is guilty of other very serious crimes including manslaughter and rape. Also, under the Crime (Sentences) Act 1997, any defendant who commits a second serious or violent offence must be given a life sentence.

A life sentence does not necessarily mean that the defendant will spend the rest of his life in prison. When a life sentence is imposed, the judge will state the period of time which he thinks should be served in prison before the offender can be even considered for parole. The Lord Chief Justice will then review the case and set the minimum term. In some exceptional cases, where the defendant has committed several murders, the Home Secretary has indicated that it is unlikely that the person will ever be released from prison.

Offenders under the age of 21 can be ordered to be detained at Her Majesty's pleasure. This has a similar effect as a life sentence but offenders are more likely to be released after a few years as it is recognised that they are more capable of being reformed.

limitation clause in a contract limits the amount of damages payable by a person who breaches (breaks) the contract.

limitation of actions: the time limit for starting court proceedings. The length of the time limit depends on the case being started:

- a claim to recover land must be brought within 12 years (subject to restrictions under the Land Registration Act 2002);

- a claim for breach of contract or in tort, where the loss has been solely financial, must be brought within six years;

- a claim in tort where the *claimant* has suffered death or physical (personal) injury must be brought within three years of the tort being committed or three years from when the claimant realised or ought to have realised he could bring a claim. This covers situations where the claimant has worked in an unhealthy environment but has not developed a disease which has been caused by this until several years afterwards. Time only begins to run from the time at which the disease develops and it is realised what has caused it;

- a claim in defamation must be brought within one year.

Where the claimant is a minor (under 18), the time limits do not start until he becomes 18, e.g. a six-year-old who has been injured by a tort has until he is 21 to start court proceedings (or his parents can sue on his behalf).

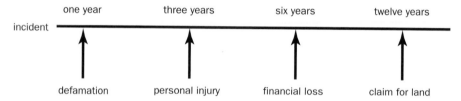

limited company: an artificial legal person that has a separate legal personality from the members who are the *shareholders* (Salomon v Salomon and Co. (1897)). (See *corporate personality*.) The word 'limited' refers to the fact that the shareholders' liability for the company's debts is limited to the value of the shares that they own. Once they have paid in full for those shares, they cannot be made to pay any more if the company becomes unable to pay its debts. A company can also be limited by guarantee under which one or more persons guarantees the company's debt up to a certain limit. Beyond that limit, the person is not liable. A limited liability company can be a *public limited company* or a *private limited company*.

limited liability means that the *shareholders* of a company are only liable for paying for the shares they own and are not liable for the company's debts beyond this. A *partnership* cannot have limited liability, as at least one partner must have unlimited liability so that he is responsible for the partnership debts. It is, however, possible for other partners to have limited liability, provided there is at least one with unlimited liability.

limited partner: a partner in a partnership whose liability for the debts of the *partnership* is limited to the extent of his contribution to the partnership capital. This is allowed under the Limited Partnership Act 1907, but there must be at least one partner who is liable for all the partnership debts.

liquidated damages in contract law: a fixed amount of *damages* which is agreed by both parties when the contract is made and is payable if contract is breached. The intention is to avoid lengthy disputes in court if the contract is breached and to enable the parties to arrange insurance cover. However, if the sum agreed is very high and seems intended to penalise the party who breached the contract rather than a genuine calculation of what the innocent party would have lost, a court will decide that it is a *penalty clause* and not enforce it. Instead, the court will make its own assessment of what the financial loss was (Dunlop Pneumatic Tyre Co v New Garage and Motor Co (1915)).

literal rule: a rule of *statutory interpretation*. It involves giving words their ordinary, plain, grammatical meaning, even if it makes the law absurd. Some judges take the view that, where words in an Act of Parliament are clear, they must follow them as this is what has been enacted by Parliament. This can lead to unsatisfactory results.

Case example: Whiteley v Chappel (1868)

The defendant was charged under a law which said that it was an offence to impersonate 'any person entitled to vote'. The defendant had pretended to be a person who had died but whose name was still on the list of voters. The court found the defendant not guilty of the offence, as the literal meaning of the words 'any person entitled to vote' did not include someone who was dead as they were no longer entitled to vote!

See also *golden rule* and *mischief rule*.

litigant: a person who is taking or defending a civil case in the courts.

litigant in person: a *litigant* who has not got a lawyer, but is representing himself in court. Because of the expense of court cases and the difficulties of obtaining *civil legal aid*, more people are representing themselves in cases in the *High Court* and Court of Appeal.

litigation: the taking of a case in the civil courts. It has been described as 'a game in which the court is the umpire'.

living apart in divorce proceedings means not living in the same household (see *household, in the same*). Normally this happens when the husband and wife live in separate houses, but it is possible to be living apart in the same house if the two parties lead separate lives with at least one of them considering that the marriage is at an end.

Case example: Fuller v Fuller (1973)

The wife set up home with her boyfriend. The husband became seriously ill and moved in with his wife and her boyfriend as a lodger. The wife cooked and washed for him, but continued to share a bedroom with her boyfriend. It was held that the wife and husband were living apart.

locus standi means that the person or organisation bringing an action for *judicial review* has sufficient interest in the matter to be allowed to make the application. For example, in R v Secretary of State, ex parte Equal Opportunities Commission (1994), the Equal Opportunities Commission was held to have sufficient interest in an action about the possible breach of European law on sex discrimination over the employment rights of part-time workers.

Lord Chancellor: a member of the government, who has usually practised as a barrister and who is appointed by the Prime Minister. The position is a breach of the doctrine of the *separation of powers* as the Lord Chancellor has a role in all three arms of state. He is:

145

- a member of the cabinet (that is the executive arm of the state);
- a member of the *House of Lords* when it is sitting to consider new law;
- a judge in the House of Lords; he is head of the *Chancery Division* of the High Court and sits as a judge on the *Judicial Committee of the Privy Council*.

He also is responsible for the appointment of lay magistrates and all lower-ranking judges. He also has influence over who is appointed to the higher judicial positions. His other responsibilities include overseeing the work of the *Legal Services Commission*, the *Law Commission*, the *Council on Tribunals*, the Public Trustee Office and the Land Registry.

In June 2003 Lord Falconer was appointed Lord Chancellor and also Secretary of State for Constitutional Affairs. It was announced that the office of Lord Chancellor was under review and may be abolished. In the meantime Lord Falconer will carry out the work of the Lord Chancellor except that he will not sit as a judge.

Lord Chancellor's Department: the civil service department of which the *Lord Chancellor* is head. This department is responsible for the administration of the courts.

Lord Chief Justice: the most senior judge after the *Lord Chancellor*. He is president of the Criminal Division of the *Court of Appeal* and the senior judge of the *Queen's Bench Division* of the High Court. He is usually appointed from the judges of the Court of Appeal. The appointment is made by the monarch.

Lords Justices of Appeal: the judges in the *Court of Appeal*. They are appointed from those who have had the right to appear as an advocate in the *High Court* for at least ten years or from existing High Court judges.

Lords of Appeal in Ordinary: the judges who sit in the *House of Lords*. They are also known as the Law Lords. They are nominated by the Prime Minister and appointed by the monarch from those who have held high judicial office in England and Wales, Scotland or Northern Ireland for at least two years.

loss of amenity: the loss of an ability to carry out certain activities. It is a term used in tort when assessing damages. A successful claimant will be awarded damages to compensate him for anything that he can no longer do because of the tort. The court will look at his lifestyle before and after the tort and assess what he has lost, e.g. a footballer will receive more damages if he suffers a broken leg which leaves him unable to run than someone whose hobby is going to the cinema.

lump sum order: an order made by the court in family law that one spouse pay the other or a *child of the family* a lump sum. This payment can be ordered to be made in instalments.

magistrates, also known as Justices of the Peace, sit to try cases in the *Magistrates' Court*. There are two types of magistrate:

- *district judges* (Magistrates' Court), formerly called *stipendiary magistrates*, who are legally qualified, paid and sit full time in Magistrates' Courts in London and other big towns or cities such as Birmingham, Leeds and Manchester. There are about 90 district judges and they sit on their own to hear cases;

- *lay magistrates*, who are not legally qualified, unpaid except for expenses and sit part time in Magistrates' Courts throughout the country. There are about 30,000 lay magistrates and they sit in panels of two or three together to hear cases.

Magistrates' Court: local courts hearing mainly criminal cases but also with some jurisdiction over civil matters. The criminal work of these courts is:

- trying all *summary offences*, that is minor cases which can only be dealt with at the Magistrates' Court;

- trying any *triable either way offence* where the magistrates and the defendant decide that the case should be tried by the magistrates;

- sending triable either way cases to the *Crown Court* when the magistrates think that the matter should be tried there or when the defendant elects jury trial;

- sending defendants charged with a triable either way offence to the Crown Court to be sentenced when the magistrates feel their sentencing powers of a maximum of six months' imprisonment and/or £5,000 fine are not sufficient to deal with the offender. (Note that the Criminal Justice Bill 2002 has provision for magistrates sentencing powers to be increased to one year for one offence or 15 months for two or more offences);

- dealing with matters connected to criminal cases; this includes issuing warrants for the arrest of a defendant or to search premises and hearing applications for bail;

- trying all but the most serious criminal cases against young offenders aged ten to 17; these are heard in the *Youth Court*, which is a separate part of the Magistrates' Court.

The civil work of the court includes issuing licenses to pubs and restaurants to sell alcoholic drinks, enforcing payment of council taxes, hearing family cases (but not divorce), hearing cases about the welfare of children in proceedings under the Children Act 1989.

See also *lay magistrates*.

Magna Carta: the charter which gave citizens the right not to be imprisoned without trial. The original charter was granted by King John in 1215.

maintenance: in family law, regular payments made to give financial support to a spouse or the *children of the family*. Maintenance can be:

- periodic payments;
- secured periodic payments;
- a lump sum.

Arrangements for maintenance can be made privately between the parties or an application can be made to the court. This can be done:

- during divorce proceedings;
- during judicial separation proceedings;
- while the couple are married and living together (this application is made to the Magistrates' court);
- where the parents are living apart, (here, maintenance for the children can be applied for under the Children Act 1989).

Where the parents are living apart, an application can also be made to the *Child Support Agency* for them to assess and collect maintenance for the children. This is usual where the parent with whom the children are living is receiving State benefit payments.

majority verdict: in a *jury trial*, one where only ten or 11 of the jury agree on the verdict. Majority verdicts were introduced in 1967 in an effort to make it more difficult for the defendant or his friends to 'get at' the jury by bribing or intimidating some of the jurors. The majority verdict can be one of guilty or not guilty, with 11 to one or ten to two in favour of the verdict. When the jury announces its verdict in the court, the foreman must say how many of the jury agreed with the verdict. About one in every five trials by a jury results in a majority verdict.

making off without payment: an offence under s3 of the Theft Act 1978. It is committed when a person who knows that payment on the spot is required for goods or services (e.g. a taxi fare) dishonestly makes off without paying, intending to avoid payment.

malice aforethought: the *mens rea* required for *murder*. It is the *intention* to kill or cause grievous bodily harm. This means that, in order to be guilty of murder, the defendant must have killed a person either with the intention to kill or with the intention to cause grievous bodily harm. There is the criticism that an intention to cause grievous bodily harm is not as serious as an intention to kill, yet the defendant is guilty of the same crime. Despite the use of the word aforethought there is no need to show that the defendant planned an attack, it only needs to be proved that he had the intention to kill or cause grievous bodily harm at the time of the attack.

Case example: R v Vickers (1957)

The defendant broke into the cellar of a shop intending to steal. He was disturbed in the course of stealing by an elderly lady, and he kicked and punched her. She died from her injuries. It was held that Vickers was guilty of murder as he intended to cause the old lady grievous bodily harm.

malicious prosecution: a tort. To bring a claim, the claimant must show all of the following:

- the defendant prosecuted him;

- the prosecution ended in the claimant's favour (he was acquitted or the case was withdrawn by the prosecution);

- the prosecution lacked reasonable and probable cause (there were no reasonable grounds for thinking the claimant was guilty);

- the defendant acted maliciously.

Cases of malicious prosecution are usually brought against the police. Malicious prosecution is one of the civil cases in which the claimant can ask to be tried by a *jury*.

malicious wounding: an offence under s20 of the Offences against the Person Act 1861. It covers situations where the defendant has unlawfully and *maliciously* wounded someone (a *wound* is a cut of the external skin) or inflicted grievous (serious) bodily harm on them. In R v Parmenter (1991), the Court of Appeal stated that it was not necessary for the defendant to realise that a wound or serious injury might be caused. A defendant would be guilty of this offence if he foresaw that some physical harm, even a minor injury, might be caused.

maliciously: a word used to indicate the level of *mens rea* required in the definition of some offences, especially in the Offences against the Person Act 1861. The legal meaning of 'maliciously' was explained in the case of R v Cunningham (1957) and is that the defendant must either:

- have the intention to do the particular kind of harm that was in fact done; or

- be reckless as to whether that harm was done, in the sense of realising that there was a risk it would occur and going on to take that risk.

This level of mens rea is also known as *subjective recklessness* or *Cunningham recklessness*.

mandamus means 'we command' and is a royal command issued by the *Queen's Bench Division* of the *High Court* which orders the performance of a public duty. It is one of the *prerogative orders* which the court can make. An order of mandamus means that the person or body to whom it is addressed must do something that they have failed to do in accordance with their duty.

Case example: R v Hendon Justices, ex parte DPP (1992)

The magistrates at Hendon Magistrates' Court dismissed a case against a defendant because there was no one from the Crown Prosecution Service to prosecute the case. The CPS failed to attend because they had been wrongly told by a court official that the case was not due to be heard. The Queen's Bench Division issued an order for mandamus ordering the magistrates to try the case properly.

mandatory sentence: one which has to be passed on a defendant; the judge has no discretion to change it. For example, for the offence of murder, the judge has to impose a life sentence on the defendant. The Powers of Criminal Courts (Sentencing) Act 2000 also sets a mandatory sentence of life imprisonment for offenders who are convicted of a second crime of violence.

manslaughter: a criminal offence of causing the death of another person. There are two types of manslaughter:

1   Voluntary manslaughter, where the defendant intended to kill or cause grievous bodily harm, but the charge is reduced from murder to manslaughter because the defendant is able to use one of the special defences of *diminished responsibility*, *provocation* or *suicide pact*.

2   Involuntary manslaughter, where the defendant did not intend to kill, but caused the death through an unlawful and dangerous act (*constructive manslaughter*) or through *gross negligence*.

Mareva injunction: an order made where there is a risk that one party in a case will move all their assets out of the United Kingdom before the case against them is tried. The effect of a Mareva injunction is to order that third parties (such as banks) who have assets owned by the party in their control must freeze those assets so that they cannot be removed from the account. It is an *equitable remedy* and so is only made if the court thinks that it is just in all the circumstances. Under the *Civil Procedure Rules* that came into force in April 1999, a Mareva injunction is re-named a freezing injunction.

marriage: a legal relationship between a man and a woman which comes into existence when the *marriage formalities* are carried out, provided that both parties freely consent, are over 16 years of age and single at the time of the marriage and are not too closely related (not within *prohibited degrees*). Marriage carries certain legal duties and rights.

Duties	Rights
• to live together;	• to occupy the *matrimonial home*;
• to maintain each other.	• to inherit if the other spouse dies *intestate* (without leaving a will);
	• to claim from the other spouse's *estate* if left out of the will;
	• to a division of the matrimonial assets on divorce based on need rather than what has been contributed financially.

marriage, effect of a divorce on: divorce brings a marriage to a legal end once the *decree absolute* has been pronounced. The effects of this are:

• the parties are free to remarry;

• they no longer have a duty to live with each other;

• they no longer have a duty to maintain each other, apart from any settlement that has been made on divorce;

• they cannot inherit from each other under the *intestacy* rules;

• *bequests* to the other party in a will made while the marriage was in existence will not take effect.

marriage, effect of a will on: where a person makes a *will* and then later gets married, that will is considered by the law to be cancelled. This means that unless the person makes another will, they are *intestate*. It is possible to avoid this problem by making a will in contemplation of marriage. This is a will which is made when you know you are going to get married and in this will you must state that the will is being made 'in contemplation of my marriage to …', naming the person to whom you are going to get married.

marriage formalities: the steps that must be taken for a marriage to be legally valid. A religious service of marriage may or may not create a legal marriage depending on whether the formalities are carried out. For some religions, it will be necessary to have both a civil wedding at a Register Office and a religious wedding. There must be:

- parental consent if either party is between 16 and 18 years of age;

- notice or licence; this is banns in the Anglican church if the wedding is to take place in an Anglican church, or notice at a Register Office and the issue of a Superintendent Registrar's certificate if the wedding is to take place anywhere else; alternatively a licence without notice from church or Register Office;

- a ceremony; this can be:
  - in an Anglican church by a priest or deacon
  - in a Register Office or premises approved by a registrar
  - in a registered place of religious worship by a minister
  - according to Jewish or Quaker rites;

- registration.

The ceremony must be open to the public with two witnesses present and the parties must both show they agree to the marriage. It must take place between the hours of 8 a.m. and 6 p.m.

Martin order: in family law, an order that a wife has the right to live in the family house until she dies or remarries. The house is then sold and the proceeds divided between the parties. It is used in divorce when making a financial settlement between the parties.

See also *Mesher order*.

Master of the Rolls: the judge who is President of the Civil Division of the *Court of Appeal*.

maternity leave of 26 weeks is a right given to all pregnant employees. The period starts from the time the woman notifies her employer she is taking the leave, or from the actual birth. During the period, the employer does not have to pay the employee, but all other benefits under the employment continue, for example, the right to a company car and accrual of holiday entitlement.

maternity rights: rights given to women employees who are pregnant. Some of the rights depend on the length of time a woman has worked for that employer. Other rights are granted from the moment a woman starts work. The main rights are shown below.

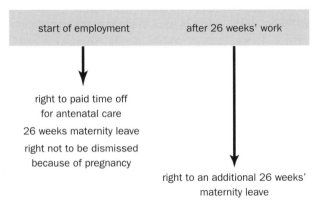

start of employment	after 26 weeks' work

right to paid time off
for antenatal care
26 weeks maternity leave
right not to be dismissed
because of pregnancy

right to an additional 26 weeks'
maternity leave

Matrimonial Causes Act 1973 s25 sets out the factors the court must take into account when deciding on the distribution of financial assets and the payment of maintenance on divorce or separation. The court will take more account of the needs of both parties and achieving a fair division than their financial contribution towards the marriage and will try to achieve a *clean break* if possible. The factors are:

- the welfare of the *children of the family* who are under the age of 18; this is the most important consideration;
- the financial resources (income) of both parties, both now and in the future; the income of a new partner can be taken into account if this makes it possible for the person paying maintenance to pay more;
- the financial obligations of both parties; an important factor here will be the support of the children of the family and, in many cases, the person with whom they live who will often retain the matrimonial home until the children leave home; where a spouse is supporting a new family, the court will try to keep a balance between the two;
- the standard of living of the parties at the time of the divorce; the court will try to maintain this as far as possible;
- the ages of both parties and the length of the marriage; cohabitation before marriage will be taken into account if it was a serious relationship;
- any physical or mental disability of either party;
- contributions made by both parties to the family's welfare, e.g. looking after the children or the family business; account will also be taken of lack of contributions;
- either party's behaviour that has been so gross and obvious that it would be inequitable (unfair) to ignore it;
- loss of future benefits, e.g. pension.

See also *financial provision on divorce*.

matrimonial home: in family law, the accommodation that the parties have treated as the family home. In many cases, married couples are joint owners or joint tenants of the home, but where only one party is the owner or tenant, the other has the right not to be evicted from it. Where the property is owned, this right needs to be registered at the Land Registry or the Land Charges Registry, otherwise, in some circumstances, the right is lost when the house is sold or mortgaged.

A court can also make *occupation orders* saying who can stay in the matrimonial home. These orders are made on the basis of who needs the accommodation rather than who has a legal right to it. These rights of occupation do not apply where the couple is not married.

McKenzie friend: a non-legally qualified person who is allowed to assist you in court and help you question witnesses and put your case to the court.

means test: a check on the amount of income and assets, such as money in a bank account or building society or the value of the house that a person has. This is important when a person is applying for *legal aid*, as only those below a certain level are eligible to receive legal aid under the government-funded schemes. See also *civil legal aid* and *criminal legal aid*.

mediation: where a neutral mediator helps the parties in a dispute to reach a compromise solution. It is a method of *alternative dispute resolution* aimed at avoiding court proceedings. The role of a mediator is to consult each party, carry offers to and fro between the parties and find out if there is any common ground between them. Mediation is only suitable if the parties are prepared to co-operate in finding a middle way to resolve the dispute.

medical treatment and the chain of causation: in most cases in criminal law where medical treatment is given to the victim of an attack, that medical treatment will not break the *chain of causation* if the victim dies. In other words, the original attacker remains liable for the death of the victim, even if the treatment was poor and contributed to, or even caused, the death.

Case example: R v Smith (1959)

The defendant stabbed the victim in a fight in army barracks. The victim was carried to the army medical station but was dropped twice on the way and at the station was given inappropriate treatment which aggravated the wound and contributed to his death. The court held that the defendant was guilty of murder as the original injury was still a 'substantial and operating cause'.

In R v Cheshire (1991) the court said that even if treatment was negligent, that would not normally absolve the original attacker of liability for the death. The attacker would only be absolved if the negligent medical treatment was independent of the attacker's acts and potent in causing death.

Case example: R v Jordan (1956)

The victim had been stabbed but was recovering well with the wounds mainly healed when he was given an overdose of a drug to which it was known that he was allergic. He died as a result of the drug. The defendant who had stabbed the victim was held not to be guilty of his murder. The hospital treatment had broken the chain of causation.

See also *causation in criminal law*.

Memorandum of Association: one of the documents required by the Companies Act 1985 to be sent to the Registrar of Companies before the company can be incorporated (created). The Memorandum of Association must state:

- the name of the company;
- the address of its registered office;
- the objects of the company;
- the liability of its members;
- the nominal capital of the company and how this is divided into shares.

mens rea means 'guilty mind' and refers to the intention element of a crime. It is the state of mind expressly or implicitly required by the definition of the offence charged. It can also be described as the required blameworthy state of mind of the defendant at the time that the *actus reus* was caused. However, the level of blameworthiness required varies from crime to crime, and the mens rea for each crime will be different. The main different levels are:

- *specific intent*, otherwise known as *intention*; this is the highest level;
- *basic intent*, otherwise known as *recklessness* and which must be sub-divided into:
  - *subjective recklessness* or *Cunningham recklessness*
  - *objective recklessness* or *Caldwell recklessness*;
- negligence.

There are also crimes for which mens rea is not required. These are called strict liability offences: just doing the actus reus will make the defendant guilty. These different levels of intention can be thought of as increasing in the need for mens rea as shown below.

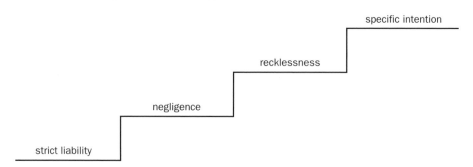

It should be noted that mens rea:

- is NOT the same as motive;
- does NOT mean in 'evil' mind;
- does NOT require knowledge that the act was forbidden by the law.

Mental Health Review Tribunal decides if the detention of a person under the Mental Health Acts is justified. An applicant to this tribunal can get legal representation from the Community Legal Service Fund.

mentally ill offenders: the mental illness of an offender will affect any criminal case against them in three different ways:

1   Because of his mental condition, the offender may not be able to understand the charge against him, to understand the difference between a guilty and a not guilty plea, to instruct lawyers or to follow the case; this is known as being unfit to plead. If it is found that the defendant is unfit to plead, the defendant cannot be tried, but the judge may make one of the orders set out below.

2   It may mean that the offender is not criminally liable for his acts. This occurs if the defendant is proved to be insane within the definition of *insanity* under the *M'Naghten rules*. Also, on a charge of murder, a person suffering from mental illness may be able to raise the defence of *diminished responsibility* and so have the charge reduced to manslaughter.

3   If a mentally ill offender is convicted of an offence (or found not guilty by reason of insanity), the courts have various options for sending that person for treatment.

The main options available to a court when dealing with a mentally ill offender are:

- supervision or probation order coupled with a requirement that the offender attends for treatment;

- a guardianship order;

- a mental health hospital order under which the offender will be detained in a mental hospital for treatment but can be discharged from there when the doctors think fit;

- a mental health hospital order with a restriction order; this order can only be made by a Crown Court and will be made where it is thought that the offender poses a risk to the public. It means that the offender can only be discharged from the hospital with the permission of the Secretary of State or the Mental Health Review Tribunal.

merchantable quality: a term used in the *Sale of Goods Act 1979* to describe the standard that goods sold in a sale of goods must reach. Since the Sale and Supply of Goods Act 1994, it has been replaced by the term *satisfactory quality*.

mere puff: a vaguely worded statement or advertisement which is not intended to be taken seriously. It is not specific enough to be an *offer*.

Case example: Carlill v Carbolic Smoke Ball Co (1893)

The company claimed that its advertisement saying that no one who used their smoke ball would get flu was a mere puff. It was held that the further statement that the company had deposited £1,000 with their bankers to show their sincerity was enough to turn a mere puff into an offer.

merits test applies to applications for legal representation. In *civil cases*, the merits test means that the applicant must satisfy the Legal Services Commission that the case has a reasonable chance of winning and that they would achieve more than a trivial advantage by taking the case. In *criminal cases*, the test is whether it is in the interests of justice for the defendant to be given legal aid. The criteria used for assessing this are set out in the Access to Justice Act 1999 and often called the *Widgery criteria* after the judge who first proposed them.

Mesher order: in family law, an order that the wife and children can stay in the family home until the youngest child finishes full-time education, or another appropriate cut-off point. The house will then be sold and the proceeds divided between the wife and husband. The order is used in divorce when settling financial provision between the parties and aims to provide the wife and children with a home without depriving the husband of all interest in the house.

See also *Martin order*.

mesne profits: benefits a landowner has lost because he has been deprived of possession of his land by a person who had no right to be there. When bringing a court action for recovery of his land, the owner can also claim for any rent he would have been able to charge, damage to his property and the costs of bringing the action.

minimum sentences are those where the Government has set a minimum length of prison sentence which must be given to certain repeat offenders. There is a minimum sentence of seven years for offenders aged 18 or over who are convicted on three separate occasions of dealing in class A drugs. There is also a minimum sentence of three years for those convicted of burglary of a residential building on three separate occasions.

Ministry of Justice: in our government there is no Ministry of Justice and so the responsibility for the legal system is divided between the *Lord Chancellor's Department* and the Home Office. In addition, the *Attorney-General* is responsible for legal advice to the government, and the *Parliamentary Counsel*, who draft Bills, are part of the Prime Minister's office. This division of duties can create problems and means that there is no particular department with responsibility for law reform. It has been suggested that all of the justice system should be brought under one Ministry of Justice, as this would make the system more efficient and more accountable. The main problem with this proposal is that the workload would be very great and there would also be a conflict of interest in some areas such as already exists in the Home Office where the Home Secretary is responsible for civil rights but also for the police.

minor: a person under the age of 18 (Family Law Reform Act 1969). There are restrictions on what a minor can do, set by Parliament; for example, it is not possible to marry under the age of 16. Also the law gives added protection to stop a minor being taking advantage of; for example, a contract made by a minor is not normally enforceable. See also *minors' contracts*.

minority protection: in company law, gives some protection to the minority of *shareholders*. The main protection comes from s459 of the Companies Act 1985, which gives a right to petition if the affairs of the company are being conducted in such a way as is unfairly prejudicial to interests of member(s). It is also possible for the minority to apply for a just and equitable *winding up* of the company. Where there is a *fraud on the minority*, there are additional remedies (see also *Foss v Harbottle rule, exceptions to*).

minors' contracts: contracts where one of the parties is under the age of 18. These contracts are covered by the Minors Contracts Act 1987 which was passed to protect minors by making many minors' contracts unenforceable. The Act states that a minor may, if he wishes, change his mind about a contract that he has entered into unless it is:

- a contract to buy *necessaries* (goods that he needs) and he has already taken delivery of them, in which case he is expected to pay a reasonable price for them, whatever the price originally agreed was;

- a *beneficial contract of service* (a contract of employment from which he is learning a skill).

Where there is a contract to buy goods which are not necessaries, the minor can change his mind but must return the goods to the seller. If he has sold the goods to someone else, the minor must give back the money he got for them or whatever he bought instead.

Minors can take out loans if they have an adult to provide a guarantee. Contracts by a minor to do with land, marriage, partnerships or the purchase of shares are enforceable unless the minor repudiates them once he reaches the age of 18.

miscarriages of justice refer to criminal cases in which a defendant is wrongly convicted. This is particularly serious where the defendant is then imprisoned for a number of years as a result of the conviction. In the 1970s, a number of miscarriages of justice occurred, often due to doubtful police interviewing techniques. Other miscarriages of justice occurred where the prosecution did not disclose that it had evidence which supported the defendant's innocence. To try and prevent further miscarriages of justice, a number of measures have been taken. The main ones are:

- The *Police and Criminal Evidence Act 1984*, which was passed to give protection to those detained for questioning. In particular, the police are required to keep records of all that happens while a person is detained for questioning (see also *custody officer*) and to tape record all interviews.

- The Criminal Procedure and Investigations Act 1996 places a duty on the prosecution to disclose to the defence any material which might 'undermine the case against the accused'.

- The setting up of the independent *Criminal Cases Review Commission* to investigate possible miscarriages of justice.

mischief rule: a rule of *statutory interpretation* which allows judges to look beyond the words of the Act of Parliament which are in dispute and to try to discover why the law was passed. The rule originates from Heydon's case (1584), which said a judge should:

- look to see what the gap in the law was which the Act of Parliament intended to put right;

- consider what remedy was intended to put that gap or 'mischief' right;

- interpret the law so as to remedy the 'mischief'.

Case example: Smith v Hughes (1960)

The Street Offences Act 1959 made it an offence for a 'prostitute to loiter or solicit in the street or public place for the purpose of prostitution'. Prostitutes who were soliciting by attracting the attention of men in the street from the windows or balcony of a house were held to be guilty of the offence even though they (the prostitutes) were in a house and not 'in the street or public place'. The judge said that the Act had been passed to protect the public from being solicited by prostitutes and as the public in the street were being solicited it did not matter that the prostitutes were in a house.

See also *literal rule* and *golden rule*.

misdirection: where a judge makes a mistake in explaining the law to the jury. If the error is serious enough to possibly have affected their decision, then the misdirection is a ground on which the defendant can appeal against his conviction.

misleading prices: under the Consumer Protection Act 1987, it is a criminal offence to give a consumer buying goods, services or accommodation misleading information about:

- price: for example where an item has a wrong price ticket and the customer is charged a higher price at the cash desk, an offence has been committed; but it is not an offence if the shop, realising its mistake, charges the lower price on the ticket at the cash desk.;

- any conditions attached to the price;

- future prices (for example, where a store says an item is for sale at a low price for only one month);

- price comparisons (for example, if an item is reduced, the ticket must give the original price and the reduced price, and the item must have been available to consumers at the original price for at least 28 consecutive days in the last six months).

misrepresentation: a false statement of existing facts as they are at the time (a *representation*) made by one party during negotiations leading to a contract which induces another party to enter into the contract. If the other party ignores the representation and enters into the contract for different reasons, there is no misrepresentation however false the statement (Attwood v Small (1838)).

The following false statements have been held not to be representations:

- a statement made immediately before the contract was made. This becomes a *term* of the contract and the injured party can sue for breach of contract.

- a statement to which special importance was given. This also becomes a term of the contract.

- a *mere puff* or vague advertising claim not expected to be taken seriously;

- a statement as to what the law is;

- an opinion rather than a statement of fact, unless given by an expert (Bissett v Wilkinson (1927));

- a statement giving the seller's intention for the future unless he knows at the time he makes it that it is not true (Edgington v Fitzmaurice (1885));

- remaining silent, unless there is a *fiduciary relationship* between the parties;

- remaining silent when information given earlier is now inaccurate because of subsequent events.

The misrepresentation may have been made:

- by mistake (*innocent misrepresentation*): injured party can rescind (cancel) contract;

- through lack of care (*negligent misrepresentation*): injured party can rescind contract and claim damages;

- deliberately (*fraudulent misrepresentation*): injured party can rescind contract and claim damages.

See also *rescission for misrepresentation*.

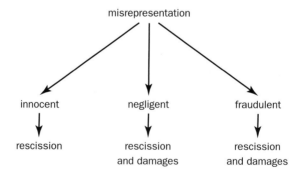

It is possible for a contract to exclude liability for innocent or negligent misrepresentation as long as this is reasonable (Misrepresentation Act 1967).

mistake may be a defence to a crime if the effect of the mistake is that:

- the defendant did not have the *mens rea* for the offence; for example, a person picks up a suitcase mistaking it for his own; in this situation, the mistake means that he is not being dishonest and so has not got the mens rea to be guilty of *theft*;

- the defendant would have been able to use another defence if the facts had been as he mistakenly believed them to be.

Case example: R v Beckford (1987)

The defendant was a police officer who was sent to arrest a man who was reported to have been threatening another person with a gun. The officer thought he saw a gun in the man's hand and shot at him, killing him. It was then discovered that the man did not in fact have a gun. The Privy Council quashed the police officer's conviction for murder on the basis that the officer's mistake in believing that the man had a gun would have given him the defence of self-defence.

The other main rules about mistake as a defence to a crime are:

- the mistake must be a mistake of fact and not of law;

- the mistake must be honestly held, though it need not be reasonable;

- a drunken mistake does not give a defendant a defence if the effect of the mistake was in relation to the need for self-defence (R v O'Grady (1987)).

mistake and its effect on a contract: a mistake made by one or both parties to a contract during its formation about an essential part of the contract so that there is no real agreement. The mistake can be:

1 *Common mistake*: both parties have made the same mistake. This makes the contract *void* unless it is a mistake as to the quality of the goods, when the contract usually remains valid.

2 *Unilateral mistake*: this can be where both parties have made mistakes, but different ones and they are at crosspurposes. This makes the contract void. It can also be where one party has made a mistake. Here the contract remains valid (except in some cases of *mistake as to the identity* of the other party).

mistake as to identity: usually occurs where a person enters into a contract with someone who gives a false name. The contract will normally be valid because there was an intention to enter into a contract with that person, whatever his name; the only mistake that has been made is about his creditworthiness. It may be *void* if the intention had been to deal only with a specific person. It is easier to show this if the negotiations leading up to the contract are through the post (Cundy v Lindsay (1878)) or at a distance (Shogun Finance Ltd v Hudson (2001)).

Case example: Ingram v Little (1961)

The sellers of a car refused to accept a cheque from the buyer until he proved his identity. When this turned out to be false, the contract was held to be void as the sellers had intended to contract with one person only.

Case example: Lewis v Avery (1971)

The buyer of a car paid by cheque. To persuade the seller to let him take away the car before the cheque was cleared, he showed false identification papers. It was held that the seller had intended to deal with the person in front of him and the contract was valid.

There is very little difference between the two cases, and in Lewis v Avery, the Court of Appeal indicated that only in exceptional cases would the contract be void. In both cases, if the buyer of the car had not already sold the car on to someone else, the seller would have been able to claim *misrepresentation*.

mistake in equity: in contract law, a substantial mistake made by the parties to a contract which does not make the contract *void* under *common mistake* or *unilateral mistake* but the court considers it unfair to uphold the contract. Established in Solle v Butcher (1950), it was overruled by the Court of Appeal in 2002 (Great Peace Shipping v Tsaviris) and is no longer applied.

mitigation in a criminal case: a speech made when the defendant has pleaded guilty or been found guilty. It involves explaining to the court circumstances about the crime, the defendant or the defendant's family which might persuade the judge (or magistrates) to give the defendant a more lenient sentence. For example, the fact that a defendant has pleaded guilty allows a court to reduce the sentence that would otherwise have been passed by up to one third.

mitigation of loss in contract law: keeping losses to a minimum. When a contract has been breached, the innocent party is expected to do what is reasonable to keep his losses to a minimum, for example by finding an alternative buyer. When damages are assessed, it will be assumed that he has done this, and they will be limited to any extra cost incurred because of the breach, e.g. the cost of re-advertising the goods, any shortfall in the new price.

M'Naghten Rules: rules which set out when a defendant may be able to use the defence of *insanity* to a criminal charge. The Rules date from 1843 and were formulated by the judges in the House of Lords after M'Naghten had been found not guilty of murder when, suffering from mental illness which caused delusions, he attempted to shoot Sir Robert Peel but instead killed his secretary.

The Rules state that everyone is presumed sane until the contrary is proved. This means that it is for the defence to prove that the defendant is insane. In order to establish that the defendant is insane, the M'Naghten Rules state that it must be shown that he was 'labouring under such a defect of reason, from disease of the mind, as not to know the nature and quality of the act he was doing or, if he did know it, that he did not know he was doing wrong'.

mobility clause: a term in a *contract of employment* under which an employer can require the employee to work at a different place. The employee is legally obliged to accept such a change, unless the employer acts unreasonably in all the circumstances.

Case example: United Bank Ltd v Akhtar (1989)

A bank employee had a term in his contract which said that 'the bank may from time to time require an employee to be transferred temporarily to any place of business which the bank may have in the UK'. The bank gave the employee only six days' notice that he would be required to move from their Leeds branch to the Birmingham branch. It was held that such short notice was unreasonable.

mode of trial hearing: held at the *Magistrates' Court* to decide whether a defendant charged with a *triable either way offence* should be tried by the magistrates or at the Crown Court. See also *plea before venue*.

Montesquieu's theory of the separation of powers: the theory that there are three primary functions of a state and that the only way to safeguard the liberty of citizens is by keeping these three functions separate. In this way, the power exercised by each of the 'arms' of the state is independent of the other and each can keep a check on the others so that there should be no abuse of power. The three arms of state are:

- the *legislature*, who makes the law (this is Parliament);
- the executive, who administers the law (this is government departments and ministers); and
- the *judiciary*, who applies the law.

Some countries, such as the United States of America, have a written constitution which enforces this theory. In the United Kingdom, there is no written constitution but, nevertheless, the three arms of state are roughly separated, with Parliament being the legislative body, the Cabinet being the executive and the judiciary being independent of these two. The main criticism in our system concerns the *Lord Chancellor*, whose position overlaps all three functions.

morality and law overlap but are not the same. Morality is a set of rules or values that are held by a community, and such moral standards are likely to have an effect on the law. However, the law may allow conduct which some people would consider is morally wrong. An example of this is the Abortion Act 1967 which allows abortions to take place under certain circumstances. Some people regard abortion as morally wrong. On the other hand, the law may forbid certain conduct which is not viewed as morally wrong. The relationship between law and morality is best thought of as overlapping.

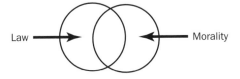

A major debate is whether euthanasia (mercy killing) should be allowed where a person is terminally ill. Many people believe that it is immoral to deliberately kill someone, even if that person is seriously ill and unlikely to recover. The law does not permit a direct act which kills such a patient, yet in Airedale NHS Trust v Bland, (1993) the House of Lords ruled that medical staff could withdraw feeding tubes from a patient who was in a persistent vegetative state. Stopping feeding the patient would inevitably cause him to die, but it was held that it was in his best interests to remove life support systems from him and allow him to die naturally.

Some academics believe that there should be a clear separation of law and morality (see also *Hart-Devlin debate*).

mortgage: in land law, a relationship between a land owner and a money lender such as a building society where the building society lends money in return for some kind of security in the property, usually a charge on the property. It can also be used to refer to the security that is given to the money lender.

mortgagee: a person or institution, such as a building society, which lends a land owner money in return for a charge on the land.

mortgagor: a person who borrows money in return for a charge on his land.

multi-discipline partnerships refers to partnerships between solicitors and/or barristers and other professionals such as accountants. The idea behind them is that clients would be able to get all the advice they needed from one place in a 'one-stop' shop. Section 66 of the Courts and Legal Services Act 1990 allows such partnerships to be formed, but the governing bodies of solicitors and barristers still retain rules which forbid this type of partnership.

multi-track cases: those where the dispute involves a claim of over £15,000 or lower claims of unusual complexity. Allocation to this track will be made by a judge, who will set the timetable for the case. The judge will effectively be a case-manager, directing and controlling the legal work conducted by both sides and monitoring the procedures adopted.

murder: the unlawful killing of a human being with *malice aforethought*. The points that must be proved to establish a murder charge are that:

- the defendant killed the victim (see also *causation in criminal law*);
- the killing was unlawful, i.e. there was no legal justification for it, such as *self-defence*;
- the victim was a person 'in being'; this means that killing a foetus is not murder, though injuring a child in the womb so that, although it is born alive, it then dies of its injury could be murder (Attorney-General's Reference (No 3 of 1994));
- the defendant must intend to kill or cause grievous bodily harm; this is what is meant by malice aforethought; if the defendant intends to kill or cause grievous bodily harm to one person, but actually kills someone else, the defendant is still said to have intention under the principle of *transferred malice*.

See also *foresight of consequences*.

mutual wills: wills made by two or more people in which they leave their property to the same beneficiaries and they agree not to revoke the wills. This can occur with a husband and wife, where both make a will leaving their property to each other, and after both have died, the property is to go to their daughter.

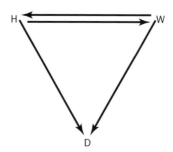

The problem is that the law recognises that any will can be revoked (cancelled) or changed at any time during the testator's lifetime so that, after one of the will-makers has died, the survivor can change his or her will and break the mutual agreement. In these circumstances, the law may decide that there is a *constructive trust* so that those who inherit under the new will have to give the benefit of the property to whomever would have inherited under the mutual wills.

Do you need revision help and advice?

Go to pages 259–99 for a range of revision appendices that include plenty of exam advice and tips.

natural justice: the idea that certain basic rules are fundamental to any decision-making process. The two main rules of natural justice are:

- no one should be a judge in his own case;
- both sides have a right to be heard.

If there is a breach of these rules of natural justice, the aggrieved party can apply for *judicial review* of the decision concerned.

Case example: In Re Pinochet Ugarte (1999)

The House of Lords set aside an earlier decision that General Pinochet could be extradited (sent) to Spain for trial on charges of torture which occurred while he was head of state of Chile. The decision was set aside because one of the judges was a director of the charitable arm of Amnesty. Amnesty had been made a party to the case and argued for the extradition. The House of Lords said that this gave the judge an interest in the outcome of the case and so he should not have taken part in deciding the matter.

natural law: based on the theory that law and morality should coincide. It assumes that there is a law which comes from some divine power and that this ought to be the law. If law does not follow morality, some theorists would say that the law should not be obeyed. The opposite point of view is held by positivists (see also the *Hart-Fuller debate*).

necessaries: in contract law, goods which the buyer needs at the time of purchase and which are suitable for his 'condition in life'. More expensive items will be considered necessaries if the buyer comes from a wealthy background (Nash v Inman (1908)). A minor or a person who is drunk or suffering from a mental disorder will be bound by a contract to buy necessaries but will only be expected to pay a reasonable price for them.

necessity as a defence to a criminal charge: the idea that the defendant's criminal act is justified as the defendant had to do it to avoid a worse evil. Although, in theory, it is accepted that there should be such a defence, in practice the courts have scarcely ever recognised it.

Case example: R v Dudley and Stevens (1881)

The defendants and two others were adrift in an open boat after being shipwrecked. After several days without food or water, the defendants killed and ate the cabin boy. This enabled them to survive until they were picked up by another boat. At their trial for murder, they pleaded necessity, as without killing the boy, they would have died. The court rejected the defence of necessity.

In recent cases, there has been some recognition that the defence may be successful. For example, in Re F (1990), the court was asked to declare that it would be lawful to sterilise a mental patient who had insufficient understanding to give consent to the operation. Lord Goff said that the common law principle of necessity could justify action which would be otherwise unlawful. In Re A (conjoined twins) (2000) the Court of Appeal were asked to rule on whether it was lawful to go ahead with an operation to separate conjoined twins when it was known that the operation would kill the weaker twin. One of the judges considered the defence of necessity and referred back to the four factors given in Stephen's Digest of Criminal Law in 1883. These factors are:

- the act was done only in order to avoid consequences which could not otherwise be avoided;
- those consequences, if they happened, would have inflicted inevitable and irreparable evil;
- that no more was done than was reasonably necessary for that purpose;
- that the evil inflicted by it was not disproportionate to the evil avoided.

The court held that the death of the weaker twin could be justified on the basis of necessity, since without the separation both twins would die. The courts have also developed a defence of *duress of circumstances*, which appears to be necessity under another name.

necessity in tort: a defence which is used in *trespass*. The defendant will not be liable if he can show he acted as he did without the consent of the claimant to stop further harm happening, for example, going onto a neighbour's land to put out a dangerous fire or treating an unconscious person to save their life.

negative equity: the position when the value of a *mortgage* on property is more than the value of the property. This situation will occur when the price of houses, flats, etc. goes down, after a mortgage has been obtained on the higher price.

negligence: a type of *tort* under which a person whose property has been damaged or who has suffered injury through someone else's careless action can claim *damages* (compensation) from him. To bring a claim, the injured person must show that:

- the person who caused the injury had a responsibility towards him in law (he was owed a *duty of care*);
- the person who caused the injury had acted in a negligent way (there was a *breach of the duty of care*);
- the injuries were a direct result of these negligent actions (see also *causation in negligence*).

Usually the claim is for physical injury to the person or damage to his property or for psychiatric injury (*nervous shock*), but occasionally a claim can be made for financial loss on its own (pure *economic loss*).

Defences to a claim in negligence are:

- *volenti non fit injuria*: the claimant had willingly taken the risk of being hurt;
- *contributory negligence*: the claimant was partly to blame for the accident or his injuries;
- *ex turpi causa non oritur actio*: the claimant was injured while carrying out an illegal activity;
- *inevitable accident*: no reasonable precautions could have prevented the accident.

negligent misrepresentation: in contract law, a *misrepresentation* made by one party to a contract to the other which has been made without bothering to check its truth. When this has happened, the person who has suffered loss as a result can rescind (cancel) the contract and claim *damages* under the Misrepresentation Act 1967. The Act makes it easy to bring a claim, and the defendant will be liable unless he can show that:

- he believed that what he said was true;
- he had reasonable grounds for believing that it was true.

The Act does not cover situations where the misrepresentation was made by someone who is not party to the contract or where the contract was *void ab initio* and claims must be made under common law instead. The claimant will be successful if he can show:

- the person making the representation had special skill; and
- he knew that the claimant would rely on the statement; and
- it was reasonable for the claimant to rely on it.

Damages will be assessed on a tort basis rather than a contract basis (see also *damages in contract* and *damages in tort*).

negligent misstatement: a statement, written or oral, which is inaccurate because the person making it has been negligent and which causes the person who relies on it to suffer financial loss. A claim can be brought for negligent misstatement where:

- the defendant made an inaccurate statement; this must be a considered statement rather than a casual remark and one which gives the benefit of his skill and judgement;
- the defendant knew or ought to have known when making the statement, that the claimant would rely on it;
- the claimant does rely on it and suffers financial loss;
- the claimant used the information for the purposes for which it was prepared;
- it is fair, just and reasonable to impose a duty of care on the defendant (*Hedley Byrne v Heller (1961)* and *Caparo Industries plc v Dickman (1990)*).

The number of people who can claim for negligent misstatement is more restricted than those who can bring a claim for negligence. The relationship between the claimant and defendant must be so close as to be equivalent to contract (a *special relationship*). Where a contract does exist between the parties, a claim can also be made for *misrepresentation*.

negotiable instrument: a written promise to pay a certain amount of money which can be given to someone else who will then be able to enforce the promise although he was not a party to the original agreement.

negotiation: the process of trying to come to an agreement, it can be used to avoid a dispute and lengthy court proceedings. The negotiation can be directly between the parties or may be done by lawyers on their behalf.

neighbour principle in negligence: used to define to whom a legal responsibility (*duty of care*) is owed. In *Donoghue v Stevenson (1932)*, Lord Atkin said that a duty of care was owed to a neighbour and that neighbours are: 'persons who are so closely and directly affected by my act that I ought reasonably to have them in contemplation as being so affected when I am directing my mind to the acts or omissions which are called in question'.

Once it has been established that the claimant was within the reasonable contemplation of the defendant, the claimant must then show the following to establish that the defendant owed him a duty of care:

- *proximity*;
- that it is just, fair and reasonable to hold that there is a duty of care;
- there are no public policy reasons for deciding that a duty of care should not exist.

See also *duty of care in negligence*.

nemo dat quod non habet: a Latin phrase meaning 'nobody can give what they have not got themselves'. This applies in contract law where a person who buys goods only becomes the legal owner of them if the seller has legal ownership (*good title*) himself. If he does not, the buyer will not become the legal owner of the goods despite the fact he has paid money for them. For example: a thief steals goods and then sells them. Because the thief does not have legal ownership, the buyer cannot become the legal owner and the goods remain the property of the original owner and must be returned to him.

nemo judex in res sua: a rule of *natural justice* which means that no man should be a judge in his own case.

nervous shock in negligence: psychiatric damage, rather than just emotional upset, caused by the sudden sight or sound of a horrifying event (Alcock v Chief Constable of South Yorkshire (1991)). The right to claim depends on whether the victim was actively involved in the event or a passive observer.

Primary victim: Actively involved	Secondary victim: Passive observer who just sees the event
Claim can be made if:	Claim can be made if:
- the claimant was exposed to physical danger or reasonably believed himself to be exposed to physical danger; and - it could be reasonably foreseen that someone in his position would suffer physical harm; and - he suffered nervous shock.	- the claimant saw a close relative injured with whom he has a relationship of 'love and affection'; and - he was physically close to the scene of the accident; and - he saw the accident happen or the results shortly afterwards; and - he suffered nervous shock as a result.

net effect approach: used in divorce when deciding on a division of financial assets. The court may decide to look at the end result of any division rather than relying on a mathematical division such as the *one-third principle*.

Newton hearing occurs where a defendant has pleaded guilty to a criminal charge but does not accept the prosecution's version of the facts of his criminal act. The court will hear evidence so that it can decide what the real version is. This can be important, as it may affect the length of sentence which is imposed on the defendant.

no win, no fee agreements are conditional fee agreements where solicitor and client agree that if the case is lost there will be no fee, but if the case is won the client will pay the normal fee plus a success fee.

nolle prosequi means 'do not prosecute' and is an order that the Attorney-General can make to prevent a prosecution from continuing. In 1998, there was criticism when this power was used to stop proceedings against a judge who had been charged with fraud. The judge had been tried, but the jury had failed to reach a verdict. The nolle prosequi prevented the prosecution from seeking a re-trial.

nominal damages: a small amount of money awarded to a winning claimant in a case. This recognises that his rights have been infringed, but he has not suffered any real financial loss. Nominal damages may be awarded in cases of trespass where no actual damage has occurred. They may also be given in *defamation* cases where it decided that the statement was defamatory, but that it did not seriously harm the claimant's reputation.

non-compensatory damages: damages in tort which are not directly related to the actual loss suffered. They are:

- *contemptuous damages* to show that the court considers the claimant should not have brought the case;
- *nominal damages* to show there has been a technical infringement of the claimant's rights but he has suffered no loss;
- *exemplary damages* or *punitive damages* to punish the defendant for committing the tort or to deprive him of any benefit he has gained by it.

non-dangerous species: a species that is not a *dangerous species* under the *Animals Act 1971*. The *keeper* of a non-dangerous animal will not be liable unless he knew that the animal had characteristics that would make it likely to cause that type of damage (or that any damage it might cause would be likely to be severe) or he knew that that species was likely to cause that type of damage at a certain times (or that any damage caused would be likely to be severe).

non est factum: a Latin phrase meaning 'not my deed', used where a party to a contract wants to show he should not be bound by it because he did not understand what he was signing. The contract will be declared *void* if he can show:

- he was unable to understand a contract document without it being explained; and
- the document he signed was substantially different from what he thought he was signing; and
- he did not act carelessly.

A plea of non est factum is rarely successful, but the person signing may also be able to argue that there had been *misrepresentation* or *undue influence*.

non-insane automatism: a defence to a criminal charge. A defendant in a state of non-insane automatism has a complete defence and will be found not guilty. This is because he committed the act while he was not conscious of what he was doing because of some external factor, such as being hit on the head by a brick.

Case example: R v Quick (1973)

The defendant was a diabetic who assaulted another person while suffering from hypoglycaemia (low blood sugar) because of the insulin he had taken to control the diabetes. It was held that the drug was an external factor which had caused him to be in an automatic state and that he was not guilty.

If the *automatism* is self-induced, then the defendant will not have a defence to crimes of basic intent where recklessness is sufficient for the *mens rea* of the crime (R v Bailey (1983)). It is also important to distinguish between non-insane automatism and *insane automatism*, as the latter is caused by an internal factor and held to come under the rules of *insanity*.

non-molestation order: a court order used in family law prohibiting a family member, cohabitee or ex-cohabitee molesting other members of the family. Molesting is any form of serious pestering or harassment or any form of conduct of which the court disapproves.

Case example: Horner v Horner (1982)

A husband was held to have molested his wife when he repeatedly made disparaging remarks about her on the telephone to the school where she taught. He also put up disparaging posters on the railings outside the school.

non-pecuniary damages: in tort, damages that cannot be precisely itemised, for example, damages for pain and suffering or *loss of amenity*.

noscitur a sociis: a rule of language used in *statutory interpretation*. It means that a word is 'known by the company it keeps' and indicates that the surrounding words and phrases have to be considered in deciding what a particular word or phrase means.

Case example: Inland Revenue Commissioners v Frere (1965)

A section of an Act set out rules for 'interest, annuities or other annual interest'. It was held that the word 'interest' meant 'annual interest' as the rest of the words were all to do with annual interest.

novus actus interveniens: a Latin phrase meaning 'an intervening new act'. It is used in *negligence* to refer to an act which happens after the original negligent act which breaks the *chain of causation* so that the defendant is not liable for the claimant's injuries even though he started off the chain of events which led to them. This second act can be:

- a negligent act by a third party (unless it is a natural and probable consequence of the defendant's actions);
- a negligent act by the claimant if he has acted unreasonably;
- an illness unrelated to the original injury (Jobling v Associated Dairies (1982));
- a natural event, e.g. a storm.

Case example: Rouse v Squires (1973)

The defendant caused an accident on a motorway through his negligent driving. The claimant, who was assisting at the scene of the accident, was killed by the negligent driving of a second car driver. It was held that the defendant's driving was an operative cause of the claimant's death because it was very likely that someone would assist at the scene and that they would be exposed to risk in doing so.

Where the claimant is a *rescuer*, the courts are very reluctant to find that he acted so unreasonably that his actions broke the chain of causation.

nuisance: an act, or more usually, a series of acts by one person which interferes with the life of another. There are two types of nuisance:

- *private nuisance* occurs when a person's use of his land is unreasonably affected by activities carried out by a neighbour on the neighbour's property;

- *public nuisance* occurs when a person carries out an act which materially affects the comfort and convenience of a whole class of Her Majesty's subjects.

Private nuisance	Public nuisance
• Nuisance may only affect one person.	• Nuisance must affect a whole group of people.
• Person affected brings claim.	• Person particularly affected brings claim OR Attorney-General can bring a criminal prosecution.
• Claimant can only claim if his enjoyment of his own land is interfered with.	• Claimant can claim for injury incurred on land which is not his; this is often the highway.
• Claimant can claim for physical injury or for loss of enjoyment.	• Claimant normally only claims for physical injury and must show that he suffered more than anyone else in the group affected.

Case example: Halsey v Esso Petroleum Co Ltd (1961)

Acid fumes from Esso's refinery damaged washing drying in the claimant's garden and his car which was parked in the road in front of his house. The claimant was able to sue in private nuisance for the damage to the washing which was on his land and in public nuisance for the damage to his car which was not on his land.

nuisance and trespass to land, a comparison

Nuisance	Trespass to land
• Caused by the defendant's actions on his own land.	• Defendant comes onto the claimant's land or places objects on the claimant's land.
• Defendant normally owner or tenant of nearby land.	• Defendant does not have to be an occupier of land.
• There usually has to be a series of acts unless physical damage has been caused.	• One act is sufficient.
• Can be a crime if enough people affected.	• Only a crime if the trespasser intends to disrupt a lawful activity.

nullity (decree of): a declaration that a marriage is *void*. It is different from divorce, which brings a valid marriage to an end, but in many ways the effects are the same, in that the parties can remarry, children are legitimate and parties can claim maintenance.

Many applications for a decree of nullity are brought on religious grounds by people who do not approve of divorce, but divorce is often more straightforward and less embarrassing. In 1995, there were 153,317 divorces and 516 nullity decrees.

What other subjects are you studying?

A–Zs cover 18 different subjects. See the inside back cover for a list of all the titles in the series and how to order.

obiter dicta means other things said. It refers to any part of the judge's speech at the end of a case which does not form a *binding precedent*. The part in which the judge sets out his legal principles for deciding the case is called the *ratio decidendi*. The remainder of the judgment is the obiter dicta. Obiter dicta can be persuasive precedent; this means that subsequent judges may decide to follow it, even though they do not have to.

Case example: R v Howe (1987)

The House of Lords decided that duress could not be a defence to a charge of murder; in the course of the judgment, they also commented that duress should not be available as a defence to a charge of attempted murder. This was only obiter dicta, as the case of Howe was about a murder and not about attempted murder. In R v Gotts (1992), a defendant who was charged with attempted murder tried to rely on the defence of duress; the Court of Appeal said he could not as they thought the obiter dicta in R v Howe was right. They did not have to follow it, but they were 'persuaded' by it.

objective recklessness in criminal law, is where the defendant does not realise there is a risk of certain consequences occurring as a result of his actions, but an ordinary, prudent person would have seen that risk (see also *Caldwell recklessness*).

objective test: a test used in contract, tort and criminal cases where the court asks, 'Would the ordinary person have realised …?' It is irrelevant what the defendant thought at the time. If the ordinary person would have realised, the defendant will be liable or guilty even if he had not realised himself the consequences of his actions. When the word 'reasonable' is used, the court will use the objective test, e.g. 'reasonably foreseeable' in *duty of care* and when assessing *damages in contract* (see also *Caldwell recklessness*).

oblique intention: a concept in criminal law referring to the situation where an offender has one aim in mind but, in order to achieve that aim, also causes other consequences. He does not have *direct intention* to cause these other consequences, but he may have oblique intention. For example, if he puts a bomb on a plane to blow up the cargo so that he can obtain the insurance money on it, that is his direct intention. However, he realises that when the plane explodes in mid-air, the crew and passengers on the plane will be killed; this is his oblique intention. He does not want it to happen; it is not his main aim. See also *foresight of consequences*.

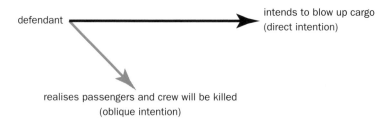

obtaining a money transfer by deception: an offence under s15A of the Theft Act 1968. A person is guilty of this offence if, by deception, he causes an amount of money to be debited from one account and, as a result, an amount of money to be credited to another account. The section was added to the Theft Act 1968 by the Theft Act 1996. This was because there had been a ruling by the House of Lords that causing money to be transferred in this way was not always an offence of *obtaining property by deception,* as paper transactions were not within the meaning of the word 'property'.

obtaining a pecuniary advantage by deception: an offence under s16 of the Theft Act 1968. Pecuniary advantage has a very narrow meaning. It covers situations where the defendant:

- is allowed to borrow money by way of overdraft or take out an insurance policy or annuity;

- earns money (or more money) through a job;

- wins money by betting.

If, as a result of a deception and meaning to be dishonest, the defendant does any of these then he is guilty of the offence. An example would be where the defendant lies about his qualifications to obtain a job.

obtaining property by deception: an offence under s15 of the Theft Act 1968. To be guilty, the defendant must:

- use deception; this can be by words or by conduct, e.g. using someone else's credit card and pretending to be that person;

- obtain property belonging to another; this includes any goods or money;

- do this *dishonestly* and intending to deprive the other person permanently of the property.

obtaining services by deception: an offence under s1 of the Theft Act 1978. 'Services' means anything done by another person which is a benefit to the defendant. This includes very ordinary things such as a haircut, gardening work, window cleaning or the use of a room in a hotel. If the defendant obtains such a service *dishonestly* and by deception, then the offence has been committed.

occupation order: a court order used in family law to exclude a member of a family from the family home in order to protect the rest of the family from their violence or severe harassment. The order states who is entitled to be in the home and who is to be excluded. The exclusion can also be extended to cover an area around the home. The order is intended to be a short-term measure until any disputes about the home are settled by the court in *divorce* or other proceedings, but an order can last indefinitely. The factors that the court will take into account are:

- the housing needs and resources of both parties and any relevant child;

- the financial resources of both parties;

- the likely effect of any order on the family's health, safety and well-being;

- the conduct of the parties.

The court must exclude a family member who is likely to cause significant harm to other family members, unless that person can show that they, and any children living with them, would suffer greater harm than the victim by being made to leave.

Where the parties are unmarried and the person wanting the order has no legal rights in the home (e.g. is not the owner or joint owner or a tenant or has not contributed financially to the purchase of the house), the order can only last for one year. When making its decision, the court will look at the nature of the couple's relationship and who has parental responsibility for any children. Greater rights are given to applicants who have a legal right to the home.

occupier: in *occupiers' liability*, any person who has control over premises. This can be:

- the owner who occupies the premises;
- a tenant;
- a licensee;
- anyone who has right to limit access to premises, e.g. building contractors on a building site.

More than one person may be responsible for premises at the same time.

Case example: Wheat v Lacon & Co Ltd (1966)

A public house was owned by a brewery with a manager having a licence to live on the premises. The claimant was fatally injured by a fall in the manager's living accommodation. It was held that both the brewery and the manager were occupiers under the Occupiers' Liability Act 1957.

occupiers' liability: a term used in *tort* to describe the duty that the *occupier* of *premises* has to anyone who comes onto his land to make sure they are not injured by anything that is there. The occupier has a greater responsibility towards *visitors* than towards *trespassers*. These duties are set out in two different Acts: the Occupiers Liability Act 1957 and the Occupiers Liability Act 1984.

Duty owed to visitors	Duty owed to trespassers (non-visitors)
• Occupiers' Liability Act 1957.	• Occupiers' Liability Act 1984.
• Occupier has a duty to all visitors.	• Occupier has a duty if:
	– he is aware or reasonably believes that a danger exists;
• Occupier has a duty to take such care as is reasonable in all the circumstances to see that the visitor will be reasonably safe (s2(2)). Case law shows that this is much higher than the duty to trespassers.	– he knows or reasonably believes that there are likely to be non-visitors on his land;
	– the risk is one which he may reasonably be expected to offer the non-visitor some protection against (s1(5)).
• Occupier expected to take greater care of child visitors (s2(3)(a)).	• Occupier has a duty to take such care as is reasonable in all the circumstances to see that the non-visitor does not suffer injury on the premises.

Continued on next page

Duty owed to visitors	Duty owed to trespassers (non-visitors)
• Occupier responsible for physical injury to visitor and damage to his property.	• Occupier expected to take greater care of child non-visitors (BRB v Herrington (1972)). • Occupier responsible for physical injury to non-visitor only.

An occupier is not responsible for:

- injury to a visitor caused by defective work carried out by specialist independent contractors he has employed, provided he has taken reasonable steps to ensure they are suitably qualified and he has checked that their work has been properly carried out so far as the ordinary person can tell;

- injury to specialist independent contractors he has employed, where they have been carrying out work which they specialise in and which carries particular risks which they ought to know about.

offensive weapon: any article made or adapted for use for causing injury to the person, or intended for such use by the person having it with him. This last part makes the definition very wide ranging, as it includes items such as screwdrivers or metal combs, if the prosecution can show that the defendant intended to use it to cause injury.

offer: a definite proposal to enter into a contract. The *offeror* intends the offer to form a binding contract if that offer is accepted by the person to whom it is made. Offers can be:

- oral

- written

- by conduct

If the details of the proposal are vague or the person making it only intends to start negotiations, it is an *invitation to treat* rather than an offer. A *reward poster or advertisement* is an offer rather than an invitation to treat if the terms are clear (*Carlill v Carbolic Smokeball Co (1893)*). Goods on the shelves of self-service stores, advertisements in newspapers, catalogues and an invitation from an auctioneer for bids have been held not to be offers.

offer of amends: a defence in *defamation*. It is only available to someone who took all reasonable care, acted without malice and who did not realise the statement he published was defamatory or realise circumstances that would make the statement defamatory by *innuendo* (*unintentional defamation*).

If the defendant has offered to:

- make a suitable correction of the statement;

- make a sufficient apology to the defamed person;

- publish a correction and apology in a suitable manner;

- pay compensation and any legal costs;

and this has been refused, he will have a defence if he is then sued for defamation.

offeree: a person to whom an *offer* is made in contract law.

offeror: a person who makes an *offer* in contract law.

Office for the Supervision of Solicitors: responsible for investigating complaints against solicitors such as inefficiency, delay or overcharging. It was set up in 1996 to replace the

Solicitors' Complaints Bureau which was itself criticised for inefficiency and delay. The Office for Supervision of Solicitors is funded by the solicitors themselves and is, therefore, thought not to be sufficiently independent when investigating complaints.

Office of Fair Trading: set up by the Fair Trading Act 1973 to:

- review current trading practices and make proposals for reform;
- pursue traders who are acting in a way that is detrimental to consumers' interests and, if necessary, take proceedings against them in the Restrictive Practices Court;
- license credit suppliers.

The head of the Office of Fair Trading is the *Director-General of Fair Trading*.

officious bystander test: in deciding whether a term is implied into a contract the court will ask itself, 'If an officious bystander was listening to the two parties to a *contract* discussing its terms and pointed out to them that a *term* should be included, would they have both thought it so obvious that they would have turned on him in irritation and said 'Oh, of course'?' It is used by a court to decide whether a term should be inserted into a contract by the court, even though that point was not discussed before the contract was made. If the court is satisfied that the only reason the point had not been discussed was because it was so obvious to both parties that it did not need discussing, and it was the intention of both parties that the term should be included, it will be implied into the contract by the court (The Moorcock (1889)).

ombudsman: a person who has been appointed to investigate complaints about a certain area, such as local administration, banking or the health service. An ombudsman can only investigate matters, such as inefficiency, delay or rudeness, for which there is no legal remedy. If the complainant could take the matter to court, e.g. for *breach of contract*, then the ombudsman has no power to deal with that complaint. See also *Parliamentary Commissioner for Administration*.

omissions as actus reus: in most cases, the failure to act does not make the person criminally liable. This was clearly explained by Stephen, a legal writer in the 19th century, when he wrote:

> 'A sees B drowning and is able to save him by holding out his hand. A abstains from doing so in order that B may be drowned. A has committed no offence.'

There are, however, some exceptions when an omission or failure to act will make the person criminally liable. These are where the defendant:

- is under a contractual duty to do something, especially if the failure to act is likely to put people's lives in danger;
- is closely related to the victim, so that the law holds the defendant responsible for caring for the victim; this is usually a parent/child relationship where the parents are under a duty to feed and care for young children;
- has undertaken to care for another who is incapable of looking after themselves; failure to care or to summon help for that person may make the defendant criminally liable if the person dies through lack of care (R v Stone and Dobinson (1977));
- is under a duty to act because of holding a public office;
- has caused a dangerous situation to arise; in this case the defendant is only under a duty to do something where it is possible; e.g. call the fire brigade.

A statutory crime can also make a person liable for failing to act. An example is failing to provide a specimen of breath for a breath test under the Road Traffic Acts.

one-third principle: was used in *divorce* when deciding on a division of financial assets. The court would, as a starting off point, divide the capital assets and income of both parties so that the husband received two thirds and the wife received one third. The court would then take into account the factors set out in s25 of the Matrimonial Causes Act 1973. Since *White v White* greater emphasis has been placed on a more equal division of assets.

Orders in Council: a form of *delegated legislation* made by the Queen and Privy Council. Orders in Council allow the government to make law when Parliament is not sitting and there is a need for law as an emergency.

original precedent: a decision on a point of law in a case where that particular point of law has never been decided in any case before (see also *judicial precedent*).

ouster order (or injunction): a court order used in family law to stop an abusive family member entering the family home. Sometimes the order also forbids him from coming within a certain distance of the home. This order has now been replaced by an *occupation order* under the *Family Law Act 1996*.

out-of-court settlement: an agreement between the parties in a *civil case* which resolves their dispute. Such an agreement may be made any time before the judge gives the final decision. In most cases, the lawyers for the parties will try to reach a negotiated settlement. Sometimes, an agreement will be reached quickly; in other cases, the settlement will not be made until the parties are actually at court waiting for the trial to start. This late agreement is often referred to as a 'court door' settlement.

outraging public decency: a crime created by judicial decisions. It is something which goes beyond offending or even shocking people. In R v Gibson (1991), the defendants were convicted of this offence when an exhibit of a modelled head in an art gallery had earrings made from real, freeze-dried human foetuses.

overruling: a term used in *judicial precedent* where a court states that the legal rule (precedent) made by a previous court is wrong and creates a different legal rule in its place. The earlier precedent is said to have been overruled. A court higher in the court hierarchy can overrule a precedent set by a lower court, for example, the House of Lords can overrule a precedent set by the Court of Appeal. In addition, the House of Lords can use the *practice statement* to overrule its own past decisions.

PACE stands for *Police and Criminal Evidence Act 1984*.

Package Travel Package Holidays and Package Tours Regulations 1992 cover packages which are prearranged at an inclusive price and cover over 24 hours or an overnight stay. The regulations state:

- package organisers and retailers must not give misleading descriptions;
- the organisers and retailers are strictly liable for the performance of the package whether they provide the service themselves or someone else does;
- any member of the party can sue, not just the person who booked the package;
- breach of the regulations can lead to both a civil case and a criminal prosecution.

There are also regulations for ensuring the security of deposits paid and the repatriation of consumers in the event of insolvency of the retailer or organiser.

para-legal services are those provided by people who have had some training in law but are not fully qualified. Examples are *legal executives* and *licensed conveyancers*.

parental responsibility towards a child is a duty to:

- take care of the child's physical well-being;
- ensure the child is educated up to the age of 16;
- maintain the child financially.

Where both parents were married to each other at the time of conception or birth, they share parental responsibility equally. Where the parents are unmarried, the mother has sole parental responsibility (except for maintenance) unless a court has made a *parental responsibility order* or a *parental responsibility agreement* has been negotiated. Normally, the order or agreement extends parental responsibility to the father, but other people such as a grandmother can also be given parental responsibility.

Parental responsibility only comes to an end when the child:

- is adopted; or
- becomes 18; or
- marries; or
- joins the armed forces.

parental responsibility agreement: an agreement between the unmarried parents of a child that the father will have *parental responsibility*. The agreement must be in a set form and the parents' signatures must be witnessed by a magistrate or a court official. The form is then filed at the Principal Registry of the Family Division of the High Court. Once the agreement has been signed, it can only be cancelled by a court order. See also *parental responsibility order*.

parental responsibility order: a court order giving parental responsibility for a child to the unmarried father. The effect is to put the father in the same position as if the child's parents had been married. The father applies to the court, and an order will normally be made as long as this will promote the child's welfare (see also *welfare principle*). Where unmarried parents are in agreement, they may also apply together for the father to have parental responsibility under a *parental responsibility agreement*.

Parental responsibility can also be given by the court to anyone involved with the child, e.g. grandparents, so that several people can have parental responsibility at the same time.

parenting order: this is intended to offer training and support to parents to help change their children's offending behaviour. In this way it is more practical than the existing provisions which merely make a parent responsible for their child's offending behaviour. A court may make a parenting order under s8 of the Crime and Disorder Act 1998 where:

- the court makes a child safety order;
- the court makes an anti-social behaviour order (or sex offender order) in respect of a child;
- a child or young person is convicted of an offence;
- a parent is convicted of an offence relating to truancy under the Education Act 1996.

An order should only be made if it is desirable in the interests of preventing the conduct which gave rise to the order.

Where a person under the age of 16 is convicted of an offence, the court should make a parenting order unless it is satisfied that it is not desirable in the interests of preventing the conduct which gave rise to the order. In this case the court must state in open court that it is not satisfied and explain why not.

The parent can be required to attend counselling or guidance sessions, no more than once a week, for up to three months. In addition, the parent may be required to comply with conditions imposed by the courts; for example, escort the child to school or ensure that a responsible adult is present in the home in the evening to supervise the child.

Parliament: our law-making body. It consists of the House of Commons, in which elected Members of Parliament sit, and the House of Lords, which is a non-elected body where, traditionally, those who inherit a title sit. The composition of the House of Lords is likely to be reformed so that hereditary peers will no longer have a right to sit there.

Parliamentary Commissioner for Administration has the responsibility for investigating complaints about maladministration by government departments and agencies. He is also known as the Ombudsman. He investigates complaints about such matters as unreasonable delay in answering letters or dealing with an application, inefficiency or rudeness, but cannot investigate any matter where the complainant could take court proceedings.

A criticism is that individuals cannot complain directly to the Ombudsman, but must take their complaint to their Member of Parliament who will decide if it should be referred to the Ombudsman. This creates an extra hurdle for the complainant and may mean that some genuine complaints are not passed on to the Ombudsman.

Parliamentary Counsel: the legally qualified civil servants who are responsible for drafting proposed laws for the government to put before Parliament. The draft law, when it goes before Parliament, is called a *Bill*, and will only become law as an *Act of Parliament* if it passes all the stages in Parliament.

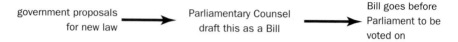

government proposals → Parliamentary Counsel → Bill goes before
for new law   draft this as a Bill   Parliament to be
                                                  voted on

parol evidence rule refers to evidence given in a dispute about a contract which is spoken. Where the contract is a written one, it is usually held that all the details of the contract are contained in the written document. This means that oral (spoken) evidence that something different or extra was agreed will not be accepted by a court. Both parties will be bound by the contract whether they have read it all or not (L'Estrange v Graucob (1934)).

An exception is made if it is shown that the written contract is not an accurate record of what both parties agreed (see also *rectification*).

parole: a term given to the early release of those serving a prison sentence. It is also called a release on licence. During this period, the prisoner can be recalled to jail if his behaviour warrants this, as his original sentence has not yet ended. See also *electronic tagging of released prisoners*.

part payment: a payment made by one party of a contract to the other, usually at the beginning of the contract or while it is being carried out. It is part of the agreed price and, unlike a *deposit*, it can be claimed back by the payer if he decides not to carry on with the contract. The other party can only keep back an amount which covers any money he has lost as a result of entering into the contract.

In deciding whether a payment is a part payment or a deposit, the court will usually accept the description the parties have given it, even if they did not understand the legal difference between the two.

part performance of a contract: the carrying out of only part of the contract; this amounts to a *breach of contract* unless:

- nearly all the contract has been carried out, leaving very little to be done (substantial performance); the other party will still be entitled to *damages*;
- the other party has freely accepted the part performance; payment for the work done will be made on a *quantum meruit* basis;
- the other party has wrongly prevented the contract being completed;
- the work is carried out in stages or the contract can be divided into different parts (severable contract);
- the contract cannot been completed because of circumstances beyond the control of either parties (*frustration*).

participation in a crime: the law considers that both those who are the *principal offenders* in a crime and those who assisted the principal by *aiding, abetting, counselling* or *procuring* are all guilty of committing the crime. They will be charged with the same crime and, if guilty, face the same punishment, though, in practice, judges will usually pass a heavier sentence on the principal offender (see also *secondary participation*).

partners: those who operate their business as a *partnership*. The minimum number of partners in a partnership is two and the maximum is normally 20, though some professions such as solicitors, are allowed to have as many partners as they wish. Usually all the partners will put capital into the business and have the right to share in the profits. Partners are equally responsible for the business debts, though it is possible to have a limited partner who has only limited liability for debts, provided there is at least one partner with unlimited liability.

partnership: defined in s1 of the Partnership Act 1890 as 'the relation which subsists between persons carrying on business in common with a view of profit'. It is not necessary to have any written partnership agreement; in fact, people may be operating a business that the law regards as a partnership without realising that this is so. If there is a business carried on in common by between 2 and 20 people with a view to making a profit, then the definition in s1 is satisfied and the law implies a partnership.

If the partners do not have a formal agreement or *deed of partnership*, then the Partnership Act 1890 sets out rules for the partnership. These rules include:

* all partners are entitled to take part in the running of the business and will share the profits equally;
* any differences between the partners are to be decided by a majority of the partners, but no change can be made to the nature of the business without the consent of all the partners;
* a new partner can only be brought into the business if all the existing partners agree.

past consideration: in contract law, an act or other form of *consideration* which has already happened at the time the agreement is reached. Because the other party to the contract is gaining no new benefit, he is not deemed to be getting any consideration and therefore no contract has come into existence.

Case example: Re McArdle (1951)

A couple spent money on improving the family home. The other members of the family then signed a document saying that, in consideration of the couple carrying out the improvements, they would be paid £488. It was held that as they had already carried out the improvements when the agreement was reached, they did not provide any consideration and that the promise to pay was a *bare promise* and unenforceable.

There is an exception to the rule which operates only if:

* an act is carried out by one party at the request of the other party; and
* at the time there was a firm but unspoken agreement it would be paid for; and
* after it is carried out, the other party promises to pay for it.

In these circumstances, the court will enforce that promise (Lampleigh v Brathwait (1615)).

paternity means fatherhood. If the mother of a child is married, it is assumed that her husband is the father unless it is proved that he is not. This is usually done by blood tests or DNA testing. If the mother is unmarried, the paternity of the child may need to be decided by a court. This is likely to occur where the mother is claiming maintenance for the child from the father or the father is applying for *parental responsibility*.

Where a child is conceived through artificial insemination, using a donor's semen, the child is considered to be the child of the married couple and not the doner's, unless the husband did not consent to artificial insemination being used. The same rule applies to unmarried couples if they have been treated together at a fertility clinic.

The father of a child has a duty to maintain the child until he is 18. In addition the married father of a child and the unmarried father of a child who has parental responsibility under a court order or by agreement has a duty to:

- care for the child's physical well-being;

- ensure the child is educated up to the age of 16.

pecuniary advantage: see *obtaining a pecuniary advantage by deception*

penalty clause in a contract sets out the amount of damages payable if the contract is breached (broken). Unlike *liquidated damages*, it is not a genuine pre-estimation of what the financial loss will be in the event of a breach, but is intended to penalise (punish) the party in breach. The courts will not enforce a penalty clause and will limit the amount of damages payable to a sum which reflects the wronged party's actual financial loss.

The courts will usually decide that a clause is a penalty clause if the sum named is much higher than any likely loss caused by a breach of contract.

pension attachment order: an order made on divorce that a divorcing spouse be paid a percentage of the other spouse's pension payments. These pension payments to the ex-spouse will cease if the ex-spouse remarries or the person receiving the pension dies. The ex-spouse will not receive any pension payments until the other spouse retires.

pension sharing order: an order made on divorce that a divorcing spouse be given a proportion of the other spouse's accumulated pension rights. A new independent pension will be set up for the divorcing spouse which will not be lost on remarriage or the death of the other spouse.

Pepper v Hart (1993): the case in which the House of Lords decided that they could look at *Hansard* (the record of the debates in Parliament) when trying to interpret the meaning of words in an Act of Parliament. However, there were conditions attached to when Hansard should be consulted and exactly what could be considered. These were:

- Hansard could only be consulted if the legislation is ambiguous or obscure or leads to an absurdity;

- only statements by the promoter of the Bill together with such other material as was necessary to understand the promoter's statements could be considered;

- those statements had to be clear.

per incuriam means 'through want of care' or 'by mistake'. It is a phrase which is used to refer to a decision of a court that has been made without consideration of an Act of Parliament or other law which would have affected the decision. A decision made per incuriam does not create a *binding precedent*. See also *Young's case*.

performance of a contract is the carrying out of what has been agreed in the contract by the parties (or someone else on their behalf). The performance of the contract must exactly match what has been agreed, and any variation will amount to a *breach of contract* (Cutter v Powell (1795)).

There are some exceptions to the rule that performance must exactly match the contract:

- Substantial performance: where the difference between what was agreed and what was done is very minor. The party who has not completely carried out the contract will not be held to have breached the contract but any money he is owed will be reduced to reflect the fact that he has not completed the contract (Hoenig v Isaacs (1952)).

- *Part performance*: where only part of the contract has been carried out, but the other party chooses to accept what has been done. This is only valid if he is not under financial or other pressure to agree to this. The defaulting party will then be entitled to payment for what he has done (it is assessed on a *quantum meruit* basis).

- Prevented performance: if one party stops the other party from completing the contract, the other party is entitled to payment for what he has done.

- Severable contracts: where the contract specifies payments at different stages of performance. Payment becomes due when each stage is reached rather than at completion of the performance.

periodic payments: regular payments made on divorce or separation by one of the parties to the marriage to the other, either for their own maintenance or for the maintenance of any *child of the family*. The payments can be ordered to be made for a fixed period or indefinitely, and the recipient can apply for the sum to be varied later.

periodic payments order: an order made by the court in family law that one spouse pay the other or a *child of the family* regular maintenance payments of a specified amount, e.g. £500 per month. The court can order that these are made by direct debit or standing order and can also make an *attachment of earnings order* under which the employer deducts the payments from the employee's pay and sends them to the court. The order can last indefinitely or for a fixed period of time, but comes to an end if the recipient remarries. The sum specified can be altered.

perjury: the making of a statement on oath in court by a witness who either knows that the statement is not true or does not believe it to be true. Perjury is a criminal offence under s1 of the Perjury Act 1911.

personal injuries litigation refers to cases in which the claimant is claiming *damages* for physical or mental injury caused by the other party. The claim will usually be under the tort of *negligence*, but can arise from various situations. The most common types of personal injury litigation are where injuries have been caused in a road traffic crash or through medical negligence or in an accident at work.

If the claim is for less than £50,000, the case must be started in the *County Court*. A claim for a higher amount can be taken in either the County Court or the *High Court*. Many cases will settle without the need for a trial, but when the case does go to trial, there are severe delays. It is estimated that the average time between the incident which caused the injuries and the case being heard in court is three years in the County Court and five years in the High Court.

personal property: all property except for land (apart from leases which are personal property).

personal representative: an *executor* or an *administrator* who has been appointed to deal with the estate of a person who has died.

personalty: see *personal property*.

persuasive precedent: a legal principle which does not have to be followed by a court which is deciding a later case, but may persuade that court to follow it. Persuasive precedent comes from a number of sources:

- statements made *obiter dicta* in the course of an earlier judgment;
- decisions of the *Judicial Committee of the Privy Council*;
- a decision by a court lower in the hierarchy than the court considering the present case;
- decisions of courts in other countries, especially Commonwealth countries;
- a dissenting judgment, that is one made by a judge in the Court of Appeal or House of Lords who disagrees with the majority of the panel of judges; often such a judge will set out reasons for his view of the law; courts in later cases may decide that this view has persuaded them.

petitioner: a spouse seeking a divorce or judicial separation. He or she is so called because he or she starts off the proceedings by filing a petition with the court. The other spouse is called the *respondent*.

Pinnel's case (1602) established the rule that where one party to a contract owes the other party money, the debt will not be discharged by paying only part of the money owed even if the other party has agreed it will be. The debtor has provided no *consideration* for the new agreement, so that it is a *bare promise*, not a contract and is unenforceable.

Exceptions:

- when the debtor provides further consideration, e.g. paying early;
- when all the creditors agree to accept a lesser amount when the debtor cannot pay all his debts;
- when the debt is paid by a third party and it is agreed that this is in final settlement;
- when the debtor has relied on the creditor's promise not to enforce the rest of the debt (see also *promissory estoppel*).

plaintiff: the old legal term for the person who started a *civil case* in the courts making a claim against another person.

plc stands for *public limited company*.

plea and directions hearing (pdh) takes place before a trial at the *Crown Court*. The defendant is asked whether he pleads guilty or not guilty. If the defendant pleads guilty, the judge will, if possible, decide the sentence at this hearing. If the plea is not guilty, the judge will ask the prosecution and defence to identify the key issues of law and facts in the case. This allows the judge to make any necessary directions as to how the trial should be conducted, such as which witnesses will be required to give evidence. The aim of a pdh is to prevent wasting time at the trial.

plea bargaining refers to discussions between prosecution and defence as to whether it might be possible for the defendant to plead guilty to a less serious crime than the one he is charged with. Plea bargaining also refers to unofficial (behind-the-scenes) approaches to the judge trying the case to see if the judge will indicate the level of sentence the defendant could expect to receive if he pleaded guilty.

plea before venue: the procedure used in the *Magistrates' Court* for *triable either way offences*. Before any decision is made as to whether the case should be dealt with in the

Magistrates' Court or the *Crown Court*, the defendant is asked whether he pleads guilty or not guilty. If he pleads guilty, he cannot choose to go to the Crown Court, though the magistrates may still decide to send him there for sentencing. If the defendant pleads not guilty, he has the right to elect trial by *jury* at the Crown Court.

pleadings (statement of case): the written documents filed in court and delivered alternately by the parties to one another. Until April 1999 these documents were the writ and statement of claim or summons and particulars of claim and defence. From April 1999 the documents are called the claim form, particulars of claim and defence. There may also be a counter-claim and defence to counter-claim if the defendant has a claim he wants to bring against the *claimant*. The pleadings set out the claimant's and defendant's cases, and neither party can bring up points at the trial that they have not put in their pleadings. These documents make it clear what the parties are in agreement about and what the court needs to decide. For example, the parties may agree that the defendant's car ran into the claimant's car, but the defendant disputes that he was driving negligently at the time.

Police and Criminal Evidence Act 1984: the main Act which governs police powers. It deals with such matters as powers to stop and search, arrest, detain and interview. It was passed as a result of the recommendations of the Phillips Commission on Criminal Justice. Some of the significant changes were the requirement that the police keep records of stop and search incidents and that at the police station there should be a *custody officer* to record all happenings while a suspect is detained. Strict time limits were imposed on the *detention by police* of suspects, and interviews at the police station had to be tape-recorded. The Act also gave the Home Secretary power to issue *Codes of Practice* in respect of the key police powers.

police codes of practice give guidelines on how the police should exercise the powers they have to conduct investigations of crimes by doing such things as searching, detaining and interviewing suspects. There are six codes issued under the *Police and Criminal Evidence Act 1984*. These codes are:

A   for the exercise of the police powers of stop and search;

B   for the police powers to search premises and to seize property;

C   to deal with the detention, treatment and questioning of suspects by police officers;

D   on identification procedures, such as identity parades;

E   on the tape-recording of interviews with suspects.

F   on visual recording with sound of interviews with suspects

Police Complaints Authority investigates serious complaints against the police. All complaints of conduct which is alleged to have resulted in death or serious injury must be referred to the Police Complaints Authority for independent investigation.

police interviews of suspects must be tape-recorded if the interview takes place at a police station. Suspects have the right to have a solicitor present at any interview. The only exception is where the offence being investigated is a *serious arrestable offence* and the police have reasonable grounds for believing that allowing the suspect to see a solicitor could lead to alerting others involved in the offence or interference with witnesses. In such a case the police can delay access to a solicitor for up to 36 hours. If the suspect is under 17 years old or is mentally handicapped, then there must be an appropriate adult present during the interview.

police powers of arrest: police officers can always arrest someone if they have a warrant to do this. However, it is also necessary that they should be able to arrest people in order to prevent crime or to detain a suspect. The general powers of arrest are set out in s24 of the *Police and Criminal Evidence Act 1984* (PACE). This allows the arrest of anyone who:

- has committed, or whom the police officer has reasonable grounds for suspecting has committed, an *arrestable offence*;
- is in the act of committing, or whom the police officer has reasonable grounds for suspecting to be committing, an arrestable offence;
- is about to commit, or whom the police officer has reasonable grounds for suspecting to be about to commit, an arrestable offence.

In addition, under s25 of PACE, the police have the power to arrest any suspect whose name and address cannot be discovered or whom the police suspect of giving a false name and address. They can also arrest someone if there are reasonable grounds for believing that an arrest is necessary to prevent that person from:

- causing physical injury to himself or another;
- causing loss of or damage to property;
- causing an unlawful obstruction of the highway.

The police also have the right to arrest if there is, or is likely to be, a breach of the peace. (See also *citizen's arrest*.)

police powers of detention of a person following an arrest are limited to a period of 24 hours for most crimes. For *serious arrestable offences*, this period can be extended to 36 hours by a senior police officer. After this, the time can only be extended by the magistrates, who can permit a maximum of 96 hours' detention.

Note that the Criminal Justice Bill 2002 has provisions to increase the detention time to 36 hours for all offences.

police powers to stop and search: are set out in ss1–7 of the *Police and Criminal Evidence Act 1984* (PACE). They have the right to stop people in a public place, which includes places such as pub car parks and private gardens. The police officer can only use this power if there are reasonable grounds for suspecting that the person is in possession of stolen goods or prohibited articles such as offensive weapons.

police powers to search premises: the police can enter premises without the occupier's permission and search those premises if they have a *warrant* to do so issued by the magistrates. The police also have power to enter premises without a warrant:

- to arrest a person and, following the arrest, to search the premises;
- to prevent a breach of the peace.

police station, legal advice for suspects at: a person detained at a police station has the right to be told that independent legal advice is available free of charge under the *duty solicitor* scheme. They are allowed to contact their own solicitor or the duty solicitor. This right to consult with a solicitor cannot be prevented by the police. However, in the case of *serious arrestable offences*, a senior police officer may delay the right for up to 36 hours if there are reasonable grounds for believing that if the suspect is allowed to see a solicitor, it could lead to alerting others involved in the offence or interfering with witnesses.

polygamy: a marriage between a husband and two or more wives or a wife and two or more husbands. A polygamous marriage entered into abroad will be *void* in the UK if either of the parties was domiciled in the UK at the time of the wedding.

positivism: the theory that if law is made through the correct procedures, then it is the law and has to be obeyed. This is the opposite view to those who believe in *natural law* (see also *Hart-Fuller debate*). Max *Weber* took the traditional positivist approach and developed the idea to show that law was the imposition of an order by those with recognised authority. If people chose to disobey this order, then clearly defined sanctions could be imposed.

postal rule (in contract law): a rule about when an *acceptance* which is posted takes effect. This is an exception to the normal *communication rules in contract* law. Under the postal rule, an acceptance takes effect at the moment it is posted and not when it is received. This means that the *offeror* is bound as soon as the acceptance is posted, whether or not he ever receives it.

The rule only applies if:

- the use of the post is an appropriate method of acceptance in the particular case (if the offeror has specifically excluded it, then it is not);
- the letter is properly addressed;
- the letter has been put in the post-box or handed in at a post office to an official whose job it is to receive mail.

Case example: Adams v Lindsell (1818)

The defendants wrote to the claimants offering to sell them some wool and requiring an answer in the course of the post. The claimants posted a letter of acceptance on the 5th September. The letter did not arrive at the defendants' until the 9th September. Because they expected to have heard earlier, the defendants sold the wool to someone else on the 8th September. It was held that a contract came into existence when the claimants posted their acceptance on the 5th, so the defendants were in breach of contract when they sold the wool to someone else.

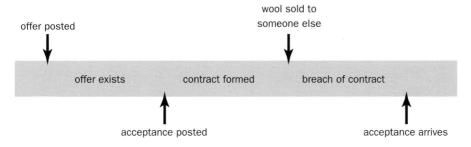

powers of arrest: given to private citizens as well as police officers. See *police powers of arrest* and *citizen's arrest*.

Practice Statement: issued by the *House of Lords* in 1966 to allow more flexibility in our system of *judicial precedent*. It was needed because the case of London Street Tramways v London County Council (1898) had ruled that the House of Lords had to follow its own past decisions. The Practice Statement said that the House of Lords proposed to treat former decisions as being normally binding but would depart from a previous decision 'when it appears right to do so'.

Initially, the House of Lords was reluctant to use the Practice Statement as it felt that certainty on the law was very important. The first use was in Conway v Rimmer (1968), but only involved a technical point of law on discovery of documents prior to a trial. The first main use was in Herrington v British Railways Board (1972) when the House of Lords refused to follow a precedent set in 1929 on the *duty of care* owed to child trespassers.

In the 1990s, the House of Lords started to use the Practice Statement more frequently with cases such as Pepper v Hart (1993), which allowed them to depart from the previous ruling that they could not look at *Hansard*, and R v Adomako (1994), which changed the law on *recklessness* in manslaughter.

pre-action protocols: set steps of procedure in a *civil case* which require parties to exchange information at an early stage in a case. This is designed to encourage settlement of the dispute at a early stage and allows claimants to assess their chances of success more readily. Where cases do go to trial, they will be better prepared than previously. Judges are expected to apply the protocols strictly and to impose sanctions on parties who do not follow them.

The first stage is a letter of claim which must be much more informative than the former letter before action. It has to be sent 'immediately sufficient information is available to substantiate a realistic claim and before issues of quantum are addressed in detail'. The other side must reply within three months, 'stating whether liability is denied, and if so, giving reasons for their denial of liability'.

This is intended to tackle one of the main causes of delay and prevent the many 'court-door' settlements which occur now.

precedent: see *judicial precedent*

pregnancy, dismissal because of: automatically *unfair dismissal* under s99 of the Employment Rights Act 1996. It is also sex discrimination under the Sex Discrimination Act 1975. This means that an employee is protected from unfair dismissal because she is pregnant from the moment she starts work. It is not necessary for her to work continuously for one year before she becomes a protected employee.

premises in occupiers' liability includes:

- land;
- buildings;
- vessels;
- vehicles;
- aircraft.

prerogative orders: those which originally belonged to the monarch and came from the idea that the monarch had the right to control what his officials did. These orders can now be applied for from the *Queen's Bench Division* of the *High Court* in *judicial review* proceedings. The three prerogative orders that can be made are:

- *certiorari*, which has the effect of quashing a decision;
- *mandamus*, which is a command to perform a public duty;
- *prohibition*, which prevents something being done.

prescription: in *private nuisance*, a right to carry on committing a nuisance because the person affected by it has done nothing to stop it for over 20 years. The 20-year period starts not when the activity started, but when the activity starts being a nuisance by adversely affecting a neighbour on his property.

Case example: Sturges v Bridgman (1879)

A confectioner had been using large pestles and mortars on his premises close to his neighbour's land for over 20 years. During this period, although there had been a lot of noise and vibration, there was no nuisance because the activity did not seriously affect the neighbour's use of his land. When the neighbour, who was a doctor, built a consulting room close to his boundary, the noise began to affect him and he started court proceedings to stop the activity. He was given the injunction he sought because, although the activity had been carried out for a long time, it had only been a nuisance for a short time. The confectioner had not acquired a prescriptive right to carry on committing a nuisance and had to stop the activity.

pre-sentence reports: reports prepared by the probation service before the court passes sentence on an offender. Such a report will give information about the offender's family and background and often suggests whether the probation officer considers the offender is suitable or not for a community-based sentence. The courts do not have to look at a pre-sentence report before passing sentence, but usually will do so, unless the offence is so serious that a custodial sentence is inevitable.

pressure groups: interest groups that campaign for new law. This can have an effect on *law reform*. An example of law which was introduced largely as the result of pressure group activity is the Disability Discrimination Act 1995.

presumption: a conclusion or inference that will be drawn unless there is evidence to disprove it. In *statutory interpretation*, there are certain presumptions which apply unless the Act being considered clearly states the opposite. The main presumptions are that:

- *mens rea* is required for a criminal offence;
- the Crown is not bound by legislation;
- Acts of Parliament do not apply retrospectively.

previous convictions: the offences for which the defendant has been found guilty in previous cases. They are important when a court has to decide on the sentence in the present case, as they may show that the defendant was not reformed by the previous sentence. Also, the fact that a defendant has a previous conviction for a similar offence can mean that he has to receive a life sentence (violent crimes) or a minimum of seven years' imprisonment (drug-dealing) or a minimum of three years' imprisonment for a third burglary conviction. Previous convictions are not normally disclosed to the jury during a trial as they are not part of the evidence in the trial, but could prejudice the jury against the defendant.

Price Marking Order 1991 sets out what information on prices must be given to the buyer. The information must be clear and in writing and must clearly refer to the item. In some cases, the unit price must be given, e.g. the labels on some foods must give the price of the item and the price per kilogram. Where the goods are kept so that only the assistant can reach them, the prices do not have to be displayed; it is sufficient if the prices are attached to the items or their boxes and can be seen when the assistant takes them out.

prima facie case means that there is a case on the face of the evidence, or at first sight of the evidence, so the matter should be fully tried.

principal offender: the person who is directly responsible for bringing about the *actus reus* of an offence. For example, if in order to burgle a house, A borrows keys from B and asks C to drive him to the house and wait outside while A commits the burglary, A is the principal offender. If B and C know that A is going to commit burglary, they are *accessories* to it or *secondary participants*. There can be joint principals in a crime. In the above situation, if C went into the house with A, A and C would be joint principals.

A person is also the principal if he uses an innocent agent to commit the actus reus for him. This could be where the principal gives a sealed envelope to his secretary and asks her to deliver it to another person. If the envelope contains a blackmailing letter, the principal is guilty of blackmail, the deliverer of the letter is an innocent agent.

prison population refers to the number of people detained in custody; the total figure used in statistics includes young offenders and those who are in custody awaiting trial. The total number in custody has been increasing rapidly since the early 1990s due to the fact that a higher percentage of those found guilty are being given prison sentences and also that the average length of sentence has increased.

prison sentences: custodial sentences passed on those aged 21 and over. Those under 21 can be detained in a detention and training centre. A sentence of *life imprisonment* has to be given for murder and also for repeat offenders who commit violent crimes. For other crimes, the sentence is normally a fixed-term sentence for a set period of time such as seven years. Offenders do not serve the whole of a fixed term sentence. Anyone sentenced to less than four years' is automatically released after they have served half of the sentence. Those given sentences of four years or more are automatically released after they have served two thirds of the sentence, but are eligible to be released for good behaviour after they have served half. (See also *electronic tagging of released prisoners*.)

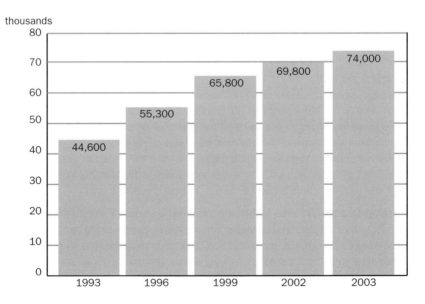

Bar chart showing increase in prison population between 1993 and 2003

privacy: a right not to have details of a person's private life made public unless it is in the public interest. No general right to privacy existed under English law until the passing of the *Human Rights Act 1998* which incorporated the *European Convention on Human Rights*, which includes a right to privacy. There have been some cases which have been successful, especially those where the claimant could show *breach of confidence*, such as private information between doctor and patient.

private Bills: draft laws which may be passed by Parliament but do not change the law for everyone. They only affect individuals or corporations. For example, in 1996 the University College London Act was passed in order to combine three medical institutes with University College.

private law: concerned with regulating relationships and solving disputes between private individuals or businesses. There are many branches of private law including:

- contract law;
- law of *tort*;
- family law;
- company law.

private limited company: any company that is not a public company. A private company may not advertise its shares for sale to the public and is not quoted on the Stock Exchange or other money market. A private company usually has two or more *shareholders*, but can have just one (Single Member Private Limited Companies Regulations 1992).

private members' Bills: those introduced into Parliament by an individual MP rather than by a government minister. Time for debating private members' Bills is usually restricted, so that only a few can be considered in each Parliamentary session. Despite this restriction, some important laws, such as the Abortion Act 1967, have been passed through this procedure.

private nuisance: the unlawful interference with a person's use and enjoyment of his land by unreasonable activities carried out by a neighbour on his own land. When deciding whether a nuisance has occurred, the courts will take into account the effect of the nuisance. There is a difference depending on whether the nuisance causes damage or not.

Nuisance interfering with the enjoyment of land, e.g. noise	Nuisance causing physical damage, e.g. fumes which damage plants
• Claimant must show that it has happened on several occasions.	• Claimant only has to show it has happened once.
• Claimant must show that the interference has been substantial. Court will take into account: – how often it has happened – the time of day – the neighbourhood – the motive of the defendant The court will not take into account: – the social utility of the activity	• Claimant only has to show that physical damage or interference has occurred.

Continued on next page

Nuisance interfering with the enjoyment of land, e.g. noise	Nuisance causing physical damage, e.g. fumes which damage plants
– the fact that the claimant is extra sensitive unless anyone would have been affected by the defendant's actions.	
• Claimant will want an *injunction* to stop the nuisance.	• Claimant will want *damages* and an injunction.

It was heard in Canary Wharf v Hunter (1997) that only the owner or tenant of the property affected can bring a claim, but this may be in breach of the *Human Rights Act*. He will normally sue the person who creates the nuisance but he may sue a landlord whose tenant is creating the nuisance, if the landlord authorises the nuisance.

The defences to a claim for private nuisance are:

- *prescription*: the defendant has been creating a nuisance which has affected the claimant for 20 years and no claim has been brought;

- statutory authority, e.g. an oil company which has the right under an Act of Parliament to run a refinery cannot be sued for nuisance unless it is negligent in the way that it runs it so that fumes are excessive;

- *necessity*;

- *Act of God*;

- *act of stranger*.

A claimant may be entitled to take action himself to stop the nuisance (*abatement*).

private prosecutions: those brought by members of the public or companies and not by the state. Big shops often conduct their own prosecutions against shoplifters, and other organisations, such as the RSPCA, will prosecute crimes involving their particular field. It is less usual for serious crimes to be privately prosecuted, as the *Crown Prosecution Service* will normally deal with these. However, it is possible for a private prosecution to be brought for any crime, even murder, where the Crown Prosecution Service do not proceed with the prosecution.

privilege in defamation: see *absolute privilege* and *qualified privilege*.

privileged wills: those for which the formalities of making a *will* are relaxed. This only applies where the *testator* is a member of the forces on active duty or is a sailor at sea. In such cases, the minimum age for making a will is 14. The will itself can be:

- oral, provided two witnesses hear what the testator says; or

- in writing without witnesses.

The reason for these rules is that in time of emergency (e.g. in a battle), it is unrealistic to have to make a formal will.

Case example: Re Jones (1981)

The testator was a soldier who was shot while on duty in Northern Ireland. On the way to hospital, he said to two officers 'If I don't make it, make sure that Anne [his fiancee] gets all my stuff.' This was held to be a valid will.

privity of contract means that only the two parties to a contract can sue each other to enforce the contract.

Case example: Dunlop Pneumatic Tyre Co Ltd v Selfridge (1915)

Dew, when buying goods from Dunlop, promised them that they would obtain a written undertaking from all retailers they sold Dunlop's goods to, not to sell them at less than list price. When Selfridge broke the undertaking, Dunlop sued Selfridge. It was held that there was no contract between them and that Dunlop could not enforce the undertakings that Selfridge had signed although it was for their benefit.

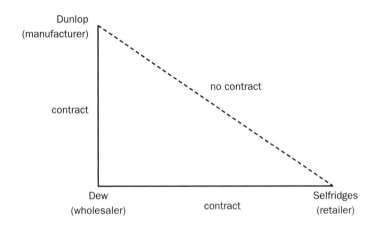

This rule does not apply where:

- there are *collateral contracts*;
- one of the parties was acting as an agent for a third party; in this case, the third party can sue to enforce the contract (see also *agency*);
- an exception has been created by *statute*, e.g. insurance policies form a contract between the insurance company and the person taking out the policy; they often name a third person who is to benefit from them, and this person can sue to enforce the contract;
- all contractual rights have been assigned to a third party; this party can then sue on the contract;
- the party in breach is sued in *negligence* rather than breach of contract;
- a person buys land knowing that when land was first sold off, the seller included a restrictive covenant in the contract of sale. Although under privity of contract this only bound the first buyer, under the rule in Tulk v Moxhay, all subsequent buyers are also bound if they know about the covenant.

These exceptions are now less important as under the Contracts (Rights of Third Parties) Act 1999, a third party can enforce a contract if it is for his benefit and there is nothing in the contract to show that the two parties had not intended him to be able to enforce it.

Privy Council: see *Judicial Committee of the Privy Council*

probate: the proving of a *will* so that the estate of the deceased can be dealt with by the executors. See also *grant of probate*.

probation orders (re-named Community Rehabilitation Orders): community sentences passed on offenders placing them under the supervision of a probation officer for up to three years. The offender must keep in regular contact with the probation officer. Extra conditions can be added to the probation order including:

- a residence order which requires the offender to live at a certain address (this could be a probation hostel);
- a treatment order requiring the offender to attend for medical or psychiatric treatment.

Under the Criminal Justice Bill 2002 it is proposed that a probation order is replaced with a *supervision requirement*. Such a requirement could be made as part of a *community order* or as an extra to follow on after a *custodial sentence*.

procuring a crime: one of the ways of *secondary participation* in a crime. In the Attorney-General's Reference (No 1) of 1975, the Court of Appeal defined procuring as 'to produce by endeavour'. They went on to say: 'You procure a thing by setting out to see that it happens and taking appropriate steps to produce that happening'. For example, putting alcohol into someone's soft drink in order to put them over the drink-drive limit. The fact that the *principal offender* (in this case the driver) does not know what has been done does not matter. The person who put the alcohol into the drink is guilty as a secondary party of drink-driving.

product liability means liability for defective products or goods where injury has been caused to a person or their property. There are various ways that a claim can be brought, as shown in this table.

	Person bringing the action	Who he can sue	Grounds for bringing claim
Sale of Goods Act 1979	Buyer who has suffered injury caused by defective goods.	Seller of goods.	Breach of s14 (implied term that goods are of satisfactory quality).
Consumer Protection 1987	Any person injured by defective goods.	Manufacturer or company who sells goods under their own brand or importer of goods into the EU.	Defective product has caused death or personal injury or damage to property over £275.
negligence	Any person injured by defective goods.	Manufacturer of goods.	Manufacturer was negligent manufacturing goods.
contract	Buyer	Seller	Breach of an express or implied term that the goods will not be defective and the damage was reasonably foreseeable.

prohibited degrees: in family law, a list of close relatives whom it is illegal to marry. A man cannot marry his mother, daughter, grandmother, sister, aunt or niece. Similarly, a woman cannot marry her father, son, grandfather, brother, uncle or nephew. It is now permissible to marry:

- a cousin;
- an ex-spouse's relatives; e.g. ex-wife's sister;
- relatives' ex-wives or ex-husbands; e.g. the ex-wife of a brother;
- step-children, provided that both parties are over 21 and the child was not treated as a child of the family while under 18;
- a son-in-law or daughter-in-law if the daughter or son to whom they had been married is dead and both parties are over 21.

prohibited steps order: in family law, an order of the court stopping a named person from carrying out an act which he or she would normally carry out as part of their parental responsibilities, e.g. taking a child abroad on holiday. The order is intended to be used to deal a particular issue and is usually made against one of the parents. It does not cover actions that are not part of parental responsibility, e.g. assault.

prohibition: one of the prerogative orders which can be made by the Queen's Bench Division of the High Court. The effect of the order is to prevent a public body from acting unlawfully or beyond their powers.

Case example: R v Telford Justices ex parte Badham (1991)

An order of prohibition was issued in order to stop the magistrates from holding committal proceedings in a rape case, where the allegations of rape had not been made until 15 years after the alleged rape.

promissory estoppel: an *equitable* principle used to stop one party to a contract from enforcing his legal rights when he has given his word that he will not. The party making the promise will be stopped from enforcing the contract if:

- one party makes a promise to the other party not to enforce part of a contract; and
- that party intends that the promise will be binding; and
- that party intends that the other party will rely on it; and
- the other party does rely on it and as a result alters his position.

Case example: Central London Property Trust Ltd v High Trees House Ltd (1956)

During the Second World War, the owners of a block of flats agreed to lower the rent payable by the tenant because he was having difficulty in sub-letting the flats. Once the war finished and all the flats had been taken, the owners sued because they were not being paid the full rent. It was held that they should be paid full rent from the time the war finished. The judge in the case, Mr Justice Denning, also said, *obiter dicta*, that the owners would not be able to claim for the war years because the tenant had relied on the owners' promise not to charge the full rent.

Because this is an *equitable* doctrine, the courts will only use it if the party to whom the promise was made has acted fairly (D & C Builders v Rees (1966)).

proof, burden of: see *burden of proof*

property (in theft) is defined as including 'money and all other property, real and personal, including things in action and other intangible property' (s4(1) Theft Act 1968). *Real property* means land but there are limitations as to when land can be stolen under s4(2) Theft Act 1968. Land can only be stolen:

- where a trustee or personal representative or other authorised person disposes of it in 'breach of the confidence reposed in him'; or

- when a person not in control of the land severs something from the land; or

- when a tenant misappropriates fixtures attached to the land.

Things in action and other intangible property include such matters as patents, copyright and a credit balance in a bank account.

Certain things cannot be stolen. These include:

- a wild creature which has not been tamed or kept in captivity or in another person's possession (s4(4) Theft Act 1968);

- electricity (but there is a separate offence of abstracting electricity (s13 Theft Act 1968));

- information or knowledge, such as the contents of an examination paper; but note that the piece of paper on which the examination is written can be stolen;

- a corpse or part of a corpse unless it has been preserved for scientific analysis (Kelly (1998)).

proprietary estoppel: an *equitable* principle that is used in cases involving land to prevent a person from enforcing his legal rights. It is used when a landowner has told or led someone else to believe that they have, or will have, an interest in his property, and as a result they have done work on it or in some other way acted to their detriment, e.g. giving up a tenancy.

Case example: Pascoe v Turner (1979)

The parties lived together as a couple for several years. The man then left to live with another woman, but told the woman that she could have the house which was in the man's name. Because she thought the house was now hers, the woman carried out various repairs. The man then tried to reclaim the house, which was still in his name. It was held that he could not now go back on his word because the woman had acted to her detriment because of what he had said. The man was ordered to transfer the house into the woman's name. The court might have instead given the woman permission to stay in the house as long as she liked. This has happened in other similar cases.

See also *promissory estoppel*.

prosecution: the agency which brings a case to court against someone alleged to have committed a crime. The main prosecution agency is the *Crown Prosecution Service*.

protection of the public: one of the aims of sentencing. Protection can be achieved by incapacitating the offender so that he cannot commit further crime. The ultimate punishment is the death sentence, though this is not now used in the United Kingdom. The main way of protecting the public is by sending the offender to prison. The Powers of Criminal Courts (Sentencing) Act 2000 states that a prison sentence can be passed for a violent or sexual offence where it is the only adequate way of protecting the public from the offender.

provisional damages: in tort, ones which are assessed on the injuries to the claimant as they are at the time of the hearing but which can be reassessed if his condition deteriorates later. Normally, the court makes an estimation of what will happen in the future and damages will be assessed on this basis. The claimant cannot reapply to the court if this estimation proves to be wrong but, where the future is unclear, the court may make an order for provisional damages and a reassessment can be made when more is known.

provocation: a special defence to a charge of murder under s3 of the Homicide Act 1957 which allows the jury to consider whether the defendant lost his self-control and killed because he was provoked by 'things done or by things said or by both together'. This covers a wide range of matters, such as being teased about a facial scar, racial abuse, being battered by one's partner or even the crying of a baby. If the defence is successful, the charge will be reduced to manslaughter.

To show there was provocation, the defence must establish that:

- the defendant suffered a sudden and temporary loss of self-control;
- the things that provoked him would also have caused a reasonable man to be provoked and do as the defendant did.

In DPP v Camplin (1978) the House of Lords ruled that the reasonable person was someone of the same age and sex as the defendant and sharing any characteristics which are relevant to the provocation.

Case example: R v Thornton (1996)

The defendant was regularly beaten by her husband. One night he came home drunk, threatened to beat her up later, then fell asleep on the settee. The defendant stabbed him while he was asleep. It was held that a final minor incident could be sufficient provocation where there had been a history of incidents. It was also held that the fact that Sarah Thornton suffered from 'battered-wife syndrome' was a characteristic to be taken into consideration.

In R v Smith (2000) the House of Lords held that characteristics were relevant to both the gravity of the provocation and the standard of self-control to be expected.

public Bills: draft laws that will, if enacted as *Acts of Parliament*, affect the public as a whole. Most government Bills come into this category, for example the Crime and Disorder Act 1998. See also *private Bills*.

Public Defence Service is a government agency which employs lawyers to represent defendants in criminal trials. This has been criticised as it means the state is acting as both prosecutor and defence.

public law: the law which governs the relationship between the individual and the state in some way. There are three main branches of public law:

- *constitutional law*;
- *administrative law*;
- criminal law.

public limited company: one which its Memorandum of Association states is a public company. It must have a share capital of not less than £50,000 and needs a Trading Certificate before it can start trading. It can offer its shares for sale on the Stock Exchange. It has to disclose more information about its accounts than a *private limited company*.

public nuisance: an unlawful act or omission which causes a *nuisance* that affects a whole group of people (a class of Her Majesty's subjects), e.g. quarrying and blasting that causes dust, noise and vibration that affects a whole neighbourhood. When the court decides whether enough people have been affected by the nuisance to make it a public nuisance, it will look at whether enough people were affected so that it would be unreasonable for an individual on his own to take action to stop it.

A person causing a public nuisance can be:

- prosecuted by the Attorney-General;
- sued by the local authority, who will ask the court for an injunction to stop the nuisance;
- sued for damages by an individual who has suffered more than the rest of the group.

Unlike private nuisance, the individual does not have to have been on his own land when he was affected by the nuisance.

Case example: Castle v St Augustine's Links (1922)

A public nuisance was created by golfers regularly hitting golf balls into the road by the side of the course. This affected everyone using the road and they amounted to a class of people. The claimant was able to sue because he suffered greater damage than everyone else when a golf ball broke the windscreen of the car he was driving and he lost the use of an eye.

public order offences: usually those that penalise group offending and try to prevent public disorder. However, some of the public order offences can be committed by a person acting on their own and they can also be committed in private. There are three main public order offences under the Public Order Act 1985. These are:

- *affray*, which can be committed by a person on his own;
- *violent disorder*, which has to be committed by at least three people together;
- *riot*, for which there must be at least 12 people involved.

In each case, the test is whether a person of reasonable firmness would fear for his own safety. I, M and H v DPP (2001) decided that there must be threat to a person present at the scene for the offence to be committed. These offences allow the police to arrest defendants before any more serious offence is caused.

publication: in *defamation*, is the making of a defamatory statement to anyone apart from the maker's spouse or the claimant. The statement can be in many forms, including print, as part of a broadcast, in a letter, by word of mouth or on the Internet. The act of publication is usually deliberate, but can also happen unintentionally. The defendant will be liable where it was foreseeable that this might happen. For example, if the defendant writes a statement on a postcard it is foreseeable it may be read by people other the person to whom it is addressed. Each time the statement is repeated, this is a further publication and a further claim for defamation can be made.

Where the statement is printed, there is a publication by the writer, the editor, the publisher or newspaper, the printer and the shop which sold the book or newspaper and anyone else involved with distributing the statement. Those not actively involved, such as the shop, have a defence if they can show that:

- they did not know the statement was defamatory; and
- there were no grounds for them to suspect that it was; and
- their lack of knowledge was not through negligence.

The same applies to Internet service providers.

puisne judges: the judges who sit in the *High Court*. They are also known as High Court judges.

punitive damages (also known as exemplary damages): damages in tort which are more than are needed to compensate the claimant for his loss and are intended to:

- punish the defendant; or
- deprive him of any benefit he has gained by it, e.g. where a newspaper deliberately prints a defamatory article calculating that their increased profits from sales will be more than they will lose in a defamation case; or
- protect the individual against oppressive conduct by government officials, such as police officers.

See also *restitutiory damages*.

pupillage: the final training stage for a barrister. It involves work shadowing an experienced barrister for a period of 12 months. During the second six months a pupil barrister may also represent clients in court.

pure economic loss: a term used in *tort* where the claimant has suffered financial loss but no personal injury or damage to property. The claimant cannot make a claim if this loss is caused by the defendant's negligent actions, but can claim if the loss is caused by the defendant's negligent statements (*negligent misstatement*). See also *economic loss in negligence*.

purposive approach: an approach to *statutory interpretation* which places the emphasis on discovering the purpose of the law concerned and interpreting it in such a way as to give effect to the purpose. It is the method of interpretation favoured by the *European Court of Justice*. It is the opposite to the *literal rule*, where the words are taken at their literal meaning, even if this creates an absurdity.

Case example: Royal College of Nursing v DHSS (1981)

The Abortion Act 1967 used the words that an abortion had to be carried out by 'registered medical practitioner'. This phrase meant a doctor. Improvements to medical technique made it possible for nurses to carry out most of the procedure. The question was whether under the wording of the Act this was legal. The House of Lords (by three judges to two) held that it was lawful. The literal meaning of the words 'registered medical practitioner' did not have to be taken. They said that the intention or purpose of Parliament was to prevent back-street abortions and make sure that abortions were carried out in hospital.

qualified privilege: a defence in *defamation* which states that where a person makes a statement because he has a moral, legal or social duty to do so, he cannot be successfully sued provided he is not acting through malice (spite).

Qualified privilege applies where the person who reports a matter has a duty to do so, and the person to whom he makes the report has a duty to receive it.

Case example: Watt v Longsdon (1930)

A manager of a company was concerned about the activities of the managing director and reported his concerns to a director. The director, in turn, passed on these concerns to the chairman but also showed the manager's letter to the managing director's wife. He also replied to the manager.

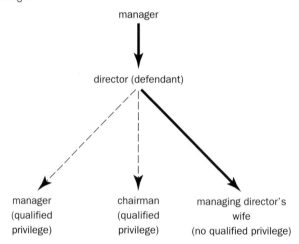

It was held that the managing director could not sue the director in defamation for the communication to the manager and the chairman, as the director had a duty to deal with concerns about the company and these were the proper people to discuss them with. However there was no duty to discuss these concerns with the managing director's wife, and this was therefore not covered by qualified privilege.

Qualified privilege also applies to fair and accurate reports made without malice of:

- parliamentary proceedings
- court proceedings
- public meetings
- matters of public interest which the public has the right to know.

quantum meruit: a Latin phrase meaning 'as much as it merits (deserves)'. It is used where a contract has not been completely carried out but payment is still due for the work that has been done. Calculation of the amount due is said to be done on a quantum meruit basis. This is done where the person carrying out the work has been wrongly prevented from completing it by the other party or the other party has willingly accepted the *part performance*.

quasi-contract arises where there is no valid contract between the parties, but work has been done or goods supplied, and it is fair that the supplier should be paid a reasonable sum for these, (for example, where a contract has been declared void because it is illegal or where no final agreement has been reached but work has been carried out anyway).

Case example: British Steel Corporation v Cleveland Bridge and Engineering (1984)

The engineering company required nodes of an unusual type. They approached British Steel and there were lengthy discussions about the specifications and the terms of the contract. While these discussions were still going on, the nodes were manufactured and delivered to the engineering company. No contract existed at the time, but it was held that British Steel should be paid a reasonable price for them.

quasi-trustee refers to someone who has not actually been appointed a trustee but whom the law treats as if they were a trustee. This is important in relation to *directors* of companies and the duties they owe to the company.

Queen's Bench Division: the biggest division of the *High Court* with over 60 judges. Cases connected to the law of contract and the law of *tort* are tried here, though this will usually only happen when the claim is for over £25,000. Smaller cases are dealt with in the *County Court*. The Queen's Bench Division also has supervisory powers and hears cases for *judicial review*. In addition, it also has two specialist courts, the *Commercial Court* and the *Admiralty Court*. For cases tried in the Queen's Bench Division, there is an appeal route available to the Court of Appeal (Civil Division).

Queen's Bench Divisional Court: the appellate court connected to the Queen's Bench Division. Two or three judges from this division will sit to hear cases. The two main functions of the Queen's Bench Divisional Court are:

- to hear appeals on a point of law from criminal cases which have been tried in the *Magistrates' Court*. This type of appeal is called an appeal 'by way of case stated';
- to hear cases of *judicial review* which are concerned with criminal cases.

The court also hears applications for *habeas corpus* where it is alleged that someone is being unlawfully detained. It is possible to appeal to the House of Lords against decisions of the Queen's Bench Divisional Court.

Queen's Counsel (QC): a senior advocate in the courts. They are usually involved with the more serious cases, often high-profile cases. Barristers or solicitors with a *certificate of advocacy* who have been qualified for at least ten years can apply to the Lord Chancellor to be appointed Queen's Counsel. There is criticism that this system of appointment is secretive and those who are not appointed are not told why they were not considered. Only about twelve per cent of QCs are women, and there are also very few from the ethnic minorities.

In 2003 the application system was suspended for a full review of the QC system.

racial discrimination: unlawful under the Race Relations Act 1976. This Act defines discrimination as:

- treating another less favourably on racial grounds (this is *direct discrimination)*; or
- applying a requirement or condition so that a considerably smaller proportion of a racial group will be able to comply with it compared to other racial groups (*indirect discrimination*).

Segregating a person because of racial grounds is also discrimination, as is *victimisation* because someone has made a complaint about discrimination.

Employers must not discriminate in any arrangement for work. This ranges from deciding who should be offered a job, through to terms of employment and opportunities for promotion. The only time discrimination is allowed is where being of a particular racial group is a *genuine occupational qualification* for the job.

rape: the offence of having sexual intercourse without the consent of the other person. Only a man can be guilty of rape, though a woman can be guilty of *aiding* and *abetting* rape. Section 1 of the Sexual Offences Act 1956 (as amended) makes it an offence for a man to rape a woman or a man. The rape can be by vaginal or anal intercourse, and the slightest penetration is sufficient. In order to be guilty, the man must know that the other person is not consenting to intercourse or be 'reckless' as to whether they consent to it. Reckless in this context means that the defendant could not care less whether the victim was consenting or not but decided to have sexual intercourse regardless (R v Satnam Singh (1983)). If a man genuinely but mistakenly believes the other person consents, then he is not guilty of rape (DPP v Morgan (1976)). A husband can be convicted of raping his wife, if she does not consent to intercourse (R v R (1991)).

ratio decidendi: the part of a *judgment* in which the judge explains the principles of law upon which his decision is based. Sir Rupert Cross defined the ratio decidendi as 'any rule expressly or implicitly treated by the judge as a necessary step in reaching his conclusion'. The ratio decidendi is an important element in the doctrine of *judicial precedent* because if the judgment is by a higher court, then all lower courts must follow it in subsequent cases.

real property: land apart from leasehold property. Land is treated differently from other property and, where the claimant is successful when claiming land, he must be given the land itself, money will not be sufficient compensation. The latin term for this is restituto in rem meaning the thing itself must be given back. Real property is also known as 'realty'.

realty: see *real property*

reasonable man test in tort: an *objective test* used to judge the standard expected from the defendant. For example, in negligence, a *duty of care* is only owed to those people that a reasonable man could foresee would be affected by his actions. This means that it is irrelevant whether the defendant himself foresaw the claimant would be affected; he will owe a duty of care if a reasonable man would have foreseen it.

The reasonable man test is also used to judge:

- whether the defendant's actions *breached the duty of care*;
- whether damage caused by the breach of the duty of care is sufficiently connected to the breach to justify compensation (see also *remoteness of damage*);
- what steps an occupier needs to take to protect people who come onto his land (*occupiers' liability*);
- the care an employer should take of his employees.

recklessness: a type of *mens rea* required to be proved for a defendant to be guilty of certain crimes. Recklessness used to have only one meaning: that the defendant realised there was a risk of the forbidden consequence occurring as a result of his conduct, but still carried on. This is called *subjective recklessness*.

The meaning of recklessness was extended by the case of R v Caldwell (1981) (see also *Caldwell recklessness*) to include the situation where the defendant had not given any thought of the possibility of there being a particular risk, but an ordinary prudent individual would have realised the risk. This is *objective recklessness*.

reconviction rates: the percentage of offenders who are convicted of a second or further offence within a certain time. Usually rates are expressed as a percentage of those who re-offend within two years of release from prison or two years from the date of conviction. These rates can be used to compare the effectiveness of different types of penalty as in the graph below. This shows that levels of re-offending are very similar for those sent to prison and those given a community penalty.

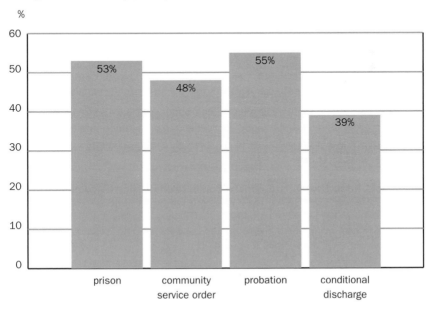

Reconviction rates for those sentenced in 1993

recorder: a part-time judge who sits as a judge for at least 20 days each year in the Crown Court or sometimes in the County Court. To be appointed as a recorder, it is necessary to have practised as a barrister or solicitor for at least ten years. Being a recorder is a recognised step to becoming a *circuit judge*.

rectification: the altering of a written contract by the courts so that it accurately reflects what both parties agreed. Normally, a written contract is held to contain all the details of the agreement and is binding on both parties, but exceptionally the court will amend the contract where it is very clear that it did not accurately record what both parties agreed. It will therefore not be granted where one or both of the parties have misunderstood the situation when they entered into the contract (*unilateral* or *common mistake*). Rectification is an *equitable remedy* and therefore will only be granted if the courts decide that it is fair in the circumstances to grant it.

redundancy: defined in s139 of the Employment Rights Act 1996 as dismissing an employee wholly or mainly because of one of the following factors:

- the employer has ceased to carry on the business for which the employee was employed either completely or in the place where the employee was employed; or
- the business no longer requires employees to carry out a particular kind of work or the need for that type of work has diminished.

If the redundancies involve more than ten employees, the employer must consult with any union involved and notify the Department of Employment. Any employee who is made redundant after working for that employer for a minimum of two years is entitled to a *redundancy payment*.

redundancy payment: a payment to compensate an employee for the loss of his job. It is calculated with reference to the length of time the employee had worked for that employer, their age and the amount they were earning. The payment is worked out as follows:

- period of work aged 18 to 21: half a week's pay per year of work
- period of work aged 22 to 40: one week's pay per year of work
- period of work aged 41 to 65: one and a half week's pay per year of work

However, there are limitations, as the maximum number of years' work counted is 20 and the maximum amount of weekly earnings is £260 (this goes up slightly each year).

regulations: laws made by the European Union under *Article 249* (*Treaty of Rome*) which are binding in every respect and directly applicable in each member state. This means that such laws automatically become law in all member states and ensures that the law is uniform in all member states.

Case example: Re Tachographs: European Commission v United Kingdom (1979)

A regulation requiring all lorries to have recording equipment registering speed, etc. was issued. The United Kingdom government decided not to bring the law into force, but to leave it to individual lorry owners to decide whether they wished to install such equipment. The European Court of Justice ruled that the regulation was law in all member states and the UK government could not disregard the law. They had to enforce it.

rehabilitation as a *sentencing aim* is the idea that the offender will be reformed by the sentence imposed on him. The hope is that this will stop the offender from re-offending in the future. Community sentences, in particular probation orders, are based on this aim of sentencing.

reliance loss: money spent by one of the parties to a contract when he is getting ready to carry out the contract. The only reason he has spent the money is because he entered into the contract. Damages are assessed on this basis in cases of *misrepresentation* and where it is impossible to calculate how the wronged party would have been better off if the contract had been completed.

Case example: Anglia Television v Reed (1972)

An actor signed a contract to appear in a film. He then changed his mind at the last minute and the film was abandoned. Anglia Television were unable to claim for the loss of profit they would have made on the film because this was an unknown figure, but they were able to claim the money they had spent on arranging the filming (reliance loss). In addition, they were allowed to claim money spent in preparation before the contract was signed, as it was held that this was something the parties knew would be lost if the contract was not carried out when it was signed.

remand in custody occurs when the defendant is not given *bail* but has to stay in prison while waiting for the next stage of the criminal process in his case. About 14 per cent of the *prison population* are defendants who have not been tried, and a number of these will be found not guilty or, even if found guilty, will not be given a prison sentence.

remand on bail means that the defendant is allowed to be at liberty while waiting for the next stage of his case to take place. Under the Bail Act 1976, there is a presumption that *bail* should be granted.

remedial justice: concerned with the remedy provided for breach of a legal rule. The ordinary person expects the law and the judges to provide a remedy when a wrong is done. This applies to both civil and criminal cases. In civil cases, the law uses the *reasonable man test* to decide what the ordinary person would expect of the law.

In criminal cases, there may be a conflict between *sentencing aims*, especial the aim of rehabilitation, and the public's desire for revenge. In R v Secretary of State for the Home Department, ex parte Thompson and Venables, two boys aged ten and 11 were convicted of murdering a two-year old child. When the Home Secretary set the tariff of how long it would be before they could apply for *parole*, he took into account public petitions which sought long sentences for the boys. The House of Lords ruled that the Home Secretary was wrong to do this.

remedies for breach of contract: there are four remedies:

- *damages*: a sum of money representing the wronged party's actual financial loss, provided that the type of loss was foreseeable by the parties;
- *rescission*: cancelling the contract;
- order for *specific performance*: court order that the party in breach of contract perform his side of the contract;
- *rectification*: court order that a written contract be amended to show the parties' true intentions.

remedies for misrepresentation: can be *rescission* (cancelling the contract) and *damages* depending on the type of misrepresentation:

- *fraudulent misrepresentation*: rescission and damages. Damages will be assessed on the basis of what is needed to put the wronged party in the position he would have been in if the fraud had not been committed. They are not assessed on the basis of putting the wronged party in the position he would have been in if the fraud was true.

- *negligent misrepresentation*: rescission and damages. Damages will be assessed on the basis of what is needed to put the wronged party in the position he would have been in if the representation had been true. A court may also award damages only and not rescission if it seems equitable (fair) to do so.

- *innocent misrepresentation*: rescission only. However, a court may award damages instead of rescission if it seems equitable (fair) to do so. This might be where the effect of the misrepresentation was very minor and rescission would be out of all proportion to the harm suffered.

In all cases, rescission will only be ordered if the wronged party has not *affirmed* the contract or allowed too much time to pass.

remedies in civil cases: usually *damages*, which are awarded as of right. However, the court has other remedies which it has discretion to order. These are the *equitable remedies* of *injunction*, *specific performance*, *rescission* and *rectification*. In some cases, the court may make a declaration about a party's status or rights.

remedies in tort: granted by a court or, in some circumstances, carried out by the claimant. Self-help remedies are not liked by the court and, if using one of these, care must be taken to act reasonably in the light of the circumstances known at the time.

Court remedies are:

- *damages*: compensation intended to put the claimant in the position he would have been in if the tort had not been committed;

- *injunction*: an order stopping the defendant doing something, usually used in *trespass*;

- restitution of property: an order that the defendant return property to the claimant.

Self-help remedies are:

- *abatement of a nuisance*: stopping a nuisance; this should not involve going onto the land of the person creating the nuisance unless it is an emergency;

- defence of property or to prevent a trespass: in some circumstances it may be reasonable to use physical force to prevent property being taken or damaged or someone coming onto land;

- re-entry on land: a person entitled to possession of land is entitled to re-enter his land, but it is a criminal offence to use violence or threats of violence or take possession of someone's home without a court order;

- recapture of chattels: the taking back of goods that have been removed;

- *self-defence*: the use of reasonable force to resist someone who is carrying out a *battery*.

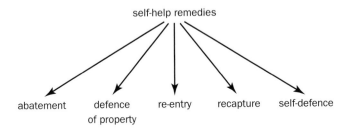

Remedies in tort

remoteness of damage: a term used in *negligence* when deciding what damage the defendant is legally responsible for. If the defendant has acted negligently, he is liable to compensate the claimant whom he has injured for any damage that is reasonably foreseeable. He is not liable for damage that is not reasonably foreseeable, even if it happens as a direct consequence of his actions; this damage is said to be too remote. See also *foreseeability and its effect on damages* and *Wagon Mound (1961)*.

reparation: where an offender has to compensate the victim of his crime in some way. This may be by returning stolen property to the victim or by paying a sum of money for damage caused.

reparation order: an order under the Powers of Criminal Courts (Sentencing) Act 2000 which a court can impose on offenders under the age of 18. An order will require the offender to make reparation as specified by the court either to:

- the community at large; or
- a person or persons who were victims of the offence or were otherwise affected by it. This can only be ordered if the victim consents.

An order is for a maximum of 24 hours work and must be completed under supervision within three months of its imposition.

repeal of a statute means that the *statute* concerned ceases to be law. A statute can only be repealed by Parliament through another Act of Parliament. Some old statutes are repealed because they are out of date and obsolete. The Law Commission has done much work in identifying old legislation which should be repealed and, as a result, Parliament passed the Statute Law Act in 1995 repealing 223 old Acts.

representation: a statement made by one party to a contract to the other which induces (persuades) him to enter into the contract. It is different from a *mere puff* because it is intended to be, and is, taken seriously. It is not a *term* of the contract because it does not become a part of the contract. A statement made during negotiations is likely to be a representation rather than a term if:

- it was made some time before the contract was made (Routledge v MacKay (1954));
- the person making it did not have any specialist knowledge of the subject matter of the contract (Oscar Chess v Williams (1957));
- the person making it suggested the other party check its truth or it was the sort of statement that is usually checked (Ecay v Godfrey (1947));
- the person to whom the statement was made did not consider it a key part of the contract (Bannerman v White (1861)).

If a representation turns out to be false, the person to whom it was made is entitled to rescind (cancel) the contract and can claim *damages* if it was made fraudulently or negligently (see also *misrepresentation*).

reprimand: action taken by the police against young offenders instead of prosecuting them. Sections 65 and 66 of the Crime and Disorder Act 1998 replaced *cautions* with a statutory scheme of reprimands and *warnings* to ensure that all police forces followed the same principles. This was aimed at preventing repeat cautioning as a reprimand can only be given if the offender has never been convicted of any offence or been previously reprimanded or warned. A reprimand can only be given if a child or young person admits they have committed an offence and the police are satisfied that it would not be in the public interest for the offender to be prosecuted.

repudiation of a contract: the rejection of a contract by a wronged party when the other party has breached (broken) the contract. The wronged party has no further duty to carry on with the contract and can claim damages. A contract can only be repudiated if the breach has been sufficiently serious, i.e. a breach of a *condition* or an *innominate term* where the consequences have been serious. See also *rescission*.

res extincta: a Latin term meaning 'an extinct thing'. In contract law, if the parties make a contract about goods which do not exist (are res extincta) at the time the contract is made, the contract is *void*. See also *mistake*.

res ipsa loquitur: a Latin phrase used in *negligence* meaning 'the thing speaks for itself' (i.e. it seems clear that there has been negligence). Normally the claimant has to prove to the court that the defendant acted negligently. This is sometimes difficult to do. But where it seems obvious that there must have been negligence, the court is entitled by the principle res ipsa loquitur to put the *burden of proof* on the defendant rather than the claimant. This means that rather than the claimant having to prove that the defendant has been negligent, the defendant will be found liable unless he can prove he was *not* negligent. The court will take this approach when the defendant was in control of the situation when the claimant was injured and the accident was one that would not normally happen without negligence.

Case example: Mahon v Osbourne (1939)

Swabs were left in the claimant after an operation. It was held that as the defendant was in control of the operation and that swabs are not normally left in a patient unless there has been negligence, it was up to the defendant to prove that he had not been negligent.

rescission of a contract: the cancelling of a contract so that the parties no longer have to carry out any further obligations under it. Rescission takes place where there has been:

- a *breach of contract*: the wronged party is entitled to rescind the contract if there has been a breach of a *condition* or an *innominate term* and the consequences of the breach are serious; or

- *misrepresentation*: the wronged party is entitled to rescind the contract whether the misrepresentation has been made fraudulently, negligently or innocently. The wronged party has a choice of carrying on with the contract or rescinding it and in fraudulent and negligent misrepresentation can also claim *damages*.

See also *rescission for breach of contract* and *rescission for misrepresentation*.

rescission for breach of contract: the cancelling of a contract which occurs when one party to the contract refuses to carry on with it because the other party has breached it. Once the contract is rescinded, neither party has a duty to do anything further under it. However, up until that point the contract still exists, so that if it contains terms regulating what will happen in the event of a breach, these will apply. The innocent party will be entitled to claim *damages* for losses he has incurred. This is also known as discharging the contract by breach or terminating the contract.

Rescission for breach of contract is different from rescission for misrepresentation, as shown in the following chart.

Rescission for breach of contract	Rescission for misrepresentation
• contract comes into existence but is ended early	• contract does not come into existence
• goods sold become buyer's	• goods sold do not become buyer's and must be returned
• damages aim to compensate for losses already suffered and those which arise because the contract has not been fully carried out	• damages aim to put the parties in position they would have been in if representation had been true (negligent misrepresentation) or back in the position they were in before the contract was agreed (fraudulent misrepresentation)

rescission for misrepresentation: the cancelling of a contract by a party who has been misled by the other party's *misrepresentation*. The contract is treated as never having come into existence, and any property that has changed hands under the contract must be returned to the original owner. Any loss incurred by carrying out the contract must be refunded by the person making the misrepresentation. A contract is rescinded by the injured party telling the other party the contract is at an end or by returning the goods obtained under the contract. If the other party cannot be found, informing the police may be sufficient (Car & Universal Finance Co v Caldwell (1965)).

In some situations, a contract cannot be rescinded even if there has been misrepresentation, although damages can still be claimed. These are where:

- there has been affirmation: the innocent party has decided to continue with the contract once he has found out about the misrepresentation;

- too much time has elapsed (except where there has been fraud);
- the goods obtained under the contract have been used so that it is impossible to give them back in substantially the same state;
- a third party has become the legal owner of the goods; this happens if goods are sold on before the contract is terminated.

Rescission can also be for breach of contract, but the effect is different. See also *rescission for breach of contract*.

rescuer in negligence cases: someone who tries to save people, including the defendant, or property which has been put at risk by the defendant's negligent actions. He will be able to claim *damages* from the defendant as long as it was reasonably foreseeable that a rescue would be attempted.

Case example: Ogwo v Taylor (1988)

The defendant negligently set fire to his house while paint stripping using a blow torch. Ogwo, a fireman, was injured while putting the fire out. It was held that it was reasonably foreseeable that, in the event of a fire, the fire brigade would be called, and Ogwo was successful in his claim.

As a matter of public policy, the defences of *volenti* and *contributory negligence* are not normally successful when a rescuer is injured. It is recognised that someone acting instinctively in an emergency may not be as careful as someone who has had time to think. However, if there are standard safety procedures which the rescuer fails to carry out, he may be found to be contributory negligent (Harrison v BRB (1981)).

residence order: a court order saying who a child is to live with. This person will have day-to-day responsibility for the child. Occasionally a joint residence order will be made in favour of two people who are living in different places. Where there is a dispute, the court will apply the *welfare principle*. It will pay most attention to the wishes of the child provided he is old enough.

Once a residence order has been made, nothing should be done to change the surname of the child or to remove him from the UK without written permission from everyone who has *parental responsibility* (this does not apply to short holidays).

residuary beneficiary: the person who inherits the remaining estate in a will. The remaining estate is what is left after funeral expenses, tax and debts and all other *legacies* have been paid out from the estate.

respondent: the term used in divorce proceedings for the spouse against whom a divorce is sought. The spouse who starts off divorce or judicial separation proceedings is called the *petitioner*.

restitution interest: the right of a party to a contract to deprive the other party, who has breached (broken) the contract, of a gain that he has unjustly made. This method of assessing *damages* is used where:

- there has been a complete failure of *consideration*, and the party in breach has made a gain, e.g. a buyer has paid for goods in advance and has not received them;
- the party in breach has made an unjust gain, although the wronged party has not suffered any real loss.

Case example: Penarth Dock Engineering v Pound (1963)

The defendants bought a floating dock from the claimants, but then refused to move it from where it was berthed as agreed in the contract. The defendants argued that damages should be minimal as the claimants had not lost any money because they would not have been able to use the berth anyway, given that it was being closed down. The court held that damages should be assessed by looking at what the defendants had gained from their breach of contract.

restitution order: in a criminal case, an order that an offender return property to its owner. For example, if the offender has stolen jewellery and is caught by the police still in possession of that jewellery and then found guilty of theft, the court can order that the jewellery be returned to its owner.

restitutionary damages: damages equivalent to the profit that the defendant has made by his breach of contract. These are only granted in exceptional cases such Att-Gen v Blake (2000) where a double agent who had breached his duty of confidentiality in his contract of employment with MI5 was paid to write a book about his life. Damages amounted to the payment he received from the publishers.

restraint of trade: restricts a person from carrying out his trade, profession or business within a certain area for a specified period of time. Restraint of trade clauses appear in:

- contracts of employment where the employer wants to prevent an employee working for a competitor either while still employed by the employer or when he leaves. The clause will usually be upheld if it only covers an area where most of the employer's clients come from and is for a reasonable length of time. The employee can be stopped from using confidential information he has acquired while working for the employer but not from using skill and knowledge he has acquired;

- contracts for the sale of a business where the buyer does not want the seller to set up in competition nearby. The clause will be upheld if the buyer has bought the goodwill of the business and wants to protect it;

- restrictive trading agreements where a wholesaler insists that the retailer only sells his goods. This will be upheld if the period of time of the agreement is reasonable. In Esso Petroleum v Harper's Garage (1968), a five-year agreement was held to be reasonable but not a 21-year agreement.

restrictive covenant: promise by one party to a contract not to do something. They are mainly found in:

- contracts of employment where an employee undertakes not to work for a competitor either during his period of employment or after he leaves. The covenant has effect even when the contract of employment comes to an end. See also *restraint of trade*;

- contracts for the sale of land where the buyer undertakes not to carry out certain acts, e.g. building more than one house on the land. In certain circumstances, not just the buyer of the land is bound by the covenant but anyone who later buys the land.

resulting trust: a trust which arises where one person is the legal owner of property but someone else has contributed towards its purchase, and both parties had intended that they would have a share in the property. No formal trust has been set up, but the court considers it would be unfair (inequitable) if the person who made the contribution did not have a share in the property. Normally, the contribution towards the purchase must be money provided for the deposit or making the mortgage payments. However, in Grant v Edwards (1986), it was held that where the house owner was only able to pay the mortgage because the other party had paid all the household bills, this was sufficient contribution although not made directly towards buying the house. There is an overlap between resulting and constructive trusts, and both are used by courts to do justice in a situation where one party has acted unfairly.

retrial: a retrial of a criminal case following a conviction by a *jury* in the *Crown Court* can be ordered where either:

- the jury in the first trial at the Crown Court failed to agree on a verdict; or
- the *Court of Appeal* on an appeal against a conviction order that the case be retried.

In either situation, the defendant will be tried in front of a new jury who will not normally be told of the first trial.

A retrial of a criminal case following an *acquittal* by a jury is very rare and can only be ordered if:

- the jury or witnesses in the original trial were interfered with by the defendant or his associates; or
- (in the future) for serious offences there is new and compelling evidence (Criminal Justice Bill 2002).

retribution: the idea of recognising that an offender has done wrong and of making the punishment fit the crime. This idea can be referred to as the offender getting his 'just deserts'. The offender deserves punishment because of his wrongdoing. The punishment must be in proportion to the crime, and this idea can be seen in the guidelines set out by the *Court of Appeal* for some offences, such as possession of illegal drugs, where different levels of sentence are suggested according to the type and amount of drug involved.

retributive theory of sentencing: based on *retribution*. The theory is that punishment should only be for retribution for the crime and not for any other purpose. This idea was expressed by Kant, when he wrote in the 19th century:

> 'Judicial punishment can never be used merely as a means to promote some other good for the criminal himself or for civil society, but instead it must in all cases be imposed on him only on the ground that he has committed a crime.'

revocation of a contract: the cancelling of a contract which occurs when a *condition* of the contract has been breached (broken). See also *rescission for breach of contract*.

revocation of an offer: the cancellation of an *offer* in contract. The *offeror* can revoke an offer at any time as long as the person to whom the offer has been made has not already accepted it. Revocation can be carried out by the offeror writing to or telling the *offeree* that the offer has been withdrawn. It can also happen if the offeree learns that the offer has been revoked from someone else (Dickinson v Dodds (1876)). It takes effect when the offeree knows about it, for example when the letter of revocation is received (see also *communication rules in contract law*).

In *unilateral contracts* (e.g. reward offers), revocation must be communicated in the same way as the original offer was. It is likely that the offeror will be unable to revoke the offer once the offeree has started carrying out the requested actions, although these will not amount to *consideration* until the action is complete (Daulia Ltd v Four Millback Nominees Ltd (1978)).

offeror posts letter
revoking offer

offer in existence   offer still exists   offer is cancelled

offeree receives letter
revoking offer

Revocation of an offer

revocation of a will has the effect of cancelling that will. A will may be revoked by:

- deliberately destroying the will;

- making a written declaration that the will is revoked; this must be signed and witnessed by two people;

- making a new will; this revokes any contradictory parts of the previous will, but does not necessarily revoke it all unless it is stated in the new will that the previous will is revoked;

- getting married; this automatically revokes any will made, unless that will stated that it was made in contemplation of the marriage.

rewards offers in contract law are *unilateral contracts*. The person offering the reward makes a general offer which a person can accept by carrying out the specified terms. He does not have to inform the person offering the reward until he has completed the required action. Once he has done so, a contract is made and he is entitled to receive the reward (even if he carries out the action for a different motive). No contract comes into existence if the action is carried out by someone who does not know about the reward and it cannot be claimed. To revoke a reward offer, it is necessary to give at least as much publicity to the revocation as was given to the reward offer.

reward poster: in contract law, this can constitute an *offer,* provided it is clear and specific enough. A person seeing a reward poster and carrying out its terms will be entitled to the reward, even though he does not tell the person offering the reward until he has completed this. His *acceptance* is the carrying out of the terms, and a contract is made when he has done this. The offer made in a reward poster can only be revoked by making sure that as much publicity is given to the *revocation* as was given to the offer.

right to silence in criminal cases, is the principle in this country is that an accused person is innocent until proved guilty. This means that it is for the prosecution to prove guilt; the accused does not have to prove his innocence. As a result, until 1994, any refusal by a suspect to answer questions could not be commented on at his trial. This was the 'right to silence'. The Criminal Justice and Public Order Act 1994 changed the law on this point. The Act states that if a defendant does not answer questions (either at the police station or in the court), his failure to do so can form part of the evidence against him. However, it cannot be the only evidence against him for a prosecution to succeed.

rights in personam: rights that can only be enforced against a specific person.

213

rights in rem: rights in respect of a piece of land which can be enforced against anyone who has an interest in the land.

rights of audience means the right to present a case in court on behalf of another person. *Barristers* have rights of audience in all courts. *Solicitors* have rights of audience in the *Magistrates' Court* and the *County Court* but only have full rights of audience in the higher courts if they have a *certificate of advocacy*. Under the Access to Justice Act 1999 solicitors will eventually be able to get full rights of audience when they qualify, but only when their training includes more emphasis on the art of presenting a case in court.

rights of occupation: in family law, a right to occupy the accommodation that a married couple has treated as their family home. Where one spouse is the sole legal owner or tenant, the other has a right not to be evicted. Where the property is owned, this right should be registered at the Land Registry or the Land Charges Registry, as otherwise, in some circumstances, it can be lost when the property is sold or mortgaged.

If there is a dispute between the couple, the court can make an *occupation order* stating who has a right to be in the property. This right does not apply to couples who are not living together.

riot: an offence under the Public Order Act 1986. For the offence to be committed, there must be 12 or more people using or threatening unlawful violence (this need not be all at precisely the same time) for a common purpose and whose conduct taken together would cause a person of reasonable firmness to fear for his personal safety.

robbery: stealing with force. It is an offence under s8 of the Theft Act 1968 which makes a person guilty of robbery if:

- he steals; and

- he uses force or puts another person in fear of force being used at the time of the *theft* or immediately before it; and

- that force is used in order to steal.

Only minimal force is needed, e.g. a push is sufficient. The important point is that the force is used in order to steal. For example, two people have a fight and one knocks the other unconscious. As he is about to leave the scene, he then decides to steal the other's watch; this is not robbery, as the force used was not 'in order to steal'. The *theft* is a quite separate incident.

Robbery can only be tried at the *Crown Court*, and the maximum sentence available to the court is life imprisonment.

Royal Assent: the final stage before a *Bill* becomes an *Act of Parliament*. After the Bill has been passed by Parliament, the formal assent of the monarch is required to make it law. The last time that a monarch refused assent was in 1707.

Royal Commissions: temporary committees set up to investigate and report on one specific area of law. They are made up of a wide cross-section of people with expertise, and/or an interest in the subject area. The chairman is often a senior judge, and the commission is usually referred to by the name of the chairman, such as the *Runciman Commission*. Once the report is made, the commission will be disbanded. Some Royal Commissions have led to major changes in the law. For example, the Royal Commission on Police Procedure (the Phillips Commission), which reported in 1981, had many of its recommendations made law in the *Police and Criminal Evidence Act 1984*.

rule of law: a doctrine which underpins our legal system. Dicey, in the Law of the Constitution, wrote that the rule of law had three main elements. These are:

- all men are equal before the law; this includes government officials;
- no one should be punished unless they have broken the law;
- the rights of the individual, such as *freedom of the person* and *freedom of speech*, are rights which come from the law.

Runciman Commission: a *Royal Commission* on Criminal Justice which reported in 1993. The Commission was set up to examine the 'effectiveness of the criminal justice system in England and Wales in securing the conviction of those guilty of criminal offences and the acquittal of those who are innocent'. The Commission had 22 research studies carried out on different areas of the criminal justice system and heard evidence from over 600 organisations. The report contained 352 recommendations for improving the system, including the continuous videoing of custody suites, the setting up of an independent body to investigate possible miscarriages of justice and modifying the selection of a jury so as to reflect the ethnic minority of a defendant or victim in the case.

Many of the recommendations have been implemented, for example the *Criminal Cases Review Commission* has been set up to investigate possible miscarriages of justice. However, some of the recommendations have not been followed. In particular, despite the Runciman Commission recommending that suspects should not have to answer police questions, this *right to silence* has been eroded by the allowing of inferences to be made from the suspect's silence.

Rushcliffe Committee recommended in 1945 the setting up of a government funded system of legal advice and representation. The main principles set out by the Committee were:

- legal aid should be available in all courts;
- it should be available not only to the poor, but also to those of moderate means;
- the scheme should be means tested;
- lawyers acting for legally aided clients should receive adequate pay.

This report led to the start of the legal aid scheme in 1949.

Rylands v Fletcher (the rule in) states that a person is responsible for damage caused by the escape of something he keeps on his land provided that:

- he has brought it onto or collected it on his land, i.e. it was not naturally there; and
- it was something that was a special use of the land bringing increased danger to others (non-natural use); and
- it was something that was likely to do a mischief if it escaped; and
- it left the defendant's land (escaped).

The defendant is liable whether he has taken reasonable care or not to prevent the escape.

Case details: Rylands v Fletcher (1866)

The defendant had a reservoir constructed on his land. His contractors found mine shafts which appeared to have been filled in. When the reservoir was filled, water seeped through the shafts into the claimant's mine. Although the defendant had not been negligent, he was found liable.

The rule in Rylands v Fletcher has developed from *nuisance*, but there are some differences as shown in this chart.

Rule in Rylands v Fletcher	Nuisance
● dangerous item brought onto land	● item can be there naturally
● item not part of the natural use of the land	● item can be part of natural use
● item must escape	● item must affect neighbour's use of his land
● item must be likely to cause physical harm	● item need only be enough to interfere with enjoyment of land

The defences available are:

● *act of a stranger*: a third party caused the escape in an unforeseen way;

● *volenti non fit injuria*: the claimant consented to the presence of the dangerous item;

● default of the claimant: the claimant caused the escape;

● statutory authority: the defendant had a right under statute to have the item on his land.

Sale and Supply of Goods Act 1994: amended s14 of the Sale of Goods Act 1979. The definition of *merchantable quality* was widened and the term changed to *satisfactory quality*. The Act also states that:

- a buyer will not be held to have accepted goods until he has had a reasonable opportunity to examine them;
- asking the seller to repair the goods does not necessarily mean the buyer has accepted the goods;
- a minor breach of ss13, 14 and 15 is only a breach of *warranty* not *condition* where the buyer is not a *consumer*.

sale of goods: the exchange of goods for money. It does not include the sale of land, the sale of money, except for curios or antiques, or an exchange of goods rather than a sale. All contracts for the sale of goods are regulated by the *Sale of Goods Act 1979*.

Sale of Goods Act 1979 (as amended) gives protection to buyers of goods by implying *conditions* into all contracts for the *sale of goods* so that they automatically become part of the contract. If these conditions are breached, the buyer is entitled to cancel the contract, receive his money back and *damages* if he has suffered any further loss or, for consumers, replacement or repair if not disproportionate. The conditions implied are:

- s12: the seller is the legal owner of the goods; this is important because if he is not, the buyer will not become the owner (cannot acquire *good title*);
- s13: the goods match their description; this applies where goods are ordered unseen through the post and also where the buyer sees the goods but relies on the description. For example, a shopper buying a tin of baked beans or a purchaser of a car described as being a 'Herald convertible white 1961' (Beale v Taylor (1967)) rely on the description that has been given;
- s14: the goods are of *satisfactory quality*; this applies except where the seller has pointed out a defect at the time of the sale or the buyer has had a look at the goods and the defect was an obvious one. The goods must also be *fit for the purpose* for which they are normally used. (This section does not apply to a sale where the seller is a private individual who does not sell goods as a business.);
- s15: where the goods have been bought after the buyer has looked at a sample, the goods must match the sample, the buyer must have an opportunity to examine the goods and the goods must not have any hidden defect.

If there has been a breach of a condition, the buyer is entitled to a reasonable amount of time in which to inspect the goods. If he keeps them after this time, he is said to have accepted the goods (see also *acceptance in a sale of goods*) and can only claim *damages*; he is no longer entitled to rescind (cancel) the contract.

If the buyer of the goods is a business, a trivial breach of s13 and s14 will be treated as a breach of a warranty rather than a condition, entitling the buyer to *damages* only. See also *Sale of Goods Act, excluding ss12–15*.

Sale of Goods Act, excluding ss12–15: the *Unfair Contract Terms Act 1977* regulates when ss12–15 can be excluded, by agreement, from a contract for the sale of goods. Where the buyer is a consumer, ss12–15 cannot be excluded by the seller. Where the buyer and seller are businesses they can agree to exclude ss13–15, if reasonable, but not s12.

Can the section be excluded?	By a business selling to a consumer	By a private individual selling to another private individual	By a business selling to another business
s12	no	no	no
s13	no	yes	yes, if reasonable
s14	no	does not apply	yes, if reasonable
s15	no	yes	yes, if reasonable

same sex couples in some areas of law, are treated in the same way as non-married heterosexual couples. In 2002, the Court of Appeal held that, under the Human Rights Act, couples of the same sex had the same rights under the Rent Act 1977 as different sex couples. In July 2003 the government proposed to introduce a *Civil Partnership Registration* scheme for same sex couples which would give them many of the rights that married couples have.

satisfactory quality: used in s14 of the *Sale of Goods Act 1979* to describe the standard expected of goods. Goods are of satisfactory quality if a reasonable person would regard them as satisfactory, taking into account any description including advertising by the manufacturer, the price and all other relevant circumstances. Factors the court will look at are the appearance and finish of the goods, their freedom from minor defects, safety, durability and fitness for all purposes for which the goods were supplied. The higher the price, the greater the quality is expected to be, whilst second-hand goods and 'seconds' are not expected to be of such a high standard.

Scott v Avery clause: a clause in a contract by which the parties agree that if they have any dispute in relation to the contract, they will go to *arbitration*. This agreement means that the courts will normally refuse to deal with any dispute; the parties must go to arbitration.

Scrutiny Committee: the Joint Select Committee on *Statutory Instruments*, responsible for reviewing statutory instruments (regulations made by government ministers and departments). However, as there are over 2,000 SIs issued each year, the Scrutiny Committee cannot check every one. In addition, any reviews it does make are based on fairly narrow grounds. The main points it will check are:

- does the statutory instrument impose a tax?
- does it have retrospective effect so that it would affect past matters?
- has it gone beyond the powers given under the *enabling Act*?

If there are any problems, the Committee has no power to make any changes. It can only inform the House of Commons and the House of Lords of its findings. There has also been criticism that ministers ignore some of the critical reports by the Scrutiny Committee.

search warrants can be issued by a magistrate under s8 of the *Police and Criminal Evidence Act 1984*. A search warrant must name the premises to be searched. The police can then enter those premises without the occupier's consent and carry out of search of them.

secondary participant, repentance of: if a secondary participant to a crime wishes to withdraw from the *joint enterprise*, it is not always enough for him just to leave the scene of the crime. He may still be guilty if the *principal offender* continues with the offence.

Case example: R v Becerra (1975)

Becerra and another man set out to commit a burglary. Becerra had given the other man a knife to use against anyone who might interrupt them. When they were inside the property, they heard someone approaching and Becerra said 'Come on, let's go' and left the building. The other man stayed and stabbed and killed the approaching person. It was held that Becerra had not done enough to withdraw effectively from the crime and he was also guilty of murder. It was suggested that for an effective withdrawal, he needed to do something positive to prevent the knife being used.

secondary participation in a crime refers to those who do not carry out the actual offence but help the *principal offender* in some way. A secondary party is charged with the same crime as the principal. To be guilty as a secondary party, the person must aid, abet, counsel or procure the crime (see also *aiding and abetting, counselling, procuring*) They must also have knowledge that the principal is going to carry out a crime and intend to help him with it. The knowledge about the crime need only be that the principal is likely to carry out a certain type of crime.

Case example: R v Bainbridge (1959)

The defendant supplied cutting equipment for use in a burglary. He did not know which premises were to be burgled, nor did he know the date on which the burglary was going to be carried out. It was held he was guilty as a secondary party.

If the principal carries out a different type of crime, for example, if they murder someone during the course of a burglary, the secondary party will only be guilty of this other crime if he realises that the principal may kill or cause serious injury. If the 'new' crime is not foreseen, then the secondary party is not guilty (R v English (1997)).

secured periodic payments order: an order made by the court in family law that one spouse pay the other or a *child of the family* regular maintenance payments of a specified amount. To guarantee that the payments are made, the payer must set up a fund of capital which can be used if the payer stops paying. The order can last indefinitely or for a fixed period of time, but comes to an end if the recipient remarries.

self-defence: a possible defence to a criminal charge, provided only such force as is reasonable in the circumstances was used. The reasonableness of the amount of force used is judged on the facts as the defendant believed them to be. If excessive force is used, the defendant has no defence (R v Clegg (1995)).

If the defendant has made an honest mistake about the need for self-defence, then he must be judged on the facts as he believed them to be (R v Williams (1984)). Evidence that the defendant is suffering from a mental condition which makes him more likely than a normal person to regard things as threatening is admissible (R v Martin (2002)).

self-defence in tort: a defence which is used in *trespass to person*. A defendant will not be liable if he acts to protect himself, someone else or property and he acts reasonably in the situation as he sees it at the time.

self-induced automatism occurs where the defendant has brought on an automatic state through his own actions; for example, if the defendant takes a prescribed drug knowing that it is likely to make him drowsy and not aware of his actions. Self-induced automatism can be a defence to a crime, but this will depend on the type of crime charged as well as the defendant's awareness of the consequences.

If the crime charged is one of *basic intent*, then self-induced automatism brought on by alcohol or illegal drugs or by the defendant's reckless conduct will not be a defence (R v Bailey (1983)). If the crime charged is one requiring *specific intent*, then the automatic state will give the defendant a defence, provided he did not have the required intention.

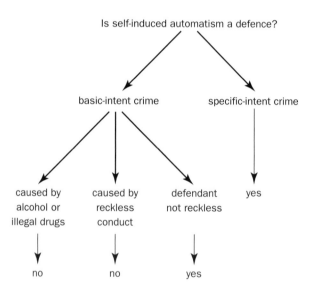

Self-induced automatism as a defence

sentencing: the decision of what penalty should be imposed on a person who is guilty of a criminal offence. In making this decision, the judge takes into consideration:

- the seriousness of the offence;

- information about the defendant, including whether he has previous convictions for similar offences;

- any mitigating circumstances (i.e. any matters that might persuade the judge to be lenient);

- *sentencing aims*.

Sentencing Advisory Panel: a panel set up by the Lord Chancellor under s81 of the Crime and Disorder Act 1998 which has the power to propose that sentencing guidelines be made or revised for a particular category of offence. In addition, when the Court of Appeal decides to make or revise sentencing guidelines, the Court must notify the Panel.

sentencing aims: there are four main sentencing aims. These are:

- *retribution*;
- *deterrence* of crime;
- *protection of the public*;
- *rehabilitation*/reform of offender.

When sentencing an offender, a judge may choose which of these aims he wishes to promote. This will depend on the type of crime committed and the defendant's circumstances. If the offender is young, the most likely aim will be reform; if the crime is a violent one, then the aim will probably be protection.

The Criminal Justice Bill 2002 includes a clause setting out the purposes of sentencing for offenders aged 18 or over. These purposes are:

- the punishment of offenders;
- the reduction of crime (including reduction by deterrence and its reduction by the reform and rehabiliation of offenders);
- the protection of the public; and
- the making of reparation by offenders to persons affected by their offences.

sentencing guidelines: sentencing guidelines are guides given by the Court of Appeal to judges in the Crown Court as to the normal length of imprisonment that should be imposed on offenders for certain types of offence.

Case example: R v Wijs (1998)

Guidance was given as to the appropriate level of sentence for importing and/or possessing amphetamines with intent to supply. The larger the amount of the drug, the greater the sentence:
- up to 500 g: up to two years imprisonment;
- more than 500 g but less than 2.5 kg: two to four years imprisonment;
- more than 2.5 kg but less than 10 kg: four to seven years imprisonment;
- more than 10 kg but less than 15 kg: seven to ten years imprisonment;
- more than 15 kg: ten years to the maximum of 14 years imprisonment.

Section 80 of the Crime and Disorder Act 1998 places the Court of Appeal's making of sentencing guidelines on a statutory footing. If the Court decides to make guidelines, it must have regard to:

- the need for consistency in sentencing;
- the sentences imposed by courts for offences of the relevant category;
- the cost of different sentences and their relative effectiveness in preventing re-offending;
- the views of the *Sentencing Advisory Panel*.

The Criminal Justice bill 2002 proposes a Sentencing Guidelines Council which will have the power to set sentencing guidelines.

separation of powers: the principle that the three functions of government of making law, enforcing the law and judging disputes about the law should be carried out by three separate groups of people. This theory was put forward by Montesquieu. He believed this separation was necessary to prevent too much power being given to one person (or group of people). See also *Montesquieu's theory of the separation of powers*.

separation order: in family law, this was to replace a *judicial separation* under the *Family Law Act 1966* using the same procedure as for a divorce.

serious arrestable offences: defined in the *Police and Criminal Evidence Act 1984 (PACE)* and include treason, murder, manslaughter, rape, hijacking, kidnapping, drug-trafficking and certain offences connected to guns or explosives. The police have extra powers when investigating such offences. In particular, the police can ask for the time limit for detaining a suspect to be extended from 24 hours up to a maximum of 96 hours.

Serious Fraud Office (SFO): a body set up by the Criminal Justice Act 1987 to investigate and prosecute large-scale fraud cases, where the amount involved is over £1 million. It is staffed by lawyers and accountants with expertise in different financial areas and has special powers to require the production of documents and information from anyone connected with an investigation.

Initially the SFO was criticised for failing to get convictions in many cases that it prosecuted. However, since the mid 1990s the SFO has had a high success rate in its prosecutions.

settlement of property order: an order made by the court in family law that one spouse settle on the other or a *child of the family* specified property, such as the matrimonial home. The effect of this is that one spouse can go on living in the matrimonial home but the other spouse still has a financial interest in it and will be entitled to a share of the proceeds once it is sold. See also *Harvey order*, *Martin order* and *Mesher order*.

settlement out of court: where the parties in a *civil case* come to an agreement over their dispute and do not need to have the matter tried in court.

severable contract: one that can be divided into different stages or parts so that payment can be claimed as each stage is completed. A building contract often specifies stage payments, and in other cases, the court may decide on the facts that a contract is severable.

several liability arises where two or more people acting independently are responsible for the same *tort*. Both are separately liable to pay the injured party full compensation, although he cannot recover more than once. See also *joint and several liability*.

sex discrimination: unlawful under the Sex Discrimination Act 1975. Discrimination means treating a person less favourably because of his sex. This is *direct discrimination*. An example would be if a garage owner refused to employ any women as mechanics. His motive for doing this does not matter; it is still direct discrimination if he refuses just because they are women or if he has another reason, such as he thought the men working at the garage would refuse to work with a woman.

It is also sex discrimination if an unjustified condition is applied which is such that only a much smaller percentage of one sex could comply with it. For example, if an employer advertises for workers with a condition that only those over six feet high can apply, it is obvious that far fewer women than men can meet this requirement, so this is *indirect discrimination*, unless the employer can show that employees have to be this height to operate certain machinery safely.

A person who claims that they have been discriminated against has the right to take the case to a tribunal and claim compensation.

sexual harassment: is defined by the European Union Code of Practice as 'unwanted conduct of a sexual nature, or other conduct based on sex, affecting the dignity of men and women at work'. In English law there is no specific law forbidding sexual harassment, but it is held to be against the Sex Discrimination Act 1976 as it involves subjecting a person to a detriment or treating them less favourably because of their sex.

Case example: Porcelli v Strathclyde Regional District Council (1984)

Two male colleagues frequently made suggestive remarks to a female worker, deliberately brushed against her and generally made her life at work so unpleasant that she asked to be transferred to another post. This was held to be discriminatory behaviour.

shareholder: someone who owns shares in a *company*. This allows them to take part in the management of the company by voting at its annual general meeting and at any extraordinary general meeting. The liability of shareholders for the debts of the company is limited to the value of the shares at the time they purchased them. So, if a shareholder has paid in full for the shares, that shareholder has no further liability for the company debts.

shares: the means by which a company raises capital. Members agree to take a certain number of shares at a set value per share and become *shareholders*. The number of shares is the measure of the members' interest in the company, and this dictates how many votes each individual member has at general meetings. The value of the shares is the extent of the member's liability for the company's debts.

silence, right to: see *right to silence*.

silent partner: a partner who has contributed capital and takes a share of the profits but is not involved in the day to day running of the *partnership*. Another name for a silent partner is a *sleeping partner*.

slander: a type of *defamation*. It is a statement which tends to lower the person referred to in the estimation of right-thinking members of society and which is in a temporary form, e.g. in speech or by gestures. (Defamatory broadcasts, although they contain speech, are libel.) A claimant bringing a claim has to show that he has suffered financial loss as a result of the slander, for example, he has lost his job, except where the allegation is that:

- he has committed a serious criminal offence;
- he is suffering from an infectious disease that would cause other people to avoid him;
- he is incompetent to fulfil his job or position;
- in the case of a woman, she is unchaste.

See also *libel* which is the permanent form of defamation.

sleeping partner: see *silent partner*.

small claims: *civil claims* for amounts of less than £5,000. Such claims are dealt with by a *district judge* in the Small Claims Court of the *County Court*. The hearing is quicker and less formal than a case in the main County Court. Litigants are encouraged to take the case themselves and not to use a lawyer.

small claims procedure: less formal than the procedure in the ordinary *County Court*. Cases are heard by a district judge and the parties are encouraged not to use a lawyer. The judge is trained to take more of an active role in the case and to ask questions and make sure that the parties are able to explain their case. However, research by Baldwin in 1996 showed that, after the increase of the limit to £3,000, the parties were more likely to use lawyers. The limit was raised again in 1999 to £5,000. See also *Woolf Report*.

sole trader: a person who is in business on his own account. He is self-employed and has sole responsibility for the running of the business. He is also liable for any debts of the business.

solicitors: one of the two legal professions, the other being *barristers*. To become a solicitor, it is usual to have a degree in law and then take the Legal Practice Course of the *Law Society*. Those with a degree in another subject must do a year's training in the core legal subjects before going on to the Legal Practice Course. After this, all would-be solicitors must serve a two-year training contract in a solicitors' firm or other legal organisation before being admitted as a solicitor.

Solicitors are allowed to form partnerships and they do a variety of work. This ranges from a sole practitioner who deals with everyday problems such as wills and *conveyancing* to large city firms who do specialist commercial work. Solicitors have *rights of audience* so that they can conduct cases in the *Magistrates' Court* and the *County Court*. Those who wish to present cases in the Crown Court or the High Court can obtain a *certificate of advocacy*.

Solicitors Complaints Bureau: set up to investigate complaints such as delay or over-charging against solicitors. By 1995, it was dealing with 26,000 complaints per year. Unfortunately, it was too inefficient, with two out of every three complainants being dissat-isfied with the way it handled complaints. As a result, it was abolished in 1996 and in its place the *Office for the Supervision of Solicitors* was set up.

Solicitors Disciplinary Tribunal hears serious complaints about solicitors and has the power to strike solicitors off, so preventing them from practising.

Solicitor-General: one of the Law Officers of the government. He is a member of the government and is the deputy to the *Attorney-General*. He carries out any functions delegated to him by the Attorney-General.

sources of law: the ways in which we get our law. The law in England and Wales comes from a variety of different places. The main sources of law are:

- case law which is the law made by the judges when they decide cases (see also *judicial precedent*).
- *Acts of Parliament*, which are the laws passed by Parliament;
- *delegated legislation*, which is law made by such people as government ministers and local authorities under powers given to them by Parliament;
- *European Union law*, which has been an increasingly important source of law since the United Kingdom joined the EU in 1973.

Historically there was another source: custom. But this very rarely provides new law today.

See Figure on page 225.

sovereignty of Parliament: the theory that Parliament has the supreme authority to make law. This is based on the idea of democratic law-making, as the House of Commons is elected by the citizens of this country. However, membership of the European Union has affected the sovereignty of Parliament. EU law now has priority over any conflicting English law. This was made clear by the Factortame case.

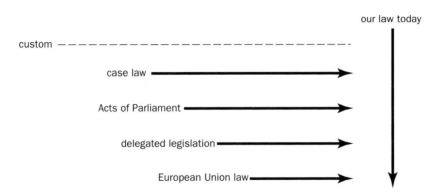

Sources of law

Case details: Factortame (1990)

Parliament had passed the Merchant Shipping Act 1988 to protect British fishermen by allowing vessels to register only if 75 per cent of the shareholders were British. The European Court of Justice held that this Act was in contravention of the EU principle of freedom of movement of workers. The court also ordered the British government to pay compensation to Spanish fishermen who had suffered financial loss as a result of not being allowed to fish in British waters.

special damage in tort is:

- in *slander*: loss of money or a material advantage, e.g. losing a job; this is something more than loss of reputation or being avoided by friends;
- in *public nuisance*: loss which is more than that suffered by other members of the group of people affected.

special damages: in tort, damages that can be itemised, e.g. loss of earnings while in hospital, damage to car. The term can also mean losses that are not an obvious consequence of the tort and need to be specified when starting a court action. Damages which cannot be itemised, such as damages for pain and suffering, are called *general damages*.

special relationship: in *negligent misstatement*, a relationship that is so close that it is almost equivalent to a contractual relationship. It arises when:

- the defendant who made the statement knew or ought to have known that it would be relied on by the claimant (this applies whether he made the statement to the claimant or to someone else, knowing that it would be passed onto the claimant); and
- the claimant used the information for the purposes for which the statement was made; and
- the claimant relied on the defendant's skill, judgment or care when making the statement; and
- it was reasonable for the claimant to rely on the defendant's statement.

Case example: Caparo Industries v Dickinson (1990)

Accountants negligently audited a company's accounts. It was held that they were responsible towards the company and the shareholders to whom the auditors had a duty to report. However, they were not liable in negligent misstatement to a person who decided, on the basis of the accounts, to make a takeover bid for the company, even though that person was a shareholder.

specific intent crimes: those for which the prosecution must prove that the defendant had a particular intention. This intention will vary with the crime committed, and there is no clear-cut way of deciding which crimes are specific intent crimes. It is easier to give examples to show what is meant by specific intent. *Murder* is a specific intent crime; the prosecution must prove that the defendant intended to kill or to cause grievous bodily harm. *Theft* is another specific intent crime; the prosecution must prove that the defendant was dishonest and that he intended to permanently deprive the other person of the property.

Another way of describing specific intent is to say that it is where *recklessness* is not enough for the *mens rea* of such crimes. See also *foresight of consequences*.

specific issues order: a court order in family law dealing with one aspect of a child's upbringing where the parents, or others with *parental responsibility*, are in disagreement. For example, the court may be asked to decide whether a child should receive private or state education.

specific performance: a court order made when there has been a breach of contract. In exceptional cases, the court may order the defendant to carry out the contract. It is usually granted where damages would not be an adequate remedy. Because it is an *equitable remedy*, it will not be granted where it would cause severe hardship or be particularly unfair to the defendant or where the claimant has acted unfairly and is trying to take an unfair advantage. The court will also not make this order where it would require the court's supervision to carry it out or would mean the defendant carrying out a personal service.

speculative damages: in contract, damages to compensate the claimant for losing a chance of acquiring a benefit. They are difficult to assess exactly because the claimant has not lost a definite benefit.

Case example: Chaplin v Hicks (1911)

An actress was prevented from attending an audition. Twelve out of the 49 actresses attending were given jobs so she lost a one in four chance of getting a job. The court awarded her damages of £100, a large sum at the time, assessed on a speculative basis.

standard form contracts: contracts which are not individually negotiated. Instead, one of the parties uses the same form of contract for all its agreements, and the other party has to accept this or not enter into the agreement at all. Powerful businesses will often use these standard form contracts to try to impose wide *exclusion clauses* on everyone they do business with. These are controlled, to a certain extent, by:

- the *Unfair Contract Terms Act 1977*: where a contract is made on one party's written standard terms of business, that party cannot rely on a clause which limits or excludes liability for his own breach of contract unless it is reasonable. He also cannot rely on a clause which says that he will not be in breach of contract if he does something which is very different from what he agreed to do;

- the courts: any exclusion clause will have to be very clear and exactly cover the breach of contract that has occurred before the court will agree that liability can be excluded. (See also *contra proferentum rule*);

- the *Unfair Terms in Consumer Contracts Regulations 1999*: where a *consumer contract* is made under the standard terms of the business selling and these terms are unfair, the consumer will not be bound by them. Terms will be held to be unfair if they cause a significant imbalance between the business and the consumer regarding their respective rights and obligations under the contract.

standard of care (in negligence) sets the standard a defendant must reach in his activity if he is not to be found to be negligent. If he is exercising a skill (e.g. driving a car, carrying out an operation), he must use the skill of an ordinary competent person qualified to do that task. If he is carrying out another activity (e.g. manufacturing goods), he must take reasonable precautions, taking into account the degree of risk of harm, the potential seriousness of any injury, the costs of precautions and the importance of the activity.

standing committee: a committee of MPs that deals with the Committee stage of a *Bill* and considers each part of it in detail. This committee then reports to the House of Commons on their suggestions for alterations to the Bill in the next stage of consideration of the proposed new law. See also *Act of Parliament.*

stare decisis means 'stand by the decision'. It is the basis of the doctrine of *judicial precedent* and it ensures that points of law decided in past cases are followed by judges in later cases. The concept of stare decisis supports the idea of certainty in the law and of fairness and justice, as like cases will be decided in a similar way.

state-of-the-art defence in the Consumer Protection Act 1987 states that a producer is not liable if, at the time of manufacture, the scientific and technical knowledge was such that a producer would not have discovered the defect. Comparison is made with other producers of similar products.

statute: another name for an *Act of Parliament*.

statutory authority: a defence in *tort*. A defendant will not be liable if he carries out an act which he had been given authority to do under an Act of Parliament. For example, television licensing officials have been given authority by Parliament to enter people's property without permission when carrying out their duties and therefore cannot be sued for trespass to land.

statutory charge allows the *Legal Services Commission* to claim back the cost of providing the claimant with legal aid from the amount of *damages* won by the claimant. This can mean that the claimant receives very little benefit from the case and is a major criticism of the way in which *civil legal aid* operates.

statutory instruments: rules or regulations made by government ministers or departments by way of *delegated legislation*.

statutory interpretation: the process by which judges have to decide the meanings of words or phrases in Acts of Parliament or other legislation. Although, when laws are drawn up, the draftsman tries to make them as clear as possible, there are still many problems which can occur so that the meaning is unclear. These are:

- a broad term: there may be words used to cover several possibilities, and it is difficult to decide exactly what it does cover;

- ambiguity: some words may have more than one meaning, and it is difficult to decide which is meant in the Act.

- a drafting error or omission: there may be a mistake which makes the meaning uncertain, or an omission so that a situation which should be included appears not to be.

- new developments: new technology may mean that an old Act of Parliament does not apparently cover the situation.
- changes in the use of language: the meanings of words change over the period of time.

Judges have different approaches to statutory interpretation. Some will take the literal meaning of the words, others will look beyond the words to try to discover what the law was meant to include. See also *literal rule*, *golden Rule*, *mischief rule* and the *purposive approach*. There are also rules of language which are used in trying to decide meanings of words and phrases. These are *ejusdem generis, expressio unius est exclusio alterius* and *noscitur a sociis*.

statutory law: law made by Parliament. An Act of Parliament is statutory law.

stipendiary magistrates: full-time paid judges in the *Magistrates' Court* at the busier courts, mostly in London and other cities. They are qualified lawyers, as they must have been a *barrister* or *solicitor* for at least seven years. They can sit to hear cases on their own, while *lay magistrates* have to sit as a panel of two or three. In 2000 stipendiary magistrates were re-named district judges (Magistrates' Court).

stop-and-search powers: under s1 of the *Police and Criminal Evidence Act (PACE)*, the police may stop and search people and vehicles in a public place, provided the policeman has reasonable grounds for suspecting that the person is in possession of stolen goods or prohibited articles (these include *offensive weapons*). The police also have power under the Misuse of Drugs Act 1971 to stop and search people whom they have reasonable grounds for believing are in possession of illegal drugs.

Under Code of Practice A, the police should not stop people just because of their age or ethnic background or other stereotyping. But there is some evidence that certain types of people are stopped more frequently by the police and that only a small percentage of those stopped are actually charged with any crime.

stop now order: a court order obtained by the *Director-General of Fair Trading* directing a trader to stop breaching one of the ten EC Directives that protect consumers. These can be obtained even if there has not been a persistent breach and the Director no longer has to try to obtain assurances first from the trader that he will stop. If the order is breached, the trader is in contempt of court and can be fined or sent to prison.

strict liability offences: those which do not require proof of *mens rea* for at least one element of the *actus reus*. This means that a defendant can be guilty if he does the act required for the crime, even though he does not have intention to do the crime. Usually, there must be intention to do part of the actus reus.

Case example: Harrow London Borough Council v Shah and Shah (1999)

A shop assistant employed in the defendants' shop sold a lottery ticket to a boy aged 13 in breach of a regulation which provided that 'no National Lottery ticket shall be sold by or to a person who has not attained the age of 16 years'. The assistant thought, reasonably, that the boy was at least 16. The defendants had done everything in their power to make sure that their staff did not sell to underage children. Despite these two points the defendants were found liable as the regulation did not require any mens rea.

In the case above the court decided that the offence was not 'truly criminal' and for that reason were more willing to decide that it was a strict liability offence. Where an offence is 'truly criminal' the modern trend is to avoid interpreting offences as being of strict liability, even if the wording of the offence does not include any requirement for mens rea (B v DPP (2000)).

Crimes in which no mens rea at all is needed are called *absolute liability* offences.

strict liability offences, justification for: most strict liability offences are regulatory crimes applying to businesses. Examples include preventing selling food that is beyond its sell-by date, or driving a vehicle with defective tyres. In both these situations, the defendant is guilty even though he did not know that the goods were out of date or that the tyres were defective. A major argument for making such crimes ones of strict liability is that it protects the public. There are, however, many arguments for and against creating crimes of strict liability. The main ones are listed below.

Pros	Cons
• protection of public	• liability should not be imposed on those
• easier to enforce	who are not blameworthy
• obliges people to adopt high standards	• wrong to penalise those who have taken care
• saves court time as there is no	• no evidence that it raises standards
need to prove intention	• takes up court time at the sentencing stage

strict liability (law of tort) means the defendant is liable even if he has taken all reasonable precautions. In most torts, the defendant is not liable unless he has been in some way at fault, but strict liability applies in cases brought:

- under the rule in *Rylands v Fletcher*;

- in *nuisance*;

- under some Acts, e.g. *Animals Act 1971* and the *Consumer Protection Act 1987*.

subjective recklessness in the criminal law means that the accused is reckless only if he had recognised that there was some risk of the particular harm occurring, but gone on to take the risk. It is subjective because it is judged from the defendant's point of view.

Case example: R v Cunningham (1957)

The defendant removed a gas meter from an unoccupied house so that he could steal the money in it. This left gas escaping. The gas seeped into the next-door house and affected the person there. Cunningham was charged with '*maliciously* administering a noxious thing so as to endanger life'. It was decided that he was not guilty, as he could only be guilty if he realised there was a risk that the gas could affect someone.

See also *Cunningham recklessness*.

subjective test: a test used in contract, tort and criminal cases where the court asks, 'What did the defendant realise ...?' The defendant is judged by what he had in mind at the time and not what an ordinary person would have thought. See also *subjective recklessness*.

substantial performance: see *performace*.

suicide pact: a partial defence to murder under s4 of the Homicide Act 1957. If a killing takes place as part of a joint suicide pact between the victim and the defendant, then the charge of murder will be reduced to one of manslaughter. This allows the judge discretion in sentencing.

summary offence: one which can only be tried at the *Magistrates' Court*. Examples of summary offences are criminal damage causing less than £5,000 worth of damage, drink-driving and driving without insurance.

summing up: the judge's speech to a jury at the end of a case. In his summing up, the judge will remind the jury of the evidence and draw their attention to the most important points. He will also direct the jury in any points of law that they need to understand in order to come to a decision in the case.

summons: a document issued from the office of a court of justice calling upon the person to whom it is addressed to attend at court.

supervision order: an order which can be imposed on a young offender under the age of 18. Its effect is to place the young person under the supervision of the local social services. Normally the young person will live at home, but the court can order that he resides in local authority accommodation for up to six months.

supervision requirement is one of the orders that are proposed for offenders aged 16 or over as part of a *community order* under the Criminal Justice Bill 2002. Such a requirement will mean that an offender has to attend appointments with a supervising officer.

Supply of Goods and Services Act 1982 gives protection to customers in situations not covered by the *Sale of Goods Act 1979*. These are where:

- goods are given in exchange for other goods;
- goods are given in exchange for a service;
- services are given in exchange for money.

Where goods are supplied by someone acting in the course of a business, the same *conditions* as those in the Sale of Goods Act 1979 are implied into the contract. A breach of an implied condition entitles the person receiving the goods to rescind (cancel) the contract and claim *damages* if he has suffered any loss. The rules about excluding these conditions are the same as in the Sale of Goods Act 1979.

Where services are supplied, the implied terms are:

- s13: the supplier will carry out the service with reasonable skill and care;
- s14: the service will be carried out within a reasonable time (if not already agreed by the parties);
- s15: the charge for the service will be reasonable (if not already agreed by the parties).

Section 15 applies to all contracts for the supply of services, not just ones where the supplier is acting in the course of a business.

A breach of an implied term entitles the injured party to rescind the contract or just claim damages, depending on how serious the effect of the breach is. Where the person who receives the services is a *consumer*, it is only possible to exclude the implied terms if this is reasonable.

Supreme Court: a proposed replacement for the House of Lords. In July 2003 the Government started consulting on separating the judicial functions of the House of Lords from the legislative function. This means that a new separate supreme court will have to be created as the final court of appeal in the English Legal System.

surety: a person who promises to pay the court a sum of money if the defendant on *bail* in a criminal case fails to turn up for the next stage of the proceedings. No money is actually paid at the time of making the promise; it is only payable if the defendant does not turn up. This is different to some other countries where the bail money must be paid before the defendant is released on bail, but is returned to the surety when the defendant attends for trial.

suspended prison sentence: a prison sentence under which the defendant does not go to prison unless he commits another offence within a certain time limit. The maximum sentence is two years (six months in the *Magistrates' Court*) and the maximum period for which it can be suspended is also two years. The Criminal Justice Act 1991 stated that a suspended sentence should only be given where the offence is so serious that an immediate custodial sentence would have been appropriate, but there are exceptional circumstances in the case that justify suspending the sentence. This Act led to a reduction in the number of suspended sentences. The Criminal Justice Bill 2002 proposes reducing the maximum term which can be suspended to 51 weeks for one offence or 65 weeks for two or more offences.

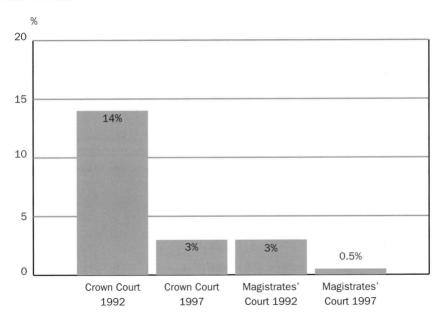

Suspended prison sentence – bar chart showing suspended sentences as a percentage of sentences imposed

---

Do you need revision help and advice?

Go to pages 259–99 for a range of revision appendices that include plenty of exam advice and tips.

taking a motor vehicle without consent: an offence under s12 of the Theft Act 1968. This section covers the taking of any 'conveyance', which is anything constructed or adapted for carrying a person or persons by land, air or water. This is wide enough to include cars, lorries, buses and motor bikes and also motor boats and aeroplanes. It does not, however, include a pedal cycle; this is a separate offence under s12(5) of the Theft Act 1968.

The prosecution does not have to prove that the defendant intended to permanently deprive the owner of the 'conveyance'; taking it without consent is the essence of the offence, so 'joy-riders' are guilty of this offence. The following can be guilty:

- the taker: this can be by pushing a vehicle rather than driving it;
- a driver: this includes anyone who took the vehicle or drove it knowing it had been taken without the owner's consent;
- a passenger who allowed themselves to be carried in it knowing it had been taken without the owner's consent.

See also *aggravated vehicle taking*.

talesman: a juror who is added to a jury when the original number of jurors summoned to the court is insufficient to form a jury. A talesman can be selected from anyone in the street or local offices provided they meet the *jury qualifications*.

tape recording of police interviews: under s60 of the *Police and Criminal Evidence Act 1984* and Code of Practice E, the police have to tape-record all interviews of suspects which take place at a police station. At the end of the interview, a master tape of the interview must be sealed in the suspect's presence to ensure that it cannot be tampered with in any way.

tariff sentences: those in which a set standard of sentencing is observed. In England and Wales, there are no strict tariffs, but there are guidelines issued by the Court of Appeal for some offences, suggesting the appropriate length of imprisonment. In some states of America there is a set tariff which operates so that the judge can only pass a sentence of a given length and has very little discretion to alter that set sentence.

tenancy: a lease. The word is usually used when the lease is a short one.

tenants in common: two (or more) people entitled to the same land together. It is different from a *joint tenancy* because each person can leave their share to whom they like and they can have different size shares in the property.

tender: a competitive bid for business. A person selling goods or looking for a supplier of goods or services will invite people to tender and will normally choose the most favourable tender. In contract law, the tender is an offer which can be accepted or rejected unless the person inviting the offers has shown a definite intention to choose the most favourable tender. In this case, the invitation to tender is an offer which the person making the tender accepts by submitting the tender.

term of a contract: a promise, statement or stipulation which forms part of the contract (e.g. the price, delivery date, condition of the goods) which is definite and an important factor for the parties when deciding whether to enter into the contract. Terms can be *conditions*, *warranties* or *innominate terms*. If a term of the contract is breached (broken), the other party is entitled to *damages* and may also be entitled to *rescission*. In deciding what the terms of a contract are, the court will look at:

- the contract itself, where it is a *written contract* (see also *non est factum* and *parol evidence rule*);
- other written terms referred to in a written contract which were intended to be part of the contract and were brought to the attention of the parties before the contract was made;
- terms in previous contracts, where the parties have frequently done business before (see also *course of dealing*);
- negotiations before the contract was made, where there is an oral contract; the points made during negotiations can be *mere puffs*, *representations* or terms. They are more likely to be terms if they were made immediately before the contract was agreed, the person making them had special knowledge of the subject and assured the other party they were true, and they were key to persuading the other party to make the contract;
- statute: terms are implied into every *consumer contract*;
- custom: terms that are normal in that trade or market place will be implied into the contract;
- what the parties must have intended when they made the contract (see also *officious bystander test*);
- what courts have recognised in past cases as standard terms; this applies particularly to landlord and tenant contracts and employment contracts.

term of years absolute: a lease. The lessee has a right to have possession of the land for a fixed period of time.

termination of a contract: the ending of a contract so that nothing further is done under it. A party to a contract is entitled to terminate it when the other party has breached (broken) it provided that the breach is a breach of a condition or a breach of an innominate term where the consequences are serious. Termination can also take place where the other party has clearly shown that he has no intention of carrying out the contract. The contract has existed up to the point at which it was terminated and, if it contains terms setting out what will happen in the event of a breach, these will apply.

termination of an offer: the bringing to an end of an *offer* in contract law. Once the offer has been terminated, it can no longer be accepted, and the *offeror* is no longer at risk of being committed to a contract.

Offers are terminated by:

- acceptance or refusal by the *offeree*;
- a *counter offer* by the offeree (Hyde v Wrench (1840));

- *revocation* or withdrawal of the offer by the offeror which reaches the offeree before he has accepted the offer (Byrne v van Tienhoven (1880));

- lapse of time: either the deadline given by the offeror for acceptance has passed or, if no deadline is given, a reasonable length of time;

- failure of a precondition where the offer is conditional;

- death of either party except where the offeree accepts the offer not knowing the offeree has died and the item being sold is an impersonal one.

See also *communication rules in contract law*.

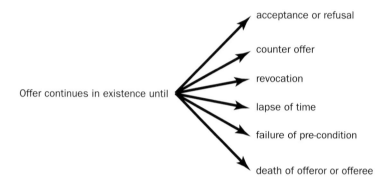

Offer continues in existence until:
- acceptance or refusal
- counter offer
- revocation
- lapse of time
- failure of pre-condition
- death of offeror or offeree

testament: another name for a *will*.

testator/testatrix: the legal term for a person who makes a will. Testatrix is the feminine form of the word 'testator' so this means a woman who has made a will. The word 'testator' can be used to refer to either a man or a woman.

testimony: the evidence given by a witness in a case.

theft: an offence under s1 of the Theft Act 1968. This section states that anyone who 'dishonestly appropriates property belonging to another with intention of permanently depriving the other of it' is guilty of theft. This means that for the *mens rea*, two points must be proved:

- that the person acted *dishonestly*; this means that he knew he was being dishonest according to ordinary standards (*Ghosh test*);

- that he intends to permanently deprive the other person of the property (this does not mean that the other has to be permanently deprived: if a thief is caught leaving a shop with stolen goods in his pockets, it is clear that he intended to permanently deprive the shop). It also covers situations where an item is 'borrowed' but by the time it is given back to the other person, it is badly damaged or in some other way worthless.

The act of stealing is the '*appropriation*' of property. This is defined in the Theft Act as any assumption of the rights of an owner. In R v Gomez (1993), it was decided that this included situations where the owner of the property handed it over to the thief because of deception. This means that any offence of *obtaining property by deception* is also theft.

third party: in contract law, somebody who is neither of the two parties to the contract. In tort, someone who is neither the person who committed the tort or the person who was injured by it.

third parties, rights under a contract: a third party may be able to enforce a contract under the Contracts (Rights of Third Parties) Act 1999 although there is no *privity* of contract where the contract was intended to confer a benefit on him and the contract makes clear that the parties intended that the third party should be able to enforce it. The third party may not exist at the time the contract was made but can still enforce it, if he is identifiable from the contract.

time immemorial: in order for a *custom* to be accepted as law, it has to be shown that it has existed since time immemorial, that is 'time beyond memory'. This was fixed by the Statute of Westminster 1275 as being since the year 1189.

time is of the essence: a phrase used in contracts to show that delivery of goods or the performance of a service must take place by a fixed date. Failure to do so will the be a *breach of contract*. Normally, performance is only expected within a reasonable time, but the parties can include a deadline in the contract and make it a *term* of the contract at the time the contract was made. One party can also make it a term later (Charles Rickards Ltd v Oppenheim (1950)).

tort: a wrong which entitles the injured party to claim compensation from the person who committed it. The main types of tort are:

- *negligence*;
- *defamation*;
- *trespass*;
- *occupiers' liability*;
- *deceit*;
- *breach of statutory duty*;
- *the rule in Rylands v Fletcher*;
- *nuisance*

tortfeasor: a person who commits a *tort*.

trade descriptions: in consumer law, a description given to goods. If this description is false, the buyer can sue for breach of s13 of the *Sale of Goods Act 1979* or for *misrepresentation*. It is also a criminal offence under the *Trades Descriptions Act 1968* to give a false description. If the seller is successfully prosecuted, the court can award the buyer compensation.

Trades Descriptions Act 1968 makes it a criminal offence for any person in the course of a trade or business to apply a false description to any goods or to supply or offer to supply any goods to which a false description has been given. The trader will be convicted whether or not he realised the description was false. However, he will escape conviction if a very clear disclaimer was given at the time the goods were offered; for example, if a market stall has a clear notice which can be seen when the buyers are looking at the goods and deciding whether to buy.

It is also an offence to knowingly or recklessly make a statement that is false about services, accommodation or facilities. This covers travel brochures, and companies can be prosecuted if they say facilities exist when they do not. They will escape prosecution, however, if the statement is about something that will happen in the future, e.g. an artist's impression of an hotel which is said will be ready next year.

Trading Standards Departments: set up and funded by Local Authorities. Their role is to check that local traders comply with consumer legislation and, if necessary, bring prosecutions where an Act has created a criminal offence, for example under the *Trades Descriptions Act 1968* and the *Consumer Protection Act 1987*. They also report to the *Office of Fair Trading* practices which seem to be unfair to consumers; this may lead to a change in the law.

training contract: the final training stage for a *solicitor*. It is a two year period in which the trainee works in a solicitors' firm or other legal organisation such as the Crown Prosecution Service getting practical experience.

transfer: the document used to transfer ownership of land from one person to another where the land has been registered at the Land Registry. A conveyance is used where the land is not registered.

transfer of property order: an order made by the court on *divorce* or *separation* that one spouse transfer to the other or to a *child of the family* specified property, such as the matrimonial home or investments. When deciding whether to make an order, the court will take into account the factors set out in the *Matrimonial Causes Act 1973 s25.*

transfer of undertakings is the change of ownership of a business. In employment law, the rights of employees are protected on such a change. The new employer is bound by the terms of the contract of employment of an employee, except as to future pension provisions. The length of time an employee worked for the previous owner of the business is counted towards *continuity of employment* so that employment rights remain protected.

transferred malice: the concept that an intention aimed at one person can be transferred to another, so making the defendant guilty.

Case example: R v Mitchell (1983)

The defendant intentionally assaulted a man in a queue in a Post Office causing him to stumble against an 89-year-old woman. She died from her injuries. Mitchell was found guilty of her manslaughter. His intention to do an unlawful act against the man was transferred to her.

However, the intention cannot usually be transferred to make the defendant guilty of a different type of offence. For example, if D throws a stone at a window meaning to break it, he has the intention required to be guilty of criminal damage. If the stone hits a person, then the intention to do criminal damage cannot be transferred to make D guilty of assault.

treasure: defined by the Treasure Act 1996 as objects over 300 years old which contain at least ten per cent gold or silver. Coins over 300 years old are also treasure if at least one of the coins contains gold or silver. Any item found with the object or the coins is also treasure. If there is a dispute as to whether an item is treasure or not, this will be decided by the Coroners' Court. Treasure belongs to the Crown, not the finder. However, the finder is usually paid a substantial reward if he reports his findings quickly.

Treaty of Rome: the Treaty which founded the *European Economic Community* (now called the *European Union (EU)*) in 1957. The Treaty sets out the aims of the Union and also governs how it is operated. The Treaty is automatically law in all member states. It has *direct effect* so that citizens of each member state can rely on its provisions. The two most important Articles in the Treaty which confer rights on individuals are:

- Article 39, which guarantees the free movement of workers throughout the EU;
- Article 141, which guarantees equal pay for equal work regardless of sex.

treaties: international agreements. By entering into a treaty, the government of the United Kingdom is undertaking to implement the laws which are the subject matter of the treaty.

trespass: a type of *tort*. It is a direct interference with someone else's person or property which cannot be justified and therefore entitles the injured person to seek compensation in the civil courts. Trespass can be:

- *trespass to person*
    - *assault*: putting someone in fear of suffering physical force
    - *battery*: directly applying physical force to another person
    - *false imprisonment*: restricting someone else's freedom of movement;
- *trespass to goods*: interfering with someone else's goods;
- *trespass to land*: directly interfering with someone else's land.

The trespass does not have to have caused any damage for an action to be brought. It is *actionable per se*. A person who carries out a trespass to person and to goods can also be charged with a criminal offence, but trespass to land can only be a crime if the trespasser intends to disrupt a lawful activity being carried out on the land.

Defences to trespass are:

- *consent*;
- *necessity*;
- *inevitable accident*;
- *statutory authority*.

trespass ab initio: a Latin phrase meaning 'trespass from the beginning'. Where a person is given a right to go onto someone else's land by an Act of Parliament (e.g. to arrest someone) or by common law (e.g. to abate a nuisance), and then commits a wrongful act, his action is treated as trespass from the moment he enters the land.

trespass to goods: in tort, an intentional, direct and unlawful interference with goods in the ownership or possession of another person. It includes damaging goods, removing them or borrowing them. No damage has to happen to the goods for a claim to be brought.

Defences to trespass to goods are:

- *statutory authority*, e.g. the police can take possession of goods in certain circumstances;
- *necessity*, to prevent immediate damage to a person or property.

trespass to land: in tort, a direct, physical and unlawful interference with land which is in the possession of another person. It includes going onto someone else's land, placing something on the land or allowing livestock to go onto the land. No damage has to have occurred for the claimant to bring a claim (it is *actionable per se*). The defendant must have intended to go on the land or have been negligent in allowing livestock to stray. It is no defence to say that he did not realise that the land was someone else's.

A B C D E F G H I J K L M N O P Q R S T U V W X Y Z

Defences to trespass to land are:

- the defendant had permission to be on the land; this applies as long as he only does what he has been allowed onto the land for and the permission had not been revoked;
- justification provided by law, e.g. the police in certain circumstances are allowed to come onto land without permission.

Remedies are:

- *damages*;
- an *injunction* to stop the trespass being repeated;
- re-entry; a landowner is entitled to take back his land provided he does not use or threaten to use violence; if the property is a home, he must obtain a court order;
- a court order for possession of the land; this is used particularly against squatters.

trespass to person: a direct and physical interference with someone else's body which cannot be justified. The *claimant* does not have to show that he actually suffered any injury as a result of the trespass to bring a claim (it is *actionable per se*).

The three types of trespass to person are:

1 Assault

This is an action which causes the claimant to fear that he is about to suffer physical violence, e.g. threatening to hit him. There must be some movement by the defendant; standing still is not enough, and the defendant must intend to frighten the claimant.

2 Battery

This is a direct and intentional application of physical force to the claimant which may or may not be forceful enough to cause injury. The defendant must intend to make physical contact, but he does not have to have any hostile intention, e.g. kissing someone without their consent is a battery.

3 False imprisonment

This is preventing someone from exercising freedom of movement. It can be by locking someone in a room, wrongfully arresting someone, or preventing a person walking in the direction he wants to go in provided there is no reasonable alternative route.

Defences which particularly apply to trespass to person are:

- *consent*: where the claimant gives genuine consent to the trespass and, in the case of serious injury, the trespass served a socially useful purpose;
- *self-defence*: the use of reasonable force to protect person or property;
- *necessity*: acting to prevent further harm, e.g. a doctor treating an unconscious patient in an emergency to save their life;
- lawful *arrest*: a person carrying out an arrest can use reasonable force and can go onto land without permission.

See also *negligence* for where the interference is indirect.

trespasser (in burglary) is anyone who has not got permission to enter a building or part of a building. The defendant must know, or be subjectively reckless, as to whether he is trespassing. Where the defendant goes beyond the permission given, he may be considered a trespasser.

Case example: R v Smith and Jones (1976)

Smith and a friend went into Smith's father's house and stole two televisions from the house. As the son of the householder he had a general permission to enter, but by stealing it was held that he had gone beyond that permission and so was a trespasser and guilty of burglary.

trespasser (non-visitor): in occupiers' liability, a person who does not have permission to be on the occupier's premises and is not therefore a *visitor*. The occupier of premises has a duty under the Occupiers' Liability Act 1984 to provide such care as is reasonable in the circumstances to make sure the non-visitor does not suffer injury, provided:

- he is aware of the danger or has reasonable grounds for believing that it exists;
- he knows or has reasonable grounds for believing that non-visitors are in the vicinity of the danger;
- the risk is one which he may reasonably be expected to offer the non-visitor some protection against.

The standard of care is less than that owed to visitors and, often a notice will be sufficient. Greater care is expected to be taken when the occupier knows the trespasser is a child (BRB v Herrington (1972)). Although this case was heard before the 1984 Act, it indicates the level of care expected towards child trespassers.

trial: the testing of a case in court.

triable either way offences: the middle range of criminal offences which can be tried either in the *Magistrates' Court* or the *Crown Court*. *Theft* and *assault occasioning actual bodily harm* are examples of triable either way offences. If a defendant pleads guilty to a triable either way offence, the *magistrates* will decide whether the case is suitable for them to deal with or whether it should be sent to the Crown Court. If a defendant pleads not guilty, he has the right to choose trial by *jury* at the Crown Court, or he can agree to the case being tried at the Magistrates' Court.

tribunals: forums for deciding disputes which are used in place of a court. There are a number of different tribunals, and each has the power to hear a specific type of case. For example, the Child Support Appeals Tribunal hears appeals against decisions on the amount an absent parent has to pay to their child.

trustee: a person who holds property on *trust* for another. The main duty of a trustee is to carry out the terms of the trust and preserve the trust property.

trust arises where property legally belongs to one person but he is under a duty to use that property only for the benefit of someone else. For example, when somebody dies, his *executors* become the legal owners of his property and can use it to pay his debts, but must then distribute what is left to the people named in the will.

What other subjects are you studying?

A–Zs cover 18 different subjects. See the inside back cover for a list of all the titles in the series and how to order.

uberrimae fidei: a Latin phrase meaning 'of the utmost good faith'. Contracts uberrimae fidei include those where there is a *fiduciary relationship* between the parties. This could be, for example, between solicitor and client, contracts for partnerships and insurance contracts. In these contracts the parties must tell each other all relevant facts, and if they fail to do so, the contract is voidable.

Case example: Woolcott v Sun Alliance and London Insurance (1978)

Mr Woolcott submitted a claim against his insurers when his house burnt down. The insurers successfully applied to have the insurance contract set aside because Mr Woolcott had failed to reveal all material facts in his application form. When asked the question 'are there any other matters which you wish to be taken into account?', he had replied 'no'. The court held that the fact he had failed to reveal that he had served 12 years for robbery was sufficient to void the contract.

UCTA stands for the *Unfair Contract Terms Act 1977*.

ultra vires means 'beyond the powers'. It is an important concept in law, as anything done beyond the powers can be challenged as not being legally valid. Three main areas in which the idea is used are:

- *delegated legislation*, where law that is ultra vires can be declared invalid;
- *judicial review*, where the fact that a decision made was beyond the powers of those making it is a reason for allowing a judicial review of that decision and quashing it;
- company law, where a company cannot do anything that is not set out in the objects of the company in the *Memorandum of Association*; if it does, this is ultra vires and it may have the effect of making a contract with the company invalid.

undue influence (on a contract) arises where one party to a contract has unfairly used his influence to persuade the other to enter into a contract which is clearly disadvantageous to him. If the court is satisfied that undue influence has been used, the contract can be set aside, provided the claimant has acted *equitably*. The claimant will have to show that:

- the defendant exerted undue influence on him (actual undue pressure); or
- there was a *fiduciary relationship* between himself and the defendant, e.g. the defendant was his solicitor. In this case, it will be assumed that the defendant exercised undue pressure (presumed undue pressure) and it will be up to him to show that he did not. He could do this, for example, by showing that the claimant received independent and competent advice or that the consideration was adequate.

See also *banking cases in contract law* for cases where wives have argued that their husbands have exercised undue pressure.

Unfair Contract Terms Act 1977 stops businesses from escaping liability by including an unreasonable *exclusion clause* in the contract. The court is given the power to say that an exclusion clause (e.g. 'Cars parked at owner's risk') which is unfair is void, although the rest of the contract remains valid.

Case example: George Mitchell v Finney Lock Seeds (1983)

A contract for the sale of seeds contained a clause stating that if the seeds were faulty, the maximum compensation would be a refund of the purchase price, £200. The seeds were planted and the whole crop failed. The total loss of profit was £61,000. It was held that the exclusion clause was not reasonable, given the size of the farmer's loss.

The courts are more likely to find that an exclusion clause is unreasonable if:

- the parties are of unequal bargaining power;
- it was not possible for the buyer to find the same goods elsewhere;
- it was not possible to obtain insurance to cover the situation;
- the price was high;
- the term was not a normal one in that trade or it had not been in previous contracts between the parties.

The Act also prevents the exclusion of:

- liability for death or personal injury through negligence in all contracts;
- liability for breach of contract or not substantially fulfilling the contract in *consumer contracts* unless reasonable;
- liability for breach of contract or not substantially fulfilling the contract where the contract is on one party's standard written terms unless reasonable;
- S12 of the *Sale of Goods Act 1979* in any contracts;
- SS13–15 of the *Sale of Goods Act 1979* in *consumer contracts;*
- SS13–15 in other contracts unless reasonable.

unfair dismissal occurs where an employer dismisses an employee without a valid reason. The reasons for which an employer can fairly dismiss an employee are set out in s98 of the Employment Rights Act 1996. They are:

- lack of capability or qualifications for the job;
- conduct of the employee which justifies dismissal; e.g. stealing from the firm;
- *redundancy;*
- that the continued employment would be a breach of the law, e.g. continuing to employ someone after it has been discovered they are an illegal immigrant;
- some other substantial reason.

The Employment Rights Act also makes it automatically unfair to dismiss because of:

- pregnancy;
- health and safety duties;
- carrying out duties of an employee representative.

To claim unfair dismissal, an employee must normally have been employed continuously for a minimum of one year. However, this does not apply to the automatically unfair reasons for dismissal.

unfair terms directive concerns unfair terms in contracts between businesses and consumers. It was made part of UK law by *statutory instrument* entitled *Unfair Terms in Consumer Contracts Regulations 1994* and updated in 1999.

Unfair Terms in Consumer Contracts Regulation 1999 stops businesses imposing any term which is unfair in *standard form contracts* for the supply of goods or services when dealing with *consumers*. The consumer will not be bound by any term which is unfair.

Terms will be held to be unfair if they:

* create a significant imbalance between the seller and the buyer to the detriment of the buyer; and

* are not in good faith.

Examples of unfair terms are set out in the regulations, e.g. excluding the legal liability of the business if it fails to perform the contract. If the contract is in writing the wording must be in plain and intelligible language. Any ambiguity in the wording of a clause will be construed (interpreted) in a way that is least favourable to the seller. See also *contra pro-ferentum rule*. Unlike the Unfair Contract Terms Act 1977, the Regulations only apply to contracts for the sale of goods or supply of services between a business and a private individual; they do not apply to contracts between businesses.

unfitness to plead occurs where a defendant in a criminal case is, because of his mental condition, unable to give, receive or understand information about the trial. If the defendant is unfit to plead, there can be a trial of the facts of the case to establish whether the defendant did the acts alleged. If it is found that he did, this is not a finding of guilt, but it gives the judge power to order that the defendant be admitted to a mental hospital or put on a supervision order.

unilateral contract: one where the person accepting an *offer* carries out the *consideration* first and then lets the *offeror* know. They are usually reward offers or specific promises made by advertisers. For example, a person offers £50 for the return of his dog. The person finding the dog returns it to the owner and then claims the £50. The contract is complete when the dog is returned, even though the owner did not know that his offer had been accepted before the consideration had been carried out. If the person finding the dog did not know about the reward when he returned the dog, there is no binding contract because he is not accepting the owner's offer. The person who knows about the reward is entitled to it, even if he carries out the consideration for different motives. See also *Carlill v Carbolic Smokeball Co (1893)*, a case concerning an advertisement.

unilateral mistake: in contract law, a fundamental misunderstanding about an important part of the contract made by one (or both) of the parties at the time the contract was agreed. The contract normally remains *valid*. The three types of unilateral mistake are:

* the *offeror* does not clearly communicate his offer and it is misunderstood by the offeree; the contract is valid (unless the offeree knew or should have known about the mistake). The contract is based on what the reasonable person would have understood the offeror to have meant.

- one party makes a mistake about the identity of the other party; normally the contract will be valid (but see also *mistake as to identity*);

- both parties make different mistakes and are at cross purposes. There has been no real offer and acceptance and the contract is void.

Case example: Raffles v Wichelhaus (1864)

Confusion arose over two ships with the same name. Although the parties appeared to be in agreement, they were each negotiating about a different ship. There was no real agreement and the contract was void.

unincorporated means that a business has not been created as a separate personality from the people who are running it. Both *partnerships* and *sole traders* are unincorporated businesses. It is an important distinction, as partners and sole traders are responsible for all the debts of their businesses while, in an incorporated business, the members have *limited liability* for the debts.

unintentional defamation: a defence in *defamation* where there has been *innocent publication* by the defendant and he has made an *offer of amends* which has been refused by the claimant.

unlawful act manslaughter: see *constructive manslaughter*.

unreasonable behaviour: in divorce law, one of the ways of proving that a marriage has irretrievably broken down. See also *behaviour*.

unsolicited goods: goods sent to a potential buyer who has not requested them. Under the *Consumer Protection (Distance Selling) Regulations 2000*, these goods are treated as an unconditional gift to the recipient and become his as soon as they arrive. This does not apply if goods are for the purposes of a business.

utilitarian theories of sentencing: based on the idea that all punishment must serve a useful purpose. This can be useful to the defendant, such as reforming him, or useful to society, for example, by imposing a long prison sentence to protect the public from the defendant. The main aims under the utilitarian view of sentencing are:

- *deterrence*;

- *protection of the public*;

- *reform* of the offender;

- *reparation* to the victim.

The utilitarian view is a forward-looking one, based on the future usefulness of the sentence. This is different to the *retributive theory of sentencing*, under which punishment is imposed just because the offender has committed a crime.

valid contract: one which is legally enforceable and cannot be terminated by one party without the other party's agreement.

variation of marriage settlement order: an order made by the court in family law where one spouse has settled (given for the recipient's lifetime) property on the other as part of a pre-nuptial agreement. This can be varied by the court on divorce. Whilst not many couples settle property on each other on marriage, this order has also been made to divert some of a husband's pension to his ex-wife (Brooks v Brooks (1996)).

veil of incorporation: a phrase used to indicate that a *corporate body* is a separate legal entity from its members. The idea is that a veil hangs between a *company* and its members to act as a screen between them so that the members are not liable for the company's debts, nor is the company liable for the acts of its individual members. However, in some cases, if there has been fraud or sharp practice or illegality, the courts will look behind the veil of incorporation and treat the corporate body and the members as one and the same person.

Case example: Gilford Motor Co. v Horne (1933)

A former employee was bound by a *restraint of trade* clause in his contract of employment which prevented him from setting up business in opposition to his former employer. In order to avoid this restriction, he started a company and used it to carry on a competing business. The court held that the setting up of the company was a 'mere cloak or a sham' to avoid the restraint and that both he personally and the company he had started were bound by the restraint of trade clause.

verdict of jury: the decision of the jury. This decision must be announced in open court so that all parties in the case can, if they wish, hear it. Where there is a jury of 12, it is possible for the verdict to be by a majority of 11 to one or ten to two.

vertical direct effect means that citizens in European Union member states can rely directly on an EU treaty, *regulation* or *directive* even if the member state has not implemented that law in their own country. Treaties and regulations always have direct effect. Directives only have vertical direct effect if:

- the time limit for the state to implement the directive has passed; and
- the directive is sufficiently clear; and
- the claim is against the state or an arm of the state.

Case example: Marshall v Southampton and South West Hampshire Area Health Authority (1986)

Miss Marshall was made to retire at the age of 62, while men doing the same work did not have to retire until the age of 65. An EU directive (the Equal Treatment Directive 76/207) required member states to bring in law banning all discrimination in work on the grounds of sex. This directive had not been fully implemented in the UK, and English law still allowed discrimination on retirement ages. The European Court of Justice held that Miss Marshall could rely on the directive to make a claim of discrimination.

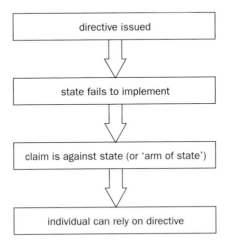

```
┌─────────────────────────────────┐
│        directive issued         │
└─────────────────────────────────┘
                 ▼
┌─────────────────────────────────┐
│      state fails to implement   │
└─────────────────────────────────┘
                 ▼
┌─────────────────────────────────┐
│ claim is against state (or 'arm of state') │
└─────────────────────────────────┘
                 ▼
┌─────────────────────────────────┐
│   individual can rely on directive  │
└─────────────────────────────────┘
```

vicarious liability (criminal law) means that one person can be liable for crimes committed by another. This is not a normal situation in criminal law and only occurs:

- where a statute uses words that are interpreted as making a person liable; words such as 'sell' will make an employer guilty as well as the person who actually sells;

- under the principle of delegation; if a manager with a licence to sell alcohol delegates the authority under that licence to another, the manager may be liable for the crimes committed by that other in relation to the licence;

- two rare common law offences – public nuisance and criminal libel.

vicarious liability (negligence): the legal responsibility of an employer for his *employee's* negligent actions. A claimant who has been injured by an employee can sue both him and his employer in negligence. The claimant will need to show that:

- he was injured through the employee's negligent actions; and

- the employee was a genuine employee and not an *independent contractor* (although an employer remains responsible for the actions of an independent contractor if he orders him to carry them out); and

- the employee was acting in the *course of his employment*; this means that he was carrying out his job, even though he was doing it in a way that he had been forbidden to do.

Case example: Fennelly v Connex South Eastern Ltd (2001)

A passenger was assaulted by a ticket inspector during a ticket inspection. The company was held to be vicariously liable although the inspector was acting in breach of the rules of the company.

If the employer has to pay damages to the successful claimant, he can claim these back from the employee, but this does not happen often in practice. See also *frolic of his own*.

victimisation: where a person is treated less favourably because a complaint has been made or proceedings have beeen brought or evidence has been given about sexual, racial or disability discrimination.

Victimisation is itself held to be discrimination. This is wide enough to protect those who were not the victims of the original discrimination, but who gave evidence about that discrimination.

violent disorder: an offence under s2 of the Public Order Act 1986. It is committed when:

- three or more people are present together; and
- they use or threaten violence for a common purpose though not necessarily at the same time; and
- this violence is such as would cause a person of reasonable firmness to fear for his personal safety.

visitor: in *occupiers' liability*, a person who has permission to come onto a person's premises. Permission can be:

- express, e.g. someone who receives an invitation;
- implied, e.g. a person delivering goods;
- through a legal right, e.g. a policeman executing a search warrant.

The *occupier* of *premises* has a duty under the Occupiers' Liability Act 1957 to take reasonable steps to make sure that the visitor is safe on his premises and must take into account the age of the visitor.

Anyone who does not have permission to be on the premises is a *trespasser* (non-visitor) and the occupier is not expected to take the same care for his safety but must still ensure he is reasonably safe.

void ab initio: a Latin phrase meaning 'void from the beginning'. In contract law, this phrase is used to describe the situation when a contract has been declared completely *void* so that any clauses in it dealing with what will happen if the contract is brought to an end because of a *breach of the contract* will not be effective. A contract used to be held to be void ab initio if the breach which brought it to an end was a fundamental breach (one which destroyed an essential part of the contract), but this is no longer the case.

Case example: Photo Productions Ltd v Securicor Ltd (1980)

A security guard supplied by Securicor to protect Photo Productions' premises set fire to them. This was held to be a fundamental breach of contract, but the *exclusion clause* in the contract was still valid.

void contract: one that has never legally come into existence. It arises where:

- there has been a *common mistake*; both parties make the same mistake about a key part of the contract;

- it would be illegal to carry out the contract (see also *illegality*);

- a mistake has been made about the document being signed as part of the contract (see also *non est factum*);

- some *minors' contracts*.

As the contract has never come into existence, the 'buyer' of any goods exchanged under the contract never acquires legal ownership (*good title*) of them. He cannot pass ownership onto a third party if he sells them on because the original 'seller' is still the owner. See also *voidable contract*.

void marriage: one which has never come into existence even though the parties have been through a wedding ceremony. The reasons for a marriage being void are:

- the parties are too closely related, e.g. brother and sister;

- one or both of the parties were under 16 at the time of the marriage;

- the proper *marriage formalities* have not been carried out, and both the parties realised this. The marriage will not be void if one of the parties genuinely believed at the time that the formalities had been complied with;

- one or both of the parties were married to someone else at the time of the marriage;

- the parties are of the same sex;

- it is a polygamous marriage and one of the parties is domiciled in the UK.

If one of these facts exist, a decree of nullity will be issued. Children of the marriage, however, will be treated as legitimate. See also *voidable marriage*.

voidable contract: one that comes into existence but which can be brought to an end by one of the parties because of the actions of the other party. It is up to the innocent party to decide whether he wants to carry on with the contract or not. A contract is voidable where there has been:

- *misrepresentation*: the innocent party has been misled by the other party;

- *duress*: the innocent party was forced to enter into the contract;

- *undue influence*: the innocent party was persuaded to enter into the contract by someone he relied on because their greater experience or trustworthy position;

- *mistake*: where it would be inequitable to allow the contract to go ahead (*mistake in equity*).

A voidable contract exists until it is terminated. Therefore, goods which have been exchanged under the contract become the property of the buyer, and he can sell them on and pass on legal ownership while the contract exists.

voidable marriage: one which is valid but there is some defect which entitles the aggrieved party to have it declared void if he wants to. The reasons for a marriage being voidable are:

- either party is permanently incapable of consummating the marriage (i.e. a spouse can bring a claim based on his own inability the consummate the marriage);

- the other party refuses to consummate the marriage;

- one of the parties did not give genuine consent to the marriage because:

- – he did not realise it was a marriage service
- – he thought he was marrying a different person
- – he was acting under duress;
- one party is unsuited to marriage because he is of unsound mind;
- the other party was suffering from VD at the time of the marriage and the aggrieved party did not know;
- the woman at the time of the marriage was pregnant by someone else and the husband did not know that she was or that the child was not his.

If one of these facts exists, a decree of nullity will be issued. Children of the marriage will, however, still be legitimate

The aggrieved party must apply to have the marriage declared void within three years unless relying on the non-consummation grounds. However, if the aggrieved party has in the past shown his intention to continue with the marriage (*approbation*), he may be refused a decree of nullity. See also *void marriage*.

volenti non fit injuria means 'no cause of action arises where someone has willingly taken a risk' (is a volunteer). It is a defence used particularly in *negligence* cases. The defendant will not be liable if he can show:

- the claimant knew there was a risk he would suffer some injury; and
- he willingly agreed to accept the risk of being injured knowing that he would not be able to bring a claim if he was injured.

The injured person must have genuinely undertaken the risk and must not be acting under pressure from his employer (Smith v Baker & Sons (1981)).

When someone is injured trying to help people put in danger as a result of the defendant's actions, the defendant cannot use the defence of volenti, even though the *rescuer* voluntarily took the risk of being injured. This applies even where the rescuer is being paid, such as a fireman or a policeman.

Under the Road Traffic Act 1988, a car driver cannot use this defence when a passenger is injured by his bad driving (except in some cases where a person accepts a lift from a driver who he knows is drunk).

This defence is similar to the defence of *consent*, which is used in *trespass to person*.

voluntary intoxication means that the defendant willingly took the intoxicating substance (alcohol, drugs, etc.). As the defendant became intoxicated voluntarily, he cannot use this as a defence where the crime involved is one of *basic intent* (generally those for which *recklessness* is sufficient for the mental element of the crime). In such a crime, the taking of the intoxicating substance is regarded as recklessness.

Case example: DPP v Majewski (1977)

The defendant had taken drugs and had drunk heavily. He was involved in a fight in a pub and had attacked the landlord and a police officer who had been called. He claimed that he was so intoxicated that he could not remember any of the assaults and that he had not intended to do them. The House of Lords confirmed his conviction as voluntary intoxication could not be a defence to offences of basic intent.

Where the crime is one of *specific intent*, the prosecution must prove that the defendant had the necessary *mens rea*. This means that voluntary intoxication can be a defence if the defendant was so drunk that he did not have the mens rea required. See also *intoxication* and *involuntary intoxication.*

voluntary manslaughter: where the defendant killed with the necessary intention to be charged with murder, but, because of one of three special defences set out in the Homicide Act 1957, that charge of murder is reduced to manslaughter. The three special defences are:

- *diminished responsibility*;
- *provocation*;
- *suicide pact.*

voluntary winding up of a company can take place if a special resolution is passed that the company be wound up (this can be for any reason) or an extraordinary resolution is passed that the company be wound up because it cannot pay its liabilities. A notice of the resolution must be advertised in the London Gazette within 14 days of its being made.

Do you know we also have A–Zs for:

- **Business Studies**
- **English Literature**
- **Economics**
- **Sociology?**

Ask for them in your local bookshop or see the inside back cover for ordering details.

Wagon Mound (1961) established the rule in *negligence* that where the defendant has been negligent, the claimant can only be compensated for the damage he has suffered which is reasonably foreseeable (i.e. damage which an ordinary person would be able to foresee might happen). Damage can be reasonably foreseeable even if it is only a possibility and unlikely to happen.

Case details: Overseas Tankship (UK) Ltd v Morts Dock & Engineering Co Ltd, The Wagon Mound (No 1) (1961)

The defendant negligently discharged fuel oil into Sydney Harbour. The claimants owned a wharf where welding was being carried out. The claimants stopped the welding when the oil was spilt but, having made enquiries and believing that the oil was not inflammatory, resumed work, making sure that inflammable material did not fall on the oil. Two days later, the oil caught fire, and the wharf and two ships moored there were damaged. The judge accepted that the fire was not foreseeable. It was held that the defendants were not liable although they had been negligent, because the damage was not reasonably foreseeable. The defendants were found liable, though, for damage to the slipway because this was reasonably foreseeable.

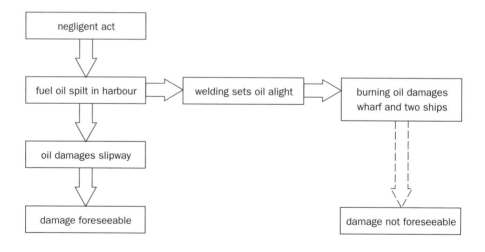

See also *foreseeability and its effect on damages in tort* and *remoteness of damage*.

waiver: an *equitable* concept used in contract law to stop a person taking unfair advantage by going back on his word. It is a form of *estoppel*.

Case example: Hickman v Haynes (1875)

The parties entered into a contract for the sale of goods and agreed a delivery date. The buyer asked the seller to delay delivery but on the second date that had been agreed, the buyer refused to accept delivery. The seller sued, and the buyer argued that the seller had been in breach of contract by failing to deliver the goods on the date set out in the contract; there was no consideration for the second agreement to delay delivery and therefore it was not binding. The court held that the buyer had waived his right to have the goods delivered on the contract date and he was therefore unsuccessful.

ward of court: a child who has come under the jurisdiction of the High Court. No important steps in the child's life can be taken without the consent of the court. Anyone can apply to make a child a ward of court, and the application takes effect straight away, without there being a hearing. The wardship lasts until a hearing is held which must take place within a month, and the court then decides whether to continue it or not.

It is not a common procedure because most disputes about children are between parents and are dealt with in divorce proceedings or under the Children Act 1989. Alternatively, care proceedings will be used if the local authority is concerned about a child. See *care order*.

Wardship is mainly used where:

- a third party is concerned about a child, e.g. a doctor who wants to treat a child in a way that is against the parents' wishes;
- the applicant wants to use the greater powers of the High Court, e.g. the High Court can order the media to keep a child's identity secret in a high profile case.

warning: action which, under the Crime and Disorder Act 1998, can be taken by the police against young offenders instead of prosecuting. An offender may be warned only if he has not been warned before or if an earlier warning was more than two years before. When warned the child or young offender must be referred to a *youth offending team*, which shall assess the case and, unless they consider it inappropriate to do so, shall arrange for the offender to participate in a rehabilitation scheme.

warrant of arrest can be issued by a magistrate to give the police authority to arrest the person named in the warrant. A warrant will only be issued if written information, supported by evidence on oath, is given to the magistrate showing that the person has committed (or there are reasonable grounds for suspecting he has committed) an offence. The offence must be one which is punishable by imprisonment. The police can only use the warrant to arrest the person named in it.

warranty: a *term* of a contract dealing with the parts that are not essential enough to be *conditions*. If a warranty is breached (broken), the other party is not entitled to rescind (cancel) the contract but can only claim *damages*. In deciding whether a term is a warranty or a condition, the court will look at what the parties had intended the term to be and whether it deals with a fundamental part of the contract. If the contract is for the sale of goods, the terms implied by the *Sale of Goods Act 1979* will be conditions not warranties.

Weber, theories of: Weber, a German sociologist, argued that the primary role of law is to maintain order in society. His view was that without the coercive power of law, order could not be maintained.

Wednesbury principles state that in *judicial review* proceedings, a decision can only be challenged on the grounds of unreasonableness if it was so unreasonable that no reasonable public body could have reached the same decision. In Council of Civil Service Unions v Minister for the Civil Service (1984), it was said that a decision had to be 'so outrageous in its defiance of logic or of accepted moral standards that no sensible person ... could have arrived at it'. This leaves a large amount of discretion to the judge hearing the judicial review proceedings.

welfare principle: used by a court when making decisions about the future of children, especially in divorce proceedings. It is set out in s1 Children Act 1996 which says that the welfare of the child is paramount, and there should be as little delay as possible in making decisions about the child. The factors the court will take into account are:

- the wishes of the child;
- his physical, emotional and educational needs;
- the likely effect on him of the change in his circumstances;
- his age, sex, background and any other characteristics;
- how capable his parents are and anyone else involved;
- what powers are available to the court.

Welfare Reform and Pensions Act (1999) makes it possible for a share of one spouse's pension entitlement to be passed to the other spouse on divorce so that he or she can set up an independent pension fund.

See *pension sharing order* and *pension attachment order.*

White Paper: a government document setting out its firm proposals for new law. Usually, a *Green Paper* is issued first with draft ideas for consultation and then a White Paper is issued with the firm proposals. There will be more consultation at this point, then the final draft will be introduced into Parliament as a *Bill* for Parliament to consider.

White v White (2001): established the approach that the court should take on divorce where a couple's assets are substantial. Using the factors in the *Matrimonial Causes Act*, S25, the court should first establish both parties' reasonable needs and should then establish what a fair division of the extra assets are, taking into account the age of both parties, the length of the marriage and both parties' contribution to the marriage giving full credit to home-making and other non-financial contributions.

Widgery criteria: those used to decide whether it is in the interests of justice for a defendant in a criminal case to receive *legal aid*. There are five criteria. These are:

1. Is the offence such that, if proved, it is likely that the court would impose a custodial sentence, or the defendant would lose his livelihood, or suffer serious damage to his reputation?
2. Does the case involve consideration of a substantial question of law?
3. Is the defendant unable to understand the proceedings or state his own case due to mental or physical disability or inadequate knowledge of English?
4. Does the nature of the defence involve tracing and interviewing witnesses, or expert cross-examination of a witness for the prosecution?

5. Is it in the interests of someone other than the defendant that the defendant should be represented?

The decision as to whether legal aid should be granted is made by the clerk of the court. There have been criticisms that clerks apply these criteria in different ways and that the rate of granting legal aid varies between courts.

will: a written document in which a person sets out what should happen to his property after his death. A will must be signed by the person making it and by two witnesses. The only exceptions to this rule are *privileged wills* made by members of the forces on active duty or by sailors at sea.

winding up: the legal operation of putting an end to the carrying on of the business of a *company*. A company can be wound up voluntarily (see also *voluntary winding up*) or compulsorily by order of the court. A compulsory winding up order can be asked for by any creditor (person or business to whom the company owes money).

On a winding up, all the assets of the company are realised and distributed amongst the creditors. If there is not enough to pay all the debts, then secured creditors are paid first and any money left over is divided proportionally among the unsecured creditors.

witness: a person who gives evidence in court. This evidence is usually given on oath but if the witness has no religious beliefs or has a conscientious objection to taking an oath, then he can make a solemn affirmation that the evidence he gives is the truth.

witnesses to a will must be competent. This means that they must be capable of seeing the *testator* sign the will and they must be able to understand the nature of the document he is signing. There is no need for a witness to know what is in the will. There must be at least two witnesses. Witnesses cannot inherit under the will, unless there are at least two other witnesses who do not inherit.

women in the legal profession: women now make up over half the new entrants to the solicitors' profession and almost half of the new entrants to the Bar. Despite this, there are very few women in senior positions in either profession. Women solicitors are more likely to be in junior positions and are on average paid less at every level of the profession. At the Bar, only about 12 per cent of *Queen's Counsel* are women.

Woolf Report on civil justice was issued in 1996. It suggested wide-ranging reforms of the way in which civil cases are conducted. It set out key objectives, which were:

*   parties to be encouraged to explore alternative ways of resolving their dispute;
*   a simpler set of rules for procedure in the courts;
*   making litigation more affordable;
*   making trials quicker.

These aims were to be achieved by:

*   increasing the limit on claims in the small claims court (this was immediately raised from £1000 to £3000 and then to £5,000);
*   a fast track for claims of up to £10,000 (later suggested to be up to £15,000);
*   simpler documents and procedures in the courts;
*   giving the judges more responsibility for managing cases;
*   more use of information technology.

These reforms came into effect in April 1999. (See also *Civil Procedure Rules*.)

wound in ss18 and 20 of the Offences against the Person Act 1861 means a cut of the whole skin. Even a minor cut is a wound. On the other hand, an internal injury that does not cause external bleeding is not a wound.

Case example: J.C.C. v Eisenhower (1984)

The defendant fired an airgun causing a pellet to strike the victim in the eye. This made the blood vessels in the eye rupture, but there was no external bleeding. The court held that this was not a wound.

If the draft *Offences against the Person Bill* put out for consultation in 1998 becomes law, there will be no distinction between a wound and any other injury. A minor wound will be classed as injury, while a serious wound will be a serious injury.

wounding with intent: an offence under s18 of the Offences against the Person Act 1861. The offence is committed if the defendant *wounds* or causes *grievous bodily harm* with intent to do so, or with intent to resist arrest or prevent someone else being arrested. This is the most serious of the offences against the person. It can only be tried at the Crown Court, and the maximum penalty is life imprisonment.

written contract: one which is written down rather than agreed by word of mouth or by actions. Normally it does not matter what form a contract is in, but in some situations, a contract must be in writing to be binding. These include:

- contracts for the sale of land;
- contracts for other dispositions of an interest in land;
- bills of exchange;
- bills of sale;
- contracts of guarantees (there must be written evidence of the contract if it is an oral one).

The rules that cover written contracts are:

- a written contract will normally held to be binding as it is, and it is not possible to give evidence in court that other terms were agreed which added to or amende d the written contract (see also *parol evidence rule*);
- both parties are bound by the terms of a written contract they have signed, whether they have read it or not (L'Estrange v Graucob (1934)).

In exceptional circumstances, however, the court may accept that the written contract does not accurately record what both parties agreed and may amend it so that it does (see also *rectification*). The court will only do this if it thinks it is *equitable* to do so.

written particulars of employment must be given by an employer to an employee within two months of the employment starting. Section 1 of the Employment Rights Act 1996 states that the principal document containing the particulars must state:

- names of the employer and the employee;
- the date on which the employment began, including if any previous employment counts towards *continuity of employment*;
- the rate of pay and whether it is to be paid weekly or monthly etc.;

- any terms and conditions relating to hours of work;
- job title or brief description of the work;
- place of employment;
- holiday entitlement.

As well as these, the employer must also give details of sick pay and pension schemes if any, the period of notice for termination of the *contract of employment*, any collective agreements in force and grievance procedures. These can be given at the same time as the principal particulars or in separate statements.

wrongful dismissal: dismissal without the correct amount of notice being given to the employee. The minimum time limits for notice are set by law and depend on the length of time the employee has worked for the employer. These are:

- after four weeks' continuous service   one week's notice
- after two years' continuous service   two weeks' notice
- for every extra year's continuous service   an additional week's notice
                                               up to a maximum of
                                               12 weeks' notice

These are minimum periods, and the contract of employment can provide for longer periods of notice. Also, for certain types of employment, the courts may decide that a longer period should be given. The employee has the right to claim for the amount of pay that would have been earned if the correct period of notice had been given.

Serious misconduct by the employee, such as stealing from the employer, can justify instant dismissal without notice.

wrongful interference with goods: see *trespass to goods*

Do you need revision help and advice?

Go to pages 259–99 for a range of revision appendices that include plenty of exam advice and tips.

year and a day rule: there used to be a rule that for an attacker to be guilty of murder, manslaughter or infanticide, the victim had to die within a year and a day of the attack. This rule was sensible when lack of medical knowledge could have made it difficult to be sure if the victim had died as a result of the injuries received in the attack. However, with modern medical techniques, especially life-support machines, it meant that a murderer could avoid liability for murder simply because the victim was kept alive on a life-support machine for more than a year and a day. The rule was abolished by the Law Reform (Year and a Day) Act 1996.

young offender: an offender under the age of 21.

Young Offenders' Institutions: offenders aged at least 18 but under 21 who are convicted of an offence which would be punishable with imprisonment in the case of a person aged 21 or over may be given a sentence of detention in a Young Offenders' Institution. The minimum sentence is 21 days and the maximum is the maximum term of imprisonment for the particular offence. If an offender becomes 21 while still serving the sentence then he or she will be transferred to an adult prison.

Young v Bristol Aeroplane, the rule in: this is a rule in *judicial precedent* which states that the *Court of Appeal* is bound by its own previous decisions. There are three exceptions to the rule when the court is not bound by a previous decision. These are:

- where there are past cases which conflict; the court may choose which to follow;
- where a decision of the House of Lords effectively overrules a previous Court of Appeal decision; the court must follow the House of Lords' decision and not its own;
- where the decision was made *per incuriam*, that is carelessly or by mistake, and an Act of Parliament or other regulation was not considered when the court made the earlier decision.

In the 1970s, Lord Denning, the then Master of the Rolls (head of the civil division of the court), wanted the Court of Appeal to have freedom, so that it was not bound by its own past decisions. In Davis v Johnson (1979), a panel of five judges sitting in the Court of Appeal refused to follow a decision made only five days earlier in another case. When the matter was appealed to the House of Lords, they re-affirmed the rule in Young v Bristol Aeroplane. So it is now clear that the Court of Appeal is bound by its own past decisions.

Youth Courts: part of the *Magistrates' Courts*. They hear cases in which those aged between ten and 17 inclusive have been charged with a criminal offence. The cases are tried in private, and the procedure is less formal than in an adult court. There is a specially trained panel of magistrates to hear these cases and there will always be at least one male and at least one female magistrate on the bench.

Youth Justice Board: set up by the Crime and Disorder Act 1998 to monitor the provision and operation of the youth justice system and services. Its main functions are to:

- advise the Home Secretary on how to prevent offending by children and young persons most effectively;
- identify, make known and promote good practice in this area.

See also *youth offending team*.

youth offender panel: a panel consisting of at least one member of the local *youth offending team* and two other people who meet with a young offender to agree a programme of behaviour, with the aim of preventing re-offending. The agreement which is reached is called a youth offender contract. The panel will monitor the offender's progress and may have further meetings at which the contract can be varied.

youth offending team: under s39 of the Crime and Disorder Act 1998 each local authority must establish one or more youth offending teams for its area. A team must include a probation officer, a local authority social worker, a police officer, a representative of the local health authority and a person nominated by the chief education officer for the area. The intention is to co-ordinate the provision of youth justice services in the area and encourage co-operation between the different agencies. Any young offender who is given a *warning* by police must be referred to the local youth offending team. Youth offending teams have to submit an annual report to the *Youth Justice Board*.

What other subjects are you studying?

A–Zs cover 18 different subjects. See the inside back cover for a list of all the titles in the series and how to order.

A B C D E F G H I J K L M N O P Q R S T U V W X **Y** Z

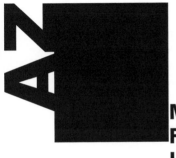

MAIN CONCEPTS REQUIRED FOR SUCCESS IN AQA A/AS LEVEL LAW EXAMS

The following pages set out lists of terms to revise for examination. When approaching exams, look up each word in the main text, making sure that you understand it and can use it correctly in context. There are revision lists for:

Unit 1 Law making

European Union law
Legislative process
Delegated legislation
Influences upon Parliament
Statutory interpretation
Judicial precedent

Unit 2 Dispute solving

Civil courts
Criminal courts
Alternatives to courts
The legal profession
Finance of advice and representation
The judges
Lay people

Unit 3 The concept of liability

Introduction to criminal liability
Introduction to tort
Sentencing
Civil damages

Unit 4a Criminal law

Murder – top ten revision terms
Voluntary manslaughter
Involuntary manslaughter
Non-fatal offences against the person
Defences

Unit 4b Contract

Formation
Contract terms
Vitiating factors
Discharge of contract
Remedies

Unit 5a Criminal law

Theft, robbery and burglary
Deception offences
Criminal damage
Defences

Unit 5b Law of tort

Negligence
Occupiers' liability
Nuisance
Strict and vicarious liability
Defences

Unit 5c Protection of human rights

Rights
Restrictions
Enforcement
Underlying concepts

Unit 5d Consumer protection

Consumer contracts
Consumer legislation
Exclusion clauses
Criminal law and tort
Enforcement, sanctions and remedies

Unit 6 Concepts of law

Law and morals
Law and justice
Balancing conflicting interests
Fault
Judicial creativity

Unit 1 Law making

European Union law
TOP 15 REVISION TERMS

Article 234 (Treaty of Rome)
Article 249 (Treaty of Rome)
Council of Ministers
direct applicability
direct effect
directives
European Commission
European Court of Justice

European Parliament
Francovitch principle
horizontal direct effect
regulations
sovereignty of Parliament
Treaty of Rome
vertical direct effect

Legislative process
TOP 8 REVISION TERMS

Acts of Parliament
Green Paper
Parliament
Parliamentary Counsel

private members' bills
Royal Assent
sovereignty of Parliament
White Paper

Delegated legislation
TOP 6 REVISION TERMS

bylaws
delegated legislation
enabling Act

Orders in Council
Scrutiny Committee
ultra vires

Influences upon Parliament
TOP 5 REVISION TERMS

Green Paper
Law Commission
law reform

pressure groups
Royal Commissions

Statutory interpretation
TOP 10 REVISION TERMS

ejusdem generis rule
extrinsic aids to statutory interpretation
golden rule
Interpretation Act 1978
intrinsic aids to statutory interpretation

literal rule
mischief rule
Pepper v Hart (1993)
purposive approach
statutory interpretation

Judicial precedent
TOP 10 REVISION TERMS

binding precedent

distinguishing (in judicial precedent)

hierarchy of the courts

judicial precedent

obiter dicta

persuasive precedent

Practice Statement

ratio decidendi

stare decisis

Young v Bristol Aeroplane, the rule in

Unit 2 Dispute solving

Civil courts
TOP 16 REVISION TERMS

appeals

civil appeals

civil proceedings

civil courts

County Courts

Court of Appeal

divisional courts

fast track cases

High Court of Justice

House of Lords

leapfrog appeal

multi-track cases

Queen's Bench Division

settlement out of court

small claims procedure

Woolf Report

Criminal courts
TOP 12 REVISION TERMS

bail

committals for sentence

committal proceedings

criminal appeals

Crown Court

indictable offences

Magistrates' Court

mode of trial hearing

plea before venue

remand in custody

summary offence

triable either way offences

Alternatives to courts
TOP 12 REVISION TERMS

administrative tribunals

Alternative Dispute Resolution

arbitration

Centre for Dispute Resolution

commercial arbitration

conciliation

employment tribunals

lay members of tribunals

mediation

negotiation

Ombudsmen

tribunals

The legal profession
TOP 18 REVISION TERMS

Bar Council

Bar Vocational Course

barristers

certificate of advocacy

fusion of the legal profession

Inns of Court

legal executives

Legal Practice Course

legal services

Legal Services Ombudsman

Office for the Supervision of Solicitors

pupillage

Queen's Counsel (QC)

rights of audience

solicitors

Solicitors Disciplinary Tribunal

training contract

women in the legal profession

Finance of advice and representation
TOP 16 REVISION TERMS

access to justice

Citizens' Advice Bureaux

civil legal aid

conditional fees

Criminal Defence Service

criminal legal aid

community legal service (CLS) fund

duty solicitor schemes

law centres

legal advice

Legal Services Commission

means test

merits test

police station, legal advice for suspects at

Public Defence Service

Widgery criteria

The judges
TOP 12 REVISION TERMS

circuit judges

district judge

district judge (Magistrates' Court)

immunity from suit

independence of the judiciary

judges, appointment of

Judicial Appointments Commission

Judicial Studies Board

Law Lords

Lord Chancellor

Lords Justices of Appeal

recorder

Lay people
TOP 14 REVISION TERMS

juries in civil cases

juries in criminal cases

jury equity

jury qualifications

jury, role of

jury selection

jury trial, advantages and disadvantages of

jury vetting

Justices' Clerk

lay magistrates

lay participation in the legal system

magistrates

Magistrates' Court

majority verdict

Unit 3 The concept of liability

Introduction to criminal liability
TOP 20 REVISION TERMS

actual bodily harm

actus reus

assault (criminal law)

assault occasioning actual bodily harm

battery (criminal law)

causation in criminal law

coincidence of actus reus and mens rea

Cunningham recklessness

foresight of consequences

grievous bodily harm

intention

malicious wounding

medical treatment and the chain of causation

mens rea

omissions as actus reus

strict liability offences

strict liability offences, justification for

subjective recklessness

transferred malice

wounding with intent

Introduction to tort
TOP 14 REVISION TERMS

breach of duty of care in negligence

Bolam test

'but for' test in negligence

Caparo test (in negligence)

damage in negligence (remoteness of)

Donoghue v Stevenson (1932)

duty of care in negligence

eggshell skull rule in negligence

foreseeability and its effect on damages in tort

foreseeablility and the duty of care

negligence

remoteness of damage

standard of care (in negligence)

Wagon Mound (1961)

Sentencing

Civil damages

Unit 4a Criminal law

Murder and voluntary manslaughter

Involuntary manslaughter

Non-fatal offences against the person
TOP 10 REVISION TERMS

actual bodily harm

assault (criminal law)

assault occasioning actual bodily harm

battery (criminal law)

consent and offences against the person

Cunningham recklessness

grievous bodily harm

malicious wounding

maliciously

wounding with intent

Defences
TOP 14 REVISION TERMS

automatism

consent and offences against the person

insane automatism

insanity as a defence to a crime

intoxication

involuntary intoxication

mentally ill offenders

M'Naghten Rules

mistake

non-insane automatism

self-defence

self-induced automatism

unfitness to plead

voluntary intoxication

Unit 4b Contract

Formation
TOP 20 TERMS

acceptance

agreement

Carlill v Carbolic Smoke Ball Co (1893)

collateral contract

communication rules in contract

consideration

contract

counter-offer

existing contractual duty

good consideration

honour clause

intention to create legal relations

invitation to treat

offer

past consideration

Pinnel's case (1602)

postal rule (in contract law)

privity of contract

revocation of an offer

termination of an offer

Contract terms

Vitiating factors

Discharge of contract

Remedies

Unit 5a Criminal law

Theft, robbery and burglary
TOP 10 REVISION TERMS

appropriation

belonging to another (theft)

dishonesty

burglary

Ghosh test

intention to permanently deprive (in theft)

property (in theft)

robbery

theft

trespasser (in burglary)

Deception offences
TOP 6 REVISION TERMS

deception offences

dishonesty

evading a liability

making off without payment

obtaining property by deception

obtaining services by deception

Criminal damage
TOP 6 REVISION TERMS

aggravated criminal damage

arson

Caldwell recklessness

criminal damage

destroy or damage

objective recklessness

Defences
TOP 8 REVISION TERMS

duress as a defence to a criminal charge

duress of circumstances

intoxication

involuntary intoxication

mistake

necessity (as a defence to a crime)

self-defence

voluntary intoxication

Unit 5b Law of tort

TOP 15 REVISION TERMS

breach of duty of care in negligence
Caparo test
damage in negligence (remoteness of)
duty of care in negligence
economic loss in negligence
eggshell rule in negligence
foreseeability and its effect on damages in tort
foreseeability and the duty of care

Hedley Byrne v Heller & Partners (1964)
negligence
negligent misstatement
nervous shock in negligence
remoteness of damage
standard of care
Wagon Mound (1961)

Occupiers' liability
TOP 4 REVISION TERMS

occupier
premises

trespasser
visitor

Nuisance
TOP 5 REVISION TERMS

abatement of a nuisance
nuisance
prescription

private nuisance
public nuisance

Strict and vicarious liability
TOP 7 REVISION TERMS

Consumer Protection Act 1987
defective product
frolic of his own
product liability

Rylands v Fletcher (the rule in)
strict liability (law of tort)
vicarious liability (negligence)

Defences
TOP 2 REVISION TERMS

consent in tort

contributory negligence

Unit 5c Protection of human rights

Rights
TOP 6 REVISION TERMS

European Convention on Human Rights

freedom of association

freedom of speech

freedom of the person

Human Rights Act 1998

privacy

Restrictions
TOP 12 REVISION TERMS

affray

defamation

harassment as a crime

police powers of arrest

police powers to stop and search

public order offences

riot

trespass

trespass to goods

trespass to land

trespass to the person

violent disorder

Enforcement/Underlying concepts
TOP 6 REVISION TERMS

civil courts

criminal courts

European Court of Human Rights

judicial review

rule of law

Wednesbury principle

Unit 5d Consumer protection

Consumer contracts
TOP 8 REVISION TERMS

acceptance

consideration

consumer

consumer contract

intention to create legal relations

offer

privity of contract

standard form contracts

Consumer legislation
TOP 10 REVISION TERMS

consumer protection
Consumer Protection Act 1987
implied terms
Sale of Goods Act 1979
Sale of Goods, exclusion of ss12–15

Supply of Goods and Services Act 1982
satisfactory quality
Unfair Contract Terms Act 1977
unfair terms directive
Unfair Terms in Contracts Regulations 1999

Exclusion clauses
TOP 5 REVISION TERMS

exclusion clause
Sale of Goods Act 1979, exclusion of ss12-15
Unfair Contract Terms Act 1977

unfair terms directive
Unfair Terms in Contracts Regulations 1999

Criminal law and tort
TOP 5 REVISION TERMS

Consumer Protection Act 1987
negligence
strict liability (law of tort)

trade descriptions
Trade Descriptions Act 1968

Enforcement, sanctions and remedies
TOP 5 REVISION TERMS

County Court
damages
ombudsman

small claims
Trading Standards Departments

Unit 6 Concepts of law

Law and morals
TOP 6 REVISION TERMS

Hart–Devlin debate
Hart–Fuller debate
Hart, theories of

morality and law
natural law
positivism

Law and justice

formal justice

justice and the law

miscarriages of justice

remedial justice

Balancing conflicting interests

This is a theme across many areas of law. Examples are seen in the following entries:

bargaining power, inequality of

prescription

right to silence

Sale of Goods, excluding ss12–15

Unfair Contract Terms Act 1977

Fault

This is a theme across many areas of law. Examples are seen in the following entries:

fault based liability

intention

mens rea

Rylands v Fletcher (the rule in)

strict liability offences

strict liability (law of tort)

Judicial creativity
TOP 8 REVISION TERMS

declaratory theory of law

Dworkin, theories of

judicial precedent

mischief rule

Montesquieu's theory of the separation of powers

original precedent

purposive approach

statutory interpretation

REVISION LISTS FOR OCR A LEVEL LAW AND AS LAW

The following pages set out lists of terms to revise for examinations. When approaching exams, look up each word in the main text and memorise the key definition. Don't forget that law examination papers often ask you to apply the law, so make sure you understand it as well.

Topics on Module 2568 – Machinery of Justice

Civil courts
ADR and tribunals
Police powers
Criminal process and the criminal courts
Penal system

Topics on Module 2569 – Legal Personnel

The legal profession
The judiciary
Lay people in the legal system
Provision of legal services

Topics on Module 2570 – Sources of law

Doctrine of precedent
Legislation
Statutory interpretation
European law
Law reform

Topics on Module 2571 – Criminal law 1

General principles of actus reus and mens rea
Participation in crime
Preliminary crimes
Fatal offences against the person

Topics on Module 2572 – Criminal law 2

General defences
Non-fatal offences against the person
Offences against property

Topics on Module 2574 – Contract law 1

Offer and acceptance
Consideration
Legal intent and capacity to form a contract
Contents of a contract

Topics on Module 2575 – Contract law 2

Privity of contract
Vitiating factors
Discharge of contracts
Remedies

Topics on Module 2577 – Law of torts 1

Negligence
Occupiers' liability
Defences
Vicarious liability

Topics on Module 2578 – Law of torts 2

Torts connected to land
Liability for animals
Trespass to the person
Remedies
The nature of the law of tort

Topics on synoptic papers

Judicial precedent – all synoptic options
Duress and necessity – Criminal law
Consideration – Contract law
Negligence and nervous shock – Law of torts

Topics on Module 2568 – Machinery of Justice

Civil courts
TOP 20 REVISION TERMS

adversarial process

appeals

Article 234 (Treaty of Rome)

civil appeals

civil proceedings

civil courts

claimant

County Court

Court of Appeal

Divisional Courts

European Court of Justice

fast track cases

High Court of Justice

House of Lords

leapfrog appeal

multi-track cases

Queen's Bench Division

settlement out of court

small claims procedure

Woolf Report

ADR and tribunals
TOP 10 REVISION TERMS

administrative tribunals

Alternative Dispute Resolution

arbitration

Centre for Dispute Resolution

commercial arbitration

conciliation

employment tribunals

mediation

negotiation

tribunals

Police powers
TOP 12 REVISION TERMS

arrestable offence

custody officer

detention by police

fingerprinting

intimate search

Police and Criminal Evidence Act 1984

police codes of practice

police interviews of suspects

police powers of arrest

right to silence

stop and search powers

tape recording of police interviews

Criminal process and the criminal courts
TOP 12 REVISION TERMS

bail

committal proceedings

committals for sentence

criminal appeals

Crown Court

indictable offences

Magistrates' Court

mode of trial hearing

plea before venue

remand in custody

summary offence

triable either way offences

Penal system
TOP 16 REVISION TERMS

bind over order

community sentences

compensation order

conditional discharge

custodial sentences

denunciation of crime

deterrence of crime

electronic tagging

fines

life sentence

protection of the public

rehabilitation

reparation

retribution

sentencing aims

youth offender panel

Topics on Module 2569 – Legal personnel

The legal profession
TOP 18 REVISION TERMS

barristers

Bar Council

Bar Vocational Course

certificate of advocacy

fusion of the legal profession

Inns of Court

legal executives

Legal Practice Course

legal services

Legal Services Ombudsman

Office for the Supervision of Solicitors

pupillage

Queen's Counsel (QC)

rights of audience

solicitors

Solicitors' Disciplinary Tribunal

training contract

women in the legal profession

The judiciary
TOP 12 REVISION TERMS

circuit judges

district judge

district judge (Magistrates' Court)

immunity from suit

independence of the judiciary

judges, appointment of

Judicial Appointments Commission

Judicial Studies Board

Law Lords

Lord Chancellor

Lords Justices of Appeal

recorder

Lay people in the legal system
TOP 14 REVISION TERMS

juries in civil cases

juries in criminal cases

jury equity

jury qualifications

jury, role of

jury selection

jury trial, advantages and disadvantages of

jury vetting

Justices' Clerk

lay magistrates

lay participation in the legal system

magistrates

Magistrates' Court

majority verdict

Provision of legal services
TOP 16 REVISION TERMS

access to justice

Citizens' Advice Bureaux

civil legal aid

conditional fees

Criminal Defence Service

criminal legal aid

community Legal Service

duty solicitor schemes

law centres

legal advice

Legal Services Commission

means test

merits test

police station, legal advice for suspects at

Public Defence Service

Widgery criteria

Topics on Module 2570 – Sources of law

Doctrine of precedent
TOP 10 REVISION TERMS

binding precedent

distinguishing (in judicial precedent)

hierarchy of the courts

judicial precedent

obiter dicta

persuasive precedent

Practice Statement

ratio decidendi

stare decisis

Young v Bristol Aeroplane, the rule in

Legislation
TOP 12 REVISION TERMS

Acts of Parliament

bylaws

delegated legislation

enabling Act

Green Paper

Orders in Council

Parliament

Royal Assent

Scrutiny Committee

sovereignty of Parliament

White Paper

ultra vires

Statutory interpretation
TOP 10 REVISION TERMS

ejusdem generis rule

extrinsic aids to statutory interpretation

golden rule

Interpretation Act 1978

intrinsic aids to statutory interpretation

literal rule

mischief rule

Pepper v Hart (1993)

purposive approach

statutory interpretation

European law
TOP 15 REVISION TERMS

Article 234 (Treaty of Rome)

Article 249 (Treaty of Rome)

Council of Ministers

direct applicability

direct effect

directives

European Commission

European Court of Justice

European Parliament

Francovitch principle

horizontal direct effect

regulations

sovereignty of Parliament

Treaty of Rome

vertical direct effect

Law reform
TOP 5 REVISION TERMS

Green Paper

Law Commission

law reform

pressure groups

Royal Commissions

OCR REVISION LISTINGS

Topics on Module 2571 – Criminal Law 1

General principles of actus reus and mens rea
TOP 16 REVISION TERMS

absolute liability

actus reus

Caldwell recklessness

causation in criminal law

coincidence of actus reus and mens rea

Cunningham recklessness

foresight of consequences

intention

medical treatment and the chain of causation

mens rea

omissions as actus reus

recklessness

strict liability offences

strict liability offences, justification for

subjective recklessness

transferred malice

Participation in crime
TOP 7 REVISION TERMS

aiding and abetting

counselling as secondary participation in a crime

joint enterprise

principal offender

procuring a crime

secondary participation in a crime

secondary participant, repentance of

Preliminary crimes
TOP 5 REVISION TERMS

attempt

conspiracy

impossible attempts

inchoate offences

iincitement

Fatal offences against the person
TOP 12 REVISION TERMS

constructive manslaughter

diminished responsibility

foresight of consequences

gross negligence manslaughter

involuntary manslaughter

manslaughter

malice aforethought

medical treatment and the chain of causation

murder

provocation

suicide pact

voluntary manslaughter

Topics on Module 2572 – Criminal Law 2

General defences
TOP 15 REVISION TERMS

automatism

consent and offences against the person

duress as a defence to a criminal charge

duress of circumstances

insane automatism

insanity as a defence to a crime

intoxication

involuntary intoxication

mistake

M'Naghten Rules

necessity as a defence to a criminal charge

non-insane automatism

self defence

self-induced automatism

voluntary intoxication

Non-fatal offences against the person
TOP 10 REVISION TERMS

actual bodily harm

assault (criminal law)

assault occasioning actual bodily harm

battery (criminal law)

consent and offences against the person

Cunningham recklessness

grievous bodily harm

malicious wounding

maliciously

wounding with intent

Offences against property
TOP 14 REVISION TERMS

appropriation

belonging to another (theft)

Caldwell recklessness

criminal damage

destroy or damage

dishonesty

burglary

Ghosh test

intention to permanently deprive

objective recklessness

property (in theft)

robbery

theft

trespasser (in burglary)

Topics on Module 2574 – Contract Law 1

Offer and acceptance
TOP 12 REVISION TERMS

acceptance

agreement

Carlill v Carbolic Smoke Ball Co (1893)

collateral contract

communication rules in contract

contract

counter-offer

invitation to treat

offer

postal rule

revocation of an offer

termination of an offer

Consideration
TOP 7 REVISION TERMS

bare promise

consideration

existing contractual duty

good consideration

part payment

past consideration

Pinnel's case (1602)

Legal intent and capacity to form a contract
TOP 6 REVISION TERMS

beneficial contract of service

capacity in contract law

honour clause

intention to create legal relations

minors' contracts

necessaries

Contents of a contract
TOP 15 REVISION TERMS

condition as a term of the contract

course of dealings

exclusion clause

express term

freedom of contract

implied term

innominate terms

officious bystander test

Sale of Goods Act 1979 (as amended)

Sale of Goods Act, excluding ss12–15

standard form contracts

terms of a contract

Unfair Contract Terms Act 1977

Unfair Terms in Consumer Regulations 1999

warranty

Topics on Module 2575 – Contract Law 2

Privity of contract
TOP 3 REVISION TERMS

collateral contracts

privity of contract

third parties, rights under a contract

Vitiating factors
TOP 15 REVISION TERMS

banking cases in contract law

common mistake

duress (in contract law)

economic duress

fiduciary relationship

fraudulent misrepresentation

misrepresentation

mistake (and its effect on a contract)

mistake as to identity

mistake in equity

negligent misrepresentation

restraint of trade

undue influence

void contract

voidable contract

Discharge of contracts
TOP 14 REVISION TERMS

anticipatory breach of contract

breach of contract

discharge of a contract

frustration of a contract

part performance of a contract

penalty clause

rescission of a contract

performance

quantum meruit

repudiation of a contract

severable contract

termination of a contract

time is of the essence

void ab initio

Remedies
TOP 8 REVISION TERMS

damages in contract law

damages in contract and tort cases

injunction in contract law

mitigation of loss (contract law)

rectification

remedies for breach of contract

remedies for misrepresentation

specific performance

Topics on Module 2577 – Law of Torts 1

Negligence
TOP 20 REVISION TERMS

breach of duty of care in negligence

'but for' test in negligence

Caparo test (in negligence)

causation in negligence

damage in negligence (remoteness of)

Donoghue v Stevenson (1932)

duty of care in negligence

economic loss in negligence

eggshell rule in negligence

floodgates argument

foreseeability and its effect on damages in tort

foreseeability and the duty of care

Hedley Byrne v Heller & Partners (1964)

negligence

negligent misstatement

nervous shock

remoteness of damage

res ipsa loquitur

standard of care

Wagon Mound (1961)

Occupiers' liability
TOP 4 REVISION TERMS

occupier

premises

trespasser

visitor

Defences
TOP 4 REVISION TERMS

consent in tort

contributory negligence

rescuer in negligence cases

volenti non fit injuria

Vicarious liability
TOP 4 REVISION TERMS

frolic of his own

independent contractor

independent contractors, tortious liability for

vicarious liability (negligence)

Topics on Module 2578 – Law of Torts 2

Torts connected to land
TOP 12 REVISION TERMS

abatement of a nuisance

Act of God

act of stranger

licence

nuisance

nuisance and trespass to land, a comparison

prescription

private nuisance

public nuisance

Rylands v Fletcher (the rule in)

statutory authority

trespass to land

Liability for animals
TOP 4 REVISION TERMS

Animals Act 1971

assault

battery

negligence

Trespass to the person
TOP 6 REVISION TERMS

assault as a tort

battery as a tort

consent in tort

false imprisonment in trespass to person

police powers of arrest

trespass to person

Remedies
TOP 4 REVISION TERMS

damages in contract and tort cases

general damages

injunction

specific damages

The nature of the law of tort
TOP 2 REVISION TERMS

fault based liability

strict liability (law of tort)

OCR REVISION LISTINGS

TOPICS ON SYNOPTIC PAPERS

Note that these topics will be examined at all sessions up to and including the January 2005 session. For June 2005 and beyond new topics will be notified to centres.

Judicial precedent – all synoptic options
TOP 10 REVISION TERMS

binding precedent

distinguishing (in judicial precedent)

hierarchy of the courts

judicial precedent

obiter dicta

persuasive precedent

Practice Statement

ratio decidendi

stare decisis

Young v Bristol Aeroplane, the rule in

Duress and necessity – Criminal law
TOP 3 REVISION TERMS

duress as a defence to a criminal charge

duress of circumstances

necessity as a defence to a criminal charge

Consideration – Contract law
TOP 4 REVISION TERMS

consideration

existing contractual duty

good consideration

past consideration

Negligence and nervous shock – Law of torts
TOP 3 REVISION TERMS

negligence

nervous shock

rescuer in negligence cases

ADVANCED GNVQ
BUSINESS STUDIES
Business and the Law Revision lists

The authors have been through the units on business and the law to identify the key terms for revision. There is a degree of overlap in the units on law and business, so the first list is one of general principles. The other three lists give key revision terms for specific areas which are the focus of business and the law.

For end of unit tests look up the following terms, making sure that you understand the text and can memorise the definitions.

1 General principles of law affecting business – top 20 revision terms
2 Legal status of business – top 20 revision terms
3 Employment law – top 20 revision terms
4 Consumer law – top 20 revision terms

1 General principles of law affecting business
TOP 20 REVISION TERMS

alternative dispute resolution
breach of statutory duty
contract
contributory negligence
civil and criminal cases contrasted
civil remedies
commercial arbitration
consumer protection
corporate personality
County Courts

duty of care in negligence
employment tribunals
health and safety at work
occupiers' liability
small claims
small claims procedure
standard form contracts
strict liability (tort)
tort
vicarious liability

2 Legal status of business
TOP 20 REVISION TERMS

Articles of Association
certificate of incorporation
company and partnership compared
corporate personality
corporation
deed of partnership
directors
duties of directors
fiduciary duties of directors
limited company

limited liability
Memorandum of Association
partners
partnership
private limited company
public limited company
shareholder
shares
sole trader
unincorporated

3 Employment law
TOP 20 REVISION TERMS

Advisory, Conciliation and Arbitration Service
constructive dismissal
continuity of employment
contract of employment
direct discrimination
disability discrimination
dismissal from employment
employee
employee representative
employee's duties

employer's duties
employment contrasted with self-employment
employment tribunals
equal pay
health and safety at work
indirect discrimination
redundancy
unfair dismissal
written statement of employment
wrongful dismissal

4 Consumer law
TOP 20 REVISION TERMS

consumer
Consumer Credit Act 1974
Consumer Credit Act 1974, exempt agreements
consumer credit formalities
consumer protection
Consumer Protection Act 1987
defective goods
defective products
Director-General of Fair Trading
duty of care in negligence

exclusion clause
General Product Safety Regulations 1994
product liability
Sale of Goods Act 1979
Sale of Goods Act 1979, excluding ss12–15
standard form contracts
Supply of Goods and Services Act 1982
Trade Descriptions Act 1968
Unfair Contract Terms Act 1977
Unfair Terms in Consumer Contracts Regulations 1999

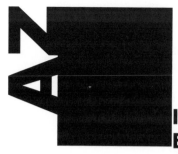

INSTITUTE OF LEGAL EXECUTIVES EXAMINATIONS REVISION LISTS

The authors have compiled lists of key terms for revision for the law papers in English legal system, criminal law, law of tort, contract and consumer law, employment law and family law. There are also lists of words which are helpful as an introduction to land law, wills and succession and business law.

Year one

English legal system – top 50 revision terms
Criminal law – top 50 revision terms
Tort – top 40 revision terms
Land law – 20 introductory terms

Year two

Contract law – top 50 revision terms
Consumer law – top 30 revision terms
Employment law – top 30 revision terms
Family law – top 50 revision terms
Wills and succession – 20 introductory terms
Business law – 20 introductory terms

Year one

English legal system
TOP 50 REVISION TERMS

Acts of Parliament

administrative tribunals

Alternative Dispute Resolution

arbitration

binding precedent

civil and criminal cases contrasted

civil appeals

Council of Ministers

County Court

Court of Appeal

criminal appeals

Crown Court

Crown Prosecution Service

delegated legislation

directives

direct effect

enabling Act

enforcement of a judgment

Equity

equitable remedies

European Union Commission

European Court of Justice

European Union law

Golden rule

hierarchy of the courts

High Court of Justice

House of Lords

indictable offences

judicial precedent

judicial review

jury, role of

Law Commission

law reform

legal personality

literal rule

Magistrates Court

mischief rule

Pepper v Hart

Practice Statement

purposive approach

regulations

remedies in civil cases

sentencing

small claims

small claims procedure

statutory interpretation

summary offences

Treaty of Rome

triable either way offences

verdict of jury

Criminal law
TOP 50 REVISION TERMS

actus reus
aiding and abetting
appropriation
attempts
automatism
burglary
capacity in criminal law
causation in criminal law
conspiracy
constructive manslaughter
criminal damage
diminished responsibility
dishonesty
duress as a defence to a crime
evading a liability
duress of circumstances
foresight of consequences
gross negligence manslaughter
impossible attempts
insane automatism
insanity as a defence to a crime
intoxication as a defence to a criminal charge
involuntary intoxication as a defence to a
criminal charge
involuntary manslaughter
making off without payment

malice aforethought
manslaughter
mens rea
mistake as a defence to a crime
M'Naghten Rules
murder
necessity as a defence to a criminal charge
obtaining property by deception
obtaining services by deception
omissions as actus reus
principal offender
property (in theft)
provocation
recklessness
robbery
secondary participation
self-defence
self induced automatism
specific intent crimes
strict liability offences
theft
transferred malice
vicarious liability (criminal law)
voluntary intoxication
voluntary manslaughter

Law of tort
TOP 40 REVISION TERMS

abatement of a nuisance
Act of God
act of stranger
chain of causation in the law of tort
consent in tort
contributory negligence
damages in negligence
Donoghue v Stevenson (1932)
duty of care in negligence
economic loss in negligence
egg shell skull rule
ex turpi causa
foreseeability and the duty of care
foreseeability and the effect on damages
frolic of his own
Hedley Byrne v Heller
inevitable accident
limitation of actions
malicious prosecution
necessity in tort

negligence
negligent misstatement
neighbour principle in negligence
nervous shock
nuisance
occupiers' liability
prescription
private nuisance
public nuisance
reasonable man in tort
remedies in tort
remoteness of damage
res ipsa loquitor
rescuer in negligence cases
Rylands v Fletcher
self defence in tort
special damage in tort
trespass
vicarious liability
volenti non fit injuria

Land law
TOP 20 REVISION TERMS

beneficial owner
beneficiary under a trust
chose in action
chose in rem
constructive trust
easement
equitable interest
joint tenancy
lease
life interest

mortgage
negative equity
personal property
real property
resulting trust
restrictive covenant
rights in personam
rights in rem
tenants in common
trusts

Law of contract
TOP 50 REVISION TERMS

acceptance
'banking' cases in contract law
bargaining power, inequality of
battle of the forms
breach of contract
capacity in contract law
certainty in contract law
communication rules in contract
condition as a term of a contract
consideration
contra proferentum rule
counter-offer
damages in contract law
discharge of a contract
duress (in contract law)
existing contractual duty
express term
freedom of contract
frustration of a contract
good consideration
illegality of contract
implied term
innominate terms
intention to create legal relations
invitation to treat
minors' contracts

misrepresentation
mistake (and its effect on contract)
mistake as to identity in contract law
offer
part performance of a contract
past consideration
performance
postal rule
privity of contract
promissory estoppel
remedies for breach of contract
repudiation of a contract
rescission of a contract
revocation of a contract
revocation of an offer
rewards
terms of a contract
termination of a contract
termination of an offer
time is of the essence
standard form contracts
Unfair Contract Terms Act 1977
Unfair Terms in Consumer Contracts Regulations 1999
written evidence of a contract

Consumer law
TOP 30 REVISION TERMS

conditional sale agreement

consumer

consumer contract

Consumer Credit Act 1974

Consumer Credit Act, exempt agreements

consumer credit agreements, formalities

consumer protection

Consumer Protection Act 1987

credit agreement

credit card

credit sale agreement

debtor–creditor agreement

debtor–creditor–seller agreement

defective goods

defective products

extortionate credit bargain

fit for purpose

General Product Liability Safety Regulations 1994

hire purchase agreement

merchantable quality

misleading prices

Package Travel Regulations 1992

Price Marking Order 1991

purchase agreement

sale of goods

Sale of Goods Act 1979

satisfactory quality

Supply of Goods and Services Act 1982

Trade Description Act 1968

Trading Standards Department

Unfair Contract Terms Act 1977

Unfair Terms in Consumer Contracts Regulations 1999

Employment law
TOP 30 REVISION TERMS

Advisory, Conciliation and Arbitration Service

collective agreements

compensatory award

constructive dismissal

continuity of employment

contract of employment

direct discrimination

disability discrimination

dismissal from employment

employee

employee representative

employee's duties

employer's duties

employment tribunals

equal pay

harassment at work

health and safety at work

Health and Safety Executive

indirect discrimination

job evaluation study

maternity leave

maternity rights

mobility clause

racial discrimination

redundancy

redundancy payment

sex discrimination

unfair dismissal

written statement of employment

wrongful dismissal

Family law
TOP 50 REVISION TERMS

adoption

adultery

ancillary relief

annulment

behaviour

care order

checklist in family law

child

child of the family

Child Support Agency

Children Act 1989

clean break principle

cohabitee

contact order

decree absolute

decree nisi

desertion

divorce

domestic violence

duress (effect on marriage)

Duxbury calculation

emergency protection order

exclusion order

Family Law Act 1966

financial provision on divorce

five facts

household, in the same

illegitimate child

legitimate child

legitimated child

living apart

lump sum order

maintenance

marriage

Martin order

Matrimonial Causes Act 1973, s25

matrimonial home

Mesher order

net effect approach

non-molestation order

nullity of marriage

occupation order

one-third-principle

parental responsibility

paternity

periodic payments

secured periodic payments

separation order

specific issues order

void marriage

voidable marriage

wardship

Wills and succession
20 INTRODUCTORY TERMS

administrator of an estate

bequest

bona vacantia

codicil

executor

formalities of making a will

grant of probate

grant of representation (inheritance)

intestacy

intestate succession

letters of administration

marriage, effect on will

mutual wills

personal property

personal representative

privileged wills

probate

residuary beneficiary

revocation of a will

witnesses to a will

Business law

20 INTRODUCTORY TERMS

Articles of Association

certificate of incorporation

company and partnership compared

corporate personality

corporation

debenture

deed of partnership

directors

duties of directors

fiduciary duties of directors

limited company

limited liability

Memorandum of Association

partners

partnership

private limited company

public limited company

shareholder

shares

unincorporated

ILEX EXAMINATIONS REVISION LISTINGS

HINTS FOR EXAM SUCCESS

There are three areas in which most candidates can help to improve their chances of a good examination result:

- good notes;
- thorough revision;
- examination technique.

In this appendix we have set out some ideas on each of these three areas.

Good notes

As you work through your course you should be making your own notes on each topic. If these notes are good they will form a useful basis for your revision. So what should you do? Our suggestion is that, as you complete each topic during the course, you rewrite your notes on that topic. This means that the topic is still fresh in your mind and, if there are any points you don't understand, it is easier to try to get them clear straightaway. When rewriting notes put them into a clear format, well spaced out. Use lots of headings and subheadings. Write case names and Acts of Parliament in different colours or highlight them. You may also decide to keep a case note book in which you list all cases on a topic. Remember that in law cases are important for the legal point they decide. You need to know the name of the case and brief facts, but the key factor is the point of law involved. If you do not manage to keep up to date on your notes during the term, then set some time aside at half-term or in the holidays to catch up. If you are studying part-time and having to cope with work and family commitments, then it is probably even more essential to be organised during the course and keep on top of your notes.

Thorough revision

Law is a subject which requires candidates to learn a considerable amount of specific knowledge. It is not a subject you can 'fudge' in answers! A question on, for example, formation of a contract can only be properly answered if the candidate knows the main legal rules thoroughly. Ideally you should try to learn each topic as you finish it. You may feel this is too far ahead of the examination and you will only forget it all. However, some of it will stick and when you come to learn that topic next time, it should get easier. If you are at school or college, you will usually have 'mock' exams part way through the course. Don't take the view that these do not matter. Learning for these is helping to form a sounder basis when it comes to revising for the real thing. (By the way, forecast grades for UCAS forms are often based on your performance in the mocks, so this is an extra incentive to work for them.)

Revision in the run-up to the exam should start early and be well planned. Start about two months before the exam. Set yourself a timetable. This should be detailed, setting out days, times and topics and balancing all the subjects you are taking. Here is an example:

Sunday 5th

12.00–1.00	Law – statutory interpretation – three rules
1.00–2.00	English – Act 1, King Lear
4.00–5.00	Economics – inflation
5.00–6.00	Law – statutory interpretation – purposive approach and extrinsic aids
8.00–9.00	English – Act 2, King Lear

When setting your revision timetable do not be too ambitious. Allow for the fact that you will want to go out with friends sometimes, or that you know you never get up early at weekends! Set small amounts to revise for each given time. Try to find out what method of revision suits you best. Some people like to write everything out again; others prefer to read through notes. It is a good idea to vary your method. Here are some suggestions for varying revision methods:

- read out loud;
- dictate your notes on to a cassette and then play them back; this is useful for those with train journeys to work or college; you can also vary this by leaving gaps at critical points and seeing if you can remember that point;
- revise with a friend and test each other;
- write essay plans;
- do timed exam questions.

PANIC TIME

You've left your revision rather late and your notes are either non-existent or in a terrible mess. Well, it may be late in the day but here are a few ideas on what to do. Use this book as your revision notes. Concentrate on learning key definitions and cases. If you have left it that late, you will not be able to learn as many topics, so go for high-profile topics and learn these as thoroughly as possible. Skim read some other topics, especially those that you found relatively easy when you did them originally. Try to make sure that you have covered as many topics as possible in the time left to you.

Examination technique

This starts before you sit the exam. First of all make sure that you are familiar with the types of question that have been asked in past exams. Get used to the examiner terms that are used. These are explained in Appendix 2.

In the exam read the questions carefully. Underline or highlight key words in questions. Take some time to plan answers and check back to the question to make sure you are keeping focused on the question. Check the number of marks allocated to each part of a question. This helps you to know the depth of answer expected. Wherever possible start with a question on one of your favourite topics. This will help you to feel more confident and, if your first answer is good, it helps to make a good impression on the examiner. Wherever possible, use relevant cases to illustrate your answers. Allocate your time so that you have a reasonable amount of time left for the last question. If you are running out of time, write the last answer in note form. It is very important to answer the required number of questions and clear notes will get some marks.

EXAMINERS' TERMS
Introduction

In order to answer examination questions it is important to know your subject, but it is also important to make sure that you answer the question as set by the examiner. In order to help you do this, key terms used in examination questions are explained below.

Advise: a word often used in a scenario style question where a situation involving one or more people is given and you are then asked to advise one (or more) of the characters. You need to explain the legal points involved in the question, come to a conclusion on the likely outcome of a case based on those legal principles and use this to advise the person(s).

Analyse: to break a topic down into its separate elements/parts. This also indicates that depth is required in the answer: a descriptive outline will not be enough. You should consider several aspects of the topic and form a conclusion based on your analysis.

Assess: weigh up two or more options or arguments or consider advantages and disadvantages and reach a conclusion. You need to justify your conclusion from the arguments you present.

Comment: draw conclusions from the facts. You need to set out relevant facts or legal principles and then point out problems or anomalies as well as advantages. Setting out the facts on their own is not enough, there must be comment on those facts.

Compare: explain the differences and the similarities between two or more things: for example, you may be asked to compare the role of juries and lay magistrates. It is not enough just to describe the role of each: you must point out the differences and the similarities.

Consider: another term which requires you to weigh up options or arguments and reach a conclusion.

Consider the liability of: in a scenario style question involving one or more characters, decide whether a character is legally liable. This requires you to identify the particular legal points involved in the scenario, explain the legal principles in detail and then form a conclusion about the person's legal liability based on those legal principles.

Critically analyse: break down the topic into its component parts and look at those parts critically. Remember that criticism is not just about negative points; criticism is the art of judging, so it is necessary to consider pros and cons of the topic.

Critically comment on: draw conclusions from facts, consider pros and cons and make a judgement. The word critically indicates that more sophisticated comment is required. Also, as in *critically analyse* remember that criticism is not just about negative points.

Define: give an explanation of the word or term given in the question. If there is an Act of Parliament setting out a definition, for example, as theft is defined in the Theft Act 1978, start with that definition, then go on to expand on it, preferably with case examples.

Describe: give a factual (and fairly detailed) account of the topic.

Discuss: means that both sides of a problem have to be explained and considered before you can come to a conclusion. The word discuss may also be used inviting you to comment on a statement or quotation. In this case you must make sure that you use the information in the statement as the basis for your discussion.

Discuss the liability of: basically the same as *consider the liability of*. The key point to remember is that you must explain the legal principles involved and base your discussion of the liability of the person(s) in the scenario on those legal principles.

Draft: draw up a specific document as required by the question. This might be a letter or a more formal document such as a claim form.

Evaluate: consider a broad range of information on the topic and come to a conclusion. Evaluation involves weighing up the points on both sides using the information you have. So you should present your evidence first (facts, legal principles, cases, research findings etc.) showing both and then come to a conclusion.

Examine: look in detail at the arguments, evidence and theories and then come to a conclusion.

Explain: make clear and illustrate the point. This means you need to demonstrate good knowledge and understanding of the facts of the topic in the question. There may be a second part to the question which then requires you to use that knowledge to *assess* or *analyse*.

Explain in your own words: this is likely to be used a data or source based paper and requires you to re-phrase the source material, literally in your own words. Merely copying out bits of the source material will not gain marks. Giving examples in your explanation can help to make sure that you do use your own words.

Illustrate your answer with relevant cases: this means you need to cite decided cases in your answer. To do this effectively you need to be able to give the case name, a brief outline of the facts of the case and explain the legal point of the case and why it is relevant to the question. Also remember that although this command specifically asks for cases, you should always use relevant cases in answer to other questions.

Outline: to give a brief explanation. A large amount of detail is not required. Check the mark allocation to help you judge how much you should include.

Suggest: put forward ideas. For example, in a question asking you to suggest how the law on a particular point could be reformed, you need to put forward ideas for reform. You should also explain and justify your suggestions.

To what extent: reach a judgement about the degree to which a statement or theory is true. This requires you to explain your points in depth in order to reach your conclusion.

EXAMINERS' TERMS